Feminist Measures

Women and Culture Series

The Women and Culture Series is dedicated to books that illuminate the lives, roles, achievements, and status of women, past or present.

Fran Leeper Buss
Dignity: Lower Income Women Tell of Their Lives and Struggles
Forged under the Sun / Forjada bajo el sol: The Life of María Elena Lucas
La Partera: Story of a Midwife

Valerie Kossew Pichanick
Harriet Martineau: The Woman and Her Work, 1802–76

Estelle B. Freedman
Their Sisters' Keepers: Women's Prison Reform in America, 1830–1930

Susan C. Bourque and Kay Barbara Warren
Women of the Andes: Patriarchy and Social Change in Two Peruvian Towns

Marion S. Goldman
Gold Diggers and Silver Miners: Prostitution and Social Life on the Comstock Lode

Page duBois
Centaurs and Amazons: Women and the Pre-History of the Great Chain of Being

Mary Kinnear
Daughters of Time: Women in the Western Tradition

Lynda K. Bundtzen
Plath's Incarnations: Woman and the Creative Process

Violet B. Haas and Carolyn C. Perrucci, editors
Women in Scientific and Engineering Professions

Sally Price
Co-wives and Calabashes

Diane Wood Middlebrook and Marilyn Yalom, editors
Coming to Light: American Women Poets in the Twentieth Century

Joanne S. Frye
Living Stories, Telling Lives: Women and the Novel in Contemporary Experience

E. Frances White
Sierra Leone's Settler Women Traders: Women on the Afro-European Frontier

Barbara Drygulski Wright, editor
Women, Work, and Technology: Transformations

Lynda Hart, editor
Making a Spectacle: Feminist Essays on Contemporary Women's Theatre

Verena Martinez-Alier
Marriage, Class and Colour in Nineteenth-Century Cuba: A Study of Racial Attitudes and Sexual Values in a Slave Society

Kathryn Strother Ratcliff et al., editors
Healing Technology: Feminist Perspectives

Mary S. Gossy
The Untold Story: Women and Theory in Golden Age Texts

Jocelyn Linnekin
Sacred Queens and Women of Consequence: Rank, Gender, and Colonialism in the Hawaiian Islands

Glenda McLeod
Virtue and Venom: Catalogs of Women from Antiquity to the Renaissance

Lynne Huffer
Another Colette: The Question of Gendered Writing

Jill Ker Conway and Susan C. Bourque, editors
The Politics of Women's Education: Perspectives from Asia, Africa, and Latin America

Lynn Keller and Cristanne Miller, editors
Feminist Measures: Soundings in Poetry and Theory

Feminist Measures
Soundings in Poetry and Theory

Lynn Keller and
Cristanne Miller, Editors

Ann Arbor
THE UNIVERSITY OF MICHIGAN PRESS

Copyright © by the University of Michigan 1994
All rights reserved
Published in the United States of America by
The University of Michigan Press
Manufactured in the United States of America
♾ Printed on acid-free paper

1997   1996   1995   1994   4   3   2   1

A CIP catalogue record for this book is available from the British Library.

Library of Congress Cataloging-in-Publication Data

Feminist measures : soundings in poetry and theory / Lynn Keller and
    Cristanne Miller, editors.
        p.   cm. — (Women and culture series)
    Includes bibliographical references and index.
    ISBN 0-472-09484-X (alk. paper). — ISBN 0-472-06484-3 (pbk. :
alk. paper)
    I. Keller, Lynn, 1952–   .   II. Miller, Cristanne.
PN1091.F46   1994
809.1′0082—dc20   94-29454
                                                                CIP

For our children
Caroline and Joseph
Catherine and Elizabeth Maxwell,
whom we hope will inherit a world of greater gender equality.

Acknowledgments

We would like foremost to thank the contributors to this volume for being a pleasure to work with and for making our task as editors so rewarding. In addition, we have received institutional support from a variety of sources that we would like to acknowledge: Pomona College for financial and word-processing assistance; the William F. Vilas Trust Estate for financial support to Lynn that assisted the project; the Alexander von Humboldt Foundation for fellowship support to Cris during the final months of preparing the manuscript for the Press; and the University of Wisconsin at Madison, Pomona College, and the Free University of Berlin for electronic-mail services and equipment, without which this project would have been far more cumbersome and costly than it has proved. We are very grateful to Mary Marchand for her painstaking and tireless editorial assistance. We would also like to thank the University of Michigan Press for its initial suggestion that we contribute a manuscript to their list, and LeAnn Fields for her enthusiastic editorial support.

Contents

Feminist Measures: Soundings in Poetry and Theory

Lynn Keller and Cristanne Miller

This volume collects previously unpublished essays by feminist critics approaching poetry as a gendered practice and considering poetic works in terms of a variety of contemporary literary theories. The essays are in multiple senses "feminist measures": they are acts of theoretically self-conscious positioning, evaluation, and measurement applied to literature traditionally written in measures; and they take measures toward the feminist end of understanding gender's role in poetic production.

The book's genesis lies in the editors' perception that poetry—and particularly the relation of poetry to recent theoretical and feminist discourses—has received inadequate critical attention in the past few decades. Most literary critics interested in theoretical problems have applied their thinking to works of narrative fiction, while feminist critics, whether or not theoretically inclined, have also tended to focus largely on fiction and drama. A comparatively small number of essays and books combining critical discussion of poetry with the development of various kinds of feminist and theoretical discourse have appeared during the past twenty years. For the most part, their impact on the larger field of literary study has been modest. We hope that the collective force of a volume that brings together a number of essays by scholars and poets interested in theoretical approaches to poetry—particularly feminist theories and women's poetry—will spur recognition of both current and previous criticism in this vein. By presenting critical/theoretical discourse in colloquial and experimental as well as traditionally analytic forms, we also seek to interrogate the boundaries between "theoretical" and "literary" work. Questions of genre, then, are central to *Feminist Measures* in several ways: because of the essays' focus on particular poetic genres; because of the essays' collective critique of the privileging of any single notion of theory; and because both the poetry discussed and the theory invoked often call genre boundaries into question. We hope that the collection's challenging of rigid and exclusive applications of genre categories will stimulate further gender-conscious theorizing of poetry and that it will foster greater interest in poetry, broadly conceived, within the academic community.

In this introduction we speculate on the reasons why poetry has so often been overlooked in certain kinds of recent critical discourse, describe briefly some of the publishing history that leads up to and makes possible a collection like this one, and, in the process of introducing the essays to follow, sketch our sense of some central issues and stances characterizing this moment in feminist criticism of poetry. This volume responds to the complex situation of poetry within two overlapping and multifaceted institutions: contemporary critical theory and feminist literary criticism. Although historically and logically these institutions are closely intertwined, in the interest of clarity we will first address them separately.

Poetry, and particularly lyric poetry, enjoyed a critical heyday in the era of New Criticism; lyric was the well-wrought urn in which the complex ironies and ambiguities of the autonomous literary text were held in most elegant balance. As New Criticism has fallen from favor and been replaced by other methodologies and theories of literature, the lyric has yielded its position of critical prestige to narrative modes. Indeed, recent critics have observed an antipathy or tension between poetry and contemporary theory, particularly deconstruction. John Koethe, for instance, sees an incompatibility between the fundamental impulses of these forms of discourse. He argues that the "basic gesture" of deconstruction as a philosophically oriented theory is one of "*unmasking*: the illusory nature of commonly accepted ideas of language and the self is to be made apparent, and the arbitrariness of the assumptions governing expression and interpretation is to be revealed" (1991, 68). Instead of such unmasking and refusal, poetry requires at some level "an acquiescence in the affective movements and rhetorical strategies by which it is enacted" (73). Hank Lazer attributes the tension between much present practice in poetry and theory not to inherently contrary impulses but to a misguided understanding—held by both poets and critics, and going back even to Plato—of poetic discourse as something opposed to abstract or serious thinking. Attempting to heal the rift between poetry and recent theory, Lazer calls attention to their "shared context": both poetry and theory "meditate on the nature of thinking and language" (1987, 259). Both are discursive forms concerned with the relationship between signifier and signified; both are subject to the same (deconstructive) play of language. They are—or can be—in conversation. We concur. As illustrated by our volume's broadly defined categories of both poetry and theory, and by our inclusion of essays that in their own form challenge generic boundaries between poetry (and other forms of "creative writing") and theory, we too believe there need be no gulf between these modes of writing. It is the purpose of this volume to demonstrate and expand current conversation between them.

Chaviva Hošek and Patricia Parker contribute importantly to the development of this conversation in their collection *Lyric Poetry: Beyond New Criticism;* these essays "bring together a variety of recent critical practices and introduce their assumptions and strategies to the reader on New Criticism's chosen ground, the analysis of poetic texts" (1985, 7).[1] The volume—with contributions by such noted theorists as Jonathan Culler, Paul de Man, Mary Jacobus, Fredric Jameson, Barbara Johnson—focuses on such issues as lyric subjectivity, the formation of poetic and theoretical canons, and the complex relations between poetic practice and critical theory. Valuable as this project is, the collection proves in some ways problematically narrow. As Marjorie Perloff notes in "Can(n)on to the Right of Us, Can(n)on to the Left of Us," *Lyric Poetry* fails to include a single essay devoted to a woman poet, and it privileges the nineteenth-century poetic canon. No poets more recent than Auden and Stevens are discussed, and the recent coming together of poetry and theory in contemporary experimental poetries remains unacknowledged and unexamined (1990, 22–23).[2]

Perloff's critique of Hošek and Parker's collection—like a great deal of her recent criticism—suggests that attempts to revitalize interest in poetry during an era when theoretical discourse reigns supreme in the academy are hampered by the narrowness of common conceptions of poetry. In "Postmodernism and the Impasse of the Lyric," she argues that since the publication of Francis Turner Palgrave's *The Golden Treasury of the Best Songs and Lyric Poems in the English Language* in 1861, poetry has increasingly been associated with a restrictive Romantic conception of expressive lyric (1985, 176–81). The recent turn of theoretically inclined critics toward narrative may reflect widespread perception that the conventions of such lyric either were exhausted by New Critical explication or are ill suited to contemporary theories that, for instance, regard as naive the notion of a unified speaking subject such lyrics might seem to reinforce. As Perloff has noted, approaching the poem as an "expression of a moment of absolute insight, of emotion crystallized into timeless patterns" has meant excluding the kinds of poetry that can accommodate narrative, discursivity, didacticism, or humor (1985, 181). If the range of what constitutes the poetic were better recognized, poetry would no doubt appeal to a broader range of critics and theorists. Conversely, as critics like Perloff have drawn greater attention to alternative forms of poetry, such as those practiced since the early 1970s by Language poets (forms that refuse to yield meaning according to the conventions of New Critical close reading), more theoretically exciting criticism has appeared. This is partly because the Language poets and their affiliates, rather than perceiving a tension between poetry and theory, produce a highly theorized poetics and works of poetry sometimes indistinguishable from theory, or vice versa.

That recent theory provides particularly appropriate lenses for reading recent poetry is the premise of a 1991 collection edited by Anthony Easthope and John O. Thompson, *Contemporary Poetry Meets Modern Theory.* As its title implies, this volume maintains the distinction between theory and poetry through its organizational principle of " 'apply[ing]' " current theory to "individual texts by contemporary poets" (viii, vii). At the same time, Easthope and Thompson's volume assumes strong links between the two projects, especially when they are synchronous; the editors regard poststructuralist theory as particularly useful for reading modernist poetry and contemporary theory for reading contemporary poetry because the poetry "arguably has already incorporated into itself such theory, though it has done so as it should, poetically rather than as conceptual discourse" (viii).

Despite the popular appeal of some feminist poetry, the history of feminist criticism in the United States over the past twenty years also traces a pattern in which poetry has often seemed at odds with dominant interests in the field.[3] Some of the explanations for this are specific to the history of women's writing and of feminist criticism. For the last one hundred and fifty years, women writers generally preferred the novel to poetic genres. Virginia Woolf speculated that this was because the older forms of literature were fixed before women writers could significantly shape their conventions, while "the novel alone was young enough to be soft in [the woman writer's] hands" (Woolf 1929, 80). More recently, Suzanne Juhasz (1976), Sandra Gilbert and Susan Gubar (1979b), Margaret Homans (1980), and Joanne Feit Diehl (1990), among others, have suggested that this preference reflects the difficulty for women of claiming the lyric speaker's subjectivity and authority. Gilbert and Gubar, for example, argue that while the novelist

> sees herself from the *outside,* as an object, a character, a small figure in a large pattern, the lyric poet must be continually aware of herself from the *inside,* as a subject, a speaker: she must be, that is, assertive, authoritative, radiant with powerful feelings while at the same time absorbed in her own consciousness— and hence, by definition, profoundly "unwomanly," even freakish. (1979b, xxii)

Considering epic rather than lyric, Susan Stanford Friedman similarly describes that genre's norms as "public, objective, universal, heroic—coincid[ing] with western norms for the masculine" and hence generating "genre anxiety" in women writers (1986, 205).

Feminist literary critics have duplicated women writers' inclination toward narrative fiction. Having begun with a scrutiny of images of women first in works by men and then also in works by women, feminist criticism naturally turned to genres in which characters were portrayed—primarily the novel, short story, and drama. These genres that foreground the social dimensions of women's experience also offer particularly rich resources for feminist revaluation of the domestic

sphere and of the political dimensions of women's lives and interpersonal rela-
tions. Even in rescuing from obscurity neglected women authors and in identify-
ing female literary traditions, critics tended to focus on prose fiction.

Within the body of feminist criticism that *has* concerned itself with poetry, the
mode of poetry receiving most attention from the 1960s through the mid-1980s
was the personal lyric in the Romantic tradition. Given the general privileging of
the expressive lyric mentioned above, this is hardly surprising. Moreover, within
feminist criticism the lyric was represented most often by confessional first-
person poems voicing an individual's exploration of what was identified as
"female experience," ranging from female sexualities and the cycles of the female
body, to female friendships and familial relations, to the consequences of
women's oppression in patriarchy. Focusing on thematic and socially oriented
reading practices, this feminist criticism stressed the political, communal rele-
vance of representing private experience. The present collection builds upon the
accomplishments of important books and essay collections from this period.
Brief mention of some of these volumes will allow us both to acknowledge our
debts and, partly by contrast, to characterize more fully the contemporary mo-
ment in feminist criticism of poetry.

In 1979—the same year in which they transformed American feminist crit-
icism with *Madwoman in the Attic*—Gilbert and Gubar published *Shakespeare's
Sisters: Feminist Essays on Women Poets,* bringing together articles from the late
1970s examining the achievement of the "'presumptuous creatures'" who,
despite all the social strictures working against them, "offer us a vigorous and
victorious matrilineal heritage" in poetry (1979b, xxiv). Like Juhasz's 1976
Naked and Fiery Forms: Modern American Poetry by Women, a New Tradition,
which was the first feminist book of essays on multiple women poets, Gilbert and
Gubar's volume is organized chronologically and devoted almost exclusively to
studies of single poets. Both these volumes trace a distinctively female poetic
tradition, helping redefine literary history so that women can no longer be ex-
cluded from it.

In 1985 Diane Middlebrook and Marilyn Yalom continued this valuable work
in the context of women poets who are twentieth-century Americans. Exploring
what difference it makes that a poet is a woman, most of the essays in *Coming to
Light* again focused on a single poet and how she "tapped for poetry the resources
of specifically female experience in our polarized gender system" (3). The collec-
tion helped solidify the reputations of recognized poets, such as Elizabeth Bishop
and Sylvia Plath, while bringing greater attention to a few previously less known
figures, such as Lucille Clifton and Mina Loy. Alicia Ostriker's *Stealing the
Language: The Emergence of Women's Poetry in America* (1986), part of which
appeared in *Coming to Light,* identified a defiant poetic tradition of women who,
refusing to be silenced, have become "thieves of language"; Ostriker focused on

poetry of personal statement to delineate central motifs characterizing a great volume of recent women's poetry. Thanks in part to books like these, the years since have seen a significant expansion of the academic poetic canon. Feminist critics no longer feel called upon to defend the stature of such poets as Dickinson, Barrett Browning, Moore, H.D., Brooks, Plath, Bishop, Clifton, and Rich.[4]

By the mid-1980s, feminist interest in retrieving women's traditions was drawing increased attention to some of the more experimental and less obviously biographical writers, particularly those of the modernist and contemporary eras. While poetry written in confessional modes seemed well suited to the dominant tendencies in 1970s feminist criticism toward thematic and biographical analysis, this poetry that disrupted formal and linguistic traditions encouraged other types of critical analysis. Moreover, in the late 1970s and early 1980s, the introduction of the new French feminist theories (facilitated by Elaine Marks and Isabelle de Courtivron's anthology, *New French Feminisms* [1980]) shifted feminist focus toward the (possibly) gendered character of language itself and the problematics of female identity formation or subjectivity. The psychoanalytic and linguistic emphasis of much French feminism subsequently became central to many Anglo-American discussions of women's poetry.

Using the work of French feminists and other European theorists, Margaret Homans and Jan Montefiore, among others, broke new ground in pushing feminist criticism toward more explicitly theorized analysis of poetry. In *Women Writers and Poetic Identity* (1980) Homans draws upon deconstructive and psychoanalytic criticism (Derrida, Lacan, Irigaray) to explore the ramifications for nineteenth-century poets of women's association with nature and their exclusion from speaking subjectivity. Homans's focus on women poets' linguistic structures and strategies in the nineteenth century leads her to a concluding critique of the "prevailing feminist opinion . . . that poetry must report on the poet's experience as a woman, and that it must be true" (216). Looking beyond what she considers a "reductive poetry of female literalism" (231), she insists feminists should value that poetry which embraces and exploits language's inherent fictiveness. This premise has been extremely important to the last decade of thinking about women's poetics and women's poetry.

Like Homans, Montefiore in *Feminism and Poetry* (1987) examines women's often difficult negotiation of poetic tradition, particularly in terms of poetic form and language; her distinctive focus is on whether there is a tradition or style specific to women's poetry. Using mostly twentieth-century poets, Montefiore explores the possibility of gaining access to a female Imaginary and to specifically female identity and meaning, while insisting that women's poetry will always simultaneously participate in male traditions.

Not surprisingly, as American feminist criticism has turned increasingly to theory based on French semiotics or Western philosophy and psychoanalysis, some feminists have objected to the perceived elitism and hegemonic bias of such theoretical accounts of literature. A recent example of such an objection comes from Meryl Altman, who in the July 1992 *Women's Review of Books* criticizes what she sees as the "unreflective and normative heterosexism" and the erasure of the lives of women who are not mothers implied in the widespread adoption of Julia Kristeva's theory of "the maternal chora" (39). Here Altman extends Adrienne Rich's observation in "Compulsory Heterosexuality and Lesbian Existence" that "lesbian existence" has been "neglect[ed]" in "a wide range of writings, including feminist scholarship" (1986a, 27). Expressing quite different concerns, critics such as Nancy K. Miller (1988) and Susan Stanford Friedman (1991) have pointed out some political dangers pure poststructuralism may pose for members of traditionally oppressed groups; while white men can afford to abandon notions like "subject" or "author," women are among those who, for their own empowerment, need to recuperate versions of those concepts.

Feminists of color have been particularly outspoken in questioning whether allegiance to the academic discourses of theory does not simply transfer hegemony from one set of exclusive aesthetic standards to another (poststructuralist) one. Barbara Christian's "The Race For Theory" (1989) is perhaps the most famous example of a critic's attempt to expand the definition of theory so that if theory is indeed, in Gayatri Spivak's terms, "a 'cultural ideology' of a specific class and trade which must seek to reproduce itself" (1987, 113), critics would be pushed to acknowledge the theories and cultural ideologies of a range of classes and traditions. Christian argues that the current privileging of theories based on Western philosophy—and in feminist criticism the way in which French feminism has become *"authoritative discourse"*—is dangerously exclusive and dangerously separate from literature itself (1989, 233).[5] She explains:

> For people of color have always theorized—but in forms quite different from the Western form of abstract logic. And I am inclined to say that our theorizing (and I intentionally use the verb rather than the noun) is often in narrative forms, in the stories we create, in riddles and proverbs, in the play with language, since dynamic rather than fixed ideas seem more to our liking. How else have we managed to survive with such spiritedness the assault on our bodies, social institutions, countries, our very humanity? . . . My folk, in other words, have always been a race of theory—though more in the form of the hieroglyph, a written figure which is both sensual and abstract, both beautiful and communicative. (226)

Tey Diana Rebolledo similarly writes that she is

> suspicious and yes, even bored, by a criticism which seems alien to the text about which it purports to talk; by a theoretical basis of patriarchal norms or a

theory which does not take the particular concerns of minority writers and culture into account. . . . [O]ur critical discourse should come from within, within our cultural and historical perspective. (1987, 137)

Works like Christian's and Rebolledo's provide salutary cautions against reinforcing a false binary between—again invoking Spivak's formulation—"the conceptualism of pure theory and the metaphorical language of the figurative cognition of art" (1987, 115).

Christian's and Rebolledo's legitimate complaints about people of color being remarginalized within academic discourse tend toward disparagement of all "high" theory. Other critics of color address similar concerns while asserting the usefulness of poststructuralist perspectives. For example, bell hooks argues in *yearning: race, gender, and cultural politics* that "racism is perpetuated when blackness is associated solely with concrete gut level experience conceived as either opposing or having no connection to abstract thinking and the production of critical theory" (1990, 23). She condemns postmodern theory's failure to mention black experience or writing by black people. Yet rather than rejecting theory's insights, she aims to "change the nature and direction of postmodern theory" from within, making its "break with the notion of 'authority' as 'mastery over'" more than a rhetorical device: "Radical postmodernist practice, most powerfully conceptualized as a 'politics of difference,' should incorporate the voices of displaced, marginalized, exploited, and oppressed black people" (24, 25).

Trinh Minh-ha's related concern in *Woman, Native, Other: Writing Postcoloniality and Feminism* is that "theory no longer is theoretical when it loses sight of its own conditional nature, takes no risk in speculation, and circulates as a form of administrative inquisition"; the theorist must instead attempt to understand "the very social and historical reality of the tools one uses to unmask ideological mystifications—including the mystification of theory" (1989, 42). These perspectives return us to the view expressed by Lazer that poetry and theory should be recognized as engaged in the same kinds of questioning, and that philosophy/theory should be seen as located *within* the realm of literature. Trinh, hooks, and other feminist critics (especially women of color) foreground the need to place this insight in the contexts of multicultural and gender-conscious criticism, as they point to the need for theory—as well as poetry—to interrogate itself. Trinh writes:

it is still unusual to encounter instances where theory involve[s] the voiding, rather than the affirming or even reiterating, of theoretical categories. Instances where poeticalness is not primarily an aesthetic response, nor literariness merely a question of pure verbalism. And instances where the borderline between theoretical and non-theoretical writings is blurred and questioned, so that theory and poetry necessarily mesh, both determined by an awareness of the sign and the destabilization of the meaning and writing subject. (42)

Our volume seeks to reflect this sort of development in current theoretical and feminist criticism: we adopt a broadly inclusive sense of what constitutes theoretical discourse, as well as an inclusive sense of what constitutes poetry. The volume contains essays that conform as much to academic expectations of "creative writing" as to conventions of critical essays, along with essays treating experimental texts that themselves refuse to distinguish poetry from theory.

The diversity of this volume's contents reflects new developments in feminist theory and the recent expansion of publishing opportunities for women of color, lesbians, avant-garde writers, and others not well represented in canonical literature.[6] This broadening of the literary base has reinforced—and been reinforced by—the increased cultural and historical specificity of much feminist criticism; the growing body of work on theories of lesbian representation; and the importation from other disciplines, such as anthropology, film theory, and postcolonial literary studies, of concepts useful to feminist literary analysis. The concept of theory itself has also been broadened to include more pragmatically and spiritually based discourses, some of which draw upon non-western traditions. Various kinds of antihegemonic writing have encouraged reexamination of women's place within structures of language and the structures of power that linguistic systems may encode.

The early 1990s appear to us a particularly exciting moment in the history of the conjunction of poetic and theoretical discourse, especially as it emerges in feminist criticism. With several generations of feminist critics now actively engaged in the field, we have been able to include essays by some of those most influential in establishing the new directions of critical inquiry, as well as essays by younger scholars. Within the increasing heterogeneity of feminist theories and theorists as well as the expanding field of poetry commanding feminist interest— phenomena that are well represented in this volume—we nonetheless note the recurrence of particular concerns, aims, and perspectives among the essays collected here. We have not grouped the essays according to topic areas because categorizing them would obscure their rich and suggestive overlappings. Instead, we will use the closing pages of this introduction to suggest ways in which intersections among the essays' concerns configure some current issues in feminist theoretical analysis of poetry.

Feminist theory and criticism are cumulative as well as developing fields. Kinds of inquiry particularly central in earlier decades—explorations of female traditions and influence, retrieval and revaluation of lost female writers or of typically female genres—have not been abandoned but instead continue, often incorporated into other currently more urgent kinds of inquiry. In this collection Janel Mueller's examination of the first volume of English poetry to be published by a woman, Aemilia Lanyer's *Salve Deus Rex Judeorum,* reminds us of the vitality of this continuing enterprise, as well as demonstrating the usefulness of comparative historical analysis for defining feminist poetics. Where retrieval of lost writers once focused on white middle- and upper-class women, now traditions of other races and classes are also being explored; here Akasha (Gloria) Hull identifies a spiritual tradition linking African American women writers.

The current dissolution of genre distinctions makes itself evident in this collection sometimes in the literary works under discussion, sometimes in the generic traits of the critical essays themselves, and sometimes in the bringing together of literary and nonliterary or "high" and "low" genres within current critical and theoretical methodologies. The long poems that are Susan Stanford Friedman's focus exemplify the recent hybridization of literary genres, as do the works of the Language-affiliated women writers invoked by Joan Retallack—including Theresa Hak Kyung Cha's *DICTEE,* the focal text for Shelley Sunn Wong's essay. Retallack's own mode of critical discourse challenges generic expectations for literary criticism, as she uses markedly heterogeneous diction, radical juxtaposition, puns, and experimental coinages to interrogate "a historical endurance and power we call 'women's silence.'" Hull's meditation on African American women's writing resists abstract theorizing as it resists a division between theory and belief and a hierarchical separation of the spiritual from the intellectual. M. Nourbese Philip's "Dis Place   The Space Between" modifies the critical essay even more radically; Philip combines dramatic dialogue, autobiography, and poetry to explore the relation of women's sexuality to cultural geography, language, and silence, as well as to poetry. Philip's essay also demonstrates the increasingly interdisciplinary sources of contemporary theoretical insight, combining African Caribbean history, myth, and demotic speech in a forthright exploration of women's sexual powers and oppressions.

Margaret Homans's essay exemplifies a more established pattern of bringing together literary and nonliterary texts in the methodology of the New Historicism. She considers poems by Elizabeth Barrett Browning within a broadly intertextual frame of Victorian sexual ideology as revealed in the correspondence between Barrett and Robert Browning, in Queen Victoria's diary entries, and in broadsheets and cartoons portraying the queen. Homans's historically detailed scrutiny, in which the "high" literary text and its author are no longer privileged, reveals the different implications of men's and women's employment of rhetorical strategies that appear gender-neutral. Teresa McKenna, too, draws together "high" and "low" traditions in examining how contemporary Chicana/o poems modify the popular Mexican border corrido. Cristanne Miller explores a poet's use of a prestigious nonliterary discourse—that of quantum mechanics. Alice

Fulton, Miller argues, uses the insights and terminology of quantum physics to break out of the constraints of various systems of binary thinking.

As noted above, much feminist criticism in the 1990s emphasizes a need for historical and cultural specificity in feminist reading, operating from the assumption that any subject position reflects a complex set of determinants, including not just gender but also class, race, regional and ethnic heritage, religion, sexual preference, family background, and so forth. Thus, Wong insists on the ethnic specificity of Cha's text, which has been glossed over by critics interested primarily in its experimental character. Lynn Keller considers the political implications of Marilyn Hacker's foregrounding lesbian sexuality in a sonnet sequence. Mueller illuminates Lanyer's innovations by positioning them in relation to early seventeenth-century controversies about women's moral character and moral agency. Similarly, Rachel Blau DuPlessis's discussion of the "cultural work" done by Marianne Moore's and Mina Loy's lyrics builds upon Carolyn Burke's insight that those modernists wrote from the subject position of their era's New Woman. Hull traces a tradition in African American women's writing in which contemporary writers' overt spiritual connection with earlier African American women enables them to produce literature from the historical and cultural specificities of black women's lives in the United States. At once highlighting and bridging cultural differences, Elaine A. Jahner uses the work of Native American poets Joy Harjo and Linda Hogan to theorize a reading process whereby cultural specificities may be respected and understood by a cultural outsider.

DuPlessis's "Corpses of Poesy" takes historically specific inquiry into the terrain of established poetic genres, examining how several modernist women writers reconstituted a gender-laden complex of associations surrounding the lyric. As she points out, this kind of inquiry can lay the groundwork for a less androcentric literary history, in this case a new understanding of poetic modernism. Other established poetic genres that receive fresh scrutiny in this collection include the sonnet sequence and the long poem. Keller examines how Hacker's play with the sonnet sequence challenges the heterosexual and hierarchical assumptions of the sonnet tradition. Friedman explains women poets' increasing interest in the long poem in terms of the genre's interplay of narrative and lyric. The form's revision of narrative convention, Friedman argues, enables women poets to counter their exclusions from subjectivity and from the discourses of myth and history, without narrative becoming a repressive totalizing force. Wong, too, considers poetry in terms of narrative traditions, examining Cha's manipulation of various genres—including bildungsroman, epic, and autobiography—as ideologically inflected forms working against each other to generate "reciprocal critiques."

As feminist theory grows more established and more diverse, critics are more carefully scrutinizing the better-known work of some established feminist theorists and exploring their previously less well known (or untranslated) texts. Thus, Jahner places Kristeva's recent work on the uncanny in dialogue with certain Native American insights. Elizabeth Hirsh examines Irigaray's recent writing on ethics in conjunction with Rich's poetry of the early 1970s. Irigaray's argument that the only ethical position is the dialogic one of speaking to (rather than speaking of or about) another enables Hirsh to reinterpret French feminist understandings of the difficulty of speaking as a woman. Friedman critically reexamines French feminist positions on narrative, calling into question the association of narrative with a repressive social order evident in the writing of Kristeva and Hélène Cixous among other poststructuralist theorists. Juhasz turns to the theory of feminist psychologist Jessica Benjamin and to object-relations psychological studies to challenge Kristeva's identification of the semiotic with the feminine/maternal, and her consequent denial of women's access to the symbolic. Using Dickinson's poetry as her test case, Juhasz argues that women have access to the symbolic particularly through their use of metaphor. Retallack quotes avant-garde texts by men and women to question whether "the feminine" shouldn't be associated with experimental or innovative uses of language and form rather than with *sub*-text, images *sub*versive to existing patriarchal norms, or other particulars of content; in so doing, she, too, questions Kristeva's identification of the symbolic with the masculine while also interrogating the assumptions of a range of theorists, including Judith Butler and Alicia Ostriker.

Women's sexuality and its relation to their linguistic or literary production is another area of current feminist inquiry well represented in this collection. Keller's use of Butler's reinterpretation of gender, particularly in the context of lesbian and gay cultural practices, exemplifies the growing importance of lesbian theory and representation to feminist literary criticism. The essays by Philip and Miller demonstrate current reconsiderations of representations of the female body. Philip explores the physically and spiritually damaging effects on women of the significance patriarchy assigns to the "space between" a woman's legs. Miller examines the work of a poet who revises sexualized embodiments of women, in this case by representing a mode of physicality that is intensely embodied and even sexual but not always distinctly gendered.

Like notions of the body, conceptions of woman's relations to language—as speaking "I," as marginalized subject, as the bearer of language traditions, as voiceless or silenced "other"—vary widely in current feminist thinking. In her psychoanalytic approach, Hirsh examines the ethical dimensions of women's accession to the subject "I" as an interpersonal process involving listening as well as speaking to one another. In disputing the dominant psychoanalytic reading of women's relation to language, Juhasz argues that Dickinson uses metaphor to articulate within the symbolic preoedipal experience that Kristeva associates with the feminine and semiotic. McKenna, in contrast, stresses women's historical and social relation to language: she examines first a Chicano ballad that revises a masculine tradition of corrido without recuperating the absent feminine voice and then a Chicana lyric, in which a woman's attempts to articulate her shifting identifications with culturally symbolic sites—Mexico and Port Townsend, Washington—enable her to create her own "rhythms of discourse." Philip, who also positions herself within multiple cultures and languages—specifically, Standard English and demotic "bajan"—argues that silence must be assigned "a validity equal to the word."

A single volume is too little space in which to represent all the important theoretical trends of this moment or all the varieties of poetry in English. While including one essay based in Caribbean culture and writing, we have not attempted the vast project of exploring the poetry of anglophone postcolonial people outside the United States and England. Our desire to attract attention to work by contemporary poets has necessitated giving less attention to pre-twentieth-century poetry. Even so, we have not been able to treat the importance of pop culture to contemporary theory and poetry—an increasingly vital intersection evident in women's rap music and in performance art like Laurie Anderson's and Jessica Hagedorn's. Also not represented here is the growing, if still slight, interest in applying Marxist approaches to poetic texts, while Wong's invocation of Bakhtin can only suggest the growing feminist interest in adapting to feminist theorizing his ideas on dialogics.

In what is collected here, we find a drive to bring a wealth of historical information and culturally specific data to bear on poetic texts, as feminist theory moves away from essentializing and totalizing structures. We find a continuing desire—a politicizing outgrowth of deconstruction evident throughout literary studies today—to undo or complicate received binaries, including those of narrative/lyric, formalist/free verse, masculine/feminine, speech/silence, theory/poetry or theory/practice, French feminist theory/Anglo-American theory, and high/low theory or art. The authors of the essays to follow not only sound the depths and define the structures of an expanding range of poetic texts but also experiment with the soundings of their own clear, personalized voices. We hope their example will stimulate further exploration of the intersections and interactions between poetry and theory.

NOTES

1. In Britain a similar task was undertaken by editor David Murray in *Literary Theory and Poetry: Extending the Canon* (1989). Intended as an "introduction to some contemporary theoretical issues by showing them in application" and as a resource that would demonstrate "both the *range* of available poetry, and the similarities of concern between recent developments in criticism and poetry" (1), this volume has received little attention in

the United States, where it is not widely available. The collection deals primarily with twentieth-century poetry; of the nine essays included, three focus on women poets.

2. These are not the only problems Perloff notes with the Hošek and Parker collection. She is concerned, for instance, about its ahistorical approach to lyric. She also objects to the editors' understanding of theory and poetry as separable discourses, one to be applied to the other.

3. Evidence of the popularity of feminist poetry abounds. Judy Grahn, for example, observes that her "Common Woman Poems" have been "reprinted hundreds of thousands of times" informally by women's groups (Grahn 1978, 60). Book sales, too, and the large audiences at feminist poetry readings indicate that many women readers would concur with Audre Lorde's forceful assertion that "poetry is not" and never has been "a luxury" (1984, 36).

4. Marie Harris and Kathleen Aguero's collection *Gift of Tongues: Critical Challenges in Contemporary American Poetry* (1987)—along with its companion volume of contemporary poems—has furthered the current opening of the critical canon to include more diverse and multicultural authors. While this collection gives relatively little attention to gendered aspects of the production or reading of poetry and makes little use of current theoretical frameworks, it nonetheless contributes to feminist as well as nonfeminist criticism through its acknowledgment of the multiple ethnic traditions interacting in American poetry.

5. An infamous example of obviously exclusive poststructuralist feminism is provided by Toril Moi in *Sexual/Textual Politics: Feminist Literary Theory* (1985). Moi claims that black and lesbian feminist criticism makes no distinct contribution to textual theory and—in a move that reinscribes white heterosexual feminism as central—claims that the importance of "black-lesbian" feminist criticism lies only in its political role of "forc[ing] white heterosexual feminists to re-examine their own sometimes totalitarian conception of 'woman' as a homogeneous category" (86).

6. Happily, as feminist theory itself has become increasingly diverse and sophisticated, studies of women's poetry that incorporate insights of contemporary theory have begun to appear with greater frequency. Book-length examples of this varied production (leaving aside the many studies treating single poets or discussing prose as well as poetry) include Joanne Feit Diehl's *Women Poets and the American Sublime* (1990), Rachel Blau DuPlessis's *The Pink Guitar: Writing as Feminist Practice* (1990), Susan Schweik's *A Gulf So Deeply Cut: American Women Poets and the Second World War* (1991), Cheryl Walker's *Masks Outrageous and Austere: Culture, Psyche, and Persona in Modern Women Poets* (1991), Liz Yorke's *Impertinent Voices: Subversive Strategies in Contemporary Women's Poetry* (1991), and Betsy Erkkila's *The Wicked Sisters: Women Poets, Literary History, and Discord* (1992).

Craving Stories: Narrative and Lyric in Contemporary Theory and Women's Long Poems

Susan Stanford Friedman

Narrative is one of the ways in which knowledge is organized. I have always thought it was the most important way to transmit and receive knowledge. I am less certain of that now—but the craving for narrative has never lessened, and the hunger for it is as keen as it was on Mt. Sinai or Calvary or the middle of the fens.
—Toni Morrison

[I]t is in this atmosphere of doubt and conflict [in the modern age] that writers have now to create, and the fine fabric of a lyric is no more fitted to contain this point of view than a rose leaf to envelop the rugged immensity of a rock. . . . It may be possible that prose is going to take over—has, indeed, already taken over—some of the duties which were once discharged by poetry.
—Virginia Woolf

The necessity of narrative—indeed the hunger for it—evident in these epigraphs resonates with the work of narrative theorists such as Robert Caserio (1979) and Peter Brooks (1985), both of whom identify narrative as an essential mode of understanding reality. But curiously, their insistence on narrative is out of tune with the views of a number of poststructuralist theorists such as Roland Barthes ([1953] 1967, [1957] 1972), Julia Kristeva (1982, [1974] 1984), and Hélène Cixous ([1975] 1980), as well as those whom they have influenced. These theorists have variously suggested that what they loosely call "poetry," the "poetic," or the "lyric" is the avant-garde of modernity's disruptions of the symbolic order. They often associate narrative (and often the novel or prose), on the other hand, with a regressive representationalism or mimesis, with, in other words, the tyranny of the symbolic order. For many feminist poststructuralists in particular, the lyric mode and poetry (especially avant-garde poetry) are tied to the repressed feminine, maternal, and preoedipal, whereas narrative and the novel (especially the mimetic novel) are linked to the repressive masculine, paternal, and oedipal. None of these poststructuralists imagine doing away with narrative; rather, the point is that for many, a revolutionary poetic involves a transgressive disruption

of narrative. Narrative may be necessary, inevitable, but its mode of discourse is
to be resisted.

Not everyone, however, centers transgressions of the symbolic order in the
lyric. Jay Clayton (1990) notes the widespread "turn to narrative" by many
novelists of color, a phenomenon that challenges the prevailing association of the
postmodern with a repudiation of narrative ways of knowing. I would like to
bring this insight back to the question of poststructuralist privileging of the lyric.
The chasm between this craving for narrative and the refusal of it by some
poststructuralist theorists suggests a blind spot on race and ethnicity that leads to
a universalizing of an ethnocentric view of narrative as an authoritarian mode.
Writers rooted in cultures where the oral tradition remains vital are more likely to
regard narrative as food for the hungry rather than as the tyrant to be resisted. As
Leslie Marmon Silko writes in her autobiographical prose poem *Storyteller:*

> The storyteller keeps the stories
>   all the escape stories
>   she says "With these stories of ours
>   we can escape most anything,
>   with these stories we will
>   survive."
>   (Silko 1981, 247)[1]

Moreover, some writers based in cultures for which the written predominates
over the oral also exhibit the "turn to narrative" evident in many writers of color.
In her prose/poem/essay, "It Was a Dark and Stormy Night," Ursula LeGuin
argues that telling stories fulfills the necessities of memory, testimony, and sur-
vival. Associating narrative with comfort and survival, she says:

> Tell me a story, great-aunt,
> so that I can sleep.
> Tell me a story, Scheherazade,
> so that you can live.
>   (LeGuin 1981, 188)

She highlights as well the function of tales to "bear witness" in citing the state-
ment made by Primo Levi, an Auschwitz survivor: "Even in this place one can
survive, and therefore one must want to survive, to tell the story, to bear witness"
(LeGuin 1981, 193). Where LeGuin bases her defense of narrative in invocations
of the oral tradition, Marjorie Perloff in *The Dance of Intellect* (1985) argues that
postmodernism brings back into poetry the prosaic and narrative elements that

had been suppressed in the modernist privileging of the lyric.[2] In postmodern poems, this "return of story" does not, Perloff hastens to add, mean a return of the linear plot, but the often fragmented, collagelike narratives expose the equation of poetry with the lyric as an ideological construct and deconstruct a modernist separation between the poetic and the everyday, between the timeless lyrical moment and the historical.

To these debates about narrative, I want to add the hypothesis that the need for narrative also reflects issues of positionality and marginalization. A historically produced cultural imperative exists that creates a need for narrative to resist or subvert the stories told by the dominant culture. Oppositional, transgressive discourses often embrace narrative as one among many strategies of resistance. To themselves, people made peripheral by the dominant society are not "marginal," "other." But to counter the narratives of their alterity produced by the dominant society, they must tell other stories that chart their exclusions, affirm their agency (however complicit and circumscribed), and continually (re)construct their identities. Morrison's defense of narrative for African Americans articulates a broadly defined "craving for narrative" that exists for many others: "We are the subjects of our own narrative, witnesses to and participants in our own experience, and, in no way coincidentally, in the experience of those with whom we have come in contact. We are not, in fact, 'other.' We are choices" (1989, 9). Narrative can represent "choices," the insistent subjectivity of the "other," for marginalized groups in highly literate domains where the oral tradition is but a trace of a memory.

I will test this hypothesis by examining first the poststructuralist privileging of lyric over narrative and second women's poetic practice in the contemporary long poem. As a descendant of the epic and the autobiographical long poems of William Wordsworth and Walt Whitman, the twentieth-century long poem has been a defining genre for male poets—from the modernists through the "confessionals" and the postmodernists.[3] Before the current wave of feminism, however, epics and long poems by women were relatively uncommon, particularly for poems written by women who achieved any stature in the world of poetry. In the first half of the century, H.D., Mina Loy, Gertrude Stein, and Gwendolyn Brooks were key pioneers in the twentieth-century women's long poem.[4] Since the 1960s there has been a phenomenal outpouring of poetic sequences and long poems by women. However much the twentieth-century long poem by both women and men has broken the conventions of narrative poetry through a reliance on lyric sequencing, fragmentation, and paratactic juxtapositions, narrative has remained a central issue for the long poem. I will suggest that the dialectical play between narrative and lyric in the women's long poem is overdetermined by a need for narrative based in traditional Western exclusions of women from subjectivity and from the discourses of both myth and history. The result, I believe, has been a re-vision of narrative convention rather than a totalizing association of narrative with the tyranny of the social order.

Privileging the Poetic as Transgressive

In spite of a deconstructionist resistance to binaries, a number of poststructuralist theorists have reinstated preexisting and overlapping polarities between narrative and lyric, novel and poem, prose and poetry, representationalism and nonrepresentationalism, realism and surrealism, humanism and modernity. Such binaries are often asserted in ahistorical terms, without regard for the diachronic and synchronic variations in historically produced modes, genres, and discourses. Moreover, there is often an inexact slippage between modes (lyric, narrative) and genres (lyric poem, novel), or between broad discourses (poetry, prose) and specific forms (poem, fiction). What remains relatively constant in these formulations is the inevitability of an oppositional binary in which the lyric/poetic/nonmimetic continuously disrupts the narrative/novelistic/mimetic. In spite of the emphasis on process—the motion of textual practice—the revolutionary potential of language is statically located at the site of this lyric transgression of narrative.

This poststructuralist fixity is rooted in structuralism, a continuity evident in the evolution of Barthes's work. In *Writing Degree Zero*, for example, Barthes writes that "poetic language and prosaic language are sufficiently separate to be able to dispense with the very signs of their difference" ([1953] 1967, 43). "There is no humanism of modern poetry," he continues. As the site of modernity, "This erect discourse [of modern poetry] is full of terror, that is to say, it relates man not to other men [the subject of prose], but to the most inhuman images in Nature: heaven, hell, holiness, childhood, madness, pure matter, etc." (50).

In *Mythologies*, Barthes defines myth as "a mode of signification," a "type of speech" closely associated with a "signifying consciousness," history, and bourgeois ideology (Barthes [1957] 1972, 109–11). He sets up poetry, especially contemporary poetry, as the discourse that exists in opposition to myth. Because myth is coercive, Barthes theorizes, "Poetry occupies a position which is the reverse of that of myth" (158). As "motivated" speech, "myth has an imperative, buttonholing character. . . . I am subjected to its intentional force" (124). As "interpellant speech," myth summons subjectivity, occupies it. Barthes's rhetoric sensationalizes the battle of the "I" against myth: "It thus appears that it is extremely difficult to vanquish myth from the inside: for the very effort one makes in order to escape its stranglehold becomes in its turn the prey of myth: myth can always, as a last resort, signify the resistance which is brought to bear against it" (135). "Revolutionary language proper," he warns the Left, "cannot be mythical" (146). Poetry, he concludes, aids in his search for "the best weapon against myth" (135).[5]

In *Revolution in Poetic Language*, Kristeva is perhaps less apocalyptic than Barthes, but no less "revolutionary" in her call for transgression against the symbolic order. However, for her, narrative and lyric remain inevitable aspects of all discourse, ever present, but varying considerably in prominence. Weaving Lacanian psychoanalytic theory with semiotics, she regards the text as a "signifying practice" in which the two modalities of language—the semiotic and the symbolic (or thetic)—engage in dialectical interplay. With the semiotic, she associates the lyric, the feminine, the preoedipal; with the symbolic (thetic), she associates narrative, the masculine, the oedipal ([1974] 1984, 23–30). Poetry tends to foreground the semiotic; prose, the symbolic. The revolutionary potential of modernity, she believes, resides most especially in the avant-garde writers whose experimentations with the semiotic register of language hold out the promise of disrupting the symbolic order and the Law of the Father.[6]

Revolution in Poetic Language works out this dialectical semiology in some detail in a series of chapters that interconnect textual practices, subjectivity, preoedipal and oedipal configurations, (male) avant-garde writers, and the revolutionary potential of the semiotic. In opposition to "poetic language" (also "modern poetic language" and "poetic practice"), Kristeva associates narrative, "whether theatrical or novelistic," with "verisimilitude" and "classical mimesis," with "denotation" and "meaning," with "systems of science and monotheistic religion," and with "political and social signifieds" ([1974] 1984, 58–59, 88). Narrative genres in which the signifying function of the thetic/symbolic dominates include "mythic narratives, the epic, its theatrical substitutes, and even the novel (including its stage or screen adaptations), news reporting, newspaper columns, and other journalistic genres . . . legends, sagas, myths, riddles, idioms, cases, memoirs, tales, jokes" (92). In all these forms, the oedipally constituted structure of the family serves as the foundation for the "social organism" and for the "I" or "author" it signifies (90–93). As the thetic function of the text, narrative is "a projection of the paternal role in the family" (91). In *Powers of Horror*, Kristeva adds: "Narrative is, in sum, the most elaborate kind of attempt, on the part of the speaking subject, after syntactic competence, to situate his or her self among his or her desires and their taboos, that is at the interior of the oedipal triangle" (165).

While Kristeva associates narrative with the oedipal complex, she connects poetic practice, in contrast, with the preoedipal and the *chora*, the maternal body. Poetic language unleashes the semiotic's transgression of the symbolic order, initiates a "breach of the symbolic" (1984, 62–63). The semiotic cannot itself stand alone; rather it exists as a dimension within the symbolic in a state of perpetual opposition: "Though absolutely necessary, the thetic is not exclusive: the semiotic, which also precedes it, constantly tears it open" (62). As the avant-garde of revolutionary linguistic practice, "poetry is the *chora's* guerilla war against culture," in the words of Calvin Bedient's summary of Kristeva's revolutionary poetic (1990, 809).[7]

In "The Laugh of the Medusa," Cixous makes explicit what is largely implicit in Kristeva's formulation: namely, the connection of these binaries to the repression and liberation of the feminine and of women through *écriture féminine*. "Only the poets—not the novelists, allies of representationalism"—can wield "the anti-logos weapon" and "blow up the Law"; for "poetry involves gaining strength through the unconscious and because the unconscious, that other limitless country, is the place where the repressed manage to survive: women" (Cixous [1975] 1980, 250). Cixous's early work on Joyce (*The Exile of James Joyce* [1972]) and her more recent work on Brazilian novelist Clarice Lispector (1991) suggest that the kind of *écriture féminine* she promotes in her essays is precisely what she finds in the avant-garde novels of these writers. It is not the novel per se to which Cixous objects, but rather the novel's tie to representationalism, which she in turn links to narrative. What she applauds in the novels of Joyce and Lispector is precisely their lyric resistance to narrative.

Barthes, Kristeva, and Cixous all variously associate narrative and the novel with a repressive social order that the lyric and the poem can potentially disrupt. Their resistance to narrative is matched by much poststructuralist narrative theory. Leo Bersani, for example, argues in *A Future for Astyanax* (1984) that narrative is inherently authoritarian, allied to the state through its connection to mimesis and subject to perpetual disruptions from unruly desires. Representing a feminist/poststructuralist critique of narrative, Teresa de Lauretis suggests in *Alice Doesn't* (1984) that narrative is inseparable from an oedipal configuration of desire in which subjectivity is constituted as masculine. Many other feminist critics have focused on the preoedipal and/or the lyric as sites of past or potential disruption of oedipal narrative patterns.[8] Here, I would include my own essay, "Lyric Subversion of Narrative" (1989), in which I assumed the relationship between narrative and lyric in women's writing to be essentially conflictual and implicitly privileged lyric as the more subversive mode.

Writing *Penelope's Web: Gender, Modernity, H.D.'s Fiction* (1990a) has made me rethink my own resistance to narrative and that of much poststructuralist theory in general. Here I argued that the innovative lyric discourse H.D. forged in the imagist period to write herself out of the cultural script of sentimental poetess was intentionally impersonal and seemingly ungendered. During World War I, she began to write experimental narrative fiction that anticipates *écriture féminine* precisely so that she could represent herself as a woman, flagrantly gendered, in the text. Narrative—with its insistent representationalism and location of subjectivity within the coordinates of historical space and time—was essential to this experimental discourse. Where her early lyric had denied story, narrative invited the inscription of female identity as it is forged through engagement of the self with the social order. These narrative self-constructions in lyric prose made possible the complex symbiosis of narrative and lyric in H.D.'s epics and long poems of the 1940s and 1950s. In her prose, as well as in her later poetry, narrative and lyric are allies, not enemies—a play of different voices, not a war.

The implication of this turn to narrative for poststructuralist privileging of lyric as the site of subversion has its corollary in the current debate about identity politics in feminist theory. Some poststructuralist feminists, such as Alice Jardine (1985) and Peggy Kamuf (1982), have seen great potential for feminist theory in the death of the Cartesian subject and modernity's dispersal of "identity." Others, such as Nancy K. Miller, have argued that it is premature to erase the issue of identity for those denied the status of subject by the symbolic order. "Only those who have it [the status of subject] can play with not having it," Miller writes (1988, 75).

It is similarly premature, I believe, to dismiss narrative for those denied the authoritative voice and position of the storyteller by the dominant symbolic order. The poststructuralist need to shatter the "meaning" and "coherence" that narrative constructs may well originate in the privilege of those who have traditionally controlled the production of literate meanings. The attack on narrative's representationalism and mimetic reference to "real" experience risks ethnocentric cultural erasure of those writers who come from marginalized cultures rich in narrative traditions—like Silko's and Morrison's. Moreover, to miss the radical potential of narrative for writers of any group that has been absent in or trivialized by hegemonic historical discourses "prematurely forecloses the question of agency for them," to borrow Miller's formulation (1988, 106).

Having defended narrative, I hasten to add that just as *identity* has often undergone revisionist transformation in women's writing, so *narrative* has often been subject to many forms of deconstruction and reconstruction. Many women writers have, for example, resisted what Virginia Woolf called in "Modern Fiction" the "tyranny of plot . . . *in the accepted manner*" (1953, 154; emphasis added)—that is, narrative conventions that replicate the ideological scripts of the social order. Secondly, as Rachel Blau DuPlessis demonstrates in *Writing beyond the Ending* (1985), women writers have often reconfigured conventional narrative patterns so as to tell stories new to literary tradition, ones suited to the historically produced narratives of women's experiences and dreams. Thirdly, women writers whose cultures rely on a living oral tradition have transformed literate narrative by weaving strands of oral and written narrative conventions. And finally, as Morrison suggests in "Memory, Creation, and Writing": "Still, narrative is not and never has been enough, just as the object drawn on a canvas or a cave wall is never simply mimetic" (1984, 388). She argues that narrative does not preclude, in fact it positively requires, other modes of knowing, modalities such as the metaphoric, the visual, the musical, and the kinesthetic. We might recognize in her evocation of the nonnarrative the realm of the lyric, even the dimension of language that Kristeva identifies with the semiotic, the *chora,* the maternal body. Many women writers have engaged in a revisionist reconstitution of narrative by setting in play a collaborative dialogue between narrative and lyric.

Claiming the Discourses of History and Myth

The contemporary women's long poem provides a rich testing ground for the relation of narrative and lyric in women's writing. At first glance, both generic convention and twentieth-century poetic practice suggest that women poets would readily disrupt narrative and foreground lyric discourse. The generic grid within which contemporary long poems are written and read includes the epic, a genre whose conventions largely precluded a woman occupying the place of bard in the community. Women would have every reason, one would suppose, to resist conventions of epic narrative within which WOMAN often functions without subjectivity as muse, booty, occasion for masculine quest, or idealized symbol (see Friedman 1986, 1990b).

Moreover, influential twentieth-century long poems, such as Pound's *Cantos,* T. S. Eliot's *The Waste Land* and *Four Quartets,* William Carlos Williams's *Paterson,* and Hart Crane's *The Bridge,* broke with the narrative conventions of the epic through a variety of structural patterns based in juxtaposition of lyric sequences. As Margaret Dickie puts it:

> The long public poem has traditionally thrived on narrative or on argumentation for development, and the Modernists had no enthusiasm for either mode of expression. They intended to start the long poem with an image, a symbol, a fragmented translation, a mode of ecstatic affirmation. In short, they began to write the long poem as if it were to be an extended lyric. (Dickie 1986, 11)

M. L. Rosenthal and Sally M. Gall further argue that the modern poetic sequence (the term for the type of long poem they privilege) "usually includes narrative and dramatic elements, and ratiocinative ones as well, but its structure is finally lyrical" and "progressively liberated from a narrative or thematic framework" (Rosenthal and Gall 1983, 9, 11).

Other critics stress the modern long poem's existence within a horizon of expectations based in the epic (see Dembo 1966; Bernstein 1980; Miller 1979).

They consequently find narrative to be at least implicitly present, frequently as an interior quest narrative that underlies lyric juxtapositions. But whatever their differences, critics regularly see the foregrounding of lyric and muting of narrative as a consistent feature of twentieth-century long poems.[9] This feature, pioneered by the avant-garde practices that Kristeva favors, thus invites a reading of women's long poems in relationship to the poststructuralist privileging of lyric as a transgressive discourse.

The scores of long poems published by women since 1960 certainly confirm a widespread resistance to narrative as it had been formulated in the epic tradition and a frequent reliance on lyric juxtaposition and sequencing as structuring devices. But I am also struck by the positive and frequent presence of narrative in these poems as part of a project to assert female identity and agency in a world that would confine that subjectivity in forms of alterity. Narrative in these long poems takes different forms; to be aware of them, we need to understand the genre in its broadest sense.[10] Sometimes, the narrative function is direct—the poet tells a story, a sequence of events that occur within recognizable coordinates of space and time. Sometimes, the narrative dimension is indirect—the reader (re)constructs an implicit story in the ordering or juxtaposition of often loosely connected lyric sequences. And sometimes the narrative exists tenuously at the borderland between the long poem and a collection of discrete, but related, poems as a structuring principle that suggests a progression from one section or poem to another. Whether narrated by the poet or the reader, these narrative functions may be mimetic or nonmimetic, may borrow heavily from or disrupt conventional narrative forms. In all cases, narrative, in Morrison's words, "is not enough." Narrative and lyric (along with related pairs of prose and poetry, story and figure, mimetic and nonrepresentational, symbolic and semiotic) coexist dialogically—sometimes supportively or conflictually; sometimes both cooperatively and oppositionally; sometimes in a simultaneous play of voices or in a distinctly bifurcated text of prose and poetry. Whatever the shifting forms and dynamics of this collaboration, narrative and lyric cannot be accurately said to exist in a fixed binary where lyric is (always) the revolutionary force that transgresses (inherent) narrative tyranny. Rather, they coexist in a collaborative interchange of different and interdependent discourses.

In general, narrative functions in two main ways in women's contemporary long poems: first, as a claim to historical discourse and, second, as a claim to mythic discourse.[11] As the Greek roots for both *history* and *myth*[12] suggest, history and myth were initially not polar opposites—the one narrating fact, the other fiction. Both terms, moreover, are inseparable from narrative and, specifically, the kind of narrative associated with the epic tradition. As *story*, both history and myth are forms of human knowing that narrate movement (whether external or internal) through space and time (whether material or spiritual).

Taken separately or together, both history and myth have provided the dominant modality of Western epic poetry.

Long poems by men often use historical and mythic discourses,[13] but women's claim to these discourses in their contemporary long poems is overdetermined by their predominant exclusion from such discourses in the past, exclusions that have been identified and reversed by numerous feminist scholars in recent years. Women have always had a history, of course, but it is only in recent years, as a result of feminism, that women have begun to narrate that history in a systematic, sustained, and cumulative way—in a field ambiguously known as "women's history," incorporating both the past events of women's lives and the telling of those stories as a field in which women are the pioneering and predominant (though not exclusive) voices. The development of women's history in the academy parallels the reclamation of historical discourse in the contemporary women's long poem—compelled by similar reasons: a conviction that the lives of women have been systematically erased or trivialized in the dominant historical discourses; an insistence on the necessity for women to participate in the construction of history, so that women's stories, as well as women-as-storytellers, will not be lost and forgotten.[14]

Women's exclusion from myth in many cultures is tied to the religious authority men have systematically claimed as an inherent function of their maleness. Women have always been, in one form or another, active participants in the religion of their cultures. But positions of sacred authority within the community have been (with a few exceptions) reserved for men in Western tradition, at least in part because of the patriarchal repression of maternal deity and the gynophobic perception of women's bodies as polluted—to be feared and adored, desired and loathed.[15] The development of feminist theology and the growth of movements to open positions of religious leadership to women in recent years parallel the reclamation of mythic discourse in the contemporary women's long poem—compelled by similar reasons: a belief that sacred texts have degraded or repressed the feminine; an insistence on the need for women to experience and narrate the sacred.

Derridean deconstructions of history and myth—of the metaphysics of Presence, of the real and referentiality—lie behind much of the poststructuralist resistance to narrative and privileging of lyric. But for those who have been excluded from the discourses of history and myth, such deconstructions, without corresponding reconstructions, are potentially regressive, accomplishing in the realm of theory the silencing that has already been a foundation of their historical positionalities. Derridean *différance*—the endless play of signifiers without reference to signifieds, the endless deferral of reference itself—is a concept that is richly useful for the deconstruction of representation. But by itself, as an end point, it has little to offer those whose survival depends upon the reconstruction of their own histories, the reclamation, through language, of their experience of the "real." Lacanian *jouissance*—the mystical/sexual pleasure beyond representation—is equally suggestive for the identification of revelatory moments that are unnarratable, unspeakable. But as teleological utopia, *jouissance* is not enough for those who need to (re)claim the religious authority to tell the sacred stories that have been appropriated, stolen, or erased. Both mythic and historical claims on the discourses of the real and the sacred require narrative, not as a mode of knowing to be resisted, but rather as one that empowers.

Focusing on the overdetermined function of narrative discourse—both historical and mythic—suggests three broad categories within which we can read the interplay of lyric and narrative in contemporary women's long poems. The first type of long poem is the one that claims a historical discourse, whether that history is personal or societal, in past time or present time, or some combination of the two. The second type claims a mythic discourse, whether this involves revisionist or new forms of mythmaking. The third type refuses the binary of history and myth to construct a fusion or intermingling of the real and the sacred. I suggest these categories not as fixed or intentional types, but rather as useful descriptors that facilitate an examination of the presence and function of narrative discourse in these poems. To demonstrate the scope of these narrative functions, I will review some different types of historical and mythic narratives, with reference to exemplary poems.

Historical Narratives

Long poems that insist upon the "real," the historical, the experiential interestingly mirror some of the different forms of the field of women's history in the academy: biography, documentary history, and social history. Autobiography is an additional form: narratives of the self-in-history, the self-as-history, and the self-as-historian. As biographical history, for example, there are long poems that narrate the lives of heroic women whom history has forgotten or insufficiently remembered. Ruth Whitman's *The Testing of Hanna Senesh* (1986) is such a poem.[16] This first-person narrative poem draws on the journals, letters, plays, and poems of Hanna Senesh (1921–44), the Jewish-Hungarian woman who escaped from Hungary to Palestine in 1939, then returned as part of a Jewish resistance sponsored by British intelligence, and was caught and finally executed in 1944. Firmly linking the poetic to the referential, a photo of Senesh and a prose account of her life by Livia Rothkirchen precede the poem. The poem itself narrates the story of her life and death in alternating sections in two voices: first, a journalistic, proselike voice that records the external events, and then, an italicized lyric voice that articulates Senesh's inner feelings, fantasies, and memories.

The real and the imaginary, the narrative and the lyric, oppose each other, often literally on the two sides of a page. The opposition, however, is not conflictual, but rather cooperative. The italicized lyrics do not transgress the journalistic but rather supplement it.

Another kind of biographical history represents the attempt to reconstruct the never-known story of women attached to famous men, women who were "penned" (in) by masculine desire, "sentenced" into history by their association with men and by their objectifying stories (see Gilbert and Gubar 1979a, 13). Susan Howe's long poem, *The Liberties* (1983), abandons the kind of representational historical discourse of Whitman's poems in a kind of experimental array of prose and lyric voices, supplemented by a few graphics. Howe's syntactic and linguistic disruptions as well as her play with lineation and the visual page—qualities that associate her with the avant-garde Language poets—certainly suggest elements of Kristeva's semiotic. But these lyric elements do not so much transgress the narrative as they collaborate with the poet's attempt to recover the story of Hester Johnson, the Stella of Jonathan Swift's *Journal to Stella*. "*[C]inders of Eve, what is my quest?*" the poet asks. It is to tell "the whole history of her story" (Howe 1983, 81, 83). Aptly titled "*Fragments of a Liquidation*," the first section, entirely in prose, quotes from Swift's work and narrates what little is known about Stella. Since "none of Stella's letters have been saved" (67), the poet imaginatively re-creates Stella's subjectivity in a verse play and increasingly avant-garde lyrics. Central to the narrative is the poet's resurrection of another penned (in) woman, Shakespeare's Cordelia, who tells Stella, "How did we happen— because we were written" (109) and asks:

> We
>
>   storied and told
>
>   are adrift
>
> we turn away
>
>   mute.
>
>   Can you not see?
>
>   (107)

The silent spaces between these words are marks of the semiotic that help narrate the story of silence. Woven into the retold story of Stella and Cordelia is the tale of the poet's identification with and articulation of these women's histories.

Documentary history—important in the fields of film and photography, as well as history—represents the need to record a sense of particular time, place, and people that has been or is about to be lost. *Steveston* (first edition 1974), by the poet Daphne Marlatt and the photographer Robert Minden, is a long poem counterpointed with photos that documents the passing of Steveston, a once flourishing Canadian Pacific boomtown at the mouth of the Fraser River, known for its salmon fishing, cannery, and mosaic of Japanese, Chinese, Finnish, and Indian Canadians. Marlatt, a Canadian poet subsequently known for her experimental prose poems influenced by poststructuralist and Québécoise feminist theory, writes in the afterward of the second edition that the text tells Steveston's "story as a single narrative told in two distinct modes that converse with each other": the one told in photos (which synchronically document a Barthesian "presence" of people and buildings) and the other told in poems (which diachronically reflect on the flow of time) (Marlatt and Minden 1984, 92). Not only do photos and poems coexist dialogically, but the poems themselves—some written as prose poems, some as lineated lyrics—set in play a river-flow of intermingling narrative and image. The lyric sequences of space-time in word-images do not themselves progress narratively. Rather, they present fluid snapshots of the town-in-time, the history of the town from boomtown to ghost town: "Steveston: hometown still for some, a story: of belonging (or is it continuing? / lost, over and over..." (Marlatt and Minden 1984, 85).[17]

Paralleling feminist social history, some long poems set out to re-create the stories of "ordinary" women's lives, that is, the texture and feel of everyday life for the kind of women "history proper" ignores. Like social history, these poems often narrate individual stories and family histories with an implicit assumption of their representability and reflection of the larger social patterns. Perhaps inspired by Judy Grahn's influential sequence *The Common Woman Poems* ([1969] 1978), Karen Brodine's "Woman Sitting at the Machine, Thinking: A series of work poems" ([1981] 1990) counterpoints the materiality of a typesetter's daily life with the daydreams, fantasies, and memories—the "thinking"—of the "woman sitting at the machine," where "my own thoughts sneak through..." in a kind of semiotic eruption into the symbolic order of work:

> call format o five. my day so silent yet taken up with words.
> floating through the currents and cords of my wrists
> into the screen and drifting to land, beached pollywogs
>
> ....
>
> enter file execute.
>
> (Brodine [1981] 1990, 5)

(How)ever, a journal devoted to women's avant-garde poetry, published portions of Brodine's poem in 1988, a mark of the poem's place in an experimentalist tradition. While the poet's lyric fantasies transgress the prosaically rendered machine work, narrative and lyric are not fixed in perpetual opposition. The poet also relies upon prosaic verse to render the structure of oppression, the patterns of resistance; and verse that begins prosaically often shades collaboratively into the disruptions of syntactic rules that Kristeva associates with the semiotic:

she and some co-workers
today more than ever in U.S.
h i s t o r y

posed to discrimination by sex,
race, color, religious or national
o r i g i n

more women go to work in

enter the labor
70 percent of the average wage
Black women lowest paid of
to organize the continuing fight. . . .
                    (Brodine [1981] 1990, 16)[18]

The long poem as social history is closely related to long poems that narrate personal history, the story of the self, autobiography in poetic form; for stories of individual lives often claim a certain representability as history of more than one. Poems about the self-in-history probe the way personal narratives are caught up in broader societal events that define not only the individual, but an era. Denise Levertov's "Staying Alive" (1971) serves as witness to "Amerika" in crisis by narrating how the Vietnam War and the need to testify against it invades the private world of the poet. Shifting from poetry to prose, from lyric to journalistic discourse (supplemented by notes that further attest to the poem's referential base), the poem moves fluidly between the inner and outer worlds, the poet's subjectivity activated by the news of the war and the protesters. The interplay of lyric and narrative, poetry and prose, mimics the intersections of public and private; both discourses are necessary for the poet's construction of the self-as-revolutionary.[19] As Levertov explains in her preface about her assemblage of these separate poems into a single long poem: "it assembles separated parts of a whole. . . . [in] the hope of that whole being seen as having some value not as a mere 'confessional' autobiography, but as a document of some historical value, a record of one person's inner-outer experience in America during the '60s and the beginning of the '70s" (1971, ix).

Some autobiographical long poems demonstrate a sense of the self-in-history supplemented by a reflexive awareness of the self-as-history. A narrative of the self unfolds with the passing of a day, an era, a life—also, with the play of time in the processes of memory. Bernadette Mayer's *Midwinter Day*, for example, evokes Joyce's *Ulysses* not only in its first word ("Stately"), but also in its narrative of the cycle of one day's (extra)ordinary life and its revelation of the poet's subjectivity, which moves associationally through past, present, future, and fantasy and across vast numbers of cultural texts. "I had an idea to write a book," the poet says in a prose section midway through the poem,

> that would translate the detail of thought from a day to language like a dream to read as it does, everything . . . to prove the day like the dream has everything in it, to do this without remembering like a dream inciting writing continuously for as long as you can stand up till you fall down like in a story. (1982, 89)

She selects 22 December, begins in the dream-state of waking in the early morning, follows the day's events (taking care of children, doing errands, fixing meals, etc.) in Lenox, Massachusetts, and finishes in the late-night writing of the poem we read. Psychological, erotic, philosophical, religious, and literary journeys—each in turn often evoking fragments of stories—are anchored in the everyday of ordinary space-time. The poet moves fluidly through various lyric and prose discourses that supplement rather than compete with each other. Syntactic disruptions, interruptions, elisions, gaps abound—not to transgress narrative, but rather to provide, as in *Ulysses,* a kind of psychological realism to the narrative events of the day. Mayer deliberately evokes the epic horizon in her reflections on her project:

> In the past of the west and maybe further, poets told stories, they sang, they wrote epics, they composed for occasions. Inherent in the history of our lives together since I, all the while wanting to write this book, met you [poet's husband Lewis] is a story, I don't know if I can tell it, I'll go as fast as I can on the occasion of this day. (89)[20]

Mayer's imaginative journeys in the course of a day highlight a major motif of long poems that narrate the self-as-history: that is, the journey motif, central to the epic for centuries. Movement through space as well as time—with its implicit quest theme—constitutes the narrative framework for many autobiographical long poems. Daphne Marlatt's *How Hug a Stone* (1983) narrates in prose-poem sequences the poet's journey home to England, to the "mother" country of her parents, a spiritual source for the poet born in Australia, raised in Malaysia, and bringing up her son in Vancouver. Marlatt and Warland's jointly written long poem *Double Negative* records in lyric and prose-poetic form, supplemented by collages, their railroad "crossing" of the continent of Australia and their later reflections on that "narrative track" (1988, 38).[21]

As collaborative autobiography of two selves (poets and lovers—"two women outback / down under / add it up—two negatives make a positive" [Marlatt and Warland 1988, 20]), *Double Negative* foregrounds the way women's poems narrating the self-as-history engage in a re-vision of the individualistic autobiographical self that characterizes much Western male autobiography, including confessional long poems such as Robert Lowell's *Life Studies* (1959) and John Berryman's *The Dream Songs* (1969). Instead of an isolate self, many women's poems narrate a relational self in which the woman's life story is inseparably interwoven with the lives of others: lovers, children, family, and often their immediate cultural group. In Lucille Clifton's prose poem *generations: a memoir* ([1976] 1987a, 227–77), for example, the story of her self begins in the narrative of her ancestors, going back to Caroline Donald, the Dahomey woman "born in Afrika in 1823," who taught her descendants that "Things don't fall apart. Things hold. Lines connect in thin ways that last and last and lives become generations made out of pictures and words just kept" (1987a, 276). Quotations from Whitman's *Song of Myself* introduce each new generation, thereby situating *generations* in the tradition of epic autobiography. Photos of the generations reinforce the verbal text's claims on history. For Clifton, personal history is inseparable from African-American familial and communal history.22

All these different claims on historical discourse implicitly insist upon the right and necessity for the poet to engage in history making—both the interpretive narration of an era and the telling itself as a significant act in history. Some poems explicitly foreground this narrative function of the self-as-historian. Diane Glancy, for example, is an American poet of Cherokee and German-English descent. *Lone Dog's Winter Count* is a volume of discrete poems that cohere as a long poem in reference to Lone Dog's spiral representation of Dakota history from the winter of 1800–1801 to the winter of 1870–71. On this nineteenth-century buffalo hide, Glancy informs us, a pictograph for each year represents a history of Lone Dog's people, particularly the march of cataclysmic events in the developing "demise of the Indian nation" (1991, 77). Glancy's own "pictographs," which counterpoint lyric and narrative, poetry and prose, are framed by the illustration of Lone Dog's Winter Count on the cover and a concluding prose section that explains his images. Her "winter count" spans personal, familial, and tribal history in the twentieth century. Lone Dog as historian is the poet's persona, and his nineteenth-century history provides the unifying structure for her twentieth-century history of her self, her family, and her people.

Mythic and Religious Narratives

Reclamations of mythic and religious discourse in the contemporary women's long poem are less common than claims to historical discourse, but they nonetheless constitute a recurrent pattern, often in combination with discourses that insist upon the "real," on women's material existence in time. This kind of narrative discourse exists on a continuum incorporating secular legends, sacred cycles, and autobiographical spiritual journeys. Often, these long poems gain their narrative dimension from preexisting stories that the poems evoke and sometimes revoke—legends from folklore and mythological cycles, biblical stories, narratives from pre-Christian or non-Western religious traditions, and autobiographical narratives of spiritual conversion and pilgrimage. Evocation of preexistent narratives often allows the lyric voice to be foregrounded, since the weight of storytelling can be shared with the reader, who already knows the outline of the tale. Although the interplay of lyric and narrative in these long poems is as richly collaborative as it is for the historical narratives, I will, in the interest of space, identify only types of mythic discourse present in these poems, all of which exhibit a strong narrative drive of one sort or another.

Perhaps the most common kind of mythic discourse in contemporary women's long poems is the revisionist narrative—that is, the (re)telling of androcentric stories from women-centered perspectives. This revisionist impulse guided H.D.'s *Helen in Egypt* ([1961] 1974), a retelling of the Trojan War from Helen's point of view, as well as Anne Sexton's *Transformations* (1971), a volume whose satiric wit unhinges and redoes *The Brothers Grimm,* and Margaret Atwood's "Circe/Mud Poems" (1974), in which Circe tells her side of the story ("It's the story that counts," Circe tells Odysseus [Atwood 1976, 221]). In an ambitious reworking of sacred texts, Lucille Clifton's two sequences—"some jesus" ([1972] 1987a, 91–106) and the Mary/Jesus poems ([1980] 1987a, 196–210)—present a succession of condensed, highly evocative lyrics that metonymically suggest a retelling of the stories of Adam and Eve, Cain and Abel, Mary and Joseph, Jesus and his disciples, and the crucifixion. Charlotte Mandel, in *The Marriages of Jacob: A Poem-Novella* (1991), burrows into the book of Genesis, specifically into the stories of Jacob, Leah, and Rachel, for evidence of suppressed stories of women's centrality in the early history of the Jews. Her retelling of Rachel's theft of her father's teraphim—a mysterious knot in the biblical narrative—alters a foundational story of the Jewish people, the narrative of Jacob, whom God renames Israel, by recovering the history of Mother Rachel.[23]

Revisionist rescriptions of canonical mythic discourse are supplemented by resurrectionist narratives of forgotten or dis-membered traditions that the poet reclaims and re-members. Such traditions might be pre-Judaic and pre-Christian narratives that have existed palimpsestically beneath or within the sedimentations of the canonical. Along with *Helen in Egypt,* H.D.'s *Trilogy* ([1944–46] 1973) has been a defining poem of this type. Influenced by H.D., Judy Grahn in *She Who* ([1971–72] 1978) extracts from the shards of ancient female deities a primal *She,* the spirit-flesh of (re)birth who powers and empowers the poet's lyric prayers, invocations, rituals, and narratives of birthing (Grahn 1978, 75–109). "Was I not over / over ridden?" *She* asks, invoking the palimpsestic narrative: "it is a long story / will you be proud to be my version?" (Grahn 1978, 104). The poem foregrounds the lyric with ritualistic use of rhythm, rhyme, repetition— semiotic elements that intensify rather than disrupt the underlying birth narrative.[24]

Other long poems implicitly resist canonical narratives by situating themselves in non-Western traditions. In *Borderlands/ La Frontera* (1987), Gloria Anzaldúa uses mirroring prose and poetic discourses to uncover the Aztec goddesses buried within the Virgin of Gaudeloupe of Mexican and Chicano/a culture. The syncretism of Anzaldúa's text becomes the structuring principle of Louise Erdrich's *Baptism of Desire* (1989). The poems in this five-part volume can be read together as a long poem whose narrative of spiritual quest is reconstructed by the reader based on the ordering and sectioning of the discrete lyrics. The occasion for the poems is the poet's pregnancy that is finally narrated and celebrated in part 5. As preconditions for this spiritual/material gestation, parts 1 and 4 journey through Christian and Chippewa traditions (respectively), retelling, for example, the stories of Mary and Mary Magdalene (in lyrics, part 1) and the trickster figure and spirit walker Potchikoo (in prose-poem sequences, part 4). Parts 2 and 3 are syncretist weavings of Western and Indian stories and mysticism.

Erdrich's narrative focuses ultimately on the mystical/gestational "I" of the poet whose nine-month journey not only invokes the narrative of pregnancy but also replays the traditional Western form of spiritual autobiography. Blending this tradition with the journey motif of the epic, Carolyn Grassi in *Journey to Chartres* (1989) and Rena Rosenwasser in *Isle* (1992) undertake pilgrimages to France (Grassi) and the Greek Isles (Rosenwasser) in their narratives of spiritual discovery. In "The Sickness That Has No Name" in *The Annie Poems* (1987), Anne Cameron journeys from a sterile Anglo-Anglicanism to a fusion of Native American animism, fable, and feminist spirituality.

As narrative discourses, the historical and mythic are perhaps always complicitous, each regularly implicit in the other. But some long poems, like H.D.'s *Trilogy,* insist upon their interpenetration, presenting narratives in which the spiritual and material, historical and religious coexist as double layers, double voices in dialogic relation. In Grahn's *The Queen of Wands* (1982), the poet's search for Inanna, the "stolen" goddess of ancient Babylonia, leads her to find traces of her erasure and insistent presence throughout myth and history—in the stories of the mythic Helen of Troy and the historical Marilyn Monroe, among the dead in the Triangle Fire in New York and the grandmothers who sing lullabies to their babies. Texts such as Ntozake Shange's *for colored girls . . .* should also be read within the tradition of the women's long poem that weaves historical and mythic discourses. Shange's "choreopoem" (her neologism) is a collection of lyrics spoken and danced by the African American women dressed and named by the colors of the rainbow. It is implicitly structured as a spiritual journey for black women, one that gestures simultaneously at the material existence of those for whom "being alive & bein a woman & bein colored is a metaphysical dilemma" ([1977] 1980, 48) and at the spiritual dimensions of their rebirth, celebrated in the poem's final gospel lyric: "i found god in myself / & i loved her / i loved her fiercely" (67).[25]

Irena Klepfisz's *Keeper of Accounts*

To demonstrate in some greater detail the collaboratively dialogic interplay of narrative and lyric in women's long poems, I will conclude with a discussion of Irena Klepfisz's *Keeper of Accounts* (1982).[26] Asserting a claim on both historical and religious discourses, *Keeper of Accounts* is a long poem in four parts made up of discrete poems and sequences that cohere around the poet's project of survival in diaspora, specifically in the exile of the post-Holocaust world. Narrative and lyric, prose and poetry, mimesis and fable, history and religion conjoin in a mosaic of discourses in which the different components cooperate dialogically in an inscription of the poet's subjectivity. To echo Kristeva's *sujet en procès* (subject in process/on trial) (Kristeva 1984, 37), the textual practices of the poem construct a subject very much in process and on trial—caught in the processes of retrieving forgotten histories of a childhood in Poland, on trial as a Jew who survived the Holocaust by "passing" as a Polish child, who must now reclaim her Jewish legacy and identity.

Part 1, "From the Monkey House and Other Cages," is a two-part narrative poem in which two female monkeys tell the story of their captivity in the timeless space of an unnamed zoo: the first, a daughter separated from her mother, forced into sex, and then separated from her baby; the second, a lonely monkey touched momentarily by the arrival and death of a rebellious monkey. Part 2, "Different Enclosures," gets its title from the last line of part 1 (Klepfisz 1982, 24) and contains three poems in which the poet tells about her enclosure in the monotonies of clerical work and her dreams of freedom: "It is a story, I tell myself, at least / a story" (31). Part 3, "Urban Flowers," contains eight poems that center on the poet's efforts to grow flowers in the "inhospitable soil" of modern American urban life: "It is the stuff of mythology / both old and new. . . . now / we must burst forth with orange flowers / with savage hues of our captivity" (56, 49, 57). Part 4, "Inhospitable Soil," contains three lengthy sequences that, from the heuristic perspective of the poet's present life in rural Cherry Hill, New York, return to Poland before, during, and just after the war to tell the stories of capture, death, escape, and survival of the poet's family and friends. The poem, then, moves in circular fashion back in time from one kind of enclosure to another. Its repetitive rhythm is the interlocking imagery of and narrative movement from captivity to freedom, from sterility to regeneration, from death to survival.

Keeper of Accounts has a strong narrative drive in both its discrete parts and its overarching project, a drive that claims historical, mythic, and religious discourses. Many of the poems tell or contain powerful stories. The monkey narrators in part 1 tell riveting tales of intimacy, separation, loss, rebellion, and death. These two stories prefigure the poet's (re)telling of events from her child-hood in part 4: the death of her father in the uprising of the Warsaw ghetto; the separation of mother and daughter, who was left first at a Catholic orphanage and then with a Polish peasant; the mother's struggle to survive alone in the woods; her friend Elza's escape, American adoption, and final suicide; her aunt's "passing" so as to help the Jews in the ghetto and her courageous claim to Jewish identity in death.

These stories (and others—of office work, dreaming, and gardening) cohere into the larger narrative projects of the poem: the recovery of a forgotten past, the exodus from captivities, the reclamation of a Jewish identity and destiny. "So much of history," the poet writes in her final poem, an elegy for her aunt, "seems a gaping absence   at best a shadow / longing   for some greater / defini-tion   which will never come" (90). As poet-historian, Klepfisz attempts to fill that gap, to locate the "vestige   of one history forgotten and unattended" (63). While gardening, she thinks, "In the earth   are buried histories / irretrievable" (95). But her poem, written over a six-year period (1976–82), gradually retrieves the irretrievable, speaks the unspeakable histories of the Holocaust and its after-math.

The return of this repressed history is gradual and painful, won through difficult discipline. It begins with the indirect displacement of fable: the story of the caged monkeys, animals who speak and feel as women and foreshadow the women who are treated as animals. Elements of the Holocaust story are present—the enclosure, the separation of mother and daughter, death of the beloved—but this zoo story does not yet trigger the memories of Poland. The poet must first understand her bond with the monkeys through an examination of her life as a clerical worker in part 2 and then initiate the indirect process of regeneration by seeking the insistent urban flowers in part 3. Gardening in Cher-ry Hill and her mother's visit in the first poem of part 4 ("Glimpses of the Outside") bring about the first surfacing of painful childhood memories, which then follow in a rush of events in the next poem, "*Bashert.*" As the Yiddish word for "inevitable, (pre)destined," *bashert* inscribes the poet's entrapment in history and her claim to freedom by acceptance of her Jewish identity. No longer must she deny who she is to survive, as she and Elza had to do in Poland; now she can accept the inevitability of her destiny, one tied to both the death and courage of her Aunt Gina. "History," she writes, "keeps unfolding and demanding a response" (81). Her poem is that response, one that gradually allows her to confront the past that she and the present moment had forgotten. The larger narrative of the volume, consequently, is a therapeutic one.

Contributing to this healing process are the mythic and religious narratives that permeate the historical. *Keeper of Accounts* emphasizes Judaism's strong tie, as a religion, to history.[27] The Bible, especially the Torah, narrates the history of the Jewish people in relation to their God. Without explicit allusion, biblical resonances nonetheless abound in Klepfisz's history. The Garden of Eden—with its narrative of desire, expulsion, and exile—exists within the poem's urban and rural gardens as an image of paradise lost and imperfectly regained in the poet's solitary labor. "I have been a dreamer   dreaming / of a perfect garden," the poet muses in the final poem (96). The story of the exodus from slavery to the promised land governs the poem's oscillations between captivity and freedom. The displacements of diaspora resonate throughout the poet's rootlessness. God's demand for the sacrifice of Isaac and the questions of Job echo within the poet's stories of loss and injustice. The lonely discipline, visionary scope, and moral fervor of the prophets undergird the poet's harsh portrait of the modern landscape. The poet's political history evokes the condemnation of oppression and the call to freedom evident in some of the prophets, especially Amos and Isaiah. The existential hope in the face of the "mortal wounds" of history with which the poem ends—"I need to hope. And do" (95)—repeats in secular terms the faith in God's special covenant with his people that sustains the ancient Hebrews in all their many exiles. And finally, the poem performs the ritual of Kaddish, the prayer for the dead that is the obligation of those who survive.

The claim Klepfisz makes on historical and mythic discourse does not preclude a strongly lyrical, even semiotic, dimension in the poem. In contrast to Kristeva's notion of narrative and lyric in fixed opposition and transgressive interplay, the poem establishes a mosaic of lineations, dictions, tones, repetitions, rhythms, and stanzaic configurations that fluidly collaborate rather than disrupt each other. The narrative modality of the poem is not allied with the symbolic order; rather, it takes both lyrical and prosaic form to construct mythic and historical discourses that transgress the social order's silence about the Holocaust. The poet's recovery of the past and survival in the present emerge from a multiplicity of forms, each of which is necessary to the project of the poem.

"Work Sonnets with Notes and a Monologue," for example, is the central poem in part 2, the section on the poet's clerical work as an enclosure that stifles dreams. The captivity and exodus theme appears in multiple discourses separated into three parts, the first in verse, the second in sketchy note form, the third in a prose monologue that reports on a dialogue. Part 1, titled "Work Sonnets," with its alternation of discourses, is a useful example of how narrative and lyric modes collaborate in Klepfisz's text. "Work Sonnets" is a highly schematized sequence of nine sections, each of which (except the eighth) is fifteen lines. Sections i, iv, vii, and ix are short-lined, highly lyrical poems centered on a succession of objective correlatives for the poet's subjectivity: iceberg, volcano, rock, and dust. Repetition is the unifying device as each section begins and ends the same way. For example, "iceberg / I dream   yearning / to be fluid" opens the first section, followed by "volcano / I dream   yearning / to explode" in section iv (33, 35). Each section ends with the line "and day breaks." In contrast, sections ii, iii, v, vi, and viii are mimetic, prosaic, diarylike entries of the poet's activities and feelings on successive days in the office. Each begins with a summary of the day. For example, the lines "today was another day. first i typed some / letters that had to get out. then i spent / hours xeroxing" open section ii, followed by "today was my day for feeling bitter. the xerox / broke down completely   and the receptionist / put her foot down" in section iii (34). The imagistic and prosaic discourses are dialogic, but their opposition is collaborative rather than conflictual. The mimetic sections ground the lyric sections' images in history; the lyric sections free the representational scenes from the purely material. Each adds a dimension that the other lacks.

"From the Monkey House and Other Cages" (part 1) and *Bashert* (the central poem of part 4) represent another instance of paired discourses that dialogically collaborate to tell the story of captivity. The monologues of Monkey I and II tell stories in imagistic, elliptical, gap-filled lyrics that focus on sensation, color, and sound patterns based in alliteration, syntactic parallelism, and rhythmic prosody—elements that Kristeva associates with the semiotic, the *chora,* and the linguistic vestiges of desire for the maternal body. For example, Monkey I's monologue begins in preoedipal bliss marred only by the sterility of captivity:

> from the beginning
> she was always dry   though
> she'd press me close
> prying open my lips:
>
> the water warm
> the fruit   sour   brown
> apples bruised and soft.
>
> hungry for dark   i'd sit
> and wait   devour dreams
> of plain sun and sky
> large leaves   trunks   dark
> and wet with sweet thick sap.

(5)

Her monologue closes—after narrating the life cycle of separation, sexuality, reproduction, and separation—with a memory of that lost mother-daughter union in a discourse that repeats the child's rocking in the arms of the mother:

> and i can see clearly
> the sky   the bars
> as we sat together
> in a spot of sun
> and she   eyes closed
> moved me
> moved me
> to the sound of the waters
> lapping
> in the small   stone pools
> outside.
>
> (15)

These passages both thematize and perform a Kristevan semiotic—not to transgress the narrative, but rather to underscore its story of loss and longing.

"From the Monkey House and Other Cages" is a displaced, lyrical version of what the poet speaks in prose stanzas in "*Bashert.*" After opening with two lyrical prayers—for those who died and those who survived—"*Bashert*"'s first prose sequence ("Poland, 1944: My mother is walking down a road") begins with another story of separation, one that grounds Monkey I's lyrical monologue in the matter-of-fact discourse of material history:

> My mother is walking down a road. Somewhere in Poland. Walking towards an unnamed town for some kind of permit. She is carrying her Aryan identity papers. She has left me with an old peasant who is willing to say she is my grandmother.
>
> She is walking down a road. Her terror in leaving me behind, in risking the separation is swallowed now, like all other feelings.
>
> (77)

As in "Work Sonnets," the lyrical does not disrupt the journalistic; rather both discourses work together to deconstruct the binaries of animal/human, captivity/ freedom, separation/union as a foundation of the poet's *bashert*, her capacity in the final sequence of "*Bashert*" to say: "I do not shun this legacy. I claim it as mine" (86).

The spatial gaps Klepfisz uses throughout *Keeper of Accounts* demonstrate another way the poem establishes a cooperative dialogue between semiotic and symbolic discourses. These gaps slide imperceptibly between functioning as syntactic markers of grammatical pauses (a function of the symbolic modality) and as spaces that resist language as a system of signification (the semiotic modality). Some gaps, in other words, mark off grammatical units, while others function as a kind of stutter, a performance of the poet's hesitations in attempting to speak the unspeakable pain and yearnings of the Holocaust. This interplay of semiotic ellipsis and symbolic syntax is not a fixed opposition, but rather a fluid mingling that both thematizes and performs the poem's double discourse. The poet's Kaddish for Gina Klepfisz in the second sequence of "Solitary Acts" demonstrates how the pause and the stutter reinforce rather than resist each other:

> So much of history   seems
> a gaping absence   at best a shadow
> longing   for some greater
> definition   which will never come
> for what is burned   becomes air
> and ashes   nothing more.
>
> So I cling   to the knowledge of your
> distant grave   for it alone
> reminds me   prods me   to shape that shadow.
>
> (90)

In *Feminism and Poetry,* Jan Montefiore argues that "strategies of storytelling are not, finally, effective in overcoming the paradoxes of exclusion" (1987, 56). With some qualifications, she follows the French theorists who privilege lyric over narrative in her examination of women's poetry. But my review of some contemporary long poems by women suggests that the transgressive and revolutionary potential of women's poetry does not lie in a fixed rejection of narrative, whether mimetic or experimental in form, or in a negative association of narrative with the social and symbolic order that the poet must dismantle, disrupt, and (in Kristeva's formulation) tear open. Instead, the insistence on *story,* on narratives that claim historical and mythic discourse as the right and necessity of women poets, permeates the interplay of lyric and narrative in women's contemporary long poems. *Story,* however (re)defined and (re)constructed, is a precondition of agency. "Such will to be known," Klepfisz writes, "can alter history" (1982, 88). As Silko says: "There have to be stories" (1976, 29); "with these stories we will survive" (1981, 247). And as Joy Harjo writes in her poem "The Book of Myth":

When I entered the book of myths
    in your sandalwood room on a granite island,
I did not ask for a way out.

(1990, 55)

NOTES

1. See also Maxine Hong Kingston's *The Woman Warrior;* Louise Erdrich's *Tracks;* Amy Tan's *The Joy Luck Club* ("Oh, what good stories! Spilling out all over the place!" [1989, 11]) and *The Kitchen God's Wife;* Silko's *Ceremony;* Morrison's *Beloved;* and Kim Chernin's *In My Mother's House* ("Very softly, whispering, I say to her, 'Mama, tell me a story.' . . . And yes, with all the skill available to me as a writer, I will take down her tales and tell her story" [1983, 17]).

2. Perloff's use of the timeless lyric to characterize modernism ignores the enormous importance of narrative—however altered from nineteenth-century conventions—for modernism, including many modernist long poems.

3. Literary histories of the twentieth-century long poem deal almost exclusively with male poets. See, for example, Miller 1979; Bernstein 1980; Rosenthal and Gall 1983; Dickie 1986; Gardner 1989; and Baker 1991. For important exceptions, see Keller 1993 and Kamboureli 1991.

4. See, for example, H.D.'s *Trilogy* ([1944–46] 1973), *By Avon River* (1949), *Helen in Egypt* ([1961] 1974; composed 1952–55), *Sagesse* (1972; composed 1957), *Vale Ave* (1982; composed 1957), *Winter Love* (1972; composed 1959), and *Hermetic Definition* (1972; composed 1960); Gertrude Stein's *Tender Buttons* (1914; composed 1911–12), *Lifting Belly* (1953; composed 1915–17), *Patriarchal Poetry* (1953; composed 1927), and *Stanzas in Meditation* (1956; composed 1932); Mina Loy's "Anglo-Mongrels and the Rose" (composed 1923–25), never published in toto until 1982 in *The Last Lunar Baedeker;* and Gwendolyn Brooks, "A Street in Brownsville" (1945), "The Anniad" (1949), and "In the Mecca" (1968). The delayed publication dates for H.D., Loy, and Stein may reflect writers' and readers' anxiety about the coupling of women and the long poem. Edna St. Vincent Millay's *Fatal Interview* ([1931] 1988), a sequence of fifty-two sonnets organized seasonally, can also be read as a long poem.

5. In *Mythologies* ([1957] 1972), Barthes does not directly connect myth with narrative, but his demystifications of mass culture in the book analyze the operations of what are now termed cultural narratives. Moreover, the opposition he sets up between myth and poetry, as well as his selection of the term *myth* for ideology, suggest that the binary that underlies the volume is the one that appears elsewhere in Barthes's work: narrative versus lyric. See also his "The Discourse of History" ([1967] 1986, esp. 136, 140).

6. Kristeva's alliance with poetic and against novelistic modalities represents an interesting departure from Mikhail Bakhtin's formulation of the narrative/lyric opposition in *The Dialogic Imagination,* where he argues that novelistic discourse, in contrast to poetry, has a "fundamentally dialogic relationship to heteroglossia" (the heteroglossic being his version of transgressive discourse) (1981, 399).

7. Bedient 1990 argues that Kristeva's privileging of poetry, poetic practice, and the semiotic ignores the way poetry is also associated *with* (not just against) culture and meaning. But he does not deal with the opposition between narrative and poetic.

8. See especially Bersani 1984, 3–16, 51–88, 189–316; Clayton's critique of Bersani and defense of narrative (1989); de Lauretis 1984, 103–58. In *Technologies of Gender*, de Lauretis moves beyond the position of *Alice Doesn't* to "specify the modes of consciousness of a feminist subjectivity and its inscription" (1987, xi). For location of female subjectivity in the preoedipal, see, for example, DuPlessis 1985; Homans 1986; Hirsch 1989; Sprengnether 1990; and Abel 1989.

9. A few critics attempt to avoid weighting lyric in relation to narrative by stressing the play of both modes in the long poem. Keller, for example, writes that the modern long poem combines "elements of lyric and epic traditions along with resources of various prose genres" (Keller 1993, 535). Kamboureli sees the long poem as a heterogeneous mix of lyric, epic, and documentary characterized by "generic restlessness": "The long poem as I read it finds its energy in its incorporation of various genres and its simultaneous resistance to generic labels" (1991, xiii–xiv).

10. Definitions of *long poem* vary considerably. I use the term to cover a variety of forms that includes reflexively identified epics and long poems, lyric sequences of substantial length and scope, volumes of discrete poems whose coherence and/or progression are somehow marked by the poet as a whole, and texts that can be read innovatively at the borders of the genre (such as Silko's *Storyteller* (1981); Anzaldúa's *Borderlands/La Frontera* (1987); Shange's *for colored girls* . . . ([1977] 1980); and Warland's *Proper Deafinitions* (1990). For discussion of definition, see Keller 1988, 1993; Riddel's special issue of *Genre* on the long poem (1978); Li 1986; Kamboureli 1991; and Friedman 1990b.

11. A more tenuous narrative function is implicit in a meditative, philosophical/literary discourse that is particularly common in avant-garde long poems such as Howe's *Pythagorean Silence* (1982); Mayer's *Utopia* (1984); Dahlen's *A Reading* (1992); Warland's *serpent (w)rite* (1987); DuPlessis's *Drafts* (1991); and Hejinian's *The Cell* (1992). Such poems implicitly contain a narrative of dialogic play with the traditional philosophic and linguistic discourses from which women have been excluded. This important philosophical-narrative mode is beyond the scope of this essay. See DuPlessis 1990, 110–39 on Howe and Dahlen; Friedman 1990b on Warland.

12. The Greek roots for *history* and *myth* are *historia* (an account of one's inquiries, often in narrative form) and *mythos* (story, legend).

13. See, for example, Allen Ginsberg, *Howl* (1956), John Berryman, *Homage to Mistress Bradstreet* (1956), Robert Lowell, *History* (1973), and Charles Olson, *The Maximus Poems* (1983).

14. In "Women's Time" (1981) Kristeva identifies this desire to insert female subjectivity into the linear time of history (that is, the narrative of men's time) with what she calls the first stage of women's liberation. While she acknowledges the contribution of this stage, her essay posits and clearly privileges two subsequent phases—one based on feminine difference outside the symbolic order of history (women's time), one based on some point dialectically beyond the first two.

15. Such representations are not confined to Western traditions; they are present in

Confucian culture, for example. They are not, however, universal. Some American Indian cultures, such as the Laguna Pueblo people to which Silko belongs, exhibit a less gynophobic theology.

16. See also Whitman, *Tamsen Donner* (1977), *Hatsheput* (1992), and "The Passion of Lizzie Borden" (1973); Atwood, *The Journals of Susanna Moody* (1976b); Hadas, *Beside Herself* (1983); Breckenridge, *Civil Blood* (1986).

17. Another Canadian poet, Dorothy Livesay, explains her turn away from the purely lyric in her prefatory note for *The Documentaries,* her collection of long poems: "My first two books of poems, published in 1929 and 1932, were brief, imagistic and lyrical. But with the thirties came the Depression and its threats of war and dictatorship. Poetry, in English and in North America, became political. I too was fired with the desire to set down in documentary form what was happening to my Canadian generation, historically and socially" (1968, v). See Kamboureli's discussion of Marlatt (1991, 114–23) and Livesay (1991, 37–44).

18. Other long poems that can be read as social history include Brooks's "In the Mecca" ([1968] 1987); Stevenson's *Correspondences* (1974); Rich's *Twenty-One Love Poems* (1978); Brown's *Cora Fry* (1977); Silko's *Storyteller* (1981); Sherley Anne Williams's "Letters from a New England Negro" (1982); Mayer's *Midwinter Day* (1982); Dove's *Thomas and Beulah* (1986); Breckenridge's *Civil Blood* (1986); and Hejinian's *My Life* (1987).

19. For other long poems about the Vietnam era, see di Prima's *Revolutionary Letters* (1971) and Ostriker's *The Mother/Child Papers* (1980) (discussed in Friedman 1990b). See also Mitsuye Yamada's "Camp Notes" (1976), a series of lyrics that follow the narrative of her incarceration in a Japanese "relocation camp" in Idaho, daily life at the camp, and her release during the early 1940s.

20. For other autobiographical long poems narrating the self-as-history, see Derricotte's *Natural Birth* (1983), a poem that incorporates lyric and prose discourses to narrate a birth from the seventh month of pregnancy through the postpartum period; Rich's *Twenty-One Love Poems* (1978); Wakoski's *Greed* (1984); Doubiago's *Hard Country* (1982); and Pat Parker's "Goat Child" and "Womanslaughter" in *Movement in Black* (1978), sequences that are shorter in length, large in scope. In her introduction to *Movement in Black*, Judy Grahn calls them long poems and writes that "*Goat Child* was the first deliberately autobiographical poem by a woman that I had ever heard, although there was no reason (try sexism) why a woman's entire life couldn't be the storyline of a poem, a modern epic" (Parker 1978, 13–14).

21. For other journey narratives, see Doubiago's *Hard Country* (1982; discussed in Keller [1992]) and Rich's "An Atlas of the Difficult World" (1991a).

22. See also Rich, *Twenty-One Love Poems* (1978) and *Sources* (1986b); Kaufman, *Claims* (1984); Spivak, *The Jane Poems* (1974); Silko, *Storyteller* (1981); Glancy, *Lone Dog's Winter Count* (1991).

23. See also Mandel's *The Life of Mary* (1988) and Ostriker's discussion of revisionist mythmaking in women's poetry (1986, 210–38).

24. See also Lawrence's *The Inanna Poems* (1980). Di Prima's *Loba* (1978) also claims religious and mythic discourse but has few narrative elements.

25. See also Grahn's *The Queen of Swords* (1987, volume 2 in a projected four-volume epic beginning with *The Queen of Wands* [1982; discussed in Friedman 1990b]); Anzaldúa, *Borderlands/La Frontera* (1987); Mayer, *Midwinter Day* (1982); Marlatt, *How Hug a Stone* (1983); Silko, *Storyteller* (1981); DeFrees, *Imaginary Ancestors* (1990); Kaufman, *Claims* (1984).

26. I owe thanks to Meryl Schwartz, whose seminar paper on *Keeper of Accounts* as a coherent volume first directed my attention to Klepfisz.

27. Klepfisz's inscription of Judaism in this poem differs markedly from that of writers such as Kim Chernin, E. M. Broner, and I. B. Singer. In cultural and religious terms, Klepfisz does not portray the rich communal life and heritage of many Jews; nor does she connect with the specifically religious (especially mystical or Hasidic) aspects of Judaism. Nonetheless, her poem contains powerful intertexual resonances with biblical narratives.

Unnaming the Same: Theresa Hak Kyung Cha's *DICTEE*

Shelley Sunn Wong

Theresa Hak Kyung Cha's *DICTEE* is not a representative work. The writer's refusal of representative status for the text—to "represent" meaning to function as type, specimen or example—is a deliberate one, and one that has in part determined the changing fortunes of this text in the history of Asian American letters. Beginning in the 1970s, critical debates within the Asian American literary community concerning the political value of specific works of Asian American writing were argued within the terms of a cultural nationalist discourse. In the context of an Asian American identity politics that was steadily gaining ground throughout the 1970s, the two leading criteria for determining literary and political value were representativeness and authenticity. *DICTEE*, with its formal experiments and its insistent undermining of generalized understandings of representation and authenticity, presented itself as enough of an anomaly within the context of the political and cultural orthodoxy of Asian America that it was never drawn into public debate. Even though it may not have gone unread, it was certainly not talked about or written about in public forums.

Asian American critics' silence regarding *DICTEE* cannot be explained in simple terms of a critical orthodoxy resisting challenges to its authority, or of tradition-bound (and largely realist) forms resisting avant-garde experimentation. Instead, that silence needs to be understood in the context of changing frameworks of reception within the Asian American community, changes that are the result not of transitory literary fashions but, rather, the conjunction of several historical developments in the 1970s and 1980s: major demographic changes within the Asian American community from 1965 to 1985; the growing strength and influence of the women's movement; the postmodernist concern with fragmentation and multiple positionalities; and the emergence of new social movements that necessitated the rethinking of oppositional strategies. What this particular historical conjuncture meant for Asian American literature and criticism was that by the 1990s the very social and ideological coordinates that had marked an earlier framework of reception had shifted to introduce another framework that would refigure *DICTEE*'s social function. In this sense, *DICTEE* is a particularly useful work for understanding the nature of the ideological discourses that have helped shape the production and the reception of Asian American writing. Its emergence from an almost decade-long obscurity into relative prominence in Asian American literary circles exemplifies what Rita Felski speaks of as "the possibility that literary forms may take on quite different social and political meanings in relation to changing cultural perspectives and struggles over meaning and interpretation" (1989, 8). Grounding literary analysis in the recognition of historically specific cultural perspectives and interpretive frameworks (both Asian American and mainstream) enables the critic of Asian American literature to assess the potential value of a work not only in terms of formal or thematic features but also in terms of its social function at a particular historical juncture.

The shift from one framework of reception to another refigures earlier notions of representativeness and authenticity. In the prism of *DICTEE*, representativeness (founded on the identity of single type) and authenticity (predicated on original, unmediated essence) are refracted and returned as difference and mediation. My use of the word *representative* is intended to account for, but also to reach beyond, a specific instance of representation, as in the way the work of a Korean American immigrant woman writer might be said to represent, or not represent, a cultural entity named Asian America. In this discussion, "representativeness" needs to be seen against what David Lloyd has identified as the "ideological function and effect of the concept of representative man in both aesthetic and political theory" (1986, 17). Such a concept assumes a universal human essence and an evolutionary narrative that views any deviations from the acknowledged archetype as moments marking incomplete development rather than instantiations of radical difference. A primary function of this concept is reconciliation:

> Both the idea of the harmonizing force of aesthetic culture and the concept of the State as the expression of the unity of the human race arise in response to the need to provide, theoretically at least, a means to reconcile the inevitably conflicting and potentially anarchic forces of bourgeois civil society. (Lloyd 1986, 17)

In *DICTEE*, Cha rethinks representation by undermining the idea of a universal history (which necessarily grounds a concept of the representative man) that writes itself as a narrative of emancipation that proceeds by way of an ethical, developmental progress. The universality of such a history inevitably privileges identity over difference, a privileging that the Korean American immigrant woman writer, marked by differences of race, nationality, and gender, can ill afford at the cost of almost certain erasure. The casting of such an identity within developmental terms has the effect as well of "minoritizing" difference. That is to say, in the relationship between minority and majority cultures, maturity, and the political and symbolic power that accrues therein, is always assigned to the majority. Minority culture, or that which is "incompletely developed historically" (Lloyd 1986, 17), is consequently viewed within the terms of a *Bildung* that can only aspire to, and move ineluctably toward, the valorized maturity of the majority culture. *DICTEE*'s insistence on the narrator's multiple positionalities as woman, as colonial and postcolonial subject, as religious subject, and as Korean, problematizes the work in relation to a cultural nationalist sense of representative Asian American status. That insistence also functions to refuse the dominant culture's demand to represent (and by implication, to establish a formal identity with), and thereby legitimate, an ideology of cultural assimilation.

Cha's formal practices throw into relief the ways in which Asian American women writers are caught up within the politics of genre. In working outside of genres such as the autobiography or the bildungsroman, which are predicated on developmental narratives, Cha writes against interpellative narratives of assimilation and incorporation. Moreover, *DICTEE* concerns itself with poetic forms. In opening *DICTEE* with an epigraph drawn from Sappho and then following it with a catalog of (and later, invocations to) the classical Muses, Cha invokes both a lyric and an epic tradition of poetry. She does so not to reinstall these traditions as operative literary modes in the present but to cast them into mutual conflict. And at the same time that lyric is made to run up against epic, the poetic itself (as the preeminent mode of high literature) is continually being run up against the prosaic. In *DICTEE*, the different genres, or modes of literary (and cinematic) production, do not coexist harmoniously; they undermine each other through a process of reciprocal critique. Cha works with the recognition that genres are not innocent or neutral aesthetic conventions or ideal types but formal constructs that are implicated in the very processes of ideological production. Recognition of the ideological dimension of genre, with its corollary assumption that a mode of aesthetic intervention can simultaneously constitute a mode of social intervention, is crucial to critical discussion of *DICTEE*. Of equal importance is the way in which historically specific frameworks of reception situate and determine the efficacy of Cha's textual strategies as a mode of social intervention.

DICTEE advances a method of historical and aesthetic procedure that prepares a ground for interventions in the dictations of colonial and patriarchal discourses; it is a method that instantiates a writing practice that stumbles over rather than smoothes out the uneven textures of raced and gendered memory. The very first page of *DICTEE*, the frontispiece, features a grainy black and white photographic reproduction of some Korean phrases etched in stone. The inscription, taken from the wall of a coal mine in Japan, is attributed to a Korean exile, one of thousands who were pressed into various kinds of labor by the Japanese early in this century. It translates:

> Mother
> I miss you
> I am hungry
> I want to go home.

Situated within the context of colonial rule and exile, the message comes across as a raw expression of privation and desire. Situated as it is here at the beginning of *DICTEE*, a text by a Korean American immigrant woman writer, published in 1982 in the United States, the message is refocused and drawn into a new urgency and a new trajectory. The basis of that new urgency and trajectory is a radical rethinking of received notions of narrative and history. Traditionally, a frontispiece precedes the title page and provides entry into the text; the Korean inscription, reading vertically and from right to left, ending at the extreme left margin, effectively disables that traditional function. Instead of leading the reader into the work, the directional movement of the frontispiece begins to usher the reader back out of the text. Within the context of narrative development, the frontispiece thus functions not to forward the narrative but, rather, to forestall it.

This forestalling constitutes the characteristic gesture of a formal practice that proceeds by way of nonidentity, by way of insisting on critical difference. Curiously, the handful of articles on *DICTEE* that have been published to date make no reference whatsoever to the frontispiece, though it contains the only Korean script (Hangul) in the entire work. In the articles that make any reference to a beginning for *DICTEE*, that beginning is pegged at the page that is numbered 1, a page preceded by four pages consisting of a frontispiece, a title page, a dedication page, and a page listing the names of the nine classical Muses of antiquity and their respective offices. In pegging the beginning at the expected and conventional starting place, these critics overlook a crucial aspect of the radical potential of Cha's formal strategies. By having the Korean sign virtually move off the page and out of the textual composition, Cha signals the instability of that Korean sign within the larger narrative framework of American life. The gesture cracks open what I would call a discourse of wholeness, a set of ideological assumptions that has historically framed that narrative apparatus. In its history of intimate associations with harmony, order, plenitude, and comprehensiveness, wholeness has generally been deemed normative from both sides of the temporal divide: it can be seen as an originary state from which humanity—or the particular minority

group in question—has been estranged, or as the end point or telos of an ineluct-
able, if oftentimes unsteady progress. In both the reception and production of
Asian American (and, I might add, other ethnic) literature, the trope of wholeness
frequently plays itself out as an uncomplicated and desirable progress—though,
to be sure, also a stumbling and painful one—from a condition of brokenness,
estrangement, and struggle (the result of an enforced social, cultural, political,
and economic marginality) to one of reconstituted wholeness and ultimate inclu-
sion in the narrative drama of American history.

The location of a site of reconciliation and resolution within the aesthetic
work is part of the West's inheritance from Schiller's ideas about the function of
aesthetic education. For Schiller, and for a Western aesthetic tradition that draws
on German idealist philosophy, aesthetics functions to harmonize the individual
both within "himself" and with society. In this way, aesthetics enables the restor-
ation of wholeness by figuring a common human essence, that is, by representing
both an original and a prospective unity. For an Asian immigrant artist, film-
maker, and writer trained within the Western academy, that inheritance was to be
received with ambivalence. From the outset, *DICTEE* contests the ideology of
wholeness and the representativeness it hails. In the frontispiece inscription, the
longed for Korean homeland is neither recovered nor found. And in the United
States, this progress will be, for those Korean Americans who maintain the ethnic
sign, not inward toward ultimate inclusion but, rather, outward toward other-
ness. These two terms—contestation and home—will function to both construct
and deconstruct the formal trajectory of that progress. On the one hand, within a
discourse of wholeness, contestation and home can be located in a sequential, and
even causal, relationship. This would mean that, in the face of an existence cross-
inscribed by multiple modes of inequality—that is, race, class, gender, sexual
orientation—one must of necessity contest those terms of inequality if one is to
arrive at, or achieve, home. The point to remember here, however, is that home,
within this way of thinking, generally means end point or finalization.

On the other hand, outside of that discourse, contestation and home can be
located in a simultaneous emergence—that is to say, the contested and the con-
testing terrain *is* home. Home, in this sense, can never be a settled space. Cer-
tainly, within the context of Japan's colonization of Korea, home will be a situa-
tion continually being fought for and fought over, forever in the making. To see
home otherwise, as perhaps final resting place, is to invite the risk of hypostatiza-
tion and idealization. In *DICTEE*, Cha problematizes the notion of home as a
stable place: "Our destination is fixed on the perpetual motion of search" (81).
She refuses the given narrative emplotment of received history and instead, to
borrow Walter Benjamin's phrase, "brush[es] history against the grain" (1968,
257).

By now it is a commonplace that official histories have generally been the narratives of the victors and the conquerors, histories marked by "triumphal procession[s]" in which the victors stepped over "those who are lying prostrate." Consequently, as Benjamin has remarked: "There is never a document of civilization which is not at the same time a document of barbarism. And just as such a document is not free from barbarism, barbarism taints also the manner in which it was transmitted from owner to another" (1968, 256). Thus, in *DICTEE,* to brush history against the grain is to break open the myth that the transmission of history is free from barbarism. Cha calls on the diseuse (from the French, meaning "female speaker") to "break open the spell cast upon time upon time again and again" (1982, 123). This spell is the naturalization of history promulgated by colonial and patriarchal discourses, a naturalization that involves a process of neutralizing or otherwise rendering innocuous troublesome manifestations of political or cultural difference by insisting on a model of identity and its corresponding narrative structure. Or as Cha writes: "Neutralized to achieve the no-response, to make absorb, to submit to the uni-directional correspondence" (33). In the Calliope section, Cha notes that this authorizing of ideological citizenship through the naturalization of history underwrites the naturalization process that confers legal citizenship:

> One day you raise the right hand and you are American. They give you an American Pass port. The United States of America. Somewhere someone has taken my identity and replaced it with their photograph. . . . Their signature their seals. Their own image. (56)

Brushing history against the grain denaturalizes received history and colonizing systems of representation, and stands against the fact that in Korea, "Japan ha[d] become the sign. The Alphabet. The vocabulary" (32). But the weight of that resistance is felt in Cha's placement of the words "Except. Some are without" (38) on a page directly facing the photograph of a Japanese firing squad standing before three bound and blindfolded Korean captives. Denaturalizing history allows the suffering of history's losers, those who are without, to be felt and seen again.

    DICTEE instantiates an argument against progress-theories of history, theories that posit history as a master narrative that resolves and smoothes over the troublesome and irrational material of history. Such theories assign to history the status of a higher truth and, in the process, "justify the suffering which its course had brought upon individuals" (Buck-Morss 1977, 48). *DICTEE* consistently argues against theories and practices—political and aesthetic—that would rationalize the dismemberments of the past. Instead, this work cultivates the uneven textures of history, preparing, through contradictions and discontinuities, a space for the expression of damaged life. In a passage from the "Clio History" section of the book (a section devoted to the Korean-Japanese conflict), Cha notes how "History" with a capital *H* can gloss over the particularity of historical events, in this case, Japan's annexation of Korea:

> Unfathomable the words, the terminology: enemy, atrocities, conquest, betrayal, invasion, destruction. They exist only in the larger perception of History's recording, that affirmed, admittedly and unmistakably, one enemy nation has disregarded the humanity of another. Not physical enough. Not to the very flesh and bone, to the core, to the mark, to the point where it is necessary to intervene, even if to invent anew, expressions for *this* experience, for this *outcome*. (32)

Immediately following this passage, Cha implicates notions of commensurability in the continuing failure of those in power to see into the specific material conditions of suffering during this period of Korean history: "To the others, these accounts are about (one more) distant land, like (any other) distant land, without any discernable features in the narrative, (all the same) distant like any other" (33). Commensurability—that is, the idea that each one is like every other one, infinitely exchangeable, interchangeable—and the model of identity upon which it draws function as political and cultural blinders, obscuring the prickly particularities of sociopolitical life and allowing within their purview only the smooth patina of wholeness derived from an overarching sense of narrative destiny. When everything is the same, there is no urgency or need to intervene. Each national conflict is just one more within a long series. This idea of an unending series of like events ascribes a continuity to history and describes a relationship of present to past predicated on a developmental model of history that privileges temporal sequence. The conjunction of commensurability and teleological progress finds its popular expression in the idea that "things will be better by and by." But what Cha is proposing in *DICTEE* is a relationship of another order: things will only get better if one recognizes and then acts into difference and contradiction rather than rationalizing or reconciling them.

The relation of present to past, however, is not the same as that of past to present. As Benjamin writes, "[W]hile the relation of the present to the past is a purely temporal, continuous one, that of the past to the moment is dialectical" (1983–84, 7–8). It is this dialectical procedure that characterizes what I would call *DICTEE*'s poetics of cleaving, a way of proceeding marked by the ability to work both the inside and the outside of a given historical or cultural moment. In this light, the translation exercises that appear at the beginning of the book can be seen as exercises in cleaving. *Cleaving*, with its dual connotations of adherence and separation, characterizes both the translation and the dictation Cha is engaged in. Cha's practice of taking dictation from the other, of mimicking the other, involves a complicated process of resifting and reaccentuating that which addresses/is addressed to her. Her method of mimicking assumes that the word is a contested and contesting terrain, and therefore available to her own efforts to repopulate, in Bakhtinian terms, the word with her own intentions. In *DICTEE*, "She hears herself uttering again reuttering to re-vive" (1982, 150). To utter in this way is to undermine identity and to make difference visible again.

The radical potential of Cha's poetics of cleaving is manifested early on in the text in the invocation of the Muses:

> O Muse, tell me the story
> Of all these things, O Goddess, daughter of Zeus
> Beginning wherever you wish, tell even us.
>
> (7)

Cha's invocation reworks Hesiod's invocation of the Muses in that quintessential foundational text, *The Theogony*. Hesiod's lines read: "Relate these things to me, Muse whose home is Olympus, from the beginning; tell me which of them first came into being" (1953, 56). In asking the Muse to begin "wherever" she wishes rather than "from the beginning," Cha interferes with a historical practice that privileges origins and the idea of orderly patriarchal succession. With its unruly assemblage of visual and textual formats, its crossing over and between genres, its paratactic structure, and its disjunctive jump-cutting of narratives, *DICTEE* works, in Benjamin's words, to free "the enormous energy of history that lies bonded in the 'Once upon a time' of classical historical narrative" (1983–84, 9). Cha's parodic reuttering of the invocation releases the daughters of memory from their bondage to the "once upon a time" of foundational discourses yoked in the service of patriarchal genealogies.

But Cha's critique of foundational discourses hardly ends with this aspect of the liberation of the Muses. Immediately following this invocation are three sets of language-learning exercises: the first two are translation exercises from English into French, while the third is an exercise in conjugating French verbs. Following these exercises is a reprise of that first invocation, but a reprise with a difference that reorients the trajectory of the address altogether. This invocation reads:

> Tell me the story
> Of all these things.
> Beginning wherever you wish, tell even us.
>
> (11)

Here, the Muse, along with her genealogical situation, has been omitted. The earlier invocation's implicit critique of the privileging of origins and patriarchal succession is here further complicated by the disappearance of an authorizing source and tradition altogether. The absence of a specific interlocutor creates a space with the potential to accommodate multiple voicings of stories rather than a single voicing of a story. The absence also immediately casts adrift the personal pronouns in this passage. No longer bound to a long-established hierarchy of dictation from gods to man, "me," "you," and "us" are left to negotiate new referential positions. The "subject" of the dictation is required now to perform itself anew through these negotiations.

The effect of this parodic reworking of the invocation—by now twice removed from the "original" (itself no doubt already a translation from the Greek)—is to further undermine assumptions of power that are based on the valorization of temporal sequence inherent in the "once upon a time" of classical historical narrative. The removal of the prevailing tradition that had been consecrated within this "once upon a time" serves to release time itself from the grip of a singly directed, calendrical memory. The result is the possibility of entertaining alternate temporal constructs, to enable, in fact, Mnemosyne's daughters to preside over historical and social constructs other than those dictated by Western and Korean patriarchal genealogies.

Cha's use of the Muses as an organizational principle for *DICTEE* extends beyond what one critic has characterized as the feminist effort to give the Muses "the voices they might have had if they weren't always serving as cheerleaders for masculine poetic projects" (Martin 1988, 188). Stephen-Paul Martin's assumption here is that Cha, not unlike many other twentieth-century women writers, has played on a set of traditional figures derived from a common stock of Western cultural memory in order to subvert the patriarchal framework within which those figures operated. What this assumption does not take into account, however, is the cultural alterity inherent in Cha's situation as a "Korean American" woman writer. Had Martin (and other critics who have noted Cha's use of the Muses) worked with that difference in mind, they would perhaps have noted the substitution of an invented Muse—Elitere—for what would normally have been Euterpe, the Muse associated with music.[1] The installation of Elitere (an invented name deriving from neither Greek nor Latin) signals the text's intention to disorganize the construction of notions of the common, constructions that make possible totalizing identifications on the basis of seemingly definitive categories such as *woman, American,* or *writer.*[2] It is also no accident that the section of *DICTEE* presided over by Elitere should be dominated by the diseuse, who figures in this text as the very condition of alternative speaking, an alternative to both patriarchal and Western frameworks of representation.

With its resonant play on *elite* and *literare,* Elitere emerges to critique the privileged place of epic as high literature. As an oppositional gesture, Cha assigns to Elitere the office of lyric poetry. In this context, the opening epigraph from

Sappho begins to perform a double function. Acknowledged by antiquity to be the tenth Muse, Sappho presides over a lyric rather than an epic tradition. Celebrated by writers of antiquity as "the mortal Muse" "among the immortal Muses" (Campbell 1982, 27), Sappho's presence at the beginning of *DICTEE*, and the function of Elitere as the muse of lyric poetry, work to undermine some of the presumptions of epic. Cha's placement of this "tenth Muse" before her listing of the nine classical Muses inverts an established sequential relationship and begins to argue against an epic world view in which

> "beginning," "first," "founder," "ancestors," "that which occurred earlier" and so forth are not merely temporal categories but *valorized* temporal categories . . . . The epic absolute past is the single source and beginning of everything good for all later times. (Bakhtin 1981, 15)

The immortal Muses of an "absolute past" are preempted by the mortal Muse of the relative time of experience. Where the epic enshrines national tradition, the lyric sings personal experience. Where an "absolute epic distance separates the epic world from contemporary reality," the lyric moment is situated within that contemporary reality. The section of *DICTEE* presided over by Elitere begins with an incantation to free time from an absolute epic past and to assign a new agency to memory:

> Dead time. Hollow depression interred invalid
> to resurgence, resistant to memory. Waits. Apel.
> Apellation. Excavation. Let the one who is
> diseuse. Diseuse de bonne aventure. Let her call
> forth. Let her break open the spell cast upon time
> upon time again and again. (123)

Cha struggles here to locate the dialectical relation of the past to the present that would break open the inaccessibility and hierarchy of an absolute past. In his discussion of epic and the novel in *The Dialogic Imagination*, Bakhtin notes,

> By its very nature the epic world of the absolute past is inaccessible to personal experience and does not permit an individual, personal point of view or evaluation. One cannot glimpse it, grope for it, touch it; one cannot look at it from just any point of view; it is impossible to experience it, analyze it, take it apart, penetrate into its core. It is given solely as tradition, sacred and sacrosanct, evaluated in the same way by all and demanding a pious attitude toward itself. (1981, 16)

From the profane ground of the personal writing self, Cha proceeds to call down that which is deemed sacred and sacrosanct: the patriarchal cast of the Western epic tradition; the religious colonization of Korea; the male-centered narrative of Korean nationalism; monumentalist historiography. In this context, the insertion of three sets of language-learning exercises between the two epic invocations serves to "contemporize" the sacred past. In Bakhtinian terms, the epic world has been "brought low, represented on a plane equal with contemporary life, in an everyday environment, in the low language of contemporaneity" (Bakhtin 1981, 21). By way of parody, *DICTEE* clears a formal spatiotemporal plane for the halting, ungrammatical quotidian of hitherto silenced lives. Whether in the ana-tomical diagrams of the organs of speech production (74), or in the ragged shiftings of thought in the handwritten manuscript page (40–41), *DICTEE* lo-cates the condition of coming-into-language in the physicality of the body. Where the epic has come down to us as an absolutely completed and finished generic form, the personal lyric proposed by Elitere comes forward as an open-ended process, one grounded in the body and consequently susceptible to change and flux.

In using the lyric moment to critique the epic, Cha is not, however, looking to install the lyric as the preeminent mode of an oppositional poetics.[3] To the contrary, *DICTEE*'s insistence on multiple subjectivities would seem to con-tradict any effort to enshrine a mode of literary production traditionally premised on a single, unified, autonomous consciousness or identity—that of the lyric "I." In recent years, the problematic nature of that lyric "I" has come to be an increasingly vexing issue. In the wake of poststructuralist claims concerning the fragmentation of the subject, the traditional premise of a unified, autonomous lyric voice has come under siege. The lyric itself, when understood as a trans-historical or normative genre, has been the subject of radical rethinking (for example, Perloff 1990). My discussion of Cha's use of the lyric is not so much an attempt to join the current debate over lyric, or the lyric "I," as it is an effort to see how Cha's formal method generates an oppositional force by signaling the contradictions within and among literary genres.[4] *DICTEE*'s resistance to re-ceived canons of form begins by recognizing that subjects are interpellated, or called into particular subject positions, by different generic formations. The work disrupts the seductive force of these various interpellative operations by bringing them together into a zone of contention. The subject of the lyric is characterized as an autonomous, transcendent, unified self; that of the epic as the object of higher determinative forces, or the plaything of the gods. Bringing these subjects into contention makes possible resistance to modes of interpellation specific to particular genres. For Cha, neither the individual lyric self nor the reverential spectator of epic seems capable of providing a viable ground for a contestatory practice because neither sufficiently comprehends the multiple subjectivities of the Korean American immigrant woman writer. What *DICTEE* offers is a new figuration of the dialectic between individuation and ideological interpellation, which allows for human agency at the same time that it acknowledges the determinative force of external constraints and impositions.[5] Recognizing the impossibility of an Archimedean point from which to critique ideological formations, Cha locates her critique instead in the space of contradiction and conflict generated by multiple, competing modes of subject formation. It is there, in the interstices of competing discourses, that the subject that had been hailed and circumscribed by these respective discourses can be unnamed and enabled to speak.

The primary vehicle of unnaming in *DICTEE* is driven by the tropes of translation and dictation. As I suggested earlier, in *DICTEE,* the act of translation is never simply a matter of finding the "right" or "equivalent" words in French to accommodate the original words of English but instead involves cleaving—that is to say, translation always proposes an original only to insist on a simultaneous departure from the original. To engage in translation is to engage in "the repetition that will not return as the same" (Bhabha 1990, 312). The resulting difference functions not to cancel the original but to introduce a previously unaccounted for element into the linguistic equation, an element that then disturbs established relations of power implicit in the directional movement between different languages and different cultures.

Both translation and dictation require one to carry or transfer language from one medium into another. Both require distancing from an original while, paradoxically, invoking sameness or equivalence. The term *dictation* itself makes manifest the element of coercion behind the desire for equivalence, as well as pointing up the trajectory of authority and power that marks an act of translation. In the context of resistance to the logic of identity that grounds the ruling strategies of colonialism and imperialism, translation will necessarily not return as the same, thus laying bare the contradictions inherent in an insistence on homogeneity. A measure of *DICTEE*'s resistance to this external imposition of identity can be seen in the way two punctuation commands in French—"ferme les guillemets" and "ouvre les guillemets"—have been omitted from the English translation. While this omission reveals the student's failure to accurately reproduce the original, it also calls attention to the fact that the commands have been written out rather than unobtrusively inserted as punctuation marks.[6] By having the conventional markers of the boundaries of thought coexisting on the same plane of signification as the thought itself, the text announces both the arbitrary nature of a given system of demarcation and hierarchical classification, and its own refusal to reproduce that system. The writing out of the punctuation commands projects the disruptive force of the familiar become unfamiliar, and the transcendent-abstract become immanent-material, the high brought low. The lesson to repeat exactly, when learned too well, returns to interrogate and collapse the formal unity of the original. In this way, the translation exercises in the text of *DICTEE* open up the possibility of thwarting operations of equivalence and commensurability at the same time that they allow the dictated subject to claim her own ability to signify.

If the desire for equivalence grounds a strategy for producing compliant colonial subjects and perpetuating orderly patriarchal rule, then the conjugation exercises can be seen as efforts to further complicate and disrupt this particular lesson in subject formation. The exercise commands the student to "Complétez les phrases suivantes" (9). In order to complete the sentence, one needs to specify and name—through the conjugation of the verb—the single subject position from which a given action is to be performed. The task of completing the sentence, or conjugating the verb, becomes frustratingly complicated for those who simultaneously occupy multiple subject positions determined by the valences of race, class, gender, national origin, or sexuality. The "me," "you," and "us" of the invocation are not so easily assigned or negotiated if, at any given moment, one inhabits more than one referential position. The proliferation of unconjugated verbs in *DICTEE* testifies to the continuing instability and unsettledness of subject positions and to the impossibility for the Korean American immigrant woman writer of specifying, or representing herself through, single definitive positions.

From its "beginning," *DICTEE* suggests that if there is a foundational moment for minority discourse, it is to be located, paradoxically, within the antifoundational moment and space of dictation. We need only meditate here for a moment on the title of this text to gain a sense of the impossibility of securing unmediated origins. Though published in the United States and directed, presumably, toward an English-speaking audience, the first word of this text is French, *DICTEE*. Before even opening the book, the reader is required to perform an act of translation and distanciation. The maneuver inevitably displaces the original. Where the frontispiece had functioned to forestall the narrative, the title, which usually designates the beginning of a written work, functions immediately to displace the beginning.

Cha's strategy of thwarting authoritarian beginnings and endings works throughout the text to open up spaces in what had previously been the exclusive narrative domain of a monumentalist historicism, spaces for the multiple utterings of a hitherto banished quotidian. The inexorable movement along a single narrative path is challenged early on in the text by the appearance of the diseuse, a figure who is never named beyond her function of speaking and whose very condition of being is located in the telling of alternative stories. It is the diseuse who throughout the text will utter and reutter the religious, colonial, and patriarchal discourses that threaten to prescribe and proscribe all possibilities of speech for the Korean American immigrant woman. The diseuse is fundamentally disruptive: "She mimicks [*sic*] the speaking" of authoritarian discourses, a mimicking "[t]hat might resemble speech" (3) but that does not quite reproduce the original. Her method seems always to be that of unfaithful translation:

> She allows others. In place of her. . . . The others each occupying her. . . . She allows herself caught in their threading, anonymously in their thick motion in the weight of their utterance. When the amplification stops there might be an echo. She might make the attempt then. The echo part. At the pause. . . . She waits inside the pause. Inside her. Now. This very moment. Now. She takes rapidly the air, in gulfs, in preparation for the distances to come. (3–4)

It is at the moment (at the "pause") when the echo is to return that the diseuse will intervene and speak. In preparation, she takes a deep breath, but she takes the air in "gulfs" rather than gulps. Already, the practice of the subversive slip-up is engaged. "Gulfs," with its connotations of "chasms" and "gaps," instantiates the strategy of translation that situates "the distances to come." Her insistence on distanciation from the original as both precondition and result of female utterance is manifested in the injunction to "[a]bsorb it" and then to "[s]pill it," maintaining always the sense of spilling as a flowing or spreading beyond bounds, as a divulging of information indiscreetly. Spilling invokes a sense of a surplus that cannot be contained. In the colonial calculus that identifies Korean with Japanese, the "Korean" is surplus; in the racial calculus that identifies American as white, the "Korean" is surplus; in the patriarchal calculus that identifies Korean as male, the "Korean female" is surplus; and in the formal calculus that identifies a literary work with a discrete genre, *DICTEE* is surplus. In *DICTEE*'s economy of translation, the Korean American feminine is invariably rendered as surplus, as that which goes unaccounted for. In this economy, the function of the diseuse is that of a "relay," of one who "deliver[s]," but one whose delivery generates meanings in excess of what was presumed in the original. The presence of a surplus or excess necessarily skews the operation of representation.

The idea of the female as surplus emerges a few pages later in the section dealing with Catholic rituals. In the course of receiving Communion, the female communicant notes the ironies of her situation within a male-identified religion. "He," the priest, God's representative, is "the one who deciphers he the one who invokes in the Name. He the one who becomes He. Man-God" (13). A few pages later, in the recitation of the catechism, the ironies of that male identification become outright absurdities:

Q: GOD WHO HAS MADE YOU IN HIS OWN LIKENESS
: God who has made me in His Own likeness. In His Own Image in His Own Resemblance, in His Own Copy, In His Own Counterfeit Presentment, in His

Duplicate, in His Own Reproduction, in His Cast, in His Carbon, His Image and His Mirror. Pleasure in the image pleasure in the copy pleasure in the projection of likeness pleasure in the repetition. Acquiesce, to the correspondance [sic]. . . . Acquiesce, to and for the complot in the Hieratic tongue. Theirs. Into Their Tongue. (17–18)

The identification of religious subject and God is shaken asunder in a delirium of repetition that points up the impossibility of equivalence—and hence, representation—between Korean American woman and Western "Man-God."

This section dealing with the formation of the religious subject ends by simultaneously invoking and undermining that most privileged of taxonomic moments—beginnings: "And it begins" (19). The conjunction "and" supposes a relationship of coordination rather than subordination. "And" removes the possibility of foundational priority and suggests, instead, the existence of an antecedent or, as the subsequent text of *DICTEE* will reveal, several antecedents in the form of intersecting dominant discourses that contribute to the formation of the Korean American immigrant woman subject. This use of the conjunction is hardly without its literary antecedents. Pound's oft-noted use of "And" to begin *The Cantos*, for instance, signaled among other things his interest in parataxis as poetic strategy, a strategy that would allow history and the presence and weight of that which we do not know to enter the poem.[7] For Cha, the use of the coordinating conjunction and the paratactic mode it puts in place allow the text to place side by side the multiple formative discourses and the many histories that inform the Korean American woman. This mode of writing will allow the inclusion of material "*[f]rom another epic another history. From the missing narrative. From the multitude of narratives. Missing. From the chronicles. For another telling for other recitations*" (81). Thus, if the "it" in "And it begins" remains vague, its referent unlocatable, the word "begins" is no less vague and lacking in clear reference within *DICTEE*'s continuing interrogation of a notion of unmediated and singular origins.

What follows is an interrogation of taxonomy itself. The text reads:

> From A Far
> What nationality
> or what kindred and relation
> what blood relation
> what blood ties of blood
> what ancestry
> what race generation
> what house clan tribe stock strain
> what lineage extraction

> what breed sect gender denomination caste
> what stray ejection misplaced
> Tertium Quid neither one thing nor the other
> Tombe des nues de naturalized
> what transplant to dispel upon
>
> (20)

In breaking up the word *afar* as "A Far," Cha inserts distances within distances. It is from within those distances that the speaker begins to interrogate the adequacy of conventional taxonomies in assigning origin and identity. Taxonomy is taken here in the sense of the "orderly classification of plants and animals according to their presumed natural relationships." *DICTEE*'s task thus far has been to question that presumption of naturalness and to insist that the seemingly natural relationship is always mediated; to be "naturalized" through the interpellative operations of colonial, religious, or patriarchal discourses is to be decidedly unnatural. As this passage suggests, it is questionable whether identity can ever be contained within a single taxonomic moment—be it "nationality," "race," "lineage," "denomination," or, I might add, "woman"—if those classifications themselves are historically determined and variable social constructs. Confronted with a classificatory schema, any one of whose categories would too narrowly name her position within a particular system of social relations, the Korean American immigrant woman can only claim the interstitial ground of the "Tertium Quid neither one thing nor the other." By the end of this passage, received categories are no longer intact and have become, instead, labile constructs that are open to further "dispelling" in the effort to find a more adequate representation of the Korean American immigrant woman's social location(s).

DICTEE's critique of presumed natural relationships attempts to point out the extent to which origins and identity are mediated constructs. An instructive example of such mediation can be found in the "Clio History" section of the text, which opens with a photograph of Korean patriot Yu Guan Soon and, facing it, a brief statement of biographical data that reads:

YU GUAN SOON

BIRTH: By Lunar Calendar, 15, March 1903
DEATH: 12, October, 1920. 8:20 A.M.

She is born of one mother and one father. (25)

As if to put forward an uncontestable primordiality, the following page contains the Chinese character for woman, and on the facing page, the character for man. As the text notes later, Yu Guan Soon was a young woman of sixteen at the time of the 1 March 1919 mass demonstration against the Japanese occupation of Korea. She was to die a year later, a martyr to the cause of Korean nationalism. What is remarkable about the biographical data is not its testimony to the brevity and heroism of a life, or its peculiar inclusion of a disarmingly self-evident statement of physiological origin, but the way in which it reveals how a seemingly neutral or natural genealogical record is intimately bound up with a colonial record. To begin with, the dates of birth and death seem to fall within the strict parameters of calendrical time. The adherence to calendrical time is, however, complicated by the reference to the lunar calendar, a system of measurement of Chinese origin that predates the standard Gregorian calendar of the West. The reference to the lunar calendar reinforces the idea of the cultural specificity of ways of marking time and hence undermines the idea of a universal history. The supposed primordiality of the female-male dyad reveals itself to be the site of the intersection of the biological-genealogical and the colonial record. The characters for woman and man are rendered, after all, not in native Korean script (Hangul), but in Chinese characters, a legacy of a colonizing effort that preceded that of the Japanese. In the "Calliope Epic Poetry" section, a section devoted to the telling of the narrator's mother's experience as colonial subject, the appearance of the Chinese characters for *father* and *mother* similarly functions to point up the extent of colonial hegemony. In this latter case, the inclusion of Chinese characters also attests to the inscription of the Korean woman within a patriarchal discourse. As Elaine Kim notes in an essay on *DICTEE:* "Official Korean chronicles of 'what happened' were written in Chinese characters, which were off-limits to females for centuries" (1994, 14).

In *DICTEE,* origins are never quite what they seem, never quite offer the foundational stability and identity that is desired, and are never quite as unadulterated or unmediated as the historicism of the "once upon a time" would have us believe. The stories of Korean women like Yu Guan Soon or the narrator's mother have generally been buried within the terms of an historicism that variously privileges the foundational discourses of colonial, patriarchal, or nationalist systems of power. But *DICTEE*'s search for and recovery of those stories is by no means the simple attempt to recuperate an essential, founding Korean feminine identity. In telling the mother's story, the daughter/narrator recognizes that identity of origin is at best an impossibility and at worst a delusory consolation.

The radical potential for claiming a signifying space for woman/Korean/postcolonial lies in this insistence on attentiveness to multiple and often contradictory inscriptions of self rather than singular assertions of identity within a mixed-genre text. The transformation of potential into actuality, however, also depends on frameworks of reception. Thus the relative success or failure of *DICTEE*'s project of radical nonidentity needs to be assessed not simply on the basis of its presentation of a formal self-reflexivity that troubles conventional modes of representation but also on the way in which the text's relationship to an oppositional social movement—the Asian American movement—is mediated by ideological constructs that determine the production and the reception of Asian American literary works.

"We used to all be Americans," notes Evan Kemp, Jr., head of the Equal Employment Opportunity Commission, in an interview in August 1991. "Now we're African Americans, Italian Americans, Hispanic Americans, etc. I think it is a bad situation" (quoted in *San Francisco Examiner,* 19 August 1991). Kemp's lament over the passing of a prelapsarian wholeness, a lament that leads to his prediction of a forthcoming period of tumultuous race relations in the United States, is emblematic of the current problems confronting the representation of difference. Kemp's comments demonstrate the extent to which the discourse of race in the United States is circumscribed and driven by underlying fictions of identity and wholeness. Explicitly, these statements point up the dominant culture's continuing recourse to and reliance upon fictions of original identity to ground its refusal to recognize race as a salient feature of social and political life. Implicitly, however, these statements provide a conceptual salve for the very problem of racial difference that it laments by invoking a paradigm of assimilation and incorporation made possible by assuming race as a subcategory of ethnicity. The equal positioning of African Americans and Italian Americans is the defining characteristic of an ethnicity paradigm that first gained ascendancy in the 1920s and that continues, despite some modifications, through the 1980s to be the dominant paradigm within discussions of the sociology of race. The paradigm rests on what is known as "the immigrant analogy," an analogy that explains racial conflict by subsuming such conflicts within a universal typology of the different developmental stages characterizing the immigrant's assimilation into American life. This universal typology proceeds without reference to distinctions between voluntary or forced entry into the United States, and is thus able to assign equivalence to the situations of African Americans and Italian Americans.

This ethnicity paradigm has generated a framework for interpreting racial difference that reads race as a mere subset of ethnicity. Within this framework, Ellis Island, and not Angel Island, stands as the central metaphor for a distinctively American *Bildung.*[8] If the recent celebrations around the refurbishing of Ellis Island are any indication, this particular image of American *Bildung* retains a strong hold on the popular and the academic imaginations alike. The widespread appeal of this image in part accounts for both the generous reception accorded Asian American literary works that, either thematically or formally, maintain links to this developmental narrative of incorporation and the less than generous reception accorded works such as *DICTEE* that refuse such links.

Within this former category, I would situate works such as Carlos Bulosan's *America Is in the Heart* (1943), Jade Snow Wong's *Fifth Chinese Daughter* (1945), Maxine Hong Kingston's *The Woman Warrior* (1976), John Okada's *No-No Boy* ([1957] 1976), Shawn Hsu Wong's *Homebase* (1979), David Mura's *Turning Japanese: Memoirs of a Sansei* (1991), and Gish Jen's *Typical American* (1991). Despite their many differences, these narratives share a certain formal resemblance in their respective relationships to the autobiography of bildungsroman. The *Bildung* that is traced in these narratives usually involves the evolution of an individual character in his or her search for identity, both in terms of individual identity and of identification with the larger society. This identity can also be either retrospective or projective, in the sense that some protagonists are committed to recovering or retrieving a lost or submerged identity, while others anticipate the forging of a new identity.

Generally conceded to be a novel of socialization, the bildungsroman is often seen to function within the terms of an organicist teleology.[9] Read in teleological terms, Asian American autobiographies and bildungsromane present the narrative of a minority culture growing into a recognition of its place within the majority culture. Thus intercultural conflicts are resolved through a naturalized pattern of development. The progress seems a familiar one—from disunified self to coherent identity and, ultimately, identification with the larger society. As a putative representative instance of a universal human progress, the work allows the reader to identify with the Asian American protagonist's situation and thus reproduces the identity of an American *Bildung*. The framework of reception generated by a structuring ideological discourse of wholeness reads difference primarily as the prefiguration of final identity.

For Asian American writers in the 1970s and 1980s, the choice of realist forms like the autobiography and the bildungsroman was determined in part by the demand for such narratives as evidenced by the enthusiastic reception granted earlier works of this kind but also by the need to provide a corrective to what many viewed as disabling misrepresentations of Asian Americans in mainstream literature and culture. The countering of such disabling fictions required the production of positive fictions grounded in the development of an authentic Asian American identity. These realist forms allowed writers to depict the particularities of the Asian American experience and to directly thematize pressing political and social issues confronting Asian Americans. Besides providing a corrective for mainstream audiences, the resulting work enabled Asian Americans themselves to rethink, through the interplay of symbolic fictions, their individual or group situation as Asian Americans. Recognizing the literary work as the site for both the construction and the contestation of cultural meanings, and recognizing the broad-based appeal and accessibility of realist forms, Asian American writers continued throughout this period to work within these forms in

order to consolidate the Asian American identity needed to galvanize an opposi-
tional social movement. With its focus on autonomous selfhood, the autobiogra-
phy or bildungsroman enabled the representation of an Asian American subjec-
tivity absent from mainstream depictions of Asians. *DICTEE* (1982) appeared
when Asian Americans were just beginning to experience some of the social and
political gains achieved through strategies based on identity politics. In this mi-
lieu, *DICTEE*'s trenchant critique of identity and foundational discourses could
hardly have made it a representative work within the context of existing Asian
American political realities. However, perhaps because of its formal density and
complexity, a complexity that resisted reductive generalizations of meaning,
DICTEE's critics never vilified the work but simply set it aside, effectively defer-
ring its critical project.

In stressing the multiple positionalities simultaneously occupied by the
Korean American immigrant woman, *DICTEE* disturbed the model of racial
identity promulgated by male-identified Asian American nationalism. Asian
American nationalists all too often framed the struggle to constitute an Asian
American identity in terms of recovering what the editors of the influential an-
thology of Asian American writing *Aiiieeeee!* simply called Asian American
"manhood" (Chin et al. 1975, 35). Increasingly, this nationalism's inability to
address issues of gender, class, or sexuality brought it into direct conflict with the
claims and oppositional strategies of other emerging social movements, primary
among them the feminist movement. In the 1980s, as the force of the women's
movement began to be felt in the Asian American community, Asian American
women became more vocal concerning the gender bias implicit in the structure of
Asian American nationalism. The publication of *This Bridge Called My Back:
Writings by Radical Women of Color* (Moraga and Anzaldúa 1981)—which
included pieces by Mitsuye Yamada and Merle Woo—provided textual evidence
of the arrival of an emerging consciousness around Asian American women's
double subordination on the basis of race and gender.

The growing confrontation between cultural nationalism and feminism in the
1980s was but one indicator of the changed and changing nature of what Asian
American nationalism had construed as a relatively stable and homogeneous
political constituency. The liberalization of the immigration laws in 1965 and the
resulting demographic changes within the Asian American community in the
years 1965–85 were to radically transform that constituency and further under-
mine cultural nationalism's claims to representativeness. The Asian American
population prior to 1965 had been dominated by the presence of Japanese Ameri-
cans, Chinese Americans, and Filipino Americans. The defining framework and
agenda of cultural nationalism had been formulated within the historical context
of the perceived social and political needs of these three groups. From 1965 to
1985, the Asian American population increased from one million to five million

and underwent a significant redistribution along national lines.[10] Differing from earlier waves of Asian immigration in terms of class and national origin and gender ratio, this post-1965 immigration also shifted the ratio of native-born to foreign-born in Asian American communities. In the face of a radically changed constituency, Asian American cultural nationalism became less and less able to specify a common political agenda and cultural identity around which the entire Asian American population could cohere. The respective needs—economic, social, political, cultural—of an increasingly diverse population that included fourth-generation Japanese American professionals as well as first-generation Hmong farmers could hardly be addressed or accommodated within a single oppositional program.

With the advent of the new social movements of the 1980s—some centering on peoples: gays, lesbians, the physically challenged; others on issues: peace, ecology—came the dispersal of political allegiances that called into question the effectiveness of an oppositional strategy founded on the basis of racial identification alone. Asian American identity politics began to founder in this welter of difference. It is within this moment of tension, when the politics of identity confronts a politics of difference, that a space can be found in which to read *DICTEE* against the full range of its critiques of institutionalized sites of oppression. Within the institution of criticism, the declaration of a poststructuralist politics of difference purportedly marked by a turn away from received canons of literature and toward a critical practice that values difference, indeterminacy, and negation has contributed to the recent surge of interest in Cha's work.

A concern with an aesthetics and a politics of difference also appears in the work of a number of Asian American poets (such as Marilyn Chin, Garrett Hongo, Li-Young Lee, David Mura, and John Yau) whose writing has only recently become more widely known. These poets' work is often marked by an awareness of the representational and epistemological stakes involved in the changing status and form of the lyric "I." The radical decentering of the subject in recent years has undermined the claims of the "I" to be at once the transcendent bearer of truth and knowledge and the transcendent eye that views all things from nowhere. The ensuing emergence of a plurality of particular, situated knowledges (knowledges that know some things from somewhere and that are sometimes congruent, sometimes conflictual, and always partial) has enabled these writers to work with alternative modes of constituting subjectivity in the poem. These poets' emphases on heterogeneity is not simply a nod, however, to a free and indeterminate play of differences. As theorists such as Nancy Hartsock have pointed out, the poststructuralist emphasis on the decentering of the subject and the dispersal of identity into incommensurable difference can be drawn all too readily into a new epistemological trap.[11] If transcendent knowledge is no longer available, if one can no longer see everything from nowhere, perhaps one cannot really see anything at all. That is, if one cannot engage in what Donna Haraway has dubbed the "god-trick," perhaps there is no such thing as knowledge (Hartsock 1990, 17). Just at the moment, then, that the marginalized or oppressed have claimed a visibility and an epistemological viability, they are snatched away again.

While acknowledging the claims of poetic works that valorize the decentered subject and observe a radical skepticism concerning the referential function of language, Asian American poets such as Mura have pointed out the problems of universalizing the liberatory effects of that decentering. While conceding that "a lot of American poetry that relies on a sense of a unified 'I' a lyric 'I' a voice of sincerity, a voice that relies solely on a realistic aesthetic, is very old-fashioned," Mura also recognizes that the position for the minority writer will, of necessity, be "slightly different" because "if the history of [a] people has never been written down, it is essential to believe that somehow there's an experience there . . . which was left out of the history books, which was left out of the culture" (1991, 268). At the same time, Mura notes his own "skepticism about the ability of language to capture that experience simply because [he] grew up in this twentieth century with a skepticism about the way that language can lie" (1991, 268–69). Mura gestures here toward the way in which poststructuralism's skepticism about the availability of the referent has been canonized, or exaggerated to the point that the real often disappears from consideration. His insisting on the necessary possibility of creating languages relating to material experiential conditions challenges poststructuralism's tendency to so problematize a subject's relation to experience that, in Paul Smith's terms, "it has become difficult to keep sight of the political necessity of being able to not only theorize but also refer to that experience." The specificity of experiences is susceptible to absorption by "theories of language, representation and subjectivity which poststructuralism has conventionalized" (1988, 159).

Thus, while the critical and political climate of the 1990s seems to provide a more appropriate setting in which to read *DICTEE*, there remains the possibility that the appropriate will become the appropriative. As earlier Asian American writers of autobiographies and bildungsromane came to recognize through the nature of the reception of their work, what had been put forward as the subversive assertion of a distinct Asian American identity and subjectivity could be drawn all too readily into a formal identity with prevailing conceptions of a universal American *Bildung*. Deriving from the Latin root *proprius*, meaning "one's own," the act of appropriation signifies, within the terms proposed by *DICTEE* itself, the transformation of something other into one's own, the reproduction of something other in one's own image, the very act of totalizing absorption. While locating its oppositional project in the refusal to be the object of such absorption or reproduction, *DICTEE* itself remains located at an historical juncture of sociopolitical tensions and competing critical paradigms and thus, like all texts, is subject to appropriations or absorptions of one or another of its critical aspects. For example, in *Open Form and the Feminine Imagination* (1988), Stephen-Paul Martin situates Cha's writing practice within a tradition of feminist experimental writing and understands the crux of the work to be an argument against patriarchal discourse. The reduction of *DICTEE*'s multivalent critical project to a single line of argument against "masculine discourse" effectively neutralizes an oppositional politics grounded in the recognition that religious, colonial, racial, and patriarchal discourses do not function in isolation from each other but reinforce, overlap, intersect, and contradict each other in their material practices and effects. Martin's rendering of Cha's name in the chapter title, "Theresa Cha: Creating a Feminine Voice" (her Korean name "Hak Kyung," which appears on the cover of *DICTEE,* has been omitted), prefigures a discussion of *DICTEE* that will proceed without reference to race or nationality.

The possibilities for appropriation extend beyond the common practice of mistaking and substituting parts for wholes. It extends to the way in which institutional circumstances can mediate the effects of radical oppositional texts. One example of such mediation could be seen in a paper delivered at the 1990 Modern Language Association Convention that discussed *DICTEE* through the critical perspectives of both colonial discourse theory and poststructuralist theory. While invoking concepts of "hybridity," "alterity," and "difference," the critic was often unable to bind these concepts to the specific and material historical conditions out of which Cha attempted to speak the difference of the Korean American immigrant woman. In not doing so, the critic risked colonizing difference itself and rendering alterity for alterity's sake. What became apparent during the course of the presentation was the way in which radical critical paradigms (particularly those of colonial discourse theory) could be emptied of the historical and material specificity that grounds their critiques of colonial power and subsequently circulated within an institutional setting as the currency of a new critical orthodoxy.[12]

DICTEE consistently works against such absorption and incorporation, insisting instead on the necessity of expressing that which exists in excess of identity (the identity of a single genre, for instance) as surplus. What *DICTEE* comes back to repeatedly is the need for attention to those persistent clamorings of difference that threaten always to spill over the pristine foundations of the "once upon a time." In *DICTEE*, the writing out of the Korean American, the woman, the religious subject, and the postcolonial creates the stain of difference that resists absorption by an American identity; instead, the "[s]tain begins to absorb the material spilled on" (65), thus subverting the usual direction of incorporation. The practice of writing self begins in the refusal to accede to the identity of the blank page:

> Something of the ink that resembles the stain from the interior emptied onto emptied into emptied upon this boundary this surface. More. Others. When possible ever possible to puncture to scratch to imprint. Expel. Ne te cache pas. Révèle toi. Sang. Encre. Of its body's extention of its containment. (65)

In *DICTEE,* it is the diseuse who presides over the spilling of language; it is her function "to puncture to scratch" the smooth surface of a discourse of wholeness, or generic identity, that would seek to absorb rather than admit the "imprint" of difference. The last section of *DICTEE,* unlike the first nine sections, proceeds without the prefatory designation of a Muse—classical or invented. The effect of this gesture of unnaming, in a work concerned with the ways in which names are used to contain and to falsify, is to usher in a figure that might be called the Muse of stumbling invention, the very figure, or figuration, of an oppositional method that searches out not type but the atypical and unrepresentative. I am taking *invention* here in its root sense of "coming upon," for what *DICTEE* finally leaves its readers with is a method of coming upon that which had been denied and trampled by the triumphal procession of the "once upon a time." Stumbling over, or coming upon, the surplus material of history in this way constitutes one of the honest and radical motions available to those who would refuse the smooth developmental progress of a discourse of wholeness. To write the way Cha writes is to work with an enabling method of recovering the body of difference lying prostrate before the triumph of History.

NOTES

I would like to thank Barry Maxwell, Giulia Fabi, Elaine Kim, and Norma Alarcon for generously providing the critical commentary and good company without which the experience of writing would be impoverished.

1. Articles by the following people also either allude to or briefly discuss the presence of the Muses in *DICTEE:* Siegle 1989; Stephens 1986; Wald 1990; Wilson 1991.

2. I am indebted to Professor Leslie Kurke of the Department of Classics at the University of California at Berkeley for her help in determining the invented nature of this name. Given Cha's predilection for skewing resemblances in the interest of naming difference, it is worth noting the orthographic similarities between Euterpe and Elitere.

3. It is interesting to note, in this regard, that the lines attributed to Sappho are actually Cha's in(ter)vention. I would like to thank Kimberly Wurtzel for first drawing this to my attention.

4. Within the ranks of contemporary Asian American poets, Cha is hardly alone in being troubled by the status of the lyric self. I am presently at work on a piece that focuses on the lyric "I" in Asian American poetry and works from Norman Finkelstein's understanding of some of the recent changes in the conception of a lyric "I" in the context of the "cultural logic of late capitalism": "According to [Fredric] Jameson, one of the distinctions

between the modern and the postmodern can be observed in 'the dynamics of cultural pathology' which 'can be characterized as one in which the alienation of the subject is displaced by the fragmentation of the subject'" (Finkelstein 1991, 4). Putting aside for the time being the accuracy of this characterization of epistemological shifts in American poetry of the last twenty-five years, what interests me is the way in which Asian American poetry is to be situated within, or without, that cultural pathology. Was the Asian American subject ever not "fragmented"? Was, then, the lyric "I" ever available to the Asian American writer? Poets such as Marilyn Chin, Garrett Hongo, Li-Young Lee, David Mura, and John Yau have produced work that distinguishes a mainstream American and Asian American lyric "I." The recent work of Li-Young Lee (*The City in Which I Love You* [1990]) and David Mura (*After We Lost Our Way* [1989]), for instance, could be characterized as moving out of a poetics of cleaving or negation. Their poetry often bears witness to DuBois's "double consciousness" and speaks as a locus of multiple, contending voices.

5. I have found Paul Smith's efforts to locate a third term beyond the opposition of subject (that which determines) and object (that which is determined) particularly helpful in providing a means of theoretical expression for this part of my discussion of *DICTEE*. Within his operative terminology, that third term is "subject/individual" (1988, xxxiii–xxxv).

6. For an extended discussion of the "aesthetics of infidelity" in *DICTEE*, see Lisa Lowe's "Unfaithful to the Original: The Subject of *Dictée*" (1994).

7. In invoking *The Cantos* (Pound 1979) and a tradition of the American long poem that would also include Williams's *Paterson* (1963) and Olson's *The Maximus Poems* (1983), I am not suggesting that *DICTEE* would fit readily within that tradition. While *DICTEE* maintains certain formal resemblances to the long poem, it is also marked by divergences, perhaps most notably in its refusal of the presence and prerogatives of a single controlling authority.

8. Ellis Island, in New York harbor, was the site of the immigration station for arrivals from Europe, while Angel Island (and before that site came to be used, the Pacific Mail and Steamship Company's wharf), in San Francisco Bay, was the entry point for immigrants from Asia.

9. Franco Moretti makes this point in *The Way of the World: The Bildungsroman in European Culture*. He further notes that while the bildungsroman is "the symbolic form that more than any other has portrayed and promoted socialization . . . [it] is also the *most contradictory* of modern symbolic forms" because "socialization itself consists first of all in the *interiorization of contradiction*. The next step being not to 'solve' the contradiction, but rather to learn to live with it, and even transform it into a tool for survival" (1987, 10). I would argue that many Asian American bildungsromane insist precisely on keeping rather than erasing contradictions. At the same time, however, those attempts to maintain contradictions always confront the possibility of being submerged by dominant frameworks of reception that valorize reconciliation.

I am using the term bildungsroman not in the classical sense associated with Goethe's *Wilhelm Meister,* but more broadly to include novels of formation, initiation, education, and self-discovery. In an article on the novel of formation, Marianne Hirsch notes some of the characteristics of the genre. These novels tend generally to foreground "the story of a representative individual's *growth and development* within the context of a defined social order," a growth directed toward the "formation of a *total personality*, physical, emotional, intellectual and moral." With its focus on "the development of selfhood . . . this type of novel is a *story of apprenticeship. . . . Its projected resolution is an accommodation to the existing society.*" The novel generally ends with the protagonist's "*assessment of himself and his place in society*" (1979, 296, 297, 298).

10. "[I]n 1960, 52 percent [of Asian Americans] were Japanese, 27 percent Chinese, 20 percent Filipino, 1 percent Korean, and 1 percent Asian Indian. Twenty-five years later, 21 percent of Asian Americans were Chinese, 21 percent Filipino, 15 percent Japanese, 12 percent Vietnamese, 11 percent Korean, 10 percent Asian Indian, 4 percent Laotian, 3 percent Cambodian, and 3 percent 'other'" (Takaki 1989, 420).

11. In "Postmodernism and Political Change: Issues for Feminist Theory," Nancy Hartsock argues that an attention to epistemologies of situated knowledges provides a viable and contestatory alternative to both the binary oppositions (neutral versus biased reason) established by Enlightenment thought and the "dead-end oppositions set up by postmodernism's rejection of the Enlightenment" (1990, 31).

12. While the theoretical apparatus Priscilla Wald (1990) brought to bear on the reading of *DICTEE* enabled her to frame (in general terms) the liberatory possibilities of Cha's "aesthetics of displacement," it also functioned at times to elide the particularity of the historical constitution of subjectivity, and to overlook the historical conditions of a text's production and reception. Though it provided much in the way of deft readings of specific passages of *DICTEE* and helpful discussions of the problems of "narrativization" and "cultural dictation," the talk was troubling because its theoretical discourse "displaced" the subject(s) of *DICTEE*.

"Corpses of Poesy":
Some Modern Poets and Some
Gender Ideologies of Lyric

Rachel Blau DuPlessis

The writing and rewriting of gender and sexualities, Woman and Man, desire and its foci are central to modern texts; there are multiple cultural debates on these issues in the writing of the moderns.[1] Yet it is increasingly clear that "modernism's stories of its own genesis" are deeply flawed by significant exclusions (Ardis 1990, 2) of these issues and figures. This point has been made with vivacity by a number of critics.[2] The reading strategies to disengage debates on gender and sexuality, to identify affiliative relationships among artists, and to reposition women within modernism are paradoxical. These strategies are deeply indebted to gynocriticism as a still active yeast for feminist analysis. One must work to discover "missing," barely read, or resisted women writers in their own specificity, looking closely at texts (in some cases reading uncollected materials, archival evidence), trying to comprehend the moves in biography and poetics as parts of one—but not necessarily unified—practice, reading the thematic and formal choices in a multidimensional fashion, setting the work in a context provided by a woman writer's ties to other (women) writers (not necessarily saccharine ties) and to cultural traditions in general.[3]

However, I think these reading strategies must now swerve from the bifocal practice accurately outlined by Patrocinio Schweickart in her summary of an earlier feminism (1986). Schweickart sees feminist readers making a motivated, self-conscious distinction between the questions asked of and investments in male and female authors. Baldly put, feminist readers will be empathetic to female authors, resistant to male ones. The gynocritical moves are quite familiar: first, a legitimation strategy explaining authorial choices as justifiable inventions of even a limited female agency; then a social and biographical contextualization to produce that materialist, situational literary criticism which, since Woolf, has been so notable a feminist contribution. But why might writing by men not be scrutinized by feminists in its social, economic, political situation, in the cultural work and the life work it is accomplishing? The strategy Schweickart outlines for discussing texts by men involves an interesting triple move, acknowledging a very contradictory response: a critic's resistance to a text's misogyny, her complicity with and temptation by patriarchal ideology, and finally her reading of the utopian component inside a text that challenges its own gender norms.[4] But why might writing by women not evoke contradictory responses in feminist readers? Why might one not have to resist as well as affirm? If we do not use the same tools to discuss writing by both genders, we still secretly "universalize" male writing or uncritically overvalue writing by women. I am reasserting an evenhanded feminist reading practice: why should the questions asked of male and female authors differ so markedly? why should one's empathetic engagement or curiosity go only to the gender or social identities the critic practices? How can one maximize one's attention to the multiple play of changing and mobile social identities (for gender is not the only one); how create evenhanded attention honoring motivations and choices in writing by both male and female writers, and yet remain aware of the asymmetries of power (in literary production, dissemination, reception, even unto the reception of critics working on gender issues) that motivated the compensatory and vindicatory readings of gynocriticism in the first place?

The struggle around evenhandedness is not simple, because it must move as well in the opposite direction, with something of what Nancy K. Miller calls "overreading." This is interpretation that calls attention to the paradigms of exclusion, discusses at length the sexual politics and historical determinants of textual production, and focuses on the aspects of the text that allegorize the struggles around its production: "a focus on the moments in the narrative which by their representation of writing itself might be said to figure the production of the female artist" (Miller 1988, 83). In the work of Miller, Susan Stanford Friedman, Margaret Homans, and myself, this moment is often seen as a confrontation with gynetical cultural paradigms—that is, narratives, materials, structures of feeling in the history of ideas of Woman that women writing and men writing raise in their work. (There are other ideas—of race, religious culture, nationhood, for example—that also serve as cultural glue; gender, however, has done powerful service.) The contradictory critical drama between evenhandedness and overreading occurs in the service of "gendering modernism," as one central, unforgettable act in producing a new modernism (which means, at least, some new literary histories of modernism).[5] In order to do this, poetry must be brought up into high relief—never mind that a good deal of what is called "theory" these days acts as if it were only theory of fiction, and that a good deal of "literary history" is the literary history of fiction only.

Now lyrics have often been privileged by the critical assumption of their timeless, universal emotions and nonparticipation in historical debate (Homans 1985).[6] It has been relatively difficult to make them "telling," to have them tell tales of embedded ideologies and debates in the same ways that narrative has. Both the privileges of poetic genius and assumptions of a transcendent "beyond" of art cling to lyric poetry in ways that make it difficult to see the cultural work done by poems. To counter this devastating assumption of poetic neutrality or specialness, I now simply assume that all kinds of social materials and cultural narratives saturate poetic texts: the question is not whether they are there, but how to find them and what they mean. Attentive close reading coupled with historical and discursive literacy on the part of the critic may help to foreground the embedding of such materials not so much *in* poetry but *as* poetry.[7]

Because of lyric poetry's great use of gender ideologies, feminist criticism seems a special kind of tool to open poetry to the same kind of cultural analysis that has (with both Marxist critics and certain social poststructuralists, as well as with many feminists) been so fruitful a terrain for the analysis of narrative. Feminist readings will engage deeply (but never exclusively) with the "gender narratives," meaning lazily naturalized stories around sexuality and gender— stories in the sense of historically active values, ideologies, cultural myths (Barthes [1957] 1972). For the genre poetry activates notable master plots, ide- ologies, and moves fundamentally inflected with gender relations. Here Homans has been an exacting guide to one of the tropes that follows from the situation of traditional love lyrics: "masculine, heterosexual desire," with its interest in look- ing at, and framing, a silent, beautiful, distant female object of desire (1985, 570).[8] To enter the lyric as genre is to enter (at least) this plot; it is an aspect of the "political unconscious" of poetry in general, and of the romantic lyric in particu- lar (Jameson 1981).[9]

To talk about lyric, one must say something about beauty, something about love and sex, something about Woman and Man and their positionings, some- thing about active agency versus malleability. This is a cluster of foundational materials with a gender cast built into the heart of the lyric. The foundational cluster concerns voice (and silencing), power (appropriation and transcendence), nature (as opposed to formation and culture), gaze (framing, specularity, frag- mentation), and the sources of poetic matter—narratives of romance, of the sublime, scenes of inspiration, the muse as conduit (Vickers 1981). There is often a triangulated situation in the lyric: an overtly male "I," speaking as if overheard in front of an unseen but postulated, loosely male "us" about a (Beloved) "she" (Grossman 1992, 227). To change any of these pronouns ("I" speaking directly to a "you," for example; an "I" who is a "she"; readers claiming to be female) is to jostle, if only slightly, the homosocial triangle of the lyric (Sedgwick 1985). The history of poetry shows that these—the foundational cluster, the tropes that

Homans describes, the general gender narrative or pattern book of moves—are materials, to echo Annabel Patterson (1987), in which a large cultural investment has been made.

> Or if thy mistress some rich anger shows,
> Emprison her soft hand, and let her rave,
> And feed deep, deep upon her peerless eyes.
>
> (Keats 1978, 374)

The circuit of pronouns here ("I" giving advice to himself as "thou") has the effect of containing the terrific possibilities of engulfment in "her." This famous passage is exemplary in other ways. Certainly poetry is always to be beautiful, and in these beauties linked to the beauties of Woman. And Woman must be beautiful—soft and peerless and deep, even if raving, angry, hysterical, offering that impotent wealth on which Keats comments.[10] Love will be poetic. Poetry will concern love; love will suggest sex, or at least forms of desirous imprisoning, loving predation, capture of richness. To be in love, to possess that beauty, is to be inspired to write. And willy-nilly, the whole cluster is reaffirmed. To cite William Carlos Williams on his poem "To a Young Housewife": "Whenever a man sees a beautiful woman it's an occasion for poetry—compensating beauty with beauty" (1986, 479).

My play between Williams and Keats is not meant to suggest that these assumptions are timeless. That is impossible; neither history nor writing works that way; genders and sexualities are learned and reinforced. If these materials are recurrent in romantic lyric, it is because they have been, like any ideology, renewed and reasserted. A writer in the course of assuming a poetic vocation would find it hard to avoid these materials (although, of course, they are hardly the only matter of poetry); thus s/he would have to find some attitude to them: to deploy, examine, reassume, investigate, play with (jocularly, happily, critically), or comment on these materials would be one aspect of a poet's cultural charge.

Genders and sexualities were topics much in debate in the generations before the first florescence of modern poetry. Indeed, all poets and writers born in the mid-1870s to late 1880s (Stein—1874, Stevens—1879, Loy—1882, Williams—1883, Pound—1885, H.D.—1886, Moore—1887, Eliot—1888) would have had, as the backdrop of their growing up, gender-laden economic, sexual, cultural, and political discussions. There were, in this period, debates over the nature and theory of sexuality, the rise of sexology as a scientific study, a show trial of an English homosexual along with increasing definitional and psychological interest in the "intermediate sex" and same-sex object choices, a newish subject position called the New Woman, agitation about controlling births and other debates on sexuality without reproduction, divorce legislation, and finally a militant feminist campaign for the vote (Weeks 1981). There was some critique of the sexual double standard, calls for male chastity as a cure for "predatory sexuality," debilitating worries over sexually transmitted diseases such as syphilis, theoretical uneasiness about female gender development, the expansion of female higher education, practical and moral questions about free(r) female sexuality, attempts at new kinds of marriage, and a heritage of mannered, deliberate gender fluidity and effeminacy in the work of the "decadent" Victorian poets. An increasing plurality of issues and effervescent debate about sexual and gender matters preceded and accompanied the earliest publications by these authors.[11] Given the intensity of debate on issues surrounding genders and sexualities, ideologies and roles, it seems pertinent to assume that the young poets of modernism reacted—as did the young fiction writers—to these new sociocultural patterns. How did this specific set of historical debates enter and inflect traditional materials foundational to the poetic discipline? Did the poets change or comply with the gender narratives often told, and often implied in the notion of lyric?

The assumptions Williams made in his brief statement on "The Young House-wife" are extensions of this foundational cluster of gendered notions: that beautiful women often inspire poetry that it is men's task to create. He suggests that poetry is a counterbalance proper to men, offsetting or compensating for the beauty of women. That poetry is a reparation to women for their beauty, which is culturally appropriated by men for their poetry via the mechanism of the gaze (Mulvey 1989). This concept may have serious uses for the analysis of lyric poetry. Laura Mulvey proposes two key moves, both of which have their analogue in many poems in Western culture: voyeuristic investigation/ demystification of the female figure, and overvaluation of the figure turned into a fetish.[12]

Williams in general demystifies women, which seems to be a tough-minded, realist strategy, but his analysis is possessive and appropriative, tinged with voyeuristic pleasure. The woman in "The Young Housewife" is framed, "uncorseted" and "in negligee" (1986, 57): lax and yearning. In the poem, too, a man is paradoxically both freer and more constrained than the woman by virtue of this responsibility of compensation. He has the power to resist, yet remark on, the sexual undertext when she "comes to the curb / to call the ice-man, fish-man." Of the wispy young housewife, the Williams-speaker states, with great power in his deliberateness, power of naming, power of connoisseurship: "I compare her / to a fallen leaf." And the allusion "fallen leaf / fallen woman" layers two discourses. It resounds with the late-nineteenth- and early-twentieth-century tendentious comparisons of marriage to "parasitism and prostitution" (in Charlotte Perkins Gilman and Olive Schreiner, for instance, and echoed in Mina Loy's "Feminist Manifesto" [1982]). And the "fallen leaf" metaphor of use and loss is also a post–carpe diem allusion, a link of woman to nature, fatalistic in implication.

Williams proposes the fate of that one leaf in an implacable image of destruction (corresponding to Mulvey's findings that one punishes the demystified object), as

> The noiseless wheels of my car
> rush with a crackling sound over
> dried leaves as I bow and pass smiling.

(1986, 57)

And what an enigmatic smile he offers at the end: rueful pleasure, condescension, relief at escape, power masked by politeness, a predictive knowledge of her fate (either used up by, or overeager for, sexual contact). Although the props, such as cars, and the line breaks are modern, the traditional gender cluster undergirding poetry has been reaffirmed in this work about the relation of female beauty to male power.

Ezra Pound has an energetic sexual narrative in his early works, especially in *Lustra* (first published 1916). The songs, his Pan-like offspring, are "impudent," and they "dance the dance of the phallus" (Pound 1926, 85–86).[13] He is proud of them and wry about them; *Lustra* is punctuated with apostrophes to their defiant attractions and to their capacity for *épatisme*. The reader, presumed to be shocked, is placed by Pound in a feminine-squeamish role as "timorous wench" and taxed repeatedly with prudishness (81). The Women he depicts (Greek, Italian, or Provençal names; some Oriental materials) are supple, fresh, cool, yearning, "restless, ungathered," as if they could not own up to sexual desire (112). The poet does that work for them; hence *Lustra*, taken as a whole, is a chivalric answer to the sexual narratives of the New Woman (Burke 1985; Ardis 1990, 13–15). The more modern urban women are depicted with a cinematographic clarity by Pound as obliquely expressing sexual yearning about "the new morality": "her fingers were like the tissue / Of a Japanese paper napkin" (Pound 1926, 110). Conversely, they come in satiric, urbane "Roman" epigrams about their sexual sophistication. One might say that *Lustra* reinforces the double sexual standard: the more sex a man has, the more attractive he is, but the more sexually sophisticated the woman is, the less desirable she is.

Several positions on the feminine are thereby taken and factored out; the reader is especially concerned to escape from the mocking charge of sexual prudishness; s/he must thereby identify with the jocular and/or yearning masculinity that has positioned various Women in stages of sexual readiness yet has denied them overt sexual freedom. The poems argue that moderns should have no truck with sexual repression or the "enslaved-by-convention," yet they assiduously appreciate the Women waiting for the poet's sexual freedom to free them (Pound 1926, 88).

Pound also announces a particular kind of masculine task. When he wrote his early poems (he speaks in the royal or editorial "we"),

> We were in especial bored with male stupidity.
> We went forth gathering delicate thoughts,
> Our "*fantastikon*" delighted to serve us.
> We were not exasperated with women,
> for the female is ductile.
>
> (1926, 82)[14]

Despite rejecting the "stupid" elements of the masculine for the feminine, Pound says in another stanza of "The Condolence" that he and his works get more virile, more red-blooded. Happy condolence! He shrugs this off in a secretly pleased fashion. Poetry is (thankfully) not effeminate; by doing it a man becomes even more manly, even though issues of class and work are occasions for some anxiety. Why? Because even if a man rejects notions emanating from members of his own gender, poetry can position Woman. Male poets may break with "male stupidity" (unglossed) and play in feminine fields of delicacy and imagination. The gathering of delicate thoughts (a word related to the injunction to "gather ye rosebuds" in classic carpe diem works) implies a gathering of momentum from pliable helper figures—both the feminine and women/the female are available. It is a strong position to be both male oneself and masculine/feminine in one's writing, but avoiding three dangerous places of writing practice: the "male but stupid," the feminist, and the effeminate.

Gertrude Stein proposes another aspect of this foundational cluster in her essay on "Poetry and Grammar" by defining the relational plot that drives poetry.

> Poetry is concerned with using with abusing, with losing with wanting, with denying with avoiding with adoring with replacing the noun. It is doing that always doing that, doing that and doing nothing but that. Poetry is doing nothing but using losing refusing and pleasing and betraying and caressing nouns. That is what poetry does, that is what poetry has to do no matter what kind of poetry it is. And there are a great many kinds of poetry. ([1935] 1985, 231)[15]

She proposes that writing is related to the intensity and level of erotic attention one gives when one is in love, and to calling out nouns ("more violently more persistently more tormentedly") as if each were the name of a loved one (210, 232). Love, sex, and poetry are hitched in Stein's theory, as they are in Williams's and Pound's: yearning, erotic desire, and sexual acts are stated or implied, although the object of attention is neither a man nor a woman, but any noun and all nouns.

But Stein (unlike Pound and Williams) is negotiating a double territory be-
tween critique and fascination. She provides an x-ray of the ideological mecha-
nism in her ultimate "rose" poem, laying bare the device about matters of love
and sex.

> When I said.
> A rose is a rose is a rose is a rose.
> And then later made that into a ring I made poetry and what did I do I
> caressed completely caressed and addressed a noun.
>
> ([1935] 1986, 231)

The rhyme of "caressed" and "addressed" clarifies the link between the romance
plot and poetic vocation, but the object of attention is a grammatical unit. She
concludes that "any poetry all poetry" is like this, and "anybody" can see it, thus
calling attention to the common knowledge (ideology) of poetry as a genre.
Courtship, sexuality, making love, love plots, and romance are proposed in her
summary, but so is a new relation to parts of speech. She revises the foundational
plot by retooling its two poles. The love object is "nouns"; the "I" is sometimes
personal but sometimes "poetry" itself (since sometimes "I" caresses nouns, and
sometimes "poetry" does). The conclusion of this syllogism is that "I" is like the
genre; this is a powerful trumping by a female writer of traditional statements to
women nullifying their poetic practice (such as this one of Pound, quoting
Browning, to H.D.: "'You are a poem, though your poem's naught'" [H.D. 1979,
12]; see Friedman 1990a, 382–83). Still, a whole melodrama of romance is
present; it fuels the language practices of poetry.

The words themselves can be hitched in a ring. Stein's famous definition of
roses, which puns on *Eros* and *arroser* (French: to water, sprinkle, spray), was
sometimes typographically presented in a circle—in, as the old word has it, a
poesy. For *poesy* does not mean only a poetical composition, or only a poetical
synonym for poetry, or only a nosegay of flowers, but also a "motto or short
inscription in metrical, patterned, or formal language," as in *Hamlet*: "Is this a
Prologue or the Poesie of a Ring" (3.2.162). Stein has produced—in a playful
"mathematical" equation—a most succinct summary of poetry's foundational
assumptions.

One case study for the new histories of modernism concerns the ways this
foundational cluster lyric-love-sex-beauty-Woman operates in the relations
among Loy, Moore, and Pound. In 1918 Pound proposed the category *logopoeia*
to define the exact character of their work: "logopoeia or poetry that is akin to
nothing but language, which is a dance of the intelligence among words and ideas
and modification of ideas and characters" (Pound 1918, 57). It is a term that
suggests analysis, critique, and ideological interventions ("modification of

ideas") made in poetry. Logopoeia became a key critical term of his modernism, appearing, for instance, in Pound's "How to Read" ([1929] 1954) and in the *ABC of Reading* (1960).[16] It is one of three ways of creating meaning—by visual imagery (phanopoeia), by sound (melopoeia), or in logopoeia, by "using the word in some special relation to 'usage,' " playing ironically with the contexts in which one expects it. This is something like what Bakhtin (1981) calls heteroglossia—the deploying of different social registers and jargons to create, in a phrase retooled from 1918, " 'the dance of the intellect among words' " (Pound [1929] 1954, 25; 1960, 37). Often and correctly approached as the desire to bring into poetry the density of social analysis in the "prose tradition" (from such writers as Flaubert and James), or to translate into English letters the insouciant urban blues of a Laforgue, logopoeia can also be approached as originating in an intense debate with the cluster of foundational materials of poetry. That is, logopoeia also began as a feminist analysis of the gender assumptions of lyric.

Many early reviewers of logopoetic works characterize this mode: clever, ingenious, chilling, unflinchingly diagnostic, replete with "erudite allusions and crisp colloquialisms" (McCarthy 1982, 85). The mode of logopoeia can be summed up in Loy's own phrase "cerebral forager" (Loy 1982, 101). With witty and even snooty attention to etymology, spur ends (or Eliot's "butt ends") of colloquialisms, esoteric diction, scientific or rare word choices, polysyllabic "philoprogenitives," a writer of logopoeia produces a poetry of ideas and wordplay, intellectual allusions made in poetry, dissenting resistant analytics, discursive gear stripping.

But logopoeia also began, in these brilliant, critical "girls," as Pound called them, as an attack on the gender narratives of lyric poetry: femininity, beauty, a certain gaze on female objects, unironic sexual yearning, the underlying lyric narrative of romance. It is, as Burke argues, a poetry written from the subject position of New Woman; the analytic lyric, or even the nonlyric written precisely to undercut the gender narratives of lyric poetry.[17] Moreover, and more problematically, these two writers were trying to change the notion of poetic pleasure—pleasures reflected in Pound's other two categories, in sound, in beautiful imagery, in the attractive framing of attractive things, in the love plot, in the yearning for a female ideal.[18] One might theorize that these givens of poetic pleasure are so embedded in our needs as readers of poetry that their lack is seriously destabilizing.[19] This may explain both critical neglect of Loy and the lavish scrutiny of a tamed, minoritized Moore, as well as questions about any poetry that does not provide the usual pleasure in the usual ways.

The New Woman position in poetry (which I propose to track further) was, historically, formed in opposition to the romantic lyric; a resistance to normal poetic pleasures was its most radical effect. The desire not for beauty but for diagnosis—a diagnosis that undercuts poesy—is most imperiously a diagnosis of poetry's own gender assumptions. Logopoeia continued, in Pound and others, as an analytic lyric, but one that erased the feminist critique. When Pound absorbs logopoeia, he also reframes it, especially in the long poem *Hugh Selwyn Mauberley* (1926; first published 1920).

It is well known in literary history that *Mauberley* was written in response to "dilution" and "general floppiness"—an indictment of Amy Lowell and the softening of imagism (Stock 1970, 206); this is, of course, literary history written by Pound. Putting the challenge of Loy and Moore to Pound in its chronological place makes clear that *Mauberley* was also written to soften a feminist critique of the lyric, not only to stiffen (as it were) a mushy and feminized imagism.[20] In this work, the critique of social institutions and the sexual implications of writing still ends by eulogizing beauty, whether in the poem's first ending, "Envoi" (dated 1919), "Till change hath broken down / All things save Beauty alone," or in the second ending, "Medallion," which describes an exquisite woman singing an exquisite song (Pound 1926, 197). Although the poem describes a Pound figure trying to embark on a social and historical mission in poetry, and although the poem satirizes female figures (Conservatrix of Milésian) as well as male (Mr. Nixon), female illusions (salon culture) as well as male (patriotism), the appeals to beauty at the end of each section are not ironic, but are the only value to recuperate from a dying civilization. Pound's reframing meant that the critique of romance and gender relations, and the challenges to the beauties of poetry as a genre, did not remain constitutive of logopoeia; this critique became contested territory within logopoetic practice.

Let me sketch, building on Burke, some of the dimensions of a New Woman position in poetry. My title phrase, "Corpses of Poesy," comes from a short poem by Loy called "Poe," which alludes to this foundational cluster via Poe's remarkable statement, "[T]he death, then, of a beautiful woman is, unquestionably, the most poetical topic in the world" (Poe [1846] 1984, 19). In his essay, this conclusion is a triumphant synthesis, with the glue being Woman, of some of the emotional and thematic markers of poetry—death, melancholy, and beauty. Best poetry draws (with vampiric precision) on best death. We understand that beautiful women are often the objects of poetry, but by proposing that the woman be dead, or be dying before his avid eyes, Poe intensifies poetry's unreciprocated gaze on beauty, beauty's implacable passivity. Loy's poem "Poe" comments,

> a lyric elixir of death
> embalms
> the spindle spirits of your hour glass loves
> on moon spun nights
>
> sets
> icicled canopy
> for corpses of poesy

with roses and northern lights

where frozen nightingales in ilex aisles
sing burial rites

(1982, 25)[21]

This poem is a parodic examination of the accouterments and props of conventional lyricism. Poe's embalmed loves are dead women—poetical corpses—who are arrayed with roses and sung over by nightingales. Loy's poem is both imitative of a sentimentalized funeral scene and satiric of it, "burying" the "poesy" that kills and embalms and then sanctifies and celebrates women.

Most amusingly, the phrase "corpses of poesy" means simultaneously women and the lyric. It means "Women as represented by poetry," because the "hour glass loves" are poetical corpses; note the allusion to the hourglass figure of nineteenth-century tintype, and lovemaking as an hour-long activity. The other meaning of "corpses of poesy" is "the mannered poeticalness of the lyric" (i.e., "a lyric elixir" or essence). Women and the lyric seem to be interchangeable terms.

"Poesy" is, of course, an especially loaded choice of diction. Not quite a synonym for poetry, its archaic turn implies its disparaged aura. It is a poetical or literary term for poetry, and it here implies the inadequacy of the dual conventions of the literary and the flowery, lovey gender materials that fuel the lyric. As a Romantic—indeed, as a Keatsean—word its use cuts into a whole religious romance about poetry that is also linked to female figures. "The viewless wings of Poesy" in the "Ode to a Nightingale" propose the rapture, yearning, and vocational doubt at the sustaining of transcendence as Keats pursues an evanescent lyric daimon, gendered female. Or the sonnet is imagined chained, like Andromeda, but destined to be bound more interestingly in Keats's garlands, and better dressed in "Sandals more interwoven and complete / To fit the naked foot of Poesy" (Keats 1978, 368). Poesy even functions as a verb, an equation of the kiss and the poem: "So said, his erewhile timid lips grew bold, / And poesied with hers in dewy rhyme" (Keats 1978, 248). In all the Keats poesy citations, a female figure is positioned—yearned for, dressed (in aesthetic dressage), and seduced. Loy's phrase "corpses of poesy" makes this poetical positioning of the female figure a subject of pointed comment.

In relation to this notional cluster, and with her eye on its cultural work, Loy opens poetry to analytic and ironic considerations that unmask a number of the gendered institutions on which poesy is built. In the poem "Lunar Baedeker," the moon, patron of women, poetry, the night, and sexuality, is examined, anatomized, and found to be a modernist stage upon which many genders play out many sensual dramas that realign the foundational materials beauty-love-sex-poetry-Woman (Loy 1982, 8–9). The poem's discontinuous flashes, fanzine snapshots or "flock[s] of dreams" are interrupted by sets of headlines all in capital letters:

"WING SHOWS ON STARWAY / ZODIAC CAROUSEL."[22] The imagery is decadent in a mannered, circusy way, as if the phases of the moon (on which the poem is arguably based) have assumed amoral poses:

> A silver Lucifer
> serves
> cocaine in cornucopia
>
> To some somnambulists
> of adolescent thighs
> draped
> in satirical draperies.

The poem takes as its model the flashing neon bytes of advertising ("Stellectric signs"). This sees beauty as something urban, commercial, and modern, verbally fusing Stella, or women of poetic tradition, the *stella* or stars in nature and the word *electric*—which has the effect of ripping apart the association in poetry-as-usual of woman and nature. "The eye-white sky-light / white-light district / of lunar lusts" are lines that acknowledge sexuality and its undersides in terms that deromanticize it familiarly, decadently (i.e., not love, but lust; not purity, but prostitution—punning on the red-light district of sex workers). In the lines

> Delirious Avenues
> lit
> with the chandelier souls
> of infusoria
> from Pharoah's tombstones
>
> lead
> to mercurial doomsdays
>
> (1982, 8)

Loy offers a brief history of the world, with the word "mercurial" removed from questions of love to questions of species survival.[23] Here, as elsewhere, Loy tries to assimilate the findings of Darwin into love poetry, challenging poetry with the theoretical findings of sexual selection and survival of the fittest, ideas that deromanticize love.

A key move of the critique of this foundational material of poetry is made at the end, in the final four stanzas.

> Onyx-eyed Odalisques
> and ornithologists

observe
the flight
of Eros obsolete

And "Immortality"
mildews
in the museums of the moon

NOCTURNAL CYCLOPS
CRYSTAL CONCUBINE

Pocked with personification
the fossil virgin of the skies
waxes and wanes

(Loy 1982, 9)

It should not be forgotten that "bird" is British slang for young woman, and that "ornithologists" are bird-watchers. But their gaze has, in this retracking, been directed away from "Odalisques." Unlike the female figures most characteristic of the languid and Orientalized image (like Man Ray's Kiki picture, "Le Violon d'Ingres," roughly contemporaneous with the poem, and like Matisse's endless paintings of haremized women), here the odalisques are not being looked at but are looking—as scientists or journalists watching trends. They are neither gazing inwardly on their own beauty, nor being gazed at by the bird-watchers. Together the former denizens of the romance plot, its significant male and female characters, study "Eros obsolete." The narratives of romance and the conventions on which their very names draw are done for, *depassés*. So too the conventions surrounding poetry and art (fame or "Immortality") mildew at the very site in which they used to flourish—"the museums of the moon," a phrase that suggests muses and traditional art.

Given the images of light and sight, the poem is in part a retracking of the gaze; point of view is multiplied and generalized, and this multidirectional, cubist quality arrests the male-looks-at-female specularity on which poesy rests. The moon becomes male and female, cyclops and concubine, parodically phallic, parodically available. The eye speculating on the moon's virginity is not clearly male or female, but ambiguously desiring and disinterested. The very plurality, discontinuity, and unfixability of the descriptors of the moon suggest Loy might be discussed under the Irigarayan rubric of plethora or "heterogeneity," which is Irigaray's theoretical response to the term *castration* and suggests how " 'the' gaze" might be modified in another economy of understanding (Irigaray 1985a, 142).[24]

Loy's poems often "scientifically" analyze love and romance, including her and women's complex ties to those cultural narratives. There's love, with its underside of economics, power politics, or pure lust:

> We have been taught
> Love is a god
> White   with soft wings
>   Nobody shouts
> VIRGINS FOR SALE
>
> (Loy 1982, 37)

Or the "Insipid Narrative" of a "Marriage" that she ironically termed "Effectual" but that might also have involved veiled self-satire and self-judgment:

> So here we might dispense with her
> Gina being a female
> But she was more than that
> Being an incipience   a correlative
> An instigation of the reaction of man
> From the palpable to the transcendent
> Mollescent irritant of his fantasy
> Gina has her use
>
> (Loy 1982, 31)[25]

The last four lines state, in unsentimental form, approximately what Williams said when he talked about a woman arousing a man to write with her beauty.

But if Loy's sympathies go with women abused or digested by the marriage economy, she also analyzes female passivity in the devastating "At the Door of the House." This poem uses the title as a refrain, punctuating the presentation of a tarot deck, which pretends to predict to various women the satisfactions of happy endings of romances:

> And really   lady
> I should say
> It will not be long before you see him
> For there he is at the door of the house
>
> (Loy 1982, 63)

All women in the poem are "Looking for the little love-tale / That never came true / At the door of the house" (64). And if the pathetic pretensions of needy women are satirized, so elsewhere are the foundational "stories" of love poetry, the ideology of the lyric-as-fairy-tale. These critical lines are more often cited than any other Loy and "stand for" her in some sense.

> Spawn of Fantasies
> Silting the appraisable
> Pig Cupid
> His rosy snout
> Rooting erotic garbage
> "Once upon a time"

(Loy 1982, 91)

Yet Loy's critical approach to the notional cluster around Woman-love-romance-beauty-lyric-sex never gets stated without marks of her complicity and attraction to that same conventional plot, as in the long poem "Love Songs" (first published 1915–17), from which these lines come.[26]

In March 1918, when Pound published his omnibus review praising Moore and Loy together, he produced a document through which we can track his response to the foundational cluster of poetry. It is also a document whose play of ambivalence we need critically to honor, for Pound tacks back and forth in trying to deal with the fact of interesting poets being intelligent women. He said their work is "the utterance of clever people in despair. . . . It is a mind cry, more than a heart cry" (Pound 1918, 58).[27] Note the generic "people." Yet the narrative of heart versus head has long been gendered; indeed, some of the shock value for Pound is that their alleged source poet, Jules Laforgue, "shows a great deal of emotion" (and, not incidentally, often produces a narrative of the love longing of a Pierrot figure), but the women have less, or none. This lack of emotion is, in my view, Pound's identification of a lack of the normal love plot, especially in Loy, the lack of narratives of beauty as usual and the lack of conventional gender ideas that suppress female agency. The poets are praised for their intelligence and their seeking out of " 'intelligence to converse with' " rather than seeking " 'an asylum for [their] affection' "—that is, Pound sees them as resisting romance and the sentimentalities that accompany it (1918, 58); he also sees them as equals, capable of dialogue and, indeed, original. There are "traces of emotion" in Moore, in her lively poems that address a changing "you" (such as "To a Steam Roller," which Pound amusingly pretends could be to him); in the work of Loy, in contrast, a shocked and admiring Pound "detect[s] no emotion whatever" (Pound 1918, 57). But this is amazing, and reveals only what Pound considers emotion. They both certainly do have emotion—it is an ironic and delighted—even superior—glee over puncturing and analyzing; it is passion, sarcasm, anger. "Their work," Pound says, echoing Milton, "is neither simple, sensuous nor passionate." He is right on only one count. It is not simple. But Loy drastically desentimentalizes romance; hence she is taxed with "no emotion," with being nonsensuous, nonpassionate. Emotion in women is equated with those feelings proper to love plots.

On the other hand Pound recognizes that this work "has none of the stupidity beloved of the 'lyric' enthusiast," because it confronts "the human"—not conventional pieties about relationships. Here are women writers whose manner is not feminine, who rupture the assumed congruence of gender norms and subject position.[28] Yet the way these women locate their poems in relation to relationships is something about which Pound is of two minds. To have them be "human" or confront "the human" neutralizes a lot of gender dances in which Pound (see *Lustra* [Pound 1926]) has invested and will continue deeply to invest. What then is their gender narrative? They no longer play naturally in a binary of masculine/feminine but either reject the binary (Moore) or lacerate it with critical comments (Loy).

It is clear that logopoeia verges on being antibeauty; or, to cite the Pound review, it has "an arid clarity, not without its own beauty" (1918, 58). Pound finds challenging the lack of conventional beauty (in melody, in diction), but he does see a rare intellectual clarity in what they offer. In this review Pound is found gulping hard. He thinks of these women writers as intelligent, educated, cool customers. "If they have not received B.A.'s or M.A.'s or B.Sc's they do not need them." Notice how the hard-won higher education of females is both affirmed and disparaged. Pound links the educated woman and the resistance to the feminine; this means that the New Woman, entering historical time (with social agitation and political claims), was the opposite of the mythic and archetypal Woman, who was often proposed by male modernists as solutions to the problems of sexuality, of emasculated men, and so on.

Pound began noticing Moore in 1915, mainly positively, and began corresponding with her in 1918. The Moore he read included pert poems anatomizing various people, usually addressed to "you" or to animals ("My Apish Cousins," also called "The Monkeys") and expressing a lot of resistance to being overrun or colonized. In 1919, he produced an amazing statement for her (a statement that later influences material in his *Cantos*) comparing the male and the female in no uncertain terms:

> The female is a chaos,
>
> the male
>
> is a fixed point of stupidity, but only the female
> can content itself with prolonged conversation
> with but one sole other creature of its own sex
> and of its own unavoidable species

the male

is more expansive
and demands other and varied contacts.

(Pound 1950, 146–47)

The letter goes on to express a good deal of male vulnerability in terms so arch
that it is almost in code; Pound's insistent use (here and above) of "male" and
"stupidity" deserves more comment. But "the female is a chaos" would certainly
stick in the craw. Aside from the universalistic insult, Moore was prone to dislike
gender polarities and hoped to avoid such fixed binaries in the first instance.
Moore's early reviews for *The Dial*, all of which postdate this letter from Pound,
evince admiration for the erasure of gender binaries, mentioning "Giotto's supe-
riority to interest in masculinity or femininity *per se*; the inadvertent muscularity
and angelic grace of his male figures—the faces of his madonnas and female
saints, like the faces of stalwart boys" (1986, 75). Clearly stereotypes of mas-
culine and feminine were coming under her increasing scrutiny, and she was
trying to build gender-blurring bridges between the polarities of masculine and
feminine.

Given the dates of all this work—Loy's poems on romance in 1915–16,
Pound's linkage of the two women in 1918 as arid, emotionless, and fascinating
purveyors of logopoeia, his gender-thumping letter of 1919, *Mauberley* (1926;
first published 1920), and then Moore's work in the 1920s—one is left with the
possibility that Moore's poems of the 1920s, which do constitute a thematic
cluster involving the critique of romance, are a response to being linked with Loy,
and to being on the receiving end of such statements as "the female is a chaos."[29]
The works are also in dialogue with H.D. Moore's poems from the 1920s take a
direct and amused bead on such romantic lyrical conventions as beauty, the love
plot, and carpe diem motifs.

The poem "Roses Only," uncollected except in Moore's *Observations* (1924),
is a frontal consideration of a flower widely associated with beauty, the feminine,
love, and carpe diem injunctions. The rose is addressed directly in the poem,
which begins "You do not seem to realise that beauty is a liability rather than / an
asset," and ends as if in syllogistic proof, "your thorns are the best part of you"
(1924, 41). Essentially, the poem argues that the rose's intelligence exists and is an
emanation of its beauty, yet that it is not its sexual availability and beauty that
distinguish it, but rather its resistance to the tropes and the assumptions that
would place it in the lyric tradition of unsurpassed and peerless gorgeousness.
This is a deliberate attack on carpe diem motifs. Carpe diem poems typically see
thorns as the occasion for the poem: the female's sexual prickliness and virginity
are genially reproached. And, as in Williams, female beauty is seen through an
elegiac lens—the leaf is already fallen. Conventional carpe diem poems separate

the rose from her thorns; Moore's "Roses Only" reunites them. And of course the carpe diem poem readies the virgin for sexual initiation in the guise of memorializing her beauties, while Moore remarks in a countermove that "it is better to be forgotten than to be remembered too violently," plucked by a "predatory hand" (1924, 41). Moore's advice tries to resocialize the rose, to turn it away from such haunting background lyrics as "Tell them, dear, that if eyes were made for seeing, / Then Beauty is its own excuse for being" and "gather ye rosebuds while ye may."

For as we know, a rose is often sent as a message to decode within a seduction framework, an image for female beauty at its peak of perfection, and a displaced object of sexual desire. In one of the poems from *Spring and All* (1923), Williams tries to negotiate both the desire and its critique in a poem that begins "the rose is obsolete" but ends by finding that if it is reimagined as somewhat technological (made of steel or copper, exploratory), and capable of "penetrat[ing] spaces," it can claim for itself more than just passivity. He makes it a dual-sexed image (1986, 195–96). So too H.D., in "Sea Rose" (the first poem in her first book, 1916), recasts the convention of roses in poetry by positing another rose, neither lush nor "precious." This rose is not an iconic object of erotic veneration; instead it is resistant, hardened, harshly treated, but free. "Rose, harsh rose, / marred and with stint of petals" challenges the conventional flower: "Can the spice-rose / drip such acrid fragrance / hardened in a leaf?" (1983, 5).[30]

H.D., however, produces a poem with a perfection of mellifluous lyrical markers, including a succinct sound, interior rhymes, assonance and consonance. Moore makes a diction choice resistant to the poetical beauties that are linked to female beauties. Indeed, she seems to delight in antimellifluousness in "Roses Only," using unpoetic, awkward, and turgid turns of line break and hyphen:

> But rose, if you are
> brilliant, it
> is not because your petals are the without-which-nothing
> of pre-eminence. You would, minus thorns,
> look like a what-is-this, a mere
>
> peculiarity.

H.D. fights the foundational gender cluster with a critique of feminized imagery of beauty in her flower poems. Moore fights the foundational gender cluster by a further antipoetic resistance to beauty in poetic texture and theme.

Her dialogue with H.D. is another way to identify Moore's scrutiny of the feminine, beauty, love, and so on, especially as Moore's observations on H.D. (and H.D.'s on Moore) slant certain evidence interestingly. In a 1916 review, H.D. asserted that Moore wants beauty, "frail" but "hard," and is fighting the same battle as H.D. "against squalor and commercialism" with her "curiously wrought patterns, these quaint turns of thought and concealed, half-playful ironies" (H.D. 1916, 118–19). The term "quaint" is an escapee from the Pretty Poetry world by which H.D. is sometimes tempted. For, though H.D. didn't see it, "squalor and commercialism" are thoroughly viable sources for Moore:

> all the physical features of
>
> ac-
> cident—lack
>   of cornice, dynamite grooves, burns, and
>   hatchet strokes. . . .
>
> (Moore 1967, 33)

In the poem placed first in her *Complete Poems* she announces, "it is a privilege to see so / much confusion"; the line break is pointed (Moore 1967, 5). We might wonder whether in these early works beauty was important to Moore at all; certainly the works I've cited twist theme, moral, and diction away from conventions of beauty. "The opaque allusion, the simulated flight upward, / accomplishes nothing," she remarks in a turn antiliterary, antitranscendent (Moore 1967, 45). "'A right good salvo of barks,' a few strong wrinkles puckering the skin between the ears, is all we ask" (Moore 1967, 45).

Moore's review of H.D. in 1923 does not avoid her "instinctive ritual of beauty" but retracks it from softness and availability to hardness: "an aesthetic consciousness which values simultaneously, ivory and the chiseled ivory of speech" (Moore 1986, 81). Aesthetic distance is a version of gender resistance. Moore is trying hard to make H.D. into a writer allied with logopoeia and "the firmness of the intelligence." In a striking last paragraph, she suggests that the book in which H.D.'s masque-poem "Hymen" appears (a work lush with beauty, a lavish depiction of a marriage ritual, complete with bridal torches, and "honey seeking lips" and "honey-thighs" [H.D. 1983, 109]) gives evidence of a "martial, an apparently masculine tone" (Moore 1986, 82). As applied to "Hymen" itself, this comment seems like wishful thinking so acute as to be revelatory. In fact, Moore is exploring the harsher lyrics in that book, rather than the honeyed marriage ritual, dealing not at all with the long title poem. By doing so, she resists her difference from H.D.

The terms Moore proposes show what is on her mind—a way of breaking and remixing some of the conventions around Woman and the feminine. "Women are regarded as belonging necessarily to either of two classes—that of the intellectual freelance or that of the eternally sleeping beauty, effortless yet effective in the indestructible limestone keep of domesticity" (Moore 1986, 82). This fairy-tale image is one that Moore will repeatedly reject; the New Woman subject position is, instead, invoked. In H.D., Moore says admiringly, one finds even a third possibility: "the intellectual, social woman, non-public and 'feminine'" (1986, 82). This synthesis takes the best from both sides. "Feminine," isolated in quotation marks, may mean a nonpassive yet nonaggressive interest in beauty as an aesthetic, and not a gender-laden, category. H.D., in Moore's view, combines the best of New Woman and old. As well, she resists stereotypes of masculine and the feminine: having an "absence of subterfuge, cowardice, and the ambition to dominate by brute force." These two reviews are certainly self-portraits or self-projections of H.D. by H.D. and Moore by Moore. Both reviews show how much gender, mingled with the demands of the lyric, was on their minds; both reviews show that each was concerned to establish some attitude to part of the foundational cluster (beauty-the feminine-sexuality) in the lyric.

Moore's "People's Surroundings" (first published June 1922) takes on significance in this argument. Dainty, lovely, gorgeous, and floral beauties of the conventionally poetic poem are recontextualized. Beauty is just one of many possible "surroundings" to appreciate and has no special thrust, higher status, or transcendent purpose. Indeed, conventional beauty ("roses outlined in pale black on an ivory ground") is probingly examined for its hidden cost and secret story (Moore 1967, 55).

As a base line for the poetical, look at Elinor Wylie's "fairy" beauties for poetry:

> Here, if you please
> Are little gilt bees
>   In amber drops
> Which look like honey,
> Translucent and sunny,
>   From clover-tops.
>
> (Wylie 1928, 27)

Instead of these baubles—related to the original seduction baubles in Marlowe's "Come live with me . . ."—or other such luscious materials and colors in Wylie's nine-stanza poem (including mother-of-pearl, lacquer, crystal, scarlet, ivory, turquoise, pearls, opal, the inevitable filigree, and the "quicksilver dust" to which these will turn, poor things, if they are taken from "fairy-land"), one has a flanking movement in Moore.[31] Moore does offer us something very like these exaggerated feminine beauties in one section of her poem, including "furious azure," "the crimson, the copper, and the Chinese vermilion of the poincianas," and other examples of lyric gorgeousness. However, these most luscious materials and colors occur in "Bluebeard's Tower"—certainly a type of "limestone keep." The lapidary comes at a price and conceals the terrible secret of serial murders of females in a "magic mouse-trap."

this dungeon with odd notions of hospitality,
with its "chessmen carved out of moonstones,"
. . . .
like splashes of fire and silver on the pierced turquoise of the lattices
and the acacia-like lady shivering at the touch of a hand,
lost in a small collision of the orchids—
dyed quicksilver let fall,
to disappear like an obedient chameleon in fifty shades of mauve and
    amethyst.

(Moore 1967, 56)

The words "obedient," "shivering," and "disappear" in this context become
sinister markers of a terror, while "odd notions of hospitality" bespeak Moore's
restrained distancing irony. Whether sinister or ironic, the words are critical of
the notional cluster of the lyric that we have been tracking: gorgeous and exotic
beauty, a complaisant and (might one say) ductile "lady," herself "lost" in nature
like a jewel, and the clear hint of predatory sexuality. In this poem, all the Pretty
Poetic Stuff is made drastically inadequate, a surface cover for damage to women.

The "fairy-land" and clichéd poetic beauty come after another tone, another
kind of catalog, other kinds of objects, indeed several populist settings (Moore
1967, 55). This bluff, hearty, commonsensical sensibility, with its Utah and
Texas, brakes and motors, is the vocabulary of modernist realism and logopoeia.
The development of this tone depends on a critique of Pretty Poetry and its
dangers to women.

That same kind of contrast, a clash produced for the sheer pleasure of gender
fireworks, and one with deep implications for her poetics, is engineered in a poem
("New York" from December 1921) that Moore places just before "People's
Surroundings" in her *Complete Poems*.

It is a far cry from the "queen full of jewels"
and the beau with the muff,
from the gilt coach shaped like a perfume-bottle,
to the conjunction of the Monongahela and the Allegheny,
and the scholastic philosophy of the wilderness.

(Moore 1967, 54)

As in many of her poems, when faced with something like the Cinderella ro-
mance with its peculiar feminine and masculine, Moore proposes a third place for
herself to stand, not inside the gender binaries of fairy-tale romance but inside
"the savage's romance" of collage, heteroglossic diction, and tumbled-together
objects, variety and accretion. She takes the word *romance* (with its implications

of idealized love) and reassigns the word wholly to adventure and mystery (the other definition of the word).[32] It is a move in keeping with the feminist origins of logopoeia.

"Novices," first published in 1923, is a rather funny and cutting poem about young men who write working entirely from the foundational materials of romance: "in the sense in which Will Honeycomb was jilted by a duchess; / the little assumptions of the scared ego confusing the issue" (Moore 1967, 60). Will Honeycomb, a character in *The Spectator* "who looks upon Love as his particular Province" (Addison and Steele 1965, 183–84), is a foppish commentator on the many foibles of the fair sex. He is "jilted" by Lady Betty Single only by virtue of never having asked for her hand, contenting himself with public inquiries about her fortune. Moore satirizes the erstwhile satirist, associating these modern pretenders both with unmodern attitudes toward women and with impotence.[33] This is a poem skeptical of the posings of the "good and alive young men," who think that their "suavity surmounts the surf." They cannot confront the majestic challenges of real sources—the ocean and the language of the Bible, both of which Moore describes happily as a "chaos" or an "abyss" of conflictual angles and energies, whose vibrant forces have the last words. Claiming boredom (something that only exemplifies their jejune qualities for Moore), the young men can't cope with satire as a genre or the antique as a source. Far from real potency, they turn to romance materials and "write the sort of thing that would in their judgment interest a lady; / curious to know if we do not adore each letter of the alphabet that goes to make a word of it." The terms "lady" and "adore" are satiric markers of the poets' inadequacies. Outflanking and outpacing the young poetasters, Moore makes a place for herself in the scene of writing not courtship. The romance plot gets skewered, along with its adjunct—stereotypical polarized genders:

> stupid man; men are strong and no one pays any attention:
> stupid woman; women have charm, and how annoying they can be.
> (Moore 1967, 60)

A central statement of her poetics is mixed up with a critique of normal gender narratives. Romance in poetry is banal, ungenerative. It is, to return to Loy's terms, "Eros obsolete."

What to conclude from this case study in literary history? The particulars can be summarized. Loy and Moore produced a distinctive intellectual, analytic writing fueled by their articulate suspicion of foundational assumptions of gender in poetic texts and traditions. Moore interpreted H.D.'s work as embarked on the same project. This move and its fallout did not go unremarked by one of the central players in modernism's production and consumption. Pound's task was ambivalent. He cushioned poetry from that feminist critique with its blows to the gender norms of poetry in order to make poetry safe for beauty and normal pleasures once again. He also appreciated, up to a point, the work Loy and Moore were doing. He thus alternated between the phallocratic and the "palocratic."

But this case study was only presented to urge the construction of others, others that use a new feminist evenhandedness to overread cultural texts. Such work needs a paradoxical, double-reading strategy—an evenhanded application of feminist questions to all writers alongside an overreading, alert to the ways that gender asymmetries and powers play through the production and dissemination of texts. To build convincing literary histories of modernism, one must continue to examine modern poetry and the precise configurations of poets' contacts, affiliations, and mutual responses. Diction choices and other formal materials will be seen to conduct and channel personal contradictions, cultural narratives, and social debates.

NOTES

Poetry from William Carlos Williams' *Collected Poems 1909–1939*, vol. 1, copyright 1938 by New Directions Publishing Corporation, reprinted by permission of New Directions Publishing Corporation; from Ezra Pound's *Personae*, copyright 1926 by Ezra Pound, reprinted by permission of New Directions Publishing Corporation; and from H.D.'s *Collected Poems 1912–1944*, copyright 1982 by the Estate of Hilda Doolittle, reprinted by permission of New Directions Publishing Corporation. Permission for the quotations from *Observations* by Marianne Moore (The Dial Press, 1924) granted by Marianne Craig Moore, Literary Executor for the Estate of Marianne Moore, all rights reserved. From *The Complete Poems of Marianne Moore* by Marianne Moore, copyright (c) 1981 by Clive E. Driver, Literary Executor of the Estate of Marianne C. Moore, used by permission of Viking Penguin, a division of Penguin Books USA Inc. From *The Complete Prose of Marianne Moore* by Patricia C. Willis, editor, copyright (c) 1986 by Patricia C. Willis, used by permission of Viking Penguin, a division of Penguin Books USA Inc. Work by Gertrude Stein, *Lectures in America*, 209–46, copyright Random House, 1935. Boston: Beacon Press, 1985. Citations from Mina Loy, *Last Lunar Baedeker*, ed. Roger L. Conover (Jargon Society, 1982), by permission of Roger L. Conover, for the Estate of Mina Loy.

I am indebted to comments on an earlier version of this article by the editors of this volume, and to the incisive scrutiny of Susan Stanford Friedman. My thanks to Carolyn Burke for helpful comments on my Loy readings. I am also indebted to the generosity of the executor of Loy, Roger L. Conover, in allowing extensive quotations from her work.

1. My capital letters on Woman and Man are meant to indicate these concepts as a cluster of ideas in the history of ideas, not historical persons; the distinction is from Teresa de Lauretis (1984).

2. Bonnie Kime Scott makes the ringing claim that "modernism at mid-century was perhaps halfway to truth. It was unconsciously gendered masculine" (Scott 1990, 2). With due respect to her halves (male modernism) and other halves (female modernism newly arrayed) to make a whole truth, one might want to modulate both the fractions and the word truth and substitute something like gender-laden readings of the evidence at hand. In a more useful metaphor, she sees "a new scope for modernism" by writing the workings of race, class, gender, and (I would add) religious culture into modernism (Scott 1990, 4, 7). My focus here on gender is not meant to disclaim responsibilities for other kinds of cultural analysis. There are important studies of modernism and gender by Shari Benstock (1986), Svetlana Boym (1991), Carolyn Burke (1990), Marianne DeKoven (1991), Susan Stanford Friedman (1990a), Sandra Gilbert and Susan Gubar (1988), Cassandra Laity (forthcoming), Susan Schweik (1991), and Susan Rubin Suleiman (1990).

3. On nonsaccharine ties, see the two necessary—inevitable—correctives to any feminist suppression of female antagonism, hostility, difference in Betsy Erkkila's *The Wicked Sisters: Women Poets, Literary History, and Discord* (1992), and Helena Michie's *Sororophobia: Differences among Women in Literature and Culture* (1992).

4. I have modified Schweickart here; she speaks of a bifurcated response to the text's (utopian) power and to its sexism. Her analysis of resistance draws on Judith Fetterley's pioneering study *The Resisting Reader: A Feminist Approach to American Fiction* (1978).

5. To understand what this may mean and how it may be conducted, the reader is directed to the introductory pages of Susan Stanford Friedman's *Penelope's Web: Gender, Modernity, H.D.'s Fiction* (1990a), an exemplary summary.

6. Theodor Adorno makes this point without the feminism in this piece, although he makes very pertinent urfeminist remarks in *Minima Moralia* (1978, 95–96). Margaret Homans, citing Adorno, makes the point with the feminism. With a general historical sense, I am following both. Adorno argues that the lyric is a genre that conceals its historical rootedness, Homans that it also conceals and universalizes the gender of its speaker. But even to use the term *lyric* is to move delicately through a set of stories about poetry. It is a term that cannot possibly mean the same thing over time, from Sappho's "lyrics" to ours. Yet, one must argue, as does Patterson, that it is a term in which a large cultural investment has been made; one should be able to trace a part of that investment (1987, 7). Patterson does not define the pastoral, indeed suggests that this would be a vain occupation; instead she analyzes key moments of its use. I will not try to define the lyric but will look at one of its cultural uses.

7. One might phrase this as whatever level of historical literacy textual critics can achieve; this is more difficult and touchy than the current prevalence of the verb *to historicize* suggests. For example, I have hardly begun this here.

8. Homans proposes an extended Irigarayan reading of specularity as it devalues female bodies and sexuality and also proposes that female poets, faced with this culturally powerful material, were compelled to construct countertropes, replacing the primacy of the visual with tactile imagery, and replacing metaphor with metonymy. At the end of her article, she suggests that "the best way out of the binding conventions of lyric romance [may be] through renouncing lyric altogether" (Homans 1985, 590).

9. Employing Jameson's term about the novel: political, because gender relations are

relations of power, and unconscious in the sense that any cultural myth is part of a deep cultural structure.

10. Part of a poem by Charles Baudelaire seems to have rewritten this. "Semper Eadem" contains the instruction to the woman to stop thinking, to keep quiet:

> Cessez donc de chercher, o belle curieuse!
> Et, bien que votre voix soit douce, taisez-vous!
>
> Taisez-vous, ignorante! . . .
> Bouche au rire enfantin! . . .
>
> Laissez . . . mon coeur . . .
> Plonger dans vos beaux yeux comme dans un beau songe.
>
> (1961, 39)

This is certainly fond, in its epithets of stupidity or childishness; it is also clear instruction to keep silent and to cease striving so that he can "plunge" or sink into those eyes. Kamuf 1988 comments that Baudelaire silences the voice of an actual female addressee so that he can appropriate the feminine into his own voice, doubling his by eradicating hers.

11. In fact, there is evidence of the impact of these materials on some poets. H.D.'s unpublished sketch "The Suffragette," from circa 1913, gives clear evidence of her curiosity and sympathy (Friedman 1990a, 7). Moore participated in feminist campaigns for the vote (Molesworth 1990). Mina Loy epitomized the New Woman and symbolized the link of new poetry and new women, free verse and free love (Burke 1985). See Scott 1990 for more links between modernism and feminism, either directly or in reaction.

12. By citing only the surface of Mulvey's findings, and not treating its source—male anxiety about woman's "lack" or castration, as the unconsciousness of patriarchy—I am not being thorough. But I am trying to signal the importance of feminist film theory to discussions of the lyric.

13. His "songs" are repeatedly addressed, saluted, and given "commissions"—a nice pun. Another measure of the sexual frankness and effect he sought is Pound's short work "Coitus," which begins "The gilded phaloi of the crocuses / are thrusting at the spring air" (1926, 110).

14. Classicist Daniel P. Tompkins translated "fantastikon" as a thing "receptive of impressions or images."

15. Despite its date, this essay concerns her work from circa 1913–14.

16. I am certainly not the first to observe this Pound-Loy-Moore conjuncture. Carolyn Burke speaks at length about the source of logopoeia in the work of Loy and Moore (1987, 99–100; 1990, 234), specifying that their logopoeia is "gender-conscious." I am following this insight here. Burke takes it that Pound is, however, "blind to gender"—arguing that he did not see specific female issues and concerns expressed in their poetry, nor in their formal innovations, splicing and collage. "Pound's sponsorship of the two women is notable precisely because he appears to have ignored the fact that they were women" (Burke 1987, 100). She repeats this in Burke 1990. She is thus crediting the seriousness with which Pound regarded the practices of his fellow artists. This article, while drawing on some similar materials and on Burke herself, reads Pound's analysis differently, as insistently

trying to negotiate materials about gender and sexuality, including masculinity and the educated woman.

17. Indeed, the critical lyric of the Pound line and the romantic visionary lyric of the Stevens line unite in their views about the feminine, beauty, and Woman. This is a point that cannot be pursued here, but these gender issues definitely disturb the distinct division between these two poetic tendencies proposed to summarize modern poetry in Perloff 1985.

18. For Moore, notorious for cutting her poems after they appeared in print, one criterion for cuts would be the eradication of the easy pleasure of poetic beauty, as in the difference between a 1924 version of "The Octopus" and the version in her *Complete Poems* (1967), which cuts an extended passage about lovely, feminine flowers. There would not be one explanation for this cut. See also discussion of it as the removal of materials on gender and authority in Diehl 1990, 75–76.

19. Some suggestive observations may be related. Moore repeatedly denied that her work was poetry, perhaps trying thereby to evade the demands of that genre for a certain kind of gender-laden pleasure (DuPlessis 1989). Loy moved across a wide front, working in several different media, including interior decoration, dress design, and beauty culture, possibly compensating in those realms for the "beauty" she critiqued in her poetry. She pioneered a set of muscle-toning exercises of the face to improve its ability to withstand the "ravages of time," offering a technique for "the independent conservation of beauty." It is interesting to see her clasp with one hand what she rejects with the other (Loy 1982, 284); the play of Loy's ambivalences is important to credit.

20. I can't, unfortunately, pursue all of the Pound end of things here. However (irreverently—and not evenhandedly), it does seem as if Pound's attitude toward women writers, while genuine in its interest, and supportive if didactic, was also like that of miners to their canaries; if the canary didn't keel over, then the site was safe to enter and to work. Pound used H.D. as the canary for imagism, and Moore and Loy for heteroglossic log-opoeia. Amy Lowell keeled over and was discarded.

21. I have cited the complete poem. All the Loy poems I will discuss come from the sections "Early Poems: 1914–1925," "Satires: 1914–1923," or "Love Songs: 1915–1917" (Loy 1982).

22. These arresting capital letters do not appear in the version in Loy's *Lunar Baedecker* ([sic] 1923).

23. "Infusoria" are a class of protozoans that live on decaying animal and vegetable matter. As in her poem "Love Songs," here Loy uses precise, obscure terms from biology to get at forces animating us as organisms. OED: "[Infusoria] were regarded by Huxley as a primary group in the animal kingdom." Our competition, in short.

24. I don't want to argue by coincidence, but this moon has interesting analogues to Irigaray's "concave mirror," and Loy's stylistic manner could well be analyzed by Irigaray's outburst/manifesto of a female rhetoric of "radical convulsions" (Irigaray 1985a, 142).

25. Note that both Loy and Moore wrote analytic and investigative poems about marriage. This should help confirm the point discussed here: their critical examination of gender materials. I propose to treat their studies of marriage elsewhere along with D. H. Lawrence's.

26. Carolyn Burke discusses the contexts of this long poem in both articles cited here. I am not discussing that work now, as I have offered a close reading of it in DuPlessis 1992.

27. Aside from Pound 1918 this essay is also available in Tomlinson 1969 and Scott 1990. The Tomlinson selection has cut some of what Pound says.

28. Pound attributes this to "le tempérament de l'Américaine" (1918, 58). With this there's only one problem—Loy was British, naturalized American only in 1946, and had lived in both France and Italy before first coming across the Atlantic (1916); she did begin to influence American poetry by about 1914. "These girls have written a distinctly national product, they have written something which could not have come out of any other country." Because of Pound's slip about Loy's nationality, I am tempted to regard nation of origin as a cover story for gender of origin.

29. Moore did know Loy's work; in a 1926 review, she sees it as cubist and sculptural: "a sliced and cylindrical . . . use of words" (1986, 121).

30. I will only note here that Loy has a satiric poem called "English Rose" that simultaneously attacks British imperial claims and prim, feminine women, in the *Lunar Baedecker* (1923). This poem was then extended to treat Jews and her family, becoming one section of the sixty-five-page poem "Anglo-Mongrels and the Rose" (Loy 1982, 121–30).

31. There is in Edith Sitwell, too, an exaggerated, even flamboyant use of the feminine. I mean Sitwell's "Elegy on Dead Fashion," or "Prelude to a Fairy Tale," long poems that combine precision of fashion vocabularies and saccharine use of poetical vocabularies in a pastoral that is self-mockingly mannered and feminine. Female camp, really.

> And on lone crags nymphs bright as any queen
> In crinolines of tarlatine marine
> Walk where a few gauze tartan thin leaves grow
> Among the ermine leaves of the cold snow.
>
> (Sitwell 1927, 38)

Incidentally, Moore's review of H.D. has a long list of "objects and hues—Egyptian gold and silver work" (1986, 81).

32. Note also Moore's blason "Those Various Scalpels," another poem about gender challenging a genre featuring "the gaze" (1967, 51–52). Just as Moore attacks the carpe diem poem, she also alters the blason.

33. Nancy Shevlin of the University of Maryland directed me to Addison and Steele; see especially *The Spectator* 4 (1965, 183–84) and 3 (1965, 343).

Channeling the Ancestral Muse: Lucille Clifton and Dolores Kendrick

Akasha (Gloria) Hull

Narrative One

One afternoon in 1975, Lucille Clifton and her two eldest daughters—then sixteen and fourteen years old—were sitting idly at home while the four younger children napped. After rejecting an outing to the movies, they pulled down the Ouija board from the closet where they stored the family games. It was a casual item that they had played with before and gotten only "foolishness." Rica said that she would record the message; Lucille and Sidney put their hands on the board. When it began moving—faster than it ever had before—Lucille said, "Sidney!" Sidney answered, "Ma, I'm not doing that, you're doing it." Lucille said she wasn't and asked the board emphatically, "Who is it?" It responded "T . . . H," at which point the two of them removed their hands. When they tried again—this time with their eyes closed—it spelled out "THELMA." Absolutely skeptical, Clifton put the board away. A few days later, they took it down again, with Lucille challenging, "Now, this is not funny. What is happening here?" It answered, "It's me, baby. Don't worry about it. Get some rest," and then dashed off the board.[1]

Both Clifton and her daughters recognized THELMA as Lucille's mother, Thelma Moore Sayles, who had died one month before Clifton's first child was born. This unsought, unexpected supernatural contact with her mother inaugurated Clifton's conscious recognition of the spiritual realm. Her next volume of poetry, *two-headed woman* (1987a; first published 1980),[2] charts the turbulence of this awareness but ends with a calm acceptance of the truth that she has come to know:

> in populated air
> our ancestors continue.
> i have seen them.
> i have heard

96

> their shimmering voices
> singing.
>
> (1987a, 221)

Narrative Two

One night, Dolores Kendrick, who is usually a good sleeper, could not fall asleep. Getting up at three A.M., she made a cup of tea and began reading the slave narratives in Gerda Lerner's documentary history, *Black Women in White America*. She became totally immersed and was particularly ensnared by the story of Margaret Garner, a woman who in 1856 had slit the throat of one daughter and attempted to kill herself and three other children rather than be reenslaved after an unsuccessful escape for freedom (the same harrowing story from which Toni Morrison's *Beloved* germinated). Kendrick awoke the next morning with an insistent urge to write a poem based on the Garner incident. Beyond this, the voice of the woman was coming to her "loud and clear," even though she had had no previous experience with that mode of writing. The voice spoke in a dialect and used words with which Kendrick was not familiar:

> Cain't cry, 'cause I be dead,
> this old tarp 'round me,
> my flesh rottin', my bones
> dryin' out, my eyes movin'
> through some kind of cheesecloth,
> like a fog.
>
> (1989, 34)

Kendrick did not know that "tarp" was "tarpaulin" until she found it in the dictionary. So, she wrote down tarpaulin, but then realized that, no, this was a slave woman talking and she should simply listen to what she said. She decided "not to fight it," to "just go and follow what I heard."

Thus began a process whereby Kendrick sat down with a stack of black female slave narratives on her lap, read them with intense emotional involvement, and then "let the voices work" within her. What eventuated was her volume *The Women of Plums: Poems in the Voices of Slave Women* (1989).

Aside from their intrinsic interest, these narratives are remarkable for several reasons. At the most rudimentary level, they reveal how the overt spiritual connection of the two poets, Lucille Clifton and Dolores Kendrick, to black female ancestors has provided both the content and creative modality of their work. In this, they are joined by an unprecedented array of contemporary African American women writers who are likewise foregrounding the spiritual in their themes and inspiration—Toni Morrison, Alice Walker, Toni Cade Bambara, Audre Lorde, Paule Marshall, Gloria Naylor, Octavia Butler, Sonia Sanchez, to name some of the most prominent. Writing thus, all of these authors are producing literature from historical-cultural specificities of black women's lives in the United States and, more particularly, from African American spiritual traditions (reverence for the dead, acknowledging the reality of ghosts, honoring "superstition" and the unseen world, spirit possession, rootworking, giving credence to second sight and other forms of suprasensory perception, paying homage to African deities, the power of voodoo and hoodoo, and so on). Other cultures of color and strong ethnicity also, of course, embrace similar worldviews, and wherever it is found, this sensibility contradicts dominant Eurocentric ontologies. It must be said, though, that nonrational, non-Western modes of apprehending reality are being increasingly legitimated by mainstream or mass culture as it moves into New Age awareness of our human-planetary connections with larger metaphysical forces and with all beings.

These two ministories about Clifton and Kendrick also enhance our understanding of creativity and creative processes. Writers have always talked about their muses and/or the inexplicable origins of their best and most original work. However, a higher level of clarity and confession is reached when Kendrick and Alice Walker thank their characters for coming to them and Clifton quotes sentences from her automatic writing in her poems. Where in the current theorizing about poetic form and politics is there space to explicitly situate such matter(s)? Speaking more narrowly from the arena of the two writers, studying them through their supernatural consciousness spotlights their achievement in unique and appropriate ways. In addition to the great value I place on their poetry as art and cultural expression, I feel that their willingness to frankly share their spiritual selves and experiences—knowing that this is usually regarded with scepticism— is laudable. Looking first at Kendrick and then Clifton, I wish to discuss the transmission of female ancestral energy as a vital force in their lives and poetry.

Dolores Kendrick was born 7 September 1927 in Washington, D.C., where she received her B.S. in 1949 from Miner Teachers College and, after years of teaching English and poetry, her M.A.T. from Georgetown University in 1970 (Kendrick 1975, book jacket). She designed the curriculum for the School without Walls and served as its humanities coordinator for several years. Since 1972, she has been an English instructor at Phillips Exeter Academy in New Hampshire. Her poems began appearing in small magazines and literary quarterlies during the 1950s, with frequent contributions to Percy Johnston's *Dasein* throughout the 1960s. Her first book, *Through the Ceiling*, was published in the London

Paul Breman Heritage series in 1975, followed by *Now Is the Thing to Praise* (1984).

Although Kendrick long conceived of poetry as "a living force capable of working in everybody's life," she had not produced anything as extraordinary as *The Women of Plums*. Nor had she channeled voices from the spirit world. She believes that it may take years of "preparation" of one's spiritual self to be ready for that sort of experience to happen and that she herself would not have been prepared any sooner. Years of contemplative living had rendered her open to receive the voices when they came:

> I started that kind of life when I was quite young. I was a great one for going off on retreats and being alone. In fact, I have a whole book of spiritual writings, journals I have done in search of the soul, dealing with one's connection to God and the universe. I've been doing this for a long, long, long, long time. And my mother was very much that way. She raised us to believe in it and not to be afraid of that sort of thing. I just accepted it as a way of life and was extremely comfortable with it. I remember girls in college talking about parties and how strange I was because I liked to be by myself. They would say, "How can you stand being by yourself?" And I'd think, "How can you stand *not* being by yourself!"

Now, as a mature adult, she has "no problems with whatever inner voices are in [her]" and is growing even stronger in "contemplative prayer, in which you just sit and listen." She also spends a part of every summer writing at a Benedictine monastery in Boulder, Colorado.

Not a practicing spiritualist of any type, Kendrick only recalls three pre-*Plums* experiences that "may have been introductions to opening parts of me that I didn't know were there." The first occurred some years ago in an old courtyard in Aix-en-Provence, France. Though it seemed pleasant enough, she and a friend felt "funny," "weird," sensed a strange presence that prompted them to want to leave—only to discover bullet holes and a plaque that informed them that the Germans had executed a number of Frenchmen in the courtyard during World War II. This same sensing of unseen presences again occurred one Sunday when Kendrick attended mass at the Catholic church where segregation had forced her to sit in the balcony as a child. Running up to tell a choir soloist how much she had enjoyed her Met-quality singing, Kendrick felt all of the black people who had sat there, "all of our grandfathers and aunts and uncles. It was a very strange, wonderful feeling, sustaining." Her prose poem, "Now Is the Thing to Praise," concludes with a rendering of this experience:

> And I: the choirloft holding me too suddenly, opening tired wounds because I remembered my childhood in that loft . . . And I: in mid-air, stunned, wanting

to cry, wanting to lift myself away from all that pain and all that Past. And I: finding their ghosts stilled in the pausing pews, knowing they were surely the true elite, smiling, gracious, leaning upon their fine endurances, the wealth of their witness, their celebrations of longer matters. . . . And I: dazed, restored, brought to my beginnings, in joy. (1984, 27)

A third, more uncommon, incident relates to her mother, who died in February 1976. After her mother's funeral, Kendrick returned to the apartment that she had occupied with her, despite friends and family worrying about her being there alone. In the apartment, Kendrick kept a small calendar with "wonderful little sayings usually attending to our spiritual natures," which was opened to the week her mother died and the injunction, "Remember the lilies of the field." One morning she rose to discover the same phrase scrawled on the calendar in her mother's print. (Her mother had been a beautiful cursive writer but exhibited "lousy penmanship" when she tried to print.) Kendrick reports:

I thought, how did that get there? She wasn't even here when that calendar was on my desk. And I never knew or understood how it got there. I ran looking for her occasional print in her own papers and I found it and compared them and surely it was her print. I have that framed and in my room right now. That for me was scary. I just don't know how that happened. But I don't question these things.

Because of these experiences, Kendrick came to the writing of *Plums* having discovered her ability to sense spirit beings, to mystically connect with her own ancestral past, and to accept these phenomena without questioning. After her first Margaret Garner–inspired hearing, she decided "not to go entirely on instincts" but to conduct some focused historical research. At the beginning of *Plums*, she acknowledges George Rawick's Federal Writers' Project interviews, *The American Slave: A Composite Autobiography*; John Bayliss's *Black Slave Narratives*; Guy B. Johnson's *Folk Culture on St. Helena Island, South Carolina*; and the Lerner history. Essentially, however, her writing process remained the same:

Basically, I would sit down with this package of narratives and some of my research notes and I'd read them. Some of them became very painful. I began either to get angry or to come out of it crying, so I had to decide just what I was going to do.

Not wanting to write "history" or "angry poetry," she fixed on the slave women's strength, thinking about how they and the women in her own family belied the shallow and demeaning media images of African American women.

Ultimately, Kendrick has decided that she "summoned" "The Women of Plums" through the historical texts:

I would read them and some I would deal with and some I wouldn't. I got the historical outline of the character, who the person was, or the narrative, and then I would put it aside and sit down and begin to write. Now what is she saying? What is she really saying? What is the voice here? Once I got the idea of the woman in my head, I began to sit down and write the narrative in her voice, in what I was hearing from her, not in terms of who I was.

Kendrick sees her role as giving voice to women who had not been able to speak for a hundred years but admits that she cannot totally explain the "mechanics":

We know very little about the creative process. This experience has taught me that. I've always believed that I as an artist am a vehicle through which the creative energy flows, and that that links me with God. I thoroughly believe that. I don't believe I originate anything. I think God originates it and He in His wisdom has given tons of people on this planet certain talents through which they can bring their art to the surface. I think I saw that manifested very, very strongly in this particular work, and I don't understand it. And I'm not going to try to understand it. I'm just going to try to accept it because I think that there is a level of creativity that people hit that we know very little about.

She encapsulates these sentiments in an acknowledgment at the beginning of the book:

> I thank these women
> for coming, and I thank
> the good God who sent them.
>
> The Women of Plums
>
> (1989, [15])

Notable here is an intertwined but still double identification of creative cause: (1) the women themselves who came, a word suggesting actual physical movement and travel, and (2) God, who might be visualized as standing behind them, sending them forward.

Explanations notwithstanding, one fact is certain. The level of creative accomplishment that Kendrick reaches in *The Women of Plums* surpasses her prior achievements. The poems are remarkable productions that evidence their spirit-driven origins and, at their best, can deeply affect many readers. Almost all of them chronicle strenuous moments: running away from slavery, having a picnic with a dead best friend, being in love, being prostituted to white men by the master when he needs extra money, praying on the auction block to be bought with daughter and not separately, nursing the Civil War soldiers on both sides of the conflict, sleeping with the master, being beaten, being abandoned, singing lullabies to a downcast child, and so on. And the names of the women themselves sound like a litany or a conjuring: Ndzeli, Leah, Peggy, Sophie, Bethany Veney, Prunella, Jenny, Hattie, Rya, Juba, Lula, Lucy, Polly, Aunt Mary, Liza Lily, Jo, Sidney, Lottie, Anne, Julia, Gravity, Harriet, Miss Maggie, Cora Sue, Tildy, Althea, Emma, Aunt Sarah, Vera, and Sadie. As the book jacket aptly states:

> Kendrick gives each poem a distinct voice that expresses how these women used their imagination and spirituality to rise above the confines of slavery. Taken together, these poems provide a vivid indictment of the oppression of slavery and the beauty of souls that, no matter their outward bonds, refused to succumb to it. (1989)

One of the earliest authentic voices is the Garner–inspired one of "Peggy in Killing." With a section labeled "Traveling," the poem begins: "They done found me, / Lord! They done found me again!" (1989, 28). The next section, "Visions," powerfully details her reasons for refusing even at the cost of her own and her children's lives to remain unfree:

> I tried to escape
> from they dark breaths,
> they glories, hallelujahs!
> they fine houses and sweet fields,
> they murders murders murders!
> they coffins stenchin' in they smiles,
> they *come heah Peggy,*
> *dress my little one,*
> *then fix her somethin' to eat,*
> *maybe some cake and milk,*
> and mine sittin' on the stairs
> in the cold, in the dark,
> waitin' to do some waitin' on
> waitin' for the milk to sour
> and the cake to crumble,
> hearin' all this
> without a word, a whimper,
> eyes freezin' in they dreams,

> hungers freezin' in they dark,
> takin' they dreams to supper
> like candles meltin',
> after 'while no more light,
> they walkin' softly
> makin' sure they seen and not heard
> and they dreams screamin'
> in they bright, soft eyes.
>
> (29–30)

After she drowns the children, she pronounces herself "dead" and prepares to sing to the ghosts that watch her, "like a star."

Voice *is* the dominant feature of these poems. The sound of engaged, impassioned human expression drives each successive thought and line, imparting emotional and rhetorical urgency. The dialectal use of the easier-to-say "they" for *their,* dropping of g from *ing* word endings, and locutions such as "heah" for *here* couple with the common but resonant adjectives like "fine," "sweet," "soft" and everyday concrete nouns such as "houses," "cake," "stairs," "milk," "supper" to swiftly and strongly communicate, convince, overwhelm. Even the sarcasm is tellingly nonabstract. Juxtapositions of archetypal pairs—dark and light/bright, food and hunger, cold and candles, speech/sound and silence—extend the depth of meaning. The metaphoric formulations of coffins stenching in the slaveowners' smiles, the black children's eyes freezing with dreams screaming within them are plausible as folk inventiveness and, at the same time, poetically effective. These linguistic qualities also combine with the situations described in the poem(s) to impart documentable or intuitively felt historical accuracy. Whether anybody had ever recorded it or not, we know that slave children waited on cold, dark stairs to spring into service on command.

It is less easy to talk about another, otherworldly quality that inheres in most of these poems. In "Peggy in Killing," that sense of a different temporal geography, of an unfamiliar reality plane, comes partially from the intensity of her extreme or deranged state. However, it also results from our having been put in direct contact with what does amount to another world through the supernatural agency of the poem's spirit-originator, and from the totally original imaginings from this dimension, imaginings that are partially caught in lines such as:

> I burn and burn
> all inside
> turn to dust
> blow away out over

> they heads when they
> finds me cryin' in a sack.

(28)

or

> I'm travelin' in my bones
> and the Spirit swooshes out
> before I gets a chance to say
> *Amen.*

(28)

or her description of the three children's drowning as

> 'jes takin' them under
> puttin' them there
> for the water to purify
> for they own bloomin'
> under the sea.

(32–33)

These predominant qualities of historic truth, voice, and otherworldliness are evident throughout the volume. Sophie, wanting to "know the baptism of words," counts and spells her way up to literacy as she climbs the stairs, reminding herself, too, of "the period and the commas, the stops and the shorts": "Say my prayers with a period. / Listen to Missus with a comma." Aunt Mary, at ten, saw her nine-month-old sister "whupped" to death by their mistress for crying. She begins her long-cadenced recital with

> Ah wants de wind in mah sorrow de las' breathin' of mah
> lil' sister holy on mah tongue

(71)

and in a poem replete with biblical allusions, makes up her own individuated origins story, dating from her receipt of free papers from her master:

> Dat be mah
> birthin'   mah genesis   first day   be earth an'
>   star   den   wind an' sea
> den bird an' lamb   den man and woman   den
>   freedom   den Me!

(71)

The symbolic beauty of Julia carrying life-giving water perfectly under any and all conditions comes through in the simple pride of her saying:

> I walks straight into
> the mouth of a [dark] doorway,
> say, Good evenin' all,
> water's here, and I never spill
>
> a drop.
>
> (95–96)

There are some passages where inspiration and achievement lapse, where the voice loses its hard-to-define but palpable authenticity and begins to sound like Dolores Kendrick, poet, perhaps too consciously shaping the material. Some of the poems were, in her words, "made up without the benefit of research," although it may not be at all true that these are the weaker works or that they were not enriched by the same general fund of supracreativity. "Jo Abandoned," for example, is a poem where Kendrick operated from more rational control. She uses her real mother's pet name, some of her autobiography, and was "seeing her a lot in doing" the poem. Consequently, Kendrick admits: "I don't know where the voice came in and I interfered or what. I just don't know how that balanced out." The overall impression is a mixed one, some stellar and some pedestrian passages.

Generally, this is usually the case: the lapses occur in poems that also contain brilliant lines. In "Polly and Platt," Polly is stretched beyond endurance by the lust and cruelty of her master. A voice asks, parenthetically and, to my mind, quite inappropriately:

> (Was it that? Was something out there
> punishing Polly for her big spirit
> that let her sleep with a crippled
> monster, and she, with impunity?)
>
> (69)

Even the diction and grammar of these lines are more studied and contrived. They are followed by effective description, which leads ultimately to a very moving concluding glimpse of the shell Polly becomes after her too-much-maligned spirit deserts her:

> she's moving like ash, floating about
> in pieces, her head hung like a scarecrow,
>
> and her smile don't jump into your throat
> and make you happy,

the way it used to

when she was herself, walking through daisies
giving God His chores.

(70)

Most of Kendrick's commentary on the poems documents the degree to which she was not in complete control of their composition. Jokingly saying that she sometimes felt the women were standing in line crying, "My turn, my turn," Kendrick mentions Jenny as an example. Jenny brought only short pieces (three of them are in *Plums*) but would only show up when she wanted to and not when Kendrick called on her for a small poem. With "Prunella's Picnic," Kendrick did not realize until she had finished writing the poem that Prunella's friend was no longer alive:

> [Prunella] was in this kitchen talking to her friend, surviving through talking to her—and she's talking about having a picnic. And I thought, "How can she be having a picnic in the kitchen?" But then it went and it developed. At the end of the poem I looked and I said, "My God, she's dead. Tula is dead."

One poem, "Miss Maggie's Little Room," Kendrick thought she could write "all by myself" because, like Miss Maggie, she was a teacher. She completed it in less than an hour and felt very pleased with herself—only to return to it the next day and discover that it was "sheer garbage." Obviously, she had been "writing about Dolores" and had not allowed Miss Maggie to speak. So, after waiting two or three days, she sat down and started again with just the title at the top of the page: "And before long the whole thing began to come to me as though it was being dictated, a totally different poem than the one I had written in the first place."

Looking back on the process of *Plums*, Kendrick has decided that she would not want to write another such book—even though she would accept it if it happened again: "I'm just saying that I'm not going out looking for it. I would not sit in a room at night and conjure these people up and say, 'Now, I need some more of you to speak to me.' I would never do that." Her reason is that the experience was too painful, even though she knew that the women were saying "that they triumphed in the end." The ordeal of not being "yourself," of being "something else" in the service of mediumship, was also exhausting enough for her to finally stop the process: "I know that whenever you move into this realm, you are using psychic energy that you didn't even know you had. I didn't know if I had any more left, and I didn't want to find out. So I just let it go."

Her current endeavor is a volume of poetry hinging on the theme of abandonment. It revolves around the biblical Samaritan woman at the well and a 1930s Washington, D.C., woman who tragically falls down on her luck, with the two women being projected as one and the same. This work is a "totally Dolores book," written without any perceptible extra-authorial assistance. Kendrick's response to my probing about the two kinds of creative processes yielded the following exchange, with which I will close this discussion of her and *The Women of Plums*:

> DK: *The Women of Plums* hit a level of psychic intuition, or psychic revelation, that is not in this work at all. That does not make this work any less, or *Plums* any more. I think this one is simply dealing with a character the same way a novel deals with a character, and that's a different level of creativity. It may be coming from the same wellspring, but the energies involved are different.
>
> AH: It's very interesting to me that you put it that way because I have to admit that my automatic predilection would be to want to hierarchize them and say that the psychic, spiritual, revelatory work was somehow "superior" to other kinds of work.
>
> DK: I wouldn't do that. I don't believe that. I think that at this stage, as a friend of mine says, comparisons are odious. Do you like Paris better than you do Rome? I think you know what I mean, Gloria.
>
> AH: Yes, I guess I do.
>
> DK: They are different art forms to begin with—if you want to talk about the craft. But I think that what inspires them or creates them (let me use that term) are different types of energy. And that's all it is—just different. I don't think the one is any higher or better than the other.

After the episode with her mother and the Ouija board, Clifton began "feeling itchy" in her hand. She also started doing what she called "listening/hearing," and the idea came to her that she should try writing. When she did, she received automatic messages faster. On one occasion, her pen wrote: "Stop this. You're having conversations with me as if I'm alive. I am not alive. Go. Conversation is for live people." Because of the feel of the spirit, Clifton knew definitely that it was her mother. She says: "You can distinguish. . . . You know if you're in a room with someone. There's a different feeling with different people." Once she asked, "What are you? Have you crossed the void? Are you in the great beyond?" using every high-flown euphemism she could think of—and her mother said, "I'm dead." "Dead!" Lucille replied, "That's cold." She began reading about spiritual phenomena, seeking information and precedents, and realized that "it wasn't a thing that was calling me to come and do it. It was telling me not to do it."

Over a period of time, Clifton came to believe that this was, in fact, her mother, whose presence was also being felt by the rest of the family. All six of her children saw and had experiences of some sort with her. Ultimately, they came to know this dead grandmother better than they knew their father's mother, who was living in Wilmington, North Carolina. And, over a period of years, the family, in Clifton's words, "incorporated the nonvisible into our scheme for what is real. It worked for us."

Thus, from the beginning of her initiation into this spiritual world, when she thought that she was "cracking up and taking my children with me," Clifton was led to acknowledge that "perhaps these were who they say they are." At this point, she had also been in contact with other beings than her mother through the medium of automatic writing. Her hands had always seemed to her to have something "interesting," "powerful," "mysterious" about them. When she started to pay attention (which she had not always done), she noticed that if "something, someone in spirit that was not alive wished to catch my attention, I would feel it in my arm, like an electric current going down my arm." Then she would know to take notice, get a pen or whatever, because something wanted her attention. And she would give it, since experience had taught her that a product of value would result, even if it were small. Clifton notes that there was a progression for her from the slow Ouija board, to automatic writing, to not particularly having to write because she could hear—"but writing and hearing were almost like the same thing." The ability to hear was clearly not imagined: "People can say you're hallucinating, but if you've heard, then you know." She adds that this is similar to the difference between dreams and visions: If you have had a vision, you know the difference; if you have not, then you don't.

Everyone in the Clifton household—Lucille, her husband Fred (a brilliant philosopher and linguist who founded a Baltimore ashram), and their six children—was somehow attuned to suprarational reality. Because of this fact, Clifton declares in her brief autobiographical statement for Mari Evans's critical anthology, *Black Women Writers*, that "[M]y family tends to be a spiritual and even perhaps mystical one. That certainly influences my life and my work" (Clifton 1983, 138).

She renders her supernatural experience of her mother in a striking sequence of poems that concludes her volume *two-headed woman* (1987a; first published 1980). Yet, the differences between her two tellings of the story are vast. Most notably, the poetic text reveals a turmoil and tonal depth that the factuality and humor of her external narrative do not even begin to touch. Secondly, they provide an unusual opportunity to begin to see how this personal experience is transformed through creativity into magnificent—and magical—art. The condensation, unerring essence, and rich resonance of the poems effect the leap from "here" to the "beyond" that characterizes spiritual vision.

Both versions recount the same basic story of a time in life when "a shift of knowing" makes possible the breakthrough to higher levels of awareness and personal power. In a series of "perhaps" that grope to explain what is happening, Clifton hits upon the right one at the end of the poem:

> or perhaps
> in the palace of time
> our lives are a circular stair
> and i am turning

(216)

This last word, "turning"—with all of its connotations of cycles, change, karma, and universal flow—appears at significant places in her work. A relevant comparison here is her poem by that title in *an ordinary woman* (1987a; first published 1974), where she sees herself turning out of "white" and "lady" cages into her "own self / at last," "like a black fruit / in my own season" (1987a, 143). Now, the turning, the metamorphosis she is about to effect, is even more momentous because it supersedes what the Rastafarians call "earth runnings" for a more divine and cosmic dimension. This process (and process it is) involves an experiential crisis of ontology and belief, but it leads "at last" to new and certain knowledge.

Clifton heralds the change in a poem, "the light that came to lucille clifton." The use of her own, real name is startling. She had previously incorporated fanciful references to "lucy girl" in earlier poems but had never instated herself with this degree of fullness, formality, and solemnity. In a dramatic move that upsets modesty and convention, the reader is invited to see the person behind the persona, the lady behind the mask. Alicia Ostriker gives a helpful warning to readers who were trained—as she, I, and many others were and still are—"not to mistake the 'I' in a poem for a real person":

> The training has its uses, but also its limitations. For most [contemporary women poets], academic distinctions between the self and what we in the classroom call [used to call] the "persona" move to vanishing point. When a woman poet today says "I," she is likely to mean herself, as intensely as her imagination and her verbal skills permit. (1986, 12)

In this prefatory poem using her own name, Clifton talks about her shifting summer, "when even her fondest sureties / faded away" and she "could see the peril of an / unexamined life." However, she closed her eyes, "afraid to look for her / authenticity," but "a voice from the nondead past started talking." The poem ends with what can now be recognized as a direct reference to an automatic writing experience:

> she closed her ears and it spelled out in her hand
> "you might as well answer the door, my child,
> the truth is furiously knocking."
>
> (1987a, 209)

In the sequence proper, Clifton begins her story as a deponent in a civil and ecclesiastical court, using religious and legal language (and, again, her full, legal name) to "hereby testify" that in a room alone she saw a light and heard the sigh of a voice that contained another world. Asking in the next poem, "who are these strangers / peopleing this light?" she is told, "lucille / we are / the Light." Not surprisingly, the following poem begins, "mother, i am mad":

> someone calling itself Light
> has opened my inside. . . .
> someone of it is answering to
> your name.
>
> (215)

Then ensue "perhaps" and possible "explanations." "[F]riends come" and try to convince her that she is losing her mind. But she is able to say to them:

> friends
> the ones who talk to me
> their words thin as wire
> their chorus fine as crystal
> their truth direct as stone,
> they are present as air.
>
> they are there.
>
> (218)

She eschews arguing with these friends in favor of an interrogative conversation with Joan of Arc, another woman—she calls her "sister sister"—who heard voices and had visions. Clearly, even if no one else does, the two of them know what it is like.

In what is the most tortured of all these poems, "confession," Clifton kneels on the knees of her soul, admitting to an equivocal "father," whose name pleadingly begins each stanza, that she is not "equal to the faith required":

> i doubt
> i have a woman's certainties;
> bodies pulled from me,

pushed into me.
bone flesh is what i know.

(220)

She has heard the angels and discerned how to see them. She has seen his, the father's, mother standing "shoulderless and shoeless" by his side, whispering truths she could not know. She wants to know:

father
what are the actual certainties?
your mother speaks of love.

(220)

Ending in a repetitious, almost stately babel of words, she tries to run from the "surprising presence" with which she has been confronted, but "the angels stream" before her "like a torch." There is no escaping this truth. Thus, the final, quiet poem of this section sounds like a reprise or a coda:

in populated air
our ancestors continue.
i have seen them.
i have heard
their shimmering voices
singing.

(221)

Thus, Clifton documents her connection with ancestral spirit (conceived as both racial and species antecedents) and arrives at the same place in her poetry as in her life: "incorporating the nonvisible" into her scheme of things.

As a girl (born in Depew, New York, in 1937), Clifton had manifested some psychometric skills (she could, in her words, "feel what things were feeling" and could retrieve lost objects of people she knew) but until 1975 had not been particularly conscious about the extrasensory realm. Since then, her psychic awareness and abilities have increasingly manifested themselves in a range of ways. As a result of being what her dead mother called "a natural channel" (using the term in the mid-1970s before it came into popular parlance), she touch-reads people and their palms, speaks truth about matters from her mouth if she asks to do so and keeps herself from interfering with the message, casts horoscopes, bestows blessings when requested, and generally continues to negotiate the world as a two-headed woman, that is, one who possesses magical power, who can see what is here and visible as well as that which is beyond ordinary vision.

She is singularly matter-of-fact about her gifts. "Being special," she avers, "has absolutely nothing to do with anything" and is, in fact, "defeating." As her mother put it when she asked her, a bit pompously perhaps, "What shall I do with this Power?": "Think about it this way. You have a teapot, a lot of people have a teapot. Don't abuse yours and you won't break it." At particularly magnetic readings of hers, when the audience was moved to radical action, she has sometimes thought that she could be "dangerous." But it takes her only five minutes, she says, to remember that she is actually the person who still cannot program her VCR: "So, how important and interesting could I be?"

Speaking more soberly, Clifton reveals that basically what she feels is "lucky" and, paradoxically, that "it's a mixed blessing—because sometimes I might get a feeling that I don't want to have." And, besides, she maintains that whatever abilities she holds "might be gone tomorrow. I don't know." In her accepting, down-to-earth fashion, she sees herself as a multiply constituted, various person: "I'm lots of stuff. And so this [spiritual] thing coming in is just a natural, for me, part of what my life is. There are those I see, those I do not see. Fine." Not surprisingly, she believes that everyone could somehow express "that ineffable thing if they tried, thought about it, and listened." She continues: "I think that people tend to not listen. It's educated out of you. My luck is that I wasn't that educated." She admits, too, that this kind of experience, what Toni Morrison terms "discredited knowledge" (1983, 342), is almost totally invalidated. Yet she declares with quiet conviction, "If you allow room in your life for mystery, mystery will come."

Even though spiritual-mystical themes and materials were always present in Clifton's work, after *two-headed woman* (1980) they become an even more prominent feature reflected in poems that

1. present mystical experiences (transcendent meditative states, past-life glimpses, seeing auras;
2. deconstruct the current, corrupt hegemonic order as the "other" of a more real and humane, though "invisible," alternative;
3. racialize, feminize, and mysticize traditional patriarchal Christianity;
4. project her feeling of connectedness with all life—things and beings;
5. affirm hope, higher values, and joy in the midst of destruction and despair;
6. show her sense of herself as part of a large, ongoing process of time and change, to which we all bear responsibility.

Most relevant to our present topic is a final group of poems that reveal Clifton's vivid connection with her spiritual genealogy, including her African past and its geography, and also her soulful attunement to other "sisters." An early instance is this untitled tribute to heroines Harriet Tubman, Sojourner Truth, and her grandmother:

> harriet
> if i be you
> let me not forget
> to be the pistol
> pointed
> to be the madwoman
> at the rivers edge
> warning
> be free or die
> and isabell
> if i be you
> let me in my
> sojourning
> not forget
> to ask my brothers
> ain't i a woman too
> and grandmother
> if i be you
> let me not forget to
> work hard
> trust the Gods
> love my children
> and wait.

(119)

Another one of these poems is written "to merle," "skinny manysided tall on the ball / brown downtown woman," whom she last saw "on the corner of / pyramid and sphinx" ten thousand years ago (171). In her seventh volume of poetry, *The Book of Light,* Clifton imagines into being a maternal great-grandmother, about whom no historical data exist. She is, as she admits, "trying to reclaim and maybe fix a mythology for that part of my family." The poem begins with an apostrophe:

> woman who shines at the head
> of my grandmother's bed,
> brilliant woman,

then proceeds to Clifton's musings: "i like to think"

> you are the arrow
> that pierced our plain skin
> and made us fancy women;

> my wild witch gran, my magic mama,
> and even these gaudy girls.
> i like to think you gave us
> extraordinary power and to
> protect us, you became the name
> we were cautioned to forget.

and ends with her instatement of self and lineage:

> woman, i am
> lucille, which stands for light,
> daughter of thelma, daughter
> of georgia, daughter of
> dazzling you.

> (1993, 13)

This particular project of reclaiming (for self and blood/spiritual family) a mythology (in a space where history and myth are entangled, often indistinguishable categories) is one way to understand what both Clifton and Kendrick are doing in all of this work.

Clifton's communications with her mother have slackened in recent years, and the number of poems about her (never that large, considering her general impact on Clifton's life) has likewise decreased. However, a very pivotal one is "the message of thelma sayles" (1987b). This seems to be the only poem that could easily be read as a direct transcription of her mother's words. Thelma Sayles recalls the factual details of her not particularly happy existence—a husband who "turned away" and recurring fits—and concludes with succinct summary and a passionate injunction to Lucille:

> i thrashed and rolled from fit to death.
> you are my only daughter.
> when you lie awake in the evenings
> counting your birthdays
> turn the blood that clots on your tongue
> into poems. poems.

> (1987b, 53)

Thus, the links are drawn between generations of painful female experience and the writing of salvific poetry, a connection that can be seen with Clifton herself and with Kendrick.

Except for this poem, Clifton—unlike Kendrick—does not seem to have channeled the specific words and language of her work; but—like her—she analytically isolates distinct strands and modes of her creative process. Ultimately, what she says clearly shows that her creativity is inseparable from her spirituality. She states outright: "Years of experience have allowed me to trust more and more what comes to me, what I can pick up in the world, and to incorporate that into my reality structure. And I think some of that is where poems come from." Even though she believes that no one—poet or critic—can really explain the origins of poetry, she jokes, "I wish I did know where poems come from so I could go get some poems. I would like that." One of her pieces in *quilting* (1991) nicely states her case. "[W]hen i stand around among poets," it begins, "i am embarrassed mostly" by their "long white heads, the great bulge in their pants, / their certainties." She, on the other hand, only pretends to deserve her poetry happening,

> but i don't know how to do it,
> only sometimes when
> something is singing
> i listen and so far
>
> i hear.
>
> (1991, 49)

As she explains her process, it is about a spirituality-based attentiveness. She recognizes when something catches her poetic awareness: "I still feel in my arms if I am to pay attention to something. And I do." If she is in a car (she does not drive), for instance, and feels something, she will look up and around to see what should be noted. My more pointed questioning produced the following exchange:

AH: Is all of your poetry about channeling?

LC: No.

AH: Does it all result from your having felt the tingle of "pay attention"?

LC: No, no. But it all results from paying attention. I think that always I've had a mind that connected things, that could see connections. Why that is, I have no idea. I think that it all comes from all of it, Gloria. I think I use intellect governed by intuition, and I think I use intuition governed by intellect. It's not all consciously done. No poetry is all consciously done. It comes out of all of what we are.

At the beginning of the interview, Clifton talked about how central the concept of "light" was to her and how, in all of the poems in her *Book of Light* (then in progress), "there is going to be something that is at least clear." Light (with a capital *L*) is her way of designating Spirit, God, the Universe, because, she says, "It is like that. It is like the making clear what has not been clear, being able to see what has not been seen." At the conclusion of the interview, she returned to her mind's habit of discerning the connections between apparently unlike things. With the two of us working in a kind of apotheosis of harmony that pulled all the pieces together, I remarked that that was the essence of poetic metaphor, the result being light, to which she replied, "And then, you see, the connecting of the nonphysical to the physical is just another step."

NOTES

1. This essay could not have been written without the gracious cooperation of Lucille Clifton and Dolores Kendrick, both of whom I heartily thank for talking with me. I conducted a telephone interview with Kendrick on 29 December 1991 and conversed with Clifton in Santa Cruz, California, in spring 1991. All information about them not otherwise ascribed comes from these exchanges.

2. Lucille Clifton's first four volumes of poetry—*good times* (1969), *good news about the earth* (1972), *an ordinary woman* (1974), and *two-headed woman* (1980)—are collected in *good woman: poems and a memoir, 1969–1980* (1987a).

Another Look at Genre:
Diving into the Wreck of Ethics with Rich and Irigaray

Elizabeth Hirsh

Intersections of gender and genre have proved fertile ground for feminist inquiry for well over a decade. To cite only some examples, feminist critics have looked at the specific challenges faced by women writers who work in male-identified genres such as epic, and at female revisions, violations, or appropriations of genre (Davis 1980; DuPlessis 1985; Friedman 1986, 1990b; Keller 1992); have defined strategies used by women who engage in the politically meaningful mixing of ideologically opposed genres such as lyric and narrative (Friedman 1989; Hirsh 1989; Monroe 1987); have argued for and against affinities between the feminine or woman's historical experience and one genre or another (Felski 1989; Hirsch 1979; Moi 1985; Montefiore 1987); and have critiqued the gender ideology of genre as it participates in the sex-gender system as a whole, or serves to inhibit or stimulate female artistic production (Benstock 1991; Diehl 1990; DuPlessis 1992; Gerhart 1992; Hirsch 1989; Homans 1990; Jones 1990). In these studies as in literary criticism generally, the term *genre* is unstable and may be associated not only with different levels of generality but also with different and incommensurable criteria of classification. It may denote the most basic categories of literary expression (poetry, narrative, drama), or much more specialized subkinds as defined by form, function, or both (ode or sonnet, elegy or epithalamion); and it may be used either interchangeably with or in contradistinction to modal and stylistic terms such as *realism*, *metafiction*, or *the sublime*. It may be identified primarily with authorial strategies, with inherent properties of a text, or with an aspect of reading competence, a working hypothesis for the production of interpretations.

However constructed or deconstructed, the term *genre* mediates between the singularity of texts and their status as nonunique members of some class within the system of literature so conceived. In this sense, it functions like the term *gender*, and as Mary Gerhart observes, etymologically *gender* and *genre* "come from the same root word [MF *genre*, *gendre*, fr. L. *gener-*, *genus*, birth, race, kind, gender] and hold several family relationships in common" (1992, 44). A related phenomenon is the controversial status of the term *woman* in feminist thought, a term that seems axiomatic to feminism but that notoriously obscures the differences between, the diverse singularities of, *women*; in this way, the term participates in a problematic of singularity and generalization, of difference and sameness, common to both *gender* and *genre*. This problematic is illuminated by the work of Luce Irigaray, who articulates the implication of gender and genre by relating both to the category of the ethical. Irigaray implicitly links what she calls a female *genre* or genealogy—which I identify with the category woman—and the poetic, the kind of linguistic expression that Irigaray describes as calling up, calling to or *addressing* its subject, rather than *speaking about* it (as object) in the ostensibly neutral or objective manner of narrative and discursive genres. Because in Irigaray's terms the ethical primarily denotes the possibility of a relation to alterity, a relation between the self or same and the other, the poetic therefore inheres in the ethical, and vice versa.[1] More specifically, as I will argue, an ethic of sexual difference inheres in the act of poetic address. Irigaray's emphasis on structures of address suggests that *woman* and *women* are or can be related through acts of poetic exchange in which a female *I*, a female *you*, and a female *genre* (in Irigaray's terms, a *she*) are reciprocally constitutive. Thus, while feminism obviously develops historically, it also inhabits and is inhabited by another, poetic temporality in which it is perpetually beginning, perpetually calling itself into being: women among themselves call woman into being, and the mediating category woman permits this exchange. Feminists are poets, as Irigaray suggests in pieces such as "He Risks Who Risks Life Itself" (1991), and the figure of the woman-poet is crucial to feminism.[2]

With this framework in mind, the present essay returns to a constitutive moment of feminist self-expression of the Second Wave, Adrienne Rich's *Diving into the Wreck* (1973). I will try to suggest in what ways an ethic of sexual difference is implicit in Rich's poetic practice and feminist themes, despite the volume's association with long-abandoned notions of androgyny and Rich's subsequent move to an affirmation of lesbian ethics.[3] My focus is on the interface between Rich's complex ethical vision and the modes of address inscribed in and by her poems. Margaret Whitford (1991b) has argued that Irigaray's project is fundamentally dialogic and expressly requires the participation of an interlocutor. Rich's poems, similarly, call up/on a female *you* in order to constitute themselves, their own female *I* or speaking voice. This appeal, addressed as much to the reader as to the various interlocutrices represented in the poems, is mediated by an express or implied *she*, a female *genre* that emerges in and through the act of address. It embodies a gesture that is at once political, ethical, and poetic, and our response to it as readers is therefore also irreducibly ethical (as well as political and aesthetic)—a fact that the poems themselves inscribe.

Irigaray's recently translated *je, tu, nous* (1993a) continues to elaborate the central theme of her writing: that to the special (though not exclusive) detriment of women, Western culture has been characterized by the repression of the feminine and the foreclusion of sexual difference, and that the distinctive project of the present age is, in the fullest sense, to cultivate sexual difference—to find or create the means to investigate, interpret, and represent it. In this interest, Irigaray (who writes, of course, in French) conducted experiments in the speech patterns of women and men. She found that while women "address themselves to sexed interlocutors," men, as she puts it,

> don't do this but remain among themselves, between *they* (*ils*) [in French, the masculine plural pronoun, which is also the generic form], or between *I-he/they* (*je-il*[s]), which is equivalent to making a non-conscious sexual choice. (1993a, 33)

Irigaray argues that in French and many other tongues the use of the masculine pronoun to represent the general or human as such is pathogenic, not only because it falsely identifies man with the neuter or sexually neutral, but more specifically because it excludes women from the possibility of representing the female as a genre, a collective or transpersonal subject: in order to do so, women in effect must assimilate their *I* to the masculine pronoun *he*. (In French both *il* and the masculine plural *ils* are used "generically"; in English the plural *they* is ostensibly neutral, but here too the transition from the sexually marked singular form—*he* or *she*—to the sexually unmarked form—*they*—passes in effect through the masculine singular *he*, since the masculine form also functions as the "generic" singular.) Thus the "passage" from *you-she-I* (*tu-elle-je* in French) is "missing for women," Irigaray says, the only available passage between *you* and *I* being by way of a (sexually unmarked!) *he*. This circumstance holds despite the fact that the first interlocutrice, the mother, is female for both men and women. Natural "genealogies" and linguistic "passages" alike succumb to "genocide" when, in a single stroke, "the maternal *you (tu)* and the female *I (je)* are wiped out," as Irigaray says (1993a, 35). This elision in the linguistic order is more than symptomatic of the ethical failure of the culture; it actively perpetuates that failure by precluding the representation of the feminine. Obviously, the drive to obliterate sexual difference in the name of sexual liberation is, for Irigaray, grossly misconceived. "To wish to get rid of sexual difference is to call for a genocide more radical than any form of destruction there has ever been in History," she writes (1993a, 12). Moreover, the ongoing failure of sexual difference is ethically related to Man's destruction of the inhuman world, including the ecosystem, for both proceed from a failure of what Irigaray repeatedly calls "respect": the failure to establish a relationship with alterity or the other as other, rather than as the avatar, slave, or reflection of self.

Irigaray's hope is that "women, without ceasing to put sexual difference into words, [will become] more able to situate themselves as *I, I-she/they (je-elle[s])*, to represent themselves as subjects, and to talk to other women" (1993a, 33). Her discourse indicates, in fact, that the cultivation of a female *je-elle(s)* (*I-she/they*) is an urgent matter, and not only for women. Again, the relation between the *I* and its implicit *you* is always mediated by a third, generic, term: at present, *he*. Female self-representation requires the constitution of an autonomous, generic *she* as a mediating term that relates the (female) *I* to the (female) *you*, and the female *I* to the male *you* (which at present can relate only to *he*'s).

However—and it is this point I especially wish to explore here—in Irigaray the pathogenic elision of the female *genre/I* also affords women an openness to "the world" and "the other" in which the possibility of cultural regeneration can be glimpsed. Although Man lays claim linguistically and culturally to the status of the sexually neutral or nonsubjective, Irigaray finds that it is actually women who tend to speak more objectively, more "scientifically," than men, in the sense that in women's discourse the *I* (and other marks of the subjective) more often gives way or opens onto the world. Referring to her linguistic experiments in the gendering of speech patterns, Irigaray writes in an essay titled "The Three Genres,"

> Contrary to what is usually said and understood, women construct more objective phrases, whose meaning or denotation is sustained by largely extra-linguistic contexts. . . . On the male side, the *I* is affirmed in different ways and is significantly more stressed than the *you* or the *world*. On the female side, the *I* tends to leave some space for the *you* and the *world*, for the objectivity of words and things. From that point of view, women seem to be better listeners, more able to discover and manage the other and the world, more open to *objective* invention or creation, as long as they are also able to say *I*. (1993b, 175)

The final words of this passage—"as long as they are also able to say *I*"—are important, of course. Only when women's openness to the other no longer corresponds to the pathogenic elision of the female *genre* will it be truly ethical and become the source of new and remedial figurations. For Irigaray, the poetic—what I am calling the act of poetic address—seems to embody this fully ethical relation. To repeat what was said earlier, Irigaray's poet speaks *to* or calls upon her subject as such rather than speaking *about* it as object from the exclusive, ostensibly neutral, subject position. The poetic can call the female *I/genre* into being for the very reason that, like the everyday speech of women, it "tends to leave some space for the *you* and the *world*."

Like Irigaray, Rich's *Diving into the Wreck* draws connections between the failure of address between men and women and man's destruction of the natural world and himself. Also like Irigaray, the volume suggests that the ethical—or its failure—inheres in the forms of expression that call the human into being. As in Irigaray, that women and men "can't communicate" is a fact inseparable from the foreclusion of the female *genre*; it signifies a cultural and political failure, not a biological joke. Thus, a repeated trope of this germinal work of feminist poetry concerns an abortive telephone communication: a woman "trying to make a call / from a phonebooth" while the phone "rings unanswered / in a man's bedroom" (1973, 40); the poet's reported dream of phoning someone (identifiable as Rich's ex-husband, a suicide) "to say: *Be kinder to yourself*," but finding that he "would not answer" (1973, 49); the image of a telephone that "is always / ripped-out," signifying the inability of a "savage" or presocial child—or of a woman-poet—to speak, less because of their own disenfranchisement or the structure of language than because those whom they struggle to address cannot *hear* voices whose style of expression is fundamentally different from their own (1973, 59). Joined within the telephone trope are the volume's pervasive tropologies of instrumentation and technology, and of voice and dialogue, which together suggest that in order for one to speak, another must "answer," must listen, hear, attend. This the adult male figures of *Diving into the Wreck* are mostly unable to do; they cannot hear because they remain trapped within the "nightmare" of a first-person pronoun that, in giving its *genre* to the world in the guise of neut(e)rality, remains cut off both from that world and from the other (the "you"), including the community of persons (the "we"), the world of objects valued in and for their specificity, and the fertile world of animate nature. The proposition might also be reversed: these men remain trapped because they cannot hear any voice but their own. At the same time, wielding the ostensibly neuter and value-neutral language of normal science and technology—or treating language as a sexually and ethically indifferent instrument of control—the male scientists, doctors, politicians, and artists invoked by Rich wreak devastation upon themselves, others, and the world. In short, they make history.

Many poems in Rich's volume dramatize in uncompromisingly political language and violent imagery the rage of women. For this reason, they have often been stereotyped and misread—especially by academic critics such as Helen Vendler and Cary Nelson, as Craig Werner points out—as man-hating outbursts or lapses into feminist sloganeering.[4] It would be better, though, to consider the ethical character of Rich's volume in terms of what Irigaray calls "a certain *subjective pathology* from both sides of sexual difference" (1993b, 172), a double dis-ease within which Man's entrapment in the closed circle of the *I* corresponds to the lack of a female *I/genre*. Though Rich's feminism is often discussed in relation to ethics, the vital connection between her art and her political convictions has not been well articulated in theoretical terms; this is in part because, as Werner says, "Critics with an interest in literary theory evince almost no interest in her work" (1988, 126), while those that do (Margaret Homans and Cary Nelson, for example) often find her work more problematic than otherwise. Irigaray's view of sexuate[5] discourse and the ethics of speech rejoins Rich's view (circa 1973) of the pathological self-destruction of Western values and the fragile feminist possibilities that survive it. Rich's insistence on a process-oriented poetic does not, I think, invalidate such a return, nor does it preclude the necessity for careful readings of individual poems and volumes. With its apparent endorsement of androgyny in the title poem, *Diving into the Wreck* is often cited as belonging to a phase of Rich's career that, however important, was rapidly replaced with a ethic of lesbian identity as developed in her more recent work.[6] But the urgent need for female auto-affection and an ethic of sexual difference—the two themes are inseparable—is already inscribed in *Diving into the Wreck*, as becomes apparent when the volume is read with Irigaray. In distinct ways, both writers elaborate a common theme of radical feminisms: the necessary implication of sexual difference in the most fundamental questions of human value and meaning. Both relentlessly dissect the corrupt remains of patriarchal culture but also project figures of the emergent woman-poet as herald of another order, one in which the reader also figures. Their poetic practice and their idea of the poetic envision an embodied dialogue in which human value inheres in a process of continual exchange between self and other. Expressing the inseparability of the ethical and the sexual, the category of the poetic contests normative definitions that identify ethics either with repressive rules of conduct or with abstract principles.[7]

For Rich and Irigaray, a way out of the infernal circle of the masculine *I*, if there is one, may be forged initially by women only. Women's coming-to-voice, their accession to a female *I/genre* from a condition either of silence or from a mimetic, self-obliterating discourse, alone has the power to render the world habitable again for both women and men. To reclaim the world and themselves from the death-dealing subjugations of masculine pseudo-objectivity, it is necessary to fashion a genuinely sexuate discourse that can reanimate it with authentically human values. Interweaving tropes of failed and emergent speech, and of pernicious and beneficial technologies, *Diving into the Wreck* inscribes its figures within an overarching drama of subject and object pronouns that enacts the ethical vision of the volume. Spoken by a voice that is at once (or alternately) singular and plural, *Diving into the Wreck* does not take as given but rather precipitates the voice of a woman-poet not only through acts of speaking but also through acts of listening. The poems illustrate and call on us to consider "why domestic, social, and cultural relations between the sexes so often get bogged down in misunderstandings and so often reach a dead end" (1993b, 176), as Irigaray writes. In the manner of a scientific apparatus, they precisely record and document the dying, lying voices of men, the radically unsettling testimony of diverse women, and the abortive dialogue of these same women and men. Through such meticulous listening, the poems create a feedback effect that disturbs the apparent neut(e)rality of the linguistic apparatus. Thus, the poetic-female *I* of the text calls (up/on) its reader to take up an ethical—and thus necessarily sexuate—position relative to (its/her) language. If, as Rich writes in "Merced," within the nightmare of a man-made history, "To speak to another human / becomes a risk" (1973, 36), this is precisely the risk undertaken by the poet, as well as the responsibility to which her volume calls us.

In "He Risks Who Risks Life Itself," Irigaray conjures the figure of the poet as one who both "[d]escend[s] into the hell of history" and "say[s] yes to what calls him beyond the horizon" (1991, 213).[8] In its vertical movement the figure resembles the solitary yet plural "diver" of Rich's title poem ("We are, I am, you are / by cowardice or courage / the one who find our way / back to this scene" [24]), while in its horizontal motion it resembles the driver or pilot of Rich's "Song," a perennial traveler "aiming / across the Rockies" or "driving across country / day after day" (1973, 20). Describing the spatial and temporal axes that structure the perceptual world in order to pass beyond them, Irigaray's poet is *constituted* by movement, a movement that cannot be quantitatively measured or formalized: "No geometry, no accounts here. What opens up does not stop in any direction. No waymarkers in this total risk" (1991, 215). Reflecting the practical speech habits of ordinary women as described elsewhere in Irigaray's writings, this po-etic *I* is one that of its essence "makes way." Within the perpetual exchange of (her) poetic respiration, "air, breath, song" are undistinguished; "[g]iving, receiv-ing themselves/one another in the as yet unfelt/beyond reason," poets (remain) open (on)to the world, language, and the other (1991, 218). Unlike Heidegger, whose writings partly inspire this elemental vision of the poet, Irigaray also attends closely to the empirical, including experiments and surveys concerning male and female speech patterns; for her, quantitative inquiry forms an indispens-able tool of the transformation the poet portends.[9] More precisely, she creates linkages between the poetic and the empirical that alter the character of both. "[W]orking on language," she writes, "is not simply a matter of preparing statis-tical studies or establishing what is the state of affairs. I make use of scientific machinery to bring to light certain tendencies that are habitually hidden and forgotten" (1993b, 176). Turned away from the false neut(e)rality of "a tech-nocratic imperialism that cares little about the regeneration of the living world, of freedom, of the future," science, no less than the poetic, becomes a means for the creation of "human values" (1993b, 176). But if the empirical analysis of male and female speech patterns exposes pathologies, misunderstandings, and impasses, it also suggests the poetic character and potential of female speech, whose special context dependence may open the way to cosmic reconciliation, as long as women can also say "I." This possibility, as I have suggested, depends in turn upon the cultivation of a female *genre* or *she*.

Irigaray links the "open" modality of female speech to a new morphology of the female body, characterized by the famous "lips" and by the "mucous" that she says serves as a threshold between the solid and the liquid. Both of these features imply not only continual self-touching, but also continual intercourse between an "outside" and an "inside" of the female body. They project woman's morphology in/as a way that precludes the rapist mentality of traditional sexual figurations, those which solicit (her) violation by constructing the female sex according to a logic of opposition that dictates a "choice" between what is outside and what is inside, what present and what absent, between virgin and mother (or whore). Such a logic—the phallologic of castration—constructing woman as wound*ed*, solicits her wound*ing*: fetishizing the female body, it invites rape. Alternatively, Irigaray writes, "[W]hat constitutes the particularity of the female sexual world [is] a different energy, a different morphology, a special relation to mucus and to the threshold that goes from inside to outside the body, from the inside to the outside of the skin (and the universe?) without leaving a wound" (1993b, 180).

Within Irigaray's comprehensive refigurations of Western tradition, the incessant passage(s) that link female morphology and the figure of the poet are also connected to the angel-messengers of the essay "Sexual Difference," of whom she says, "They speak as messengers, but gesture seems to be their 'nature'" (1991, 174). For Irigaray it is also "gesture," evocative and expressive of the sexuate body, that marks the distinction between "style"—which expresses sexual difference—and "the pathogenic neutralization of languages" (1993b, 174) characteristic of non-poetic genres. Where those genres speak *about* their subject from a position veiled in neut(e)rality, the poet, by speaking *to* or evoking her subject, also puts herself in play, and at risk; she moves and is moved. This ethical gesture, rather than any formal or structural feature per se, marks the "generic" difference between poetic and nonpoetic utterances. Thus, while the I-lessness of women is pathological within a sexually indifferent context in which "Man gives his own gender to the universe" (1993b, 173), the greater "objectivity" implied by this condition may afford a means of constituting "a different cultural *I*" (1993b, 177), one that has survived the nightmare of history—or of autobiography. "This transformation of the autobiographical *I* into a different cultural *I* seems essential if we are to set up a new ethics of sexual difference," Irigaray writes.

If we are not to run the risk of producing a traditional moral code—abstract norms for experience, formal frameworks, or a truth that emerges from the personal experiences of someone who happens to shout louder than all the others—then it is equally crucial that we not qualify that ethics with an explanation of what is being invented and discovered therein as acts of creativity, love, freedom. (1993b, 177)

Linguistic acts may neut(e)ralize by purporting fully to explain themselves, either in theoretical terms (as method, technique, knowledge) that supposedly desubjectivize, or in autobiographical ones (as confession, immediacy, truth) that assert the subjective as absolute. Style or gesture is action or movement that cannot be reduced to any form of statement. In fact, Irigaray's comment suggests the mutual implication of "the transformation of the autobiographical I" and the emergence of "a new ethics of sexual difference," since women's accession to the subject pronoun requires the creation of a female *genre* that will shift the cultural and symbolic ground of the *I*. This is precisely the (feminist) movement, the characteristic gesture, of *Diving into the Wreck*.

Rich opens the first part of her volume with a pair of epigraphs that suggestively frame the problematic of the I. The first, from André Breton's *Nadja*, epitomizes the "tragic" self-absorption of the masculine *I*:

Perhaps my life is nothing but an image of this kind; perhaps I am doomed to retrace my steps under the illusion that I am exploring, doomed to try and learn what I should simply recognize, learning a mere fraction of what I have forgotten. (1973, 1)

The passage marks Rich's connection with the traditions of modernism and prepares for the pervasive imagery of dreams and nightmares, and the themes of uncertainty and exploration, in the poems following. But it is pointedly qualified and contested by a second epigraph, taken from George Eliot, that is as positive in its declaration as Breton's is uncertain: "*There is no private life which is not determined by a wider public life.*" In other words, the personal is political. The literary tradition here evoked is that of modernism's proverbial other, nineteenth-century realism, and the autobiographical *I* is as conspicuously absent here— along with the female sex cloaked by the pen name of Mary Ann Evans—as it is insistent in the first epigraph. The realistic novelist whose *I* "makes way" for the empirical world will inform the explorations of the emergent woman-poet as much as the radical, nightmare subjectivity of the surrealist. The two epigraphs, subjective and objective, are as such *sexed*, their apparent sexual indifference exposed, analyzed in this juxtaposition. Each in turn announces a distinct strain within the volume, which Rich will identify with two kinds of vision: the night vision of an *I* who, as in "Waking in the Dark," "walk[s] the unconscious forest," excavating nightmares or projecting visions of another world (1973, 8); and the vigilant daylight vision in "From the Prison House" of an "eye" that "is not for weeping," whose "vision / must be unblurred," whose "intent is clarity" (1973, 17)—an eye who bears witness to the nightmare of history, attesting to the social determination of consciousness and the unconscious both.

Eliot's *I*-less, objectively observant realism corresponds to the figure of a woman scientist or doctor in whom Rich projects an antidote to the male nightmare, and it contrasts with woman's traditional confinement to the part of the nurse or mother attendant upon that nightmare. "A man is asleep in the next room," she writes in "Incipience," a poem apparently addressed, at least in part, to another woman ("While we sit up smoking and talking of how to live / he turns on the bed and murmurs").

> A neurosurgeon enters his dream
> and begins to dissect his brain
> She does not look like a nurse
> she is absorbed in her work
> she has a stern, delicate face like Marie Curie
> She is not/might be either of us
>
> (1973, 12)

Framing the figure of the woman scientist are the volume's opening and closing poems. In the first, "Trying to Talk with a Man," the speaker visits a site where atomic testing is conducted accompanied by a male friend, probably a scientist involved in the tests: "You mention the danger / and list the equipment" (3–4), she says, implicitly appalled by his inability to realize the situation, his depersonalized vocabulary of enumeration. In the last poem, the five-part "Meditations for a Savage Child," the poet responds to the account given by a nineteenth-century French doctor, J-M Itard, who confined and studied "The Wild Boy of Aveyron," and tried to teach him to speak. The child is addressed by the poet, and in the third section, he apparently responds:

> When I try to speak
> my throat is cut
> and, it seems, by his hand
>
> The sounds I make are prehuman, radical
> the telephone is always
> ripped-out

> and he sleeps on
>
> (1973, 59)

Within the context of the volume, however, these words might just as well be spoken by any number of other figures, including the betrayed women of "The Phenomenology of Anger" and "Translations," the wife's twin sister of "A Primary Ground" (who "speechless / is dying in the house" [39]), or the ex-wife of "From a Survivor." In this way the wild child is identified with the emergent *I* of the woman-poet, and a collection of marginal figures—the androgyne of "The Stranger" and "Diving into the Wreck," and the figure of the woman artist Lily Briscoe from Virginia Woolf's *To the Lighthouse*, alluded to in the epigraph of "A Primary Ground," which is drawn from that novel. The wild child is also implicitly associated with "the babies at My Lai" (28) mentioned in "The Phenomenology of Anger," who are again mentioned, and who recall the victims of Hiroshima, in the final poem's image of a "child with arms / burnt to the flesh of its sides" (62).

References to the Vietnam War recur throughout the volume, and Dr. Itard's nationality links him to the French exploitation of Southeast Asia that laid the ground for a war in which "technocratic imperialism" reached nightmare proportions. The technologies of dehumanization also are recalled in allusions to the Holocaust, and in the fear it evokes for the speaker in "Merced":

> Fantasies of old age:
> they have rounded us up
> in a rest-camp for the outworn.
> Death in order, by gas,
> hypodermics daily
> to neutralize despair.
>
> (35)

To witness, record, and analyze such historic atrocities is the indispensable role of the volume's camera eye, which also scrupulously bears witness to the specific experience—the "confession" or the "testimony," as Rich puts it in "The Phenomenology of Anger"—of women. Thus the actual words of women Rich knows are reproduced in some poems, including "The Phenomenology of Anger" and "Dialogue." The relentless clarity of the volume's camera eye implicitly counteracts the cultural force of such documents as Leni Riefenstahl's film of the 1936 Berlin Olympics, *Olympia* (1938), which is recalled in "Waking in the Dark."

Clarity,

    spray

blinding and purging

spears of sun striking the water

the bodies riding the air

like gliders

the bodies in slow motion

falling
into the pool
at the Berlin Olympics

control; loss of control

the bodies rising
arching back to the tower
time reeling backward

clarity of open air
before the dark chambers
with the shower-heads

                                          (9)

That women as nurses, artists, or police officers (as in "From the Prison House") may serve the technologies of destruction is a point repeatedly emphasized. The "clarity" of Riefenstahl's artistic vision is powerful and defies the force of sexual oppression ("A woman made this film," Rich writes, "against / the law / of gravity" [1973, 9]) but is also complicitous in the Fascist ideology of health and its glorification of the youthful, rationalized, well-formed body. Imaginatively reversing the movement of Riefenstahl's film, Rich in effect causes the bodies to fly, poetically, through the air, but she also performs an analytical feat, clarifying their historic relation to the violated, inanimate "bodies" of the camps that came later.

I have suggested how Irigaray's attempts to refigure the sexuate body beyond oppositional logic are connected to her emphasis on a new ethics of speech, the role of risk and responsibility in human dialogue. In *Diving into the Wreck*, the possibility of precipitating a female *I/genre* through dialogic intercourse is related to a thematics of the body in which idealization and violation are similarly complicitous; a way out of this logic, if there is one, is often figured in a moving, fluid body, or in a female body released from the constraints of reproduction. The grotesquely outfitted diver of the title poem, with her "absurd flippers" and "awkward mask"—armed with the inevitable apparatuses of science—forms an obvious counterpoint to the exquisitely graceful and self-sufficient bodies of the Berlin athletes. But the same is true of the marine lovers of "Waking in the Dark," who "move together like underwater plants" and stream "through the slow / citylight forest ocean / stirring our body hair" (10). These lovers, whose entangled hair seems indistinguishable from the ambient plants, are "open" both to one another and to the shifting landscape(s) through which they pass. Not "control" or "power" but an art of movement ("I have to learn alone / to turn my body without force / in the deep element" [23], the diver says) defines them and also protects them from definition. Such openness distinguishes them and their landscape from the "condemned," scarred, and exploited "scenery" of poems like "Trying to Talk with a Man," "The Phenomenology of Anger," and "When We Dead Awaken."

The lovers' bodies are not explicitly sexed and possess something of the solitary diver's, the Stranger's, or the savage child's androgyny (a point to which I will return). And of course, it was not only women who suffered the ultimate violation of the camps. The logic of bodily idealization and violation, however, passes inevitably through the problematic of sexual difference. "Rape" uncompromisingly draws the connection between man's suicidal subjugation of the natural world (epitomized by the macho cop "on horseback"), the instrumentalizing of reason—"he has access to machinery that could kill you," Rich writes, referring not only to the cop's gun but also to the "typewriter" with which he records the woman's words and the bureaucratic "file" in which he files them—and the rapist mentality common to both the criminal and his victim's "confessor." Indeed, like the Nazis, the cop is noted for "certain ideals," ideals that Rich says "stand in the air, a frozen cloud / from between his unsmiling lips" (44). The rapist's violence is answered by that of the enraged murderer of "The Phenomenology of Anger," a woman who apparently enforces the feminization or wounding of her lover or husband with a blade. Assuming the murderer's voice, the poet writes,

> My hands, sticky in a new way.
> Menstrual blood
> seeming to leak from your side.
>
> Will the judges try to tell me
> which was the blood of whom?

> (28)

Another bodily wound inflicted by another criminal woman is the theme of part IV of "Meditations for a Savage Child," which quotes Itard's text concerning the appearance of a scar on the child's throat: "*A hand with the will rather than the habit of crime had wished to make an attempt on the life of this child*" (60), Itard concludes, writing in the genteel, sympathetic, and uncomprehending manner that pervades his discourse. His text is placed in dialogue with the voice of the emergent woman-poet, who relates the child's scar to the upsurge in infanticide in the eighteenth century, when "starving mothers" with no reliable means of birth control often smothered their children or abandoned them to the elements. This in turn prompts the autobiographical reflection,

> I keep thinking of the flights we used to take
> on the grapevine across the gully
> littered with beer-bottles where dragonflies flashed
>
> we were 10, 11 years old
> wild little girls with boyish bodies
> . . . .
> Later they pointed out
> the venetian blinds
> of the abortionist's house
> we shivered
>
> *Men can do things to you*
> was all they said

(60)

The exploitation of women's bodies and their enslavement to reproduction connect the eighteenth and twentieth centuries, and seal the fate of "wild children" in both ages. Similarly, the freedom of the "wholly mad" murderer of "The Phenomenology of Anger" to "smear & play with her madness / write with her fingers dipped in it / the length of a room" (27) is exposed as another kind of prison; hers is not, Rich ironically observes,

> the freedom
> you have, walking on Broadway
> to stop & turn back or go on
> 10 blocks; 20 blocks.

(27)

Incarcerated and immobilized like so many other figures in the volume, she recalls the nightmare vision of a woman in "Waking in the Dark," who charges an unspecified male with wanting to drink her blood "like milk" and to "dip your finger into it and write" (8). Both figures display "the subjective pathology" of those who can write *only* in blood—their own or that of others. Indeed, their nightmare reality seems more real than the fluid world of the lovers, whose experience, the speaker grants, is only "the saying of a dream / on waking," adding, "I wish there were somewhere / actual we could stand" (10). To precipitate such a place, belonging neither to the nightmare of history nor to the world of the unconscious, would require a dialogue between the real and the surreal, the objective and the subjective, Breton's masculine *I* and Eliot's feminine eye. The recurring telephone image suggests the impossibility of a dialogue between women and men in *Diving into the Wreck*, but this impossibility is mitigated by another crucial image, that of two women in dialogue. Such poems as "After Twenty Years" and "Dialogue" explicitly mark the emergence of a female *I/genre* that makes way to an other without self negation—indeed, that discovers itself in doing so. In the former, "Two women in the prime of life" sit "at a table by a window" (13), talking with such passion that their encounter resembles the natural forces ("snow and thunder") at work outside the window. In the female dialogue of the latter, a scene marked by "a sense of August and heat-lightning" (21), the words of one woman—who is experiencing a crisis related to her marriage—are reportorially transcribed, while the speaker of the poem, who reports them, listens to and hears her words without a quoted response. Unnamed, the women are represented only by first- and third-person (female) pronouns. The reported words with which the poem concludes echo the insistent *I* and the radical doubt of Rich's Bretonian epigraph; but by way of contrast with Breton, they imply, in context, that an intelligible cause can be found for the crisis of self-knowledge there evoked, and one that resides not in the categories of philosophy or psychology, but in the practices of history and society. More accurately, they contest the segregation of the former and the latter as part of the ethical vision of Rich's volume:

> she says: *I do not know*
> *if sex is an illusion*
>
> *I do not know*
> *who I was when I did those things*
> *or who I said I was*
> *or whether I willed to feel*
> *what I had read about*
> *or who in fact was there with me*
> *or whether I knew, even then*
> *that there was doubt about these things*
>
> (21)

The female *I* that speaks here is predicated on the openness of the other who listens, and by implication the voice that says "she says" is similarly dependent on her interlocutrice. Less explicit but no less important to the volume's ethic are poems such as "Translations," "The Mirror in Which Two Are Seen As One," "For A Sister," and "Incipience" that envision a dialogue between women as the germ of personal and social transformation. In 1973, while "sisterhood" is still a central trope of the feminist movement, Rich emphasizes the bodily and maternal roots of this trope with poems that speak of biological as well as political sisterhood, a bond posited as an alternative to repeated representations of marriage and traditional family life as spiritually lethal.

What the "sisters" of *Diving into the Wreck* specifically share and engage in dialogue *about* is the moment of their own emergence into voice, sisterhood, and political consciousness. In this sense the poems possess a ritual force that actualizes the sisterhood trope by enacting it. In Irigaray's terms, the emergence of a new cultural *I* beyond autobiography requires the creation of new social and symbolic forms that will permit the constitution of a female *genre*. "In certain cultures," Irigaray observes,

> men in groups ritually celebrate the experience of passing into manhood. In one way or another such rites continue in our own cultures. For women this initiation into sexuality is a solitary event, even when it is observed. The little girl becomes a wife or a mother alone, or at best with her mother or some substitute. Even when women are together, they rarely know how to live and speak of that passage from one state to another. They complain about what's been happening lately, they compete, they bitch, they worry out loud. . . . Of their sexual needs and desires they speak almost not at all. If they do so it is usually in terms of the wrongs done them, the hurts suffered. Women exchange bits and pieces of games that have already been played. (1993b, 180–81)

Though hardly playful, the ritual initiation into sisterhood shared by the women of *Diving into the Wreck* marks the emergence of a new female *genre*, women-identified women disengaged from the place of those wives and mothers whose whole vocation (to paraphrase "Living in the Cave") consists in filling, emptying, comforting, warming, and feeding a masculine *I*. It is through the repetition of dialogic moments between women, whether related by blood ("The Mirror in Which Two Are Seen As One") or by political commitment ("For a Sister"), that such moments assume the continuing power of ritual to call up new categories of existence.

This poetic and political alchemy is related, in turn, to a process of *un*naming enacted in many of the poems, itself a ritual disengagement from the patronym or *Nom-du-Père* through which "man gives his genre to the universe," in Irigaray's words, "as he intends to give his name to his children and his possessions"

(1993b, 173). Proper names are invoked throughout the volume, but mainly as historical and cultural reference points: Marie Curie, Cousteau, Botticelli, Thoreau, Norman Morrison. The women and men who act and speak in the present tense of the poems are identified only by pronouns; their "names do not appear," to take a phrase from the title poem. One effect of this device is to stress their situation or placement within a particular historical configuration and specifically in the social category of gender; by the same token, their constitution in relation to one another and the world, rather than in the imaginary uniqueness of a singular name, is stressed. In addition, by their anonymity these figures potentially elude the patronym that underwrites the hellish egotism of the male. In "The Ninth Symphony of Beethoven Understood At Last As a Sexual Message," the proverbial genius is heard "yelling at Joy from the tunnel of the ego," creating "music without the ghost / of another person in it" (43). This "tunnel" is elsewhere recalled in subterranean images of the allegorical cave of Plato, the all too real New York subway, and finally, the "cellar" where the prosperous bourgeois of "A Primary Ground" stores "the last wine" of his wedding. Marked by possessive, implicitly masculine, pronouns, his proprietorship extends equally to the wife and children ("your wife, your children") who "protect [him] from the abyss" (38), even as they serve to maintain the illusion that it is he who protects them. The presence, upstairs, of his wife's mute and dying "twin sister" undercuts the festivity of the family's Thanksgiving, and several poems later, in "August," the patriarchal civility of his household is implicitly equated with the poet's vision of a nightmare prehistory, "which looks like a village lit with blood / where all the fathers are crying: *My son is mine!*" (51).

Like Irigaray, Rich identifies the institution of property and the patriarchal family with the derealization of the body and its senses. The modern bourgeois father places the mark of his ego upon each member of his household, furnishings and children alike—"in every room the furniture reflects you"—like the nineteenth-century doctors who, taking possession of the "Wild Boy of Aveyron," try to teach him "to care / for objects of their caring," such as "glossed oak planks" or "glass / whirled in a fire / to impossible thinness" (55). The aesthetic refinement and elaboration of natural materials is as irrelevant to the boy as to the projected woman-poet, and reflects the process in which language as an instrument of domination and commodification reduces the specificity of things to symbolic fungibility. Thus the doctors try to teach their child "names / for things / you did not need," such as "linen on a sack of feathers" (a pillow) or "boxes with coins inside" (banks)—objects that the poet in effect *un*names in an attempt to recover their concreteness and particularity (55). The "glossed oak planks" that simultaneously exhibit and obscure the labor of those who crafted them, and are thus so highly prized by their father-owners, contrast with the modest but useful "rowboat" of "Song," with whom the poet as traveler identifies; like her, its unrefined "wood" possesses "a gift for burning" (20) rather than the fetish value of a "glossed" commodity. If, as the poet says in "A Primary Ground," "Protection is the genius" of the patriarchal household—as of patriarchal language—what she proposes as an alternative is a community of risk in which speakers (continually) exchange not *things* but, as Irigaray writes, "asking, thanking, appealing, questioning" (1993b, 170)—in short, themselves.

The elaboration of the ethical in and as a continual process of dialogue, passage, and exchange informs Rich's pervasive tropology of instrumentation. Reflecting commonplace technologies of communication like telephones, typewriters, and books, more sophisticated ones like wirephotos and underwater cameras, and also the simplest tools and weapons (including the hand), this tropology is itself a technology and as such may humanize or neutralize. Both languages and persons *are* instruments, whether of destruction or creation, according to Rich. "Trying to Talk with a Man," the opening poem, equates the testing of bombs with the testing of "ourselves," identifying the danger that ostensibly pertains to the bombs with the human actors of the poem ("talking of the danger / as if it were not ourselves / as if we were testing anything else" [4]). "Song" figures its speaker as an airplane gliding "across the Rockies," while the speaker of the title poem, having descended to the wreck of human values, simply asserts, "*we* are the half-destroyed instruments / that once held to a course" (24; emphasis added). The wreck of ethics is represented in the arrested movement of the vessel and specifically of its navigational instruments, while the bold and supple movements of the diver-poet embody the only possibility of regeneration. The diver's recorded gestures ("I have to learn alone / to turn my body without force / in the deep element") are implicitly those of the poem, whose tropes "turn" finally toward their reader in a gesture of opening and enfolding, a dialogic assertion of risk and responsibility that belies the diver's solitude:

> We are, I am, you are
> by cowardice or courage
> the one who find our way
> back to this scene.
>
> (24)

"This scene" is above all the place of meeting between "we," "I," and "you."

Like the apparent sexual indifference of the proper names attached to Rich's opening epigraphs, however, the sexual neutrality of these pronouns deserves scrutiny. Collective pronouns—*we, they,* the plural form of *you*—suggest generality without propriety, without the names and definitions governed by the *Nom du Père*; in English they also are unmarked for gender and seem to evoke a human *genre* beyond or outside sex. The recurrence of androgynous figures in Rich's text, as noted earlier—including the diver who is both "he" and "she," the "Stranger" who can identify herself only by saying "I am the androgyne / . . . the living mind you fail to describe / in your dead language" (19), or the many figures of preadolescent children—appears to reinforce this reading. Of course, Rich's next published volume, *The Dream of a Common Language*, turned back on such tropes, asserting, "These are words I cannot choose again: / *humanism androgyny*" (1978, 66). But already in *Diving into the Wreck* the inappropriateness of these terms and the necessity for a *new* cultural *I*, for a sexuate discourse, and for an ethic not of humanism or androgyny but of sexual *difference*, is implicit. Before women have a *genre/I* of their own, the tyranny and self-tyranny of the male ego continues, and only sexual dis-ease is authentically "general."

For both Rich and Irigaray, the feminine *genre* and the poetic *genre* come together not—as some rumors of "French feminism" would have it—because the poetic in any sense either dissolves or precedes sexual difference. Rather, in dialogically connecting the *I* and the *you*, the *she* also marks a distinction between the two: a distinction being that which positions them neither as wholly exterior or opposed to one another, nor as "the same" or wholly contained by one another. "*Genre* stands for the unsubstitutable position of the *I* and the *you* and of their modes of expression," Irigaray writes. "Once the difference between the *I* and the *you* is gone, then asking, thanking, appealing, questioning . . . also disappear" (1993b, 170). By this logic, a female gender would not constitute some sort of conflict-free zone removed from the multiple operations of power nor any kind of return to normative criteria of (female) behavior or (female) truth ("someone who shouts louder than all the rest"). It would certainly not denote a practical or symbolic interchangeability of women akin to the logic of commodities. An effective female gender could exist only by registering the specificities that distinguish women and women as well as those that distinguish women and men; an *I* constituted in dialogue—that is, in exchange without equivalence—would found its ethic.[10]

A turn toward the ethics of sexual difference need not represent a turn away from politics inside or outside the academy. The violence of the operations through which man "gives his own gender to the universe" in a pretense of neut(e)rality and objectivity is everywhere felt in Rich and Irigaray; their dialogics project a utopian alternative in the figure of the woman-poet, but this alternative remains rooted in the concrete speaking practices of women, practices that Irigaray investigates with her "scientific apparatus" and that Rich makes the basis for the emergence of a new feminist consciousness, a new *I*. In addition, dialogue becomes for both a powerful means of intervention into the male monopoly, the monologue that so often has passed for dialogue in Western tradition since Plato: both writers use their texts to open and when necessary to *force* a dialogue where monologue has gone unchallenged. The most famous example of this strategy in Irigaray occurs in *Speculum*'s "The Blind Spot of an Old Dream of Symmetry" (1985a), whose speaker positions herself as imaginary interlocutrice at Freud's lecture on "Femininity" (which in fact was never delivered as such, but only published); in this role, she harasses, mocks, and otherwise exposes the pervasive phallacies of his discourse.[11] Similarly, in the last part of *Diving into the Wreck*, the poet interrupts and appropriates the text of Dr. Itard, interpolating her own historical, analytical, impassioned, and imaginative gloss throughout the quoted portions of his text. At the conclusion of the volume, in turn, a young woman responds impertinently to a "distinguished" but unnamed doctor (who might be either Dr. Itard or Dr. Freud) who has just finished lecturing: raising *her* hand, she says, *"You have the power / in your hands, you control our lives"*— then asks, *"why do you want our pity too?"* (62). Her question recalls the epigraph of "A Primary Ground," taken from *To the Lighthouse*, reflecting Mr. Ramsay's insatiable need for female "sympathy." Still more specifically, her *why?* echoes that of the singer Judy Collins, whose rendition of Leonard Cohen's "Bird on a Wire" provides the epigraph to the third part of the volume, and it is in turn echoed by the poet in the concluding words of the volume: "why should the wild child / weep for the scientists // why."[12] Like the movements of the diver-poet, the young woman's gesture—a question, an appeal, a demand—repeats that of the text, and these repetitions constitute a kind of impromptu ritual that serves to collectivize the several female voices.

Speaking of Adrienne Rich's art, James McCorkle observes, "Writing holds the power of transformation, but that power is interpreted only by those who can afford to read" (1989, 128). By way of an always premature conclusion, some explicit registration or marking of my own role as a female reader and critic is required to position myself as I would like to be positioned, *within* the ethical vocation of Rich and Irigaray. However, I do not hope to make my role as such fully explicit by elaborating a "critical method" that would only serve, as Irigaray says, to neutralize the gesture of my reading—and writing, since that is of course what critics do. Moreover, despite the brave experiments and impressive accomplishments of feminist inquiry, like other women I lack the means of self-inscription, and I have acquired the habit of absenting myself from the critical discourse I write—of "giving way" to the text in a gesture of respect but also of self-neutralization, or of cloaking my subjectivity in a language of methodology that delimits but also disavows responsibility. In *The Ethics of Criticism*, Tobin Siebers argues persuasively that, in its pervasive concern with avoiding violence to the other—however this imperative is interpreted—contemporary criticism of virtually all types is fundamentally ethical: "there is finally a question of whether anyone on the current scene conceives of a criticism that is not ethical" (1988, 13). But the account of "The Ethics of Sexual Difference" is the least compelling chapter of the book, and this is perhaps because, despite Siebers's intelligent discussion of his own male gender in that chapter, the implications of sexual difference are ostensibly confined within its limits. To practice and not only to conceive or theorize criticism *as* ethical, however, would require a generalized economy of sexual difference, one that could not be contained within the confines of a chapter, and that would not be limited either to women or to men. In this sense, the ethics of criticism remains at a rudimentary stage, and will remain so until criticism normally embodies risks as well as the "choices" that Siebers emphasizes. At the same time, as Siebers says, "modern literary theory comprises a united front when it comes to the importance given to the ethics of criticism. There is something hopeful in that thought, and, without being sentimental [surely not a gender-neutral caveat!], we may consider its promise" (13).

NOTES

1. Irigaray's elaboration of the ethical in terms of the relationship between the self/same and the other is developed in many different texts—including, of course, *Éthique de la différence sexuelle*—and in dialogue with many voices, including those of professional philosophers. Of the latter, the voice of Emmanuel Levinas is perhaps most crucial to her concept of the ethical. For excellent discussions of Irigaray's relation to Levinas, see Grosz 1989 and Whitford 1991b.

2. I use the compound term *woman-poet* to designate the identification of the poet and of the emergent woman in the texts of Rich and Irigaray. In what follows I will argue that both writers reconceive the figure of the poet as sexed, female, and, by the same token, in specifically ethical terms.

3. The move toward lesbian ethics in Rich is wholly consistent with Irigaray's emphasis on the affirmation of female "autoaffection" or the self-relation of woman, which, as I will argue below, is effected linguistically in the "passage" between *you* and *I* via *she*. As Irigaray writes, "To date, women have had to remain *among themselves* not only in order for a plural to be feminine—*elles s'aiment* (they love each other), *elles sont belles* (they are beautiful)—but also for a relationship to the subjectively female world to be possible. This linguistic necessity lays the basis for certain sorts of liberation movements. . . . Single-sex strategies are essential when it comes explicitly to matters of content in discourse, but even more so in the case of the forms and laws of language" (1993a, 34).

4. "Either Rich denigrates men or she ignores them," Claire Keyes writes of *Diving into the Wreck*. "Her allegiance is with women" (1992, 134). The latter statement is certainly true, but the former, though widely echoed, is misleading. Rich indicts masculinist values as having rendered the world "uninhabitable" for both women and men; she seeks a way out that will make the world livable for human beings—that is, for sexually different persons, not mythic androgynes. As Werner indicates, the poem "Rape" particularly provokes the charge of man hating: "Rich would be the first to object to an equally stereotyped description of women," Vendler writes (1980, 243). Nelson faults the poem for lacking the "self-doubt" he praises elsewhere in Rich, asserting in 1981 that the argument of the poem "is not new, nor was it new in 1972 when the poem was written" (152). Werner correctly

insists that the poem be read within the double context of the volume as a whole and of Rich's ongoing poetic process (1988, 31–33). My own reading suggests that "Rape"'s provocation of nonfeminist readers as well as its expression of female rage in deliberately militant language are more important than whether or not its argument seems new.

5. "Sexuate" is Margaret Whitford's translation of Irigaray's *sexué*, which Whitford wisely refuses to define in abstraction from various specific uses of the term in Irigaray's discourse (Whitford 1991a, 18). For my purposes, *sexué* might also be rendered as *sexed*, in the sense of *marked by sexual difference*.

6. These writings include *The Dream of a Common Language* (1978), *A Wild Patience Has Taken Me This Far* (1981), *Your Native Land, Your Life* (1986b), *Time's Power* (1989), and *An Atlas of the Difficult World* (1991a). Rich's development of a lesbian ethic in her writing of the 1980s follows from the ethics of sexual difference that is already latent in her radical feminism of the 1970s; from an Irigarayan perspective, they could be described as two sides of the same coin.

7. McCorkle's excellent discussion of Rich's ethic emphasizes several ideas that I also develop: the inclusion of the other *in* language (1989, 118); the essential role of the reader to ethical writing (128); and what he calls the "deictic" quality of Rich's language (106). He does not emphasize the role of risk, as I do (following Irigaray), nor does he articulate the imbrication of the ethical and sexual difference, but our readings are largely consistent. Mine, of course, focuses in much greater detail on *Diving into the Wreck*.

8. In Irigaray's French, "Risque qui risque la vie même" is the first line of the untitled final section of *L'Oubli de l'air chez Martin Heidegger*. David Macey's invaluable translation of this risky text renders the line in English with a masculine pronoun, but in context it seems that Irigaray is reinscribing the figure of the poet as feminine.

9. For further discussion of Irigaray's relation to the category of the empirical, see my "Back in Analysis: How To Do Things With Irigaray," in *Engaging With Irigaray* (1994).

10. This attempt to articulate a generality or *genre* without propriety might then be seen as an alternative to two competing strains in contemporary feminist theory: those that urge a turn away from the dispersions and deconstructions of postmodernism as disempowering; and those, also arguing on political grounds, that see this reaction as itself an unwitting capitulation to the traditional categories and ideology of humanism, especially to its divorce of power and knowledge. See Bordo 1992 and Butler 1992, for example.

11. *Speculum* performs comparable operations in the text of western philosophy, notably that of Plato, the father of dialogics. For analysis of these interventions, see Whitford 1991b; Grosz 1989; Braidotti 1987; and Schwab 1991.

12. Rich makes a point of distinguishing between the text of Cohen's song and Collins's performance of it, which thrice repeats the question "Why not, why not, why not ask for more?" Here as elsewhere in the volume, the re-creative force of performance is emphasized.

Adventures in the World of the Symbolic: Emily Dickinson and Metaphor

Suzanne Juhasz

"If you were here—and Oh that you were, my Susie, we need not talk at all, our eyes would whisper for us, and your hand fast in mine, we would not ask for language," wrote Emily Dickinson in a letter to her beloved friend, Susan Gilbert (Letter 94; 11 June 1852; 1958, 1:211–12). Dickinson also wrote, in a poem that begins, "Silence is all we dread," "There's Ransom in a Voice" (1955, poem 1251). These two utterances do not denote a contradiction between desiring silence and repudiating it. Rather, they reveal a continuum about communicating that moves from a vision of experience centered on a protoconversational process of communication to an urgent demand for linguistic expression, for *words*, so as to "ransom" experience from silence. Basic to Dickinson's definition of genuine experience is that it includes or even is achieved by interpersonal communication. Dickinson tells Sue—in words—about her desire for conversation so elementary, so primary that it occurs without needing words; she tells *us* in a poem about her fear of a world without language. Language, especially as it extends primary intersubjectivity, is what ransoms experience for Dickinson, and language is where this woman writer most intensely and profoundly lived her life.

Knowing these things about Emily Dickinson, a great writer, a great woman writer, it is hard for me to accept some current and widely accepted beliefs held by many academic feminists about the nature of "woman's language." That women and language are dichotomous concepts. That language codifies culture, which is "male" or "patriarchal"; that the "female" or the "feminine" belongs some-where outside culture and is thus emblematized by silence. Or, if the feminine enters into language, that it does so as a residue of the preoedipal body and its archaic drives or "primary process functioning," by way of what Julia Kristeva has called the "semiotic" as opposed to the "symbolic." The symbolic stands for that aspect of language which we commonly associate with its production of

139

meaning—"nomination, sign, and syntax"—and yet access to the symbolic is denied to women by all of these ideas about women and language (Kristeva [1974] 1984). Or, if a woman were somehow to find herself using the symbolic, that very gesture would alter or compromise her integrity or identity. And yet, I wonder, how does Dickinson's poetry fit in here? Dickinson, who constructed a life in language, a language most certainly symbolic as well as semiotic.

Dickinson uses her letter to Sue (language) to bridge the geographical separation between them. With language she imagines how the separation between their two bodies and minds, even when physically together, might be traversed with a "reciprocal exchange of complementary messages," to quote the infant researcher Colwyn Trevarthen, in his essay "Communication and Cooperation in Early Infancy: A Description of Primary Intersubjectivity" (1979, 334). In Dickinson's vision of intimacy, talk might be unnecessary but not communication: "our eyes," she tells Susan, "would whisper for us." This is not so much silence as what Trevarthen calls "a complex form of mutual understanding," reminiscent of the "protoconversational" character of early mother-infant interaction (346). Even as Trevarthen describes "a dance of expressions and excitements" in which infant and mother partner one another, so Dickinson imagines a conversation of eye and hand expressive of loving intercourse. This kind of interaction requires the lovers to be present in person; however, a long-distance fantasy about it can be created in language.

Two facts become apparent from our perusal of Dickinson's words about words. First, not talking does not mean no interaction or communication. Loving is not a state of symbiotic merger, in which two become one, but an active and reciprocal relating, notwithstanding its use of discourse other than language per se. Second, this state is imagined and desired—from a condition of not having it. Dickinson's verbal depiction of preverbal love and intimacy suggests to me a connection between this fantasy and the original model for such a moment, the loving interaction between mother and infant—especially since Dickinson prefaces these remarks to her friend with the wish to "each become a child again" and to "bring [Susie] *home*" (emphasis added). If we follow through on this suggestion, however, we must note that Dickinson imagines this preoedipal-like moment differently from the ways in which it is explained by Freudian psychoanalytic theory. She yearns not for symbiotic merger or oneness but for interaction: something more like intersubjectivity.

The developmental psychologist Daniel Stern, in explaining intersubjectivity between infant and mother, describes a situation quite similar to the one for which Dickinson yearns:

[This is] a working notion that says something like, what is going on in my mind may be similar enough to what is going on in your mind that we can somehow communicate this (without words) and thereby experience intersubjectivity. For such an experience to occur, there must be some shared framework of meaning and means of communication such as gesture, posture, or facial expression. When it does occur, the interpersonal action has moved, in part, from overt actions and responses to the internal subjective states that lie behind the overt behaviors. (1985, 124–25)

Stern is describing an occurrence in the early months of a baby's life; his research challenges the notion of an original state of fusion from which the infant gradually separates and individuates to arrive at a sense of self and other. Rather, he suggests that a sense of self as differentiated from others is present from the beginning, and that, for these are related concepts, the infant's world is interpersonal from the start.

These new findings support the view that the infant's first order of business, in creating an interpersonal world, is to form the sense of a core self and core others. The evidence also supports the notion that this task is largely accomplished during the period between two and seven months. Further, it suggests that the capacity to have merger- or fusion-like experiences as described in psychoanalysis is secondary to and dependent upon an already existing sense of self and other. (70)

Central to this approach to earliest identity formation is the concept of recognition—achieved through communication between mother and baby in which the mother's gaze or attunement behaviors or words, in that developmental order, reify the identity of the child by attesting to her existence, both different from and like the mother herself: "oh, it's you." When the child communicates back to the mother, in the process recognizing her as a person who is there, the child likewise attests to her identity—a self in relation to an other self. This model challenges Freud's view of the first relationship as based on an oral drive, a physiological dependency, a nonspecific need for some object that might reduce tension by providing satisfaction. Instead, as Jessica Benjamin explains in *The Bonds of Love: Psychoanalysis, Feminism, and the Problem of Domination,* "[T]he idea of intersubjectivity reorients the conception of the psychic world from a subject's relation to its object toward a subject meeting another subject." In this way

the individual grows in and through the relationship to other subjects. Most important, this perspective observes that the other whom the self meets is also a self, a subject in his or her own right. It assumes that we are able and need to recognize that other subject as different and yet alike, as an other who is capable of sharing similar mental experience. (1988, 19–20)

In her letter to Sue, Dickinson is fantasizing such a moment of intersubjectivity—of love and recognition. It may be based in what she did experience with her mother: a paradigm she subsequently cast onto experiences of love. Or it may come out of a longing her own mother never did satisfy, which then influenced and organized later relationships. My tendency is to believe the latter, because not only does it make more sense in terms of her own comments about her relationship with her mother, but it makes more sense in terms of how she conducted her later loves, characterized as much by fear of actual bodily presence as by powerful fantasies of its felicitousness. The facts that she made a habit of establishing loving relationships where physical closeness could not occur, that her poetic expressions of love and desire are always concerned with ratios between distance and fulfillment, indicate to me that the situation she imagines with Sue functions for her as a desire that she did not understand to be realistically attainable and that may well have been, on one level, frightening—and this may be in large part due to what actually did transpire between Emily Norcross Dickinson and her little daughter Emily. Whatever the truth, which we cannot know, Dickinson habitually uses language as the place—probably the only place—in which she can encounter the nonverbal, primary intersubjectivity for which she longs.

Dickinson's passionate interest in communication as a means to intimacy and even identity alerts us to its centrality in her psychic economy. Silence, therefore, is for her almost always the enemy of discourse, situated at the edge or end of language. It signifies absence, not presence; it is the opposite of eyes whispering and hands held fast: it has, significantly, "no face."

> Silence is all we dread.
> There's Ransom in a Voice—
> But Silence is Infinity.
> Himself have not a face.
>
> (1955, poem 1251)

In this powerful indictment of silence, we should note that silence is identified as "Himself"—that is, gendered masculine. Dickinson does not associate it with that much-vaunted silence which some would say constitutes the female modality (stemming from the female's association with that original maternal body, that original preoedipal oneness that is signified and not signifier) in relation to language—the symbolic, culture, phallic dominance (here I borrow freely from Lacan). In Dickinson's version, silence has associations to culture, cultural oppression, in relation to woman's potential to use language in service, we might assume, of her own needs. Silence is "all we dread," a condition from which (only) a voice might ransom us. The word *ransom* is compelling. I imagine a captive maiden, an evil abductor. In such a situation, the woman, held captive by silence, is thus an icon for her own linguistic potential. What is being silenced is precisely woman's language: disavowed by all those societal forces with which we are only too familiar from feminist explication, that suppress in ways both overt and covert women's language use. What ransoms the captive maiden is a voice: her own voice, perhaps, or the voice of another woman who might speak to her or for her. Language is necessary. Language is salvation. So Dickinson, of all woman writers, believed. Her career was devoted to the task of ransoming.

In response to Dickinson's purposes and practices (and to those of other women writers I have read), I want to propose a theory about women and language that grants women access to all dimensions of language, including the symbolic, wherein resides the production of meaning. I propose that symbolic language is not antithetical to women's gendered identity, but that it has more than one aspect—or dialect or idiom: one that inscribes cultural norms or values, which we might indeed associate with "the masculine"; another that, as it communicates a "sharing of mutually created meanings about personal experience," comes out of the mother-infant matrix and can thus be associated with the feminine (Stern 1985, 172). It is significant that little girls learn speech *during* the preoedipal period and most often learn it from their mothers, who therefore function in culture. It can be shown that children learn speech *both* as a way to enter into the wider world (the domain of the father) and to expand their relationship with the mother and the more personal or relational world for which the idea of "mother" stands. I would maintain that both of these functions are aspects of the symbolic and both are potentially available to women speakers.

However, given that language as it articulates cultural hegemony creates what Daniel Stern calls an "official version" of experience—"official or socialized world knowledge as encoded in language" (1985, 178)—it clearly does privilege the communication of some experiences and suppress or repress others, others that may well be gendered feminine. For example, intimacy, connection, "we-experiences," expressed in a language that extends the nonverbal intersubjective discourse of eyes and hands into the symbolic. Since connectedness is culturally gendered feminine, separation culturally gendered masculine, what is happening is that one aspect of language dominates and denies another aspect of language. But if this is so, then the other aspect of language that is being silenced, while indeed directly linked to the experience of the mother, is neither nonlinguistic nor nonsymbolic.

If one major aspect of language acquisition for children has been its role in the continuation of the mother-infant dyad as a vehicle for mutually created meanings about shared experience, then that linguistic function might well be accessible despite (or because of) cultural admonitions against it. What we will then find is less a tension between semiotic and symbolic for women than a tension between "dialects" for women who speak and write—and a sense of doubleness. Because they usually become in some way members of the social order, they do belong to its language culture. But especially because they frequently persist (longer and more directly than do boys, as many theorists, most notably Nancy Chodorow [1978], have argued) in a mother-daughter bond based in the preoedipal relationship, the language usage that characterizes this "being-with" experience is theirs as well. Thus, we might assume that one problem that writing poses for women is to know which version or dialect of language to use, what the relationship between them should or could be in a given situation.

Dickinson appears to have appreciated full well language's potential to express we-meanings, to function as an agent of intersubjective communication and thereby extend the kind of loving interaction for which the original preoedipal relationship is paradigmatic. At the same time, she knew that symbolic language, if not the language of eyes and hands, participates in the public world of the culture at large. Her language use is characterized by her awareness of these potentially competing functions, even as it is characterized by more than one dialect. In her poetry, this doubleness at the formal level forcefully occurs at those sites where at the semantic level she balances a culturally approved notion against another that interrogates or subverts or quite simply challenges it (see Juhasz 1989, 1993). Often, we find her expressing both versions—in such a way, however, that the reader has options for interpretation. Because her language is so complex, so multiplicitous, so *figurative*, especially at points of conflict between the two "dialects," the reader can read one meaning or another, or *both*. Dickinson does not make her language decide for us.

Love is consistently the occasion for such doubleness in Dickinson's poems, as I have previously argued. This makes perfect sense, if an idea about love as a version of the preoedipal mother-infant relationship is understood as contradicting the culturally approved paradigm for love as based in the father-daughter (Oedipal) relationship. In this essay, I shall take as my text a poem in which achieved love is presented as a reincarnation of the maternal-infant moment of recognition—and as it is rendered, more conventionally, in Christian terms, as gaining God's love through going to heaven. In poem 788, "Joy to have merited the pain—," I identify the linguistic rendering of the moment of intersubjective mother-infant recognition as a *feminine dialect;* the Christian plot, the story the culture prefers, as a societal or *masculine dialect*. Additionally, I shall chart the intense linguistic figuration that negotiates these two discourses—particularly the trope of metaphor—to show how the two dialects are bridged so that both sets of meanings augment one another to create a third alternative—a place in language where the dichotomous constraints of culture are transcended.

For my final proposition in this essay is that symbolic language itself offers "bilingual" speakers such as women a vehicle for negotiating the very doubleness that defines their language usage: that vehicle is metaphor. By metaphor I mean a trope or rhetorical device, occurring at the syntactic or formal level of language, where x is spoken of as y. I am referring therefore not to a philosophical perspective but to a linguistic activity that occurs on the symbolic level, a transfer on grounds of analogy, to paraphrase Aristotle in the *Poetics*.[1] Even a hasty reading of Dickinson's poetry will impress the reader with the pronounced metaphoricity of her language: metaphor may well be its most salient linguistic feature. In the two examples of her language to which I have already referred, for example, we see ample use of metaphor. First is the phrase "our eyes would whisper for us," in that x, eyes, are spoken of as if they were y, lips. Second, we note that almost every line of the brief poem about silence is a metaphor: "Ransom in a Voice," "Silence is Infinity," "Himself have not a face."

Metaphor functions in Dickinson's language as a powerful device for establishing relationship and in the process creating new contexts and new meanings. First, its yoking of elements from different modalities—its action of carrying across—makes it particularly useful for the speaker of more than one dialect or mode of language (more than one mode of perception and value) who needs to bring them into some kind of association. Second, its stress on the activity of relationship reifies Dickinson's deep concern for communication that is intersubjective and reciprocal. Third, its role in shaping, turning, transferring language enables not merely the bringing together of disparate modes but their transformation into a new world altogether: the world of the poem, a world of language. A "holiday" from the real world—a "newly created relevance" (Miles 1967, 128). Metaphor gives resonance to the symbolic so that it can manifest desire as well as order.

By far the most influential theory about women and language for contemporary feminist criticism is that of Julia Kristeva. Feminists have critiqued her thought on the basis of its essentialism—woman = body, male = culture; or they have taken the opposite approach—that she is no feminist, because not only are the texts she chooses as radical as the works of men, but that the semiotic itself is a disruptive force that underlies all identities (see Felski 1989, 33–40). Nonetheless, her ideas about language structure and its basis in psychoanalytic concepts of human development, especially her formation of the semiotic and symbolic components of language, frequently form givens in feminist discussion. Further, as her theory reinforces Lacanian principles about language acquisition and significance, wherein the symbolic order is defined as the law of the Father, thereby necessarily excluding the feminine, it functions as a significant postmodernist extension of classical Freudian theory. Particularly in her acceptance of the drives as the structuring agency in development and of the Oedipal crisis as the most significant moment in development, Kristeva's work stands in opposition, however, to the line of thought about the first relationship that stems from object-relations psychology. For if the semiotic in language is the residue of the preoedipal relationship to the mother, Kristevan, and Freudian, ideas about the nature of that experience may well be questioned.

Especially, I want to take issue here with the belief that this early moment is characterized by a primary narcissism or autism, "daughter-mother symbiosis . . . glimpses of oneness or paranoid primary identification phantasized as primordial substance" (Kristeva 1980, 279). To the contrary, both differentiation and development have been seen in that earliest period. Object-relations theory, as it postulated attachment to an object-world rather than drive fulfillment as dominating infant need, in consequence began to pay close attention to the preoedipal mother-infant relationship. When this relationship has been studied, either in the clinical setting or in experimental situations, it has turned out to be dynamic and interactive, characterized by both connection and individuation. It is also, and this is of utmost importance here, verbal as well as nonverbal. Therefore, I should like to place Kristeva's formulations about language in the context of the work of Stern and other contemporary researchers into language acquisition.

Kristeva's central concept of language as constituted by a dynamic of semiotic and symbolic rests on the semiotic's association with the repressed preoedipal experience: it is "a mark of the workings of the drives" (Kristeva 1980, 136). Drives, she explains, "involve pre-Oedipal semiotic functions and energy discharges that connect and orient the body to the mother. . . . The oral and anal drives, both of which are oriented and structured around the mother's body, dominate this sensorimotor organization" ([1974] 1984, 27). "Language as symbolic function constitutes itself at the cost of repressing instinctual drive and continuous relation to the mother" (1980, 136). Nonetheless, "this prelinguistic, unrepresentable memory" does enter into language, especially poetic language, which "maintains itself at the cost of reactivating this repressed, instinctual, maternal element" (1980, 239; 136). This "anteriority," the "instinctual and maternal, semiotic processes," always remains "subordinate—subjacent to the principle function of naming-predicating" (1980, 136). Especially, Kristeva postulates that the semiotic, as it articulates the primary processes, is characterized by intonation and rhythm: the transfers of drive energy "can be detected in phonematic devices (such as the accumulation and repetition of phonemes or rhyme) and melodic devices (such as intonation or rhythm)" ([1974] 1984, 86, 65).

Because Kristeva's approach is insistent upon a somatic oneness between mother and infant in the preoedipal period, the simultaneity of the move into language and culture ("the 'social' and the 'symbolic' are synonymous") via the Oedipal crisis, and the resulting repression of the maternal, there is no way in her theory that the symbolic can directly speak the maternal; rather, the maternal as semiotic generates, qualifies, complicates the symbolic. The mother functions as signified to language's signifier, with the necessary gap or displacement between them operating as the condition for culture, and the symbolic, to exist at all.

Object-relations theory and its heirs place this psychoanalytic paradigm in question. Even as we no longer need assume that such a rupture between the maternal and the paternal occurs in order for the creation of individuation and identity, so we need not take for granted that the symbolic is of necessity situated in and resultant from the Oedipal crisis. "The acquisition of language has traditionally been seen as a major step in the achievement of separation and individuation, next only to acquiring locomotion. The present view asserts that the opposite is equally true, that the acquisition of language is potent in the service of union and togetherness," writes Stern (1985, 172). Indeed, Stern's work and other recent experimental investigations into language formation present a very different model altogether, a "dialogic" view of language predicated on the idea that the very process of learning to speak has much to do with the infant's "need and desire to re-establish the personal order with mother" (Dore quoted in Stern 1985, 175).

> One of the major imports of this dialogic view of language is that the very process of learning to speak is recast in terms of forming shared experiences . . . of creating a new type of "being-with" between adult and child. Just as the being-with experiences of intersubjective relatedness required the sense of two subjectivities in alignment—a sharing of inner experience of state—so, too, at this new level of verbal relatedness, the infant and mother create a being-with experience using verbal symbols—a sharing of mutually created meanings about personal experience. (Stern 1985, 172)

In other words, this new research alerts us to the possibility that language can be understood as an extension and renegotiation of the mother-infant bond, having everything rather than nothing to do with mother love. In his work on protoconversational communication between mothers and infants aged one to three months, Colwyn Trevarthen shows how an infant establishes the basis for a deep affectional tie to his mother and other constant companions by means of a "delicate and specifically human system for person-to-person communication" (1979, 321). On the basis of careful study of facial expressions and vocalizations, Trevarthen concludes that

> a complex form of mutual understanding develops even at this age. It is both naturally accepted and strongly regulated by the infant. Two-month-olds exhibit many different expressions, some highly emotional, and they make a

variety of attempts to gain the lead in an exchange with another person. They are also sensitive to subtle differences in the mother's expression. The dependent acts of the mother show that she is adapting to the infant, and apparently each pair develops a unique style of communication and a private code. But in primary intersubjectivity there is innovation of meaning by the infant as well as by the mother. Furthermore, inside the earliest communications . . . may be observed the embryonic forms of communication by speech itself. (1979, 346)

John Dore, studying mother-infant interaction during the period between babbling and the first genuinely referential words, when the infant produces "proto-language," argues that first words emerge in the infant as consequences of dialogic functions of affective expressions across members of an intimate dyad and that such words arise as solutions to maintain and negotiate relationship through dialogue (1983, 168). He shows how the mother matches the baby's expressed affect, "analoging," "complementing," or "imitating" so that the baby can observe a form for her affects, transforming the baby's expressions into intents to express those affect-states. The baby discovers a gesture for what she is feeling, albeit her affect has to "loop through" the mother to become observable. "This may be the original moment of 'cognizing' a connection between internal state and external sign for it. The behavioral form can then be reproduced when feeling the same affect, thereby allowing both baby and caregiver together to '*re*-cognize' and share the same affect state" (Dore 1983, 169).

Dore proposes that the baby's change from expressing to intending is motivated by desire to maintain some intimate state of connection with the mother, both when they have shared a pleasurable affect and, perhaps more significantly, when a misunderstanding has occurred.

> Being able to express his state intentionally allows [the baby] to invite a match of positive affect and to deny negative matches. It allows him to *test the state of their relationship*. The intent to express becomes the first cognitive tool for communicating about their relative states in their dialogue with one another. Because the same affect can be differentiated into two forms and communicated cross-modally, partnership in dialogue merges. *But the analog of affect is the foundation of dialogue*. (1983, 170)

Thus the mother accommodates to the baby's efforts and assimilates it to her forms, even as the baby accommodates to the mother's forms and assimilates them to her affects and cognition. But tension always exists from the disequilibrium of their matches, and mismatches cannot help but occur. Dore concludes that

> after intentionality emerges the only solution to mutual comprehension in dialogue is a shared system of linguistic symbols. . . . Not only uncertainty

and ambiguity, but also anxiety is reduced by being able to express states, needs, desires for objects, and so on by unequivocal symbols; that is, words that disambiguate among items desired at the right moment. Words reconstitute the dyad's intersubjectivity. (1983, 172)

Language, then, in Stern's words, permits "the old and persistent life issues of attachment, autonomy, separation, intimacy, and so on to be reencountered on the previously unavailable plane of relatedness through shared meaning of personal knowledge" (1985, 173). Nonetheless, Stern notes ways in which language is a double-edged sword, in that it is as well "a problem for the integration of self-experience and self-with-other experiences" (163). For all that language can implement the sharing of personal experience, it also "forces a space between interpersonal experience as lived and as represented" (182). Language cannot help but isolate a given aspect of experience from the "amodal flux in which it was originally experienced" (176). Kristeva might want us to see this "global experience resonant with a mix of amodal properties" as the preoedipal symbiosis of mother and infant; but when Stern describes preoedipal experience, he is describing the experience of an infant both differentiated and social, occurring in culture, not outside of it. Before language, however, such experience can be shown to be amodal, not yet reduced and focused, selected, by language.

Where Stern draws close to Kristeva, however, is when he notes that language creates an "official version" of the experience, and that "the amodal version goes underground and can only resurface when conditions suppress or outweigh the dominance of the linguistic version" (176). He refers to this process as a "slippage between personal world knowledge and official or socialized world knowledge as encoded in language" (178).

One of the consequences of this inevitable division into the accountable and the deniable is that what is deniable to others becomes more and more deniable to oneself. The path into the unconscious (both topographic and potentially dynamic) is being well laid by language. Prior to language, all of one's behaviors have equal status as far as "ownership" is concerned. With the advent of language, some behaviors now have a privileged status with regard to one having to own them. The many messages in many channels are being fragmented by language into a hierarchy of accountability/deniability. (181)

This insight has repercussion both for the individual psyche and for the relation of gender identity to language. It is both related to and different from Kristeva's central discussion of repression. For Kristeva, the mother and all that she represents must be repressed, sent to the nether worlds of the unconscious, because she is what is not culture. The preoedipal is another modality altogether and can influence the societal only through the persistence of energies of body and drive. For Stern, there is a difference between culturally privileged behaviors and experiences and those that are not, a selection and enforcement which may well initially result from the mother's behavior to the infant. The mother exists in culture, gendered and "socialized."[2] And whereas maternity itself as well as certain traditional aspects of the female role are especially conducive to "we-experiences" (the concern and capacity for devotion, intimacy, empathy, relationality, and nurturing) other qualities traditionally gendered female (passivity, insecurity, lack of self-definition) are not. D. W. Winnicott's concept of the "good enough mother" is certainly an idealization, describing nurture when all goes well (Winnicott 1965). When it does not go well, as frequently happens, the infant will have experiences that are not recognized—not attuned or mirrored. They then go underground. They are repressed and do not find a direct pathway into language. A "false self" that adapts nicely to the caregiver's demands becomes established—"as a semantic construction made of linguistic propositions about who one is and what one does and experiences." At the same time, a "true self" remains as "a conglomerate of disavowed experiences of self which cannot be linguistically encoded" (Stern 1985, 227).

Thus, there seem to be two forms of unofficial experience, both denied ready access to culturally sanctioned language practice. The first kind are associated with the "feminine"—intimate, relational, and so on: modes of behavior that are devalued but present in society. The second kind are more deeply repressed; they exist but have been cut off from language. Through the aid of good therapy or perhaps good art, however, they can be accessed. Kristeva's idea of the semiotic points to a repressed gestalt that can find its way into language, but as drive energy—rhythm or intonation. The repressed true self is, on the contrary, not an acultural nexus of experience, so that if or when it achieves linguistic expression, there seems no reason why that language might not be symbolic. What I am arguing, then, is that although preoedipal experience differs in significant ways from the modes of behavior sanctioned by the Oedipal transition, it is nonetheless representable in symbolic language.

Where does metaphor come in? Kristeva identifies it as a representative or agent of the semiotic. She describes

a breakthrough of what may be called "primary" processes, those dominated by intonation and rhythm. When this involves morphemes, it produces "stylistic figures": metaphor, metonymy, elisions, etc. Here, this intonational, rhythmic, let us say "instinctual" breakthrough is situated at the most intense place of naming—at the thetic place of an inescapable syntax that abruptly halts the maternal body's vague, autoerotic jubilation—recognizes its reflec-

tion in a mirror and shifts instinctual motility into logically structurable sig-
nifiers. (1980, 167)

Metaphor is that feature of language most closely associated with drives and the
primary processes that "displace and condense both energies and their inscrip-
tion." The principle of metaphor, as agent of condensation, is indissoluble from
the drive economy underlying it ([1974] 1984, 25, 28).

The existence of links between unconscious processes and linguistic practices,
however, does not negate their status as language. Kristeva's word "indissocia-
ble" seems inaccurate here, for it prevents metaphor from being in any way an
activity in the symbolic. To the contrary, many theorists of metaphor have under-
stood it to be just that, a sophisticated grammatical maneuver, a figure of rhetoric
that in its transactions makes alternative or figurative meanings possible and
available in the domain of the symbolic.

Kristeva, following Lacan and Freud, associates metaphor with condensation,
one major aspect of unconscious or primary process functioning. Condensation
is a useful description, in that metaphor allows us to represent in language a
complex series of associations in a relatively simple grammatical structure. For
example, Winifred Nowottny is referring to the condensative aspect of linguistic
metaphor when she writes that "with a metaphor one can make a complex
statement without complicating the grammatical construction of the sentence
that carries the statement." She gives an example:

> For if we say, "the ship ploughs the waves" [this is Aristotle's famous ur-
> metaphor], this is tantamount to saying, "The action of a ship in the waves is
> like the action of a plough in the soil," or to saying, "The ship goes through
> the waves; the plough goes through the soil; the two actions are in one or more
> respects the same," or "The ship is to the waves as the plough is to the soil."
> (1965, 56–57)

However, the action of metaphor, its ability to *carry across*, seems less condensa-
tion, as Freud describes it, than the creation of relationship. For Freud condensa-
tion functions in the dream pictures

> as though a force were at work which was subjecting the material to compres-
> sion and concentration. As a result of condensation, one element in the man-
> ifest dream may correspond to numerous elements in the latent dream-
> thoughts; but, conversely too, one element in the dream-thoughts may be
> represented by several images in the dream. (Frend 1965, 20)

Freud is insisting that the dreamwork is prelinguistic or even nonlinguistic: an
aspect of "archaic regression" in which "the subtler relations of thought—the

conjunctions and prepositions, the changes in declensions and conjugation—are dropped." He notes that "just as in a primitive language without any grammar, only the raw material of thought is expressed and abstract terms are taken back to the concrete ones that are at their basis" (20).

Freud's theory of language development is debatable; however, his distinction between primary process thinking and language is frequently followed. What I want to question here in particular is the association between condensation and metaphor, for what seems to me most significant about condensation is that it works to repress relationship rather than to highlight it. To the extent that Freud is cognizant of condensation's propensity to refer to "numerous elements," the notion of relationship is present. But in most respects it functions more like a symbol (which is what Freud says it is) than a metaphor, in that whereas symbol acts to *stand for*, metaphor creates a *relation between* (it means, in Greek, as I have noted, to carry across). What I am most interested in about Dickinson's use of metaphor is how she employs it to say at least two things at once and, even more significantly, to create a complicated relationship between the two ideas and images.

The ideas of two theorists of metaphor, Max Black in his well-known essay, "Metaphor," and Josephine Miles in *Style and Proportion: The Language of Prose and Poetry*, can best explicate how metaphor as relation (or as "interaction" in Black's vocabulary and as "proportion" in Miles's) is understood, especially in terms of the process and power of figuration in language. Black notes how "metaphor creates the similarity [rather than formulating] some similarity antecedently existing," how it generates "a new meaning, which is not quite its meaning in literal uses," a new context, which "imposes extension of meaning upon the focal word" (1962, 39). Further, "for the metaphor to work the reader must remain aware of the extension of meaning—must attend to both the old and the new meanings together" (39). In this way the reader is forced to "connect" two ideas.

Hence, Black's interaction view presents metaphor as a "filter," evoking a system of related commonplaces surrounding a word or idea and suppressing some details, emphasizing others—in short, *organizing* our view of the principal subject, which is thus "seen through" the metaphorical expression (41). The metaphorical vocabulary "filters and transforms: it not only selects, it brings forward aspects of [the principal subject] that might not be seen at all through another medium" (42). "If to call a man a wolf is to put him in a special light, we must not forget that the metaphor makes the wolf seem more human than he otherwise would" (44). Thus, Black's theory stresses both the relational aspect of the metaphor and its figurativeness.

Josephine Miles's discussion of metaphor is especially helpful in its focus on matters of relationality and figurativeness. Miles points out that what is vital in metaphor is "the sense of relative position within a group or class," the kind of transfer that Aristotle meant when he spoke of genus to genus, species to species, and genus to species. As Black uses as his exemplary metaphor "a man is a wolf," so Miles plays with "the dove is a cabbage."

> What have we done by this transference? It is a relatively superficial one, lacking depth of context, except for the endearment of *le petit chou*, yet it is characteristic in structure. *We have reversed the ordinate and subordinate qualities in the definition of dove* [emphasis added], emphasizing those of shape and texture, which do not appear essential in delimitation, and underplaying those of bird and pigeon, which set it apart from the vegetable world. By putting the dove in a cabbage cote, we have given it vegetable traits—a round and solid leafiness—and have taken away part of its birdiness—its Columbidae characteristics of beak and claw—yet have retained, with the leafiness, its feathers and its round puffed profile, *for the sake of the metaphor's own newly created relevance* [emphasis added]. In considering the dove-cabbage range—the relatively plump and ruffled within bird and vegetable worlds—we have based upon an *ad hoc* relation or proportion (more than a simple property) an *ad hoc* class. . . . This is the pride and pathos of metaphor: for its moment we are not bound by lexical boundaries. (1967, 123–24)

Consequently, metaphor, in its "wrench from essence into context," is best understood as *proportion*—"a partial yet double statement, an *as* and an *if*" (126, 127). Such a transfer is "artistic action, doing some special shaping, turning, transferring of the language, for some effect" (127). That effect, it seems to me, has much to do with the *trans*, the *meta*. "Carried to where?" asks Miles. "[T]o an alien land. This is foreign trade, as Aristotle makes clear in his list of odd uses in the *Poetics*." Not necessarily hostile but rather "simply different, irrelevant until made relevant by context."

> That is, again, the extraordinary transfer is not based on central, ordinate characteristics, but on peripheral, subordinate characteristics in relatively similar or proportionate position: not from dove to anti-dove or to hawk, but from dove to cabbage. The world of metaphor is not so much a world of vehicular tension as a world of holiday, of variety, of free-wheeling, where within the familiar limitations of every day a word can move and transport us, making first qualities last and last first, in the crosscurrent of values. (128)

Metaphor's association with relationship makes it especially valuable to Dickinson. Because she is deeply interested in communication as a technique for establishing intersubjectivity, dialogue, and relationship, because she is aware that language as social discourse contains dialects that themselves need to be brought into relation, and because metaphor has the propensity to turn relationship into transformation, metaphor frequently becomes the agent of relationality in Dickinson's poetic language. The following poem places metaphor at the center of a relational discourse that uses language to release a repressed moment of love and recognition into present consciousness.

> Joy to have merited the Pain—
> To merit the Release—
> Joy to have perished every step—
> To Compass Paradise—
>
> Pardon—to look upon thy face—
> With these old fashioned Eyes—
> Better than new—could be—for that—
> Though bought in Paradise—
>
> Because they looked on thee before—
> And thou hast looked on them—
> Prove Me—My Hazel Witnesses
> The features are the same—
>
> So fleet thou wert, when present—
> So infinite—when gone—
> An Orient's Apparition—
> Remanded of the Morn—
>
> The Height I recollect—
> 'Twas even with the Hills—
> The Depth upon my Soul was notched—
> As Floods—on Whites of Wheels—
>
> To Haunt—till Time have dropped
> His last Decade away,
> And Haunting actualize—to last
> At least—Eternity—
>
> (1955, poem 788)

"Joy" is the subject of this poem, that we know. But joy under what conditions? Gaining Heaven? Reunion with a lover? Where? When? And indeed, how? Why so many questions—or rather, so many possible answers? Why do we experience a superfluity, an excess of meanings that not so much overdetermine the poem as confuse us, in our effort to understand? Because, in the terms that this essay has suggested, Dickinson is using more than one idiom or dialect, and the vocabulary of each intersects regularly. If that is not enough, a third idiom still, which comes from the realm of neither spiritual nor secular love but uses vocabulary from nature, law, and even the supernatural, creates metaphoric crosscurrents between the other two—so that it is indeed hard to know where one is at many moments in the poem. In what world? In what *language*?

In this way Dickinson imagines and communicates how needs might be fulfilled, employing a series of interlocking dialects that make her vision at once available to and protected from different components of her "audience." If we imagine her audience as a wide spectrum of potential readers—both men and women—then we can see right away how the poem could be read by both groups, but that different interpretations might ensue. And, because she is actually a member of both communities herself—a socialized woman who can function, more or less (in Dickinson's case, a little less than more) in the culture, an antisocial (literally) woman who seeks for alternative verities within her own mind and heart—her linguistic doubleness expresses her own realities as well as those of others to whom she tries to speak. Thus, if we begin with the assumption that the poet speaks more than one dialect in the poem, and that it is the overlap or overlay of these languages that creates a meaning that may well be multiple, we can trace their several paths to see not only what but how meanings are established.

The first line of the poem situates its activity in some kind of space and time—conceptual, emotional, and in some less clear way, environmental. The stanza identifies joy as the condition of the poem—a joy that is complicated by its association with pain. Pain and reward, so that the situation is both emotional and ethical. But it is very abstract. Where is this joy being experienced? When? By whom? Under what conditions? The comparative nature of the joy alerts us to a present tense of the poem in relation to a previous past tense. First there was pain; *now* there is release. First there was perishing every step; *now* there is compassing paradise. Meriting the pain has occasioned meriting the release: "Compass[ing] Paradise." We can say with some assurance that the speaker is now feeling joy in paradise; but does she mean that literally—she has died and has earned the joy of Heaven, or figuratively—the release (however it transpired) from pain (whatever kind of pain it was) is a joy that makes this moment "Paradise"? The persistent parallelism of the opening lines does not allow us to answer this question, so that from the very start, two different situations, two different scenarios are possible. The one is culturally condoned—one suffers on earth and earns happiness and God's love in Heaven. The other is more mysterious, not an idea about a Christian afterlife at all.

The second stanza is a sudden close-up. The wide lens of compassing paradise now focuses in on "to look upon thy face." The syntactical position of "Joy" has been replaced by "Pardon." Thus I assume that a component of the joy is the pardon, so that a component of the pain was some sentence or punishment. Since the pardon granted is to [be able to] look upon thy face, the pain or sentence may very well have been not to be able to look upon thy face. (This supposition proves correct, we discover as we read further.) Thus the essence of the experience of paradise turns out to be able to *look* at someone beloved. The someone could of course be God; or not. No way to tell. The focus of the stanza is on the looking and on the eyes that do it. "Old fashioned eyes," because they are "Better." The syntax of the third line is not so much fragmentary as excited, breathless—its dashes occasioning not missing words but (simply) pauses. Dashes omitted, the line reads, "Better than new could be for that." "That" seems to refer to looking on thy face, so that we can paraphrase: these old-fashioned eyes are better for looking on thy face than new ones would be, even though they were bought in paradise.

Here is the first hint of subversiveness. If one subscribed to conventional Protestant ideology, old-fashioned eyes would *not* be better than new, for the promise of Heaven includes the belief in a transformation of earthly bodies. Dickinson is challenging conventional doctrine with a different version by privileging earthly life, bodies with eyes that "looked on thee before," eyes that "thou hast looked on." In this version of paradise the original gaze is repeated rather than transformed: "Prove Me—My Hazel Witnesses / The features are the same—." Surely there is a pun here on the word "Witnesses," meaning not only to see or know by personal presence and perception but in more specifically religious terms, to testify to Christ's immanence. Thus "witnessing" here creates a tension between the recognition of Christ's ultimate power and some other powerful recognition. (In her manuscript Dickinson also tried the phrase, "Swimming Witnesses," with "swimming" operating, I assume, as a metaphor for tears. "Hazel" is at once more literal and more personal, since it refers to the color of her own eyes.) In this stanza joy turns out to be quite simply pardon from the sentence of separation that has parted these two since that original, remarkable moment when they first looked on one another, a moment of profound intersubjectivity and connection.

That moment was so important, so formative, that Dickinson devotes the next two stanzas to describing its significance, and it is here that she reaches dramatically for metaphor's revelatory potency. Up to this point in the poem two dialects have first existed side by side (in stanza 1) and then, suddenly (in stanza 2), in a more conflictual relationship, in which a version of secular love challenged the preeminence of spiritual love. Now a third vocabulary is brought in to create metaphors that call into question the very conflict itself by transferring signification to a new plane altogether.[3]

The beloved is first described as "fleet . . . when present"; "infinite—when gone—." The loved one's identity is correlated with presence, whether actual or, afterwards, imagined, internalized. Thus I read "infinite" as expanded albeit nonliteral presence in the mind of the speaker. This situation is then further described as "An Orient's Apparition— / Remanded of the Morn—." Metaphor piles upon metaphor, making sense not logically but associationally, amplifying the original depiction of presence and absence, transitory and lasting. The metaphorical vocabulary juxtaposes words of nature, law, and the supernatural. "Orient"—the East. "Apparition"—a ghostly appearance, specter or phantom; anything that appears, especially, something remarkable or startling. "Remanded"—sent back or consigned again; especially, to send back a prisoner or accused person into custody, as to await further proceedings, or to send back a case to a lower court. "Morn"—morning. The East—in Dickinson's lexicon associated with the dawn, the exotic or "fabulous," and even with the heretical.[4]

Does "Orient" here refer to a place? A person? An ambience? Why not all? Metaphor can accomplish just that expansion of meaning through its transfers of subordinate characteristics in relatively similar or proportionate position (Miles 1967). When Orient becomes an apparition, its exoticism and its fleetingness are intensified by the association of "apparition" with both something remarkable or startling and something spectral or phantomlike.

This experience, very much a matter of *vision*, is however remanded—sent back: "of" (?) the Morn. "Of" is indeed awkward—not correct English grammar. Yet Dickinson, who knew grammar better than any of us, alters the correct forms when she has a mind to do so. What can "of" do here that "by" or "to" cannot? Its possessive function seems important, endowing "by" with a little more ownership, perhaps. The legal attributes of the term are startling in this context of natural phenomena. Dickinson, the lawyer's daughter, might well associate legal language with the culture at large. "Remanded," cutting short that glorious apparition, as the much more prolonged ordinary condition of morning curtails the dawn, might well be a way to explain the loss of the experience. Why was the beloved's presence so fleeting, why was it apparitional? Because something else intervened, cutting off the moment (repressing it, relegating it to the mind), even as "Morn" or everyday life took over—until the moment of this poem.

Yes, I would like to read the moment as emblematizing the original gaze between mother and child—the all-important "oh, it's you" moment of recognition. Yes, I would like to see the remanding as signifying a version of the Oedipal crisis, when the culture (in the form of father) intervenes between the mother and the child to create an official form of language, one that denies the significance of mother-type love as it stands for intimacy, connectedness, and intersubjectivity. Yes, I would also like to note the speaker's continuing perception of that moment—infinite albeit gone, its existence enduring somewhere in her mind or heart. Yes, I would like to call attention to the unorthodox ramifications of her desire. Yes, I believe, from the evidence of her writing in which she frequently evokes it, that the significance of that psychodynamic moment of dawn, as well as its abrupt loss, remained an ongoing desire in her life, a desire that is reified in this poem.

With metaphor Dickinson creates the amplitude and potency of that moment by shattering the control of the literal so that a new linguistic dimension evolves. We see gold and blue and dazzle and delight and loss. We see a shimmer of dawn and a ghostly Eastern potentate then shackled and sent away as the sunshine fills the sky. We see a scene in nature that is hardly natural. Language accesses a resonance of associations by creating images that would explode should we take them literally. We must accept and enter the "holiday" world of the figurative, with its "reversed ordinate and subordinate qualities," "not bound by lexical boundaries." In this way the repressed is released into language. The experience is preoedipal in content and form: amodal, intersubjective, personal. But it is not symbiosis or fusion; and it is not a transgression of the symbolic by the semiotic as much as an expansion of the symbolic by the metaphoric.

The poem continues to evoke through metaphor the aftermath of that apparitional event. A height "even with the Hills"—so high, so close to the sky; a depth so deep it was "notched upon [her] Soul." "Notched," a metaphor evoking physical alteration deeply and dramatically accomplished, further amplified by an analogy, itself complicatedly metaphoric: "As Floods—on Whites of Wheels—." Perhaps this notching is the dark line that the flooding of the Connecticut River would leave on painted buggy wheels, calling attention to the river's awesome power that is not forgotten when the water recedes.[5] The experience remains, repressed but real, after literal presence is denied.

For this imprinting of the experience on her very psyche has "Haunt[ed]" her (that word reinscribing the moment's apparitional status, occasioned by its fleeting *and* remarkable nature)—

> till Time have dropped
> His last Decade away,
> And Haunting actualize—to last
> At least—Eternity—.

This final stanza is so startling, because tenses in the verse sentence literally shift before our very eyes, so that what starts out as future becomes present—the present moment of the poem we are reading. The first two lines of the final stanza evoke the future. To paraphrase: the depth was notched upon my soul and will haunt me till the end of time. But suddenly that haunting is actualized, become both real and forever! This is the condition that the poem describes and creates, the joy that has merited the pain. The pain was the loss of the moment of recognition; the joy is its reestablishment. It is now *actual* again, as it was before. In between was the haunting, when the beloved could exist only as an aspect of the speaker's mind or soul. The poem as an instance of relational discourse has brought a moment of nonverbal intersubjectivity into language.

But if the poem describes the future turning into the present, where in time and space is it supposed to be located? One answer is in Heaven, where either earthly lovers might be reunited or the lover of God might be united with Him. But there are other more heretical terms in this poem implying that if this place/space is after death, not only is this not a Christian paradise, but the death that has transpired may be other than literal. The speaker and the beloved are "the same" as they were before, suggesting that the original condition of their life has returned. If they were literally dead, they could not be as in life, the only difference being that this time the moment is lasting forever, with no intervening remanding.

Dickinson writes other poems that evoke this condition. Poem 474 concludes with

> Not Either—noticed Death—
> Of Paradise—aware—
> Each other's Face—was all the Disc
> Each other's setting—saw—

Poem 577, which begins "If I may have it, when it's dead," concludes:

> Forgive me, if the Grave come slow—
> For Coveting to look at Thee—
> Forgive me, if to stroke thy frost
> Outvisions Paradise!

And Poem 625 describes lovers meeting after death:

> These Fleshless Lovers met—
> A Heaven in a Gaze—
> A Heaven of Heavens—the Privilege
> Of one another's Eyes—

In all of these moments as depicted in poetry, the gaze between one and the other dominates and calls into question the cultural definition of "Heaven." There are Heavens and heavens, Paradises and paradises. Heaven, paradise, is the privilege of one another's eyes, an experience that can be understood to outvision Paradise, even as it shifts the proportionate importance of maternal over paternal modalities.

This is the condition, the joy of the speaker of poem 788—and it is, finally, a moment achievable only in language, in a present tense that is not literally death and not literally Heaven but an imagined actuality—an actual figuration. It is conjured by and with and in language, especially and particularly by metaphor, that agency in the symbolic capable of moving beyond the literal to create a new, albeit regained, world.

It is metaphor, in its wrench from essence into context, its reversal of ordinate and subordinate qualities, that becomes the agent of the symbolic in language whereby the unofficial experience of intersubjectivity, connection, and maternal love might best be rendered. The resonance that metaphor evokes enables the symbolic to manifest such desire. "Our eyes would whisper for us," wrote Dickinson to Sue. "Whisper" is a metaphor, carrying elements of spoken language across to nonverbal communication and vice versa, so that the two now share common qualities rather than existing as separate experiential entities. When eyes whisper in language, the nonverbal intersubjective discourse of eyes and hands extends naturally into a common symbol system, a forging of shared or dialogic meaning. Dickinson's metaphor creates "a new form of coming together in the domain of verbal relatedness." In language, if not in the external world.

Dickinson valued language so much, feared silence so proportionately, because language enabled her to negotiate cultural conflicts and contradictions in a way that might have been quite impossible in Amherst proper. Writing a poem about the moment of maternal recognition, returning it from the repressed into present (and even future) time, gave her the power not only to have the experience herself but to offer it to others. For those who could and would read the dialect of the maternal mode, reciprocal recognition on the order that the poem describes might transpire between poet and audience. The poet's communicative act might bring her recognition—hence, a sense of identity. The poet's communication might as well recognize the reader and give *her* a sense of identity. Consequently, the communicative powers of the symbolic as well as of the preverbal or nonverbal were absolutely necessary to Dickinson, the gesture that might ransom herself and others from being remanded into silence.

NOTES

References to Dickinson's poems and letters are to Johnson's editions of 1955 and 1958, respectively; poems and letters are reprinted by permission of the publishers and the Trustees of Amherst College from *The Poems of Emily Dickinson*, Thomas H. Johnson, ed., Cambridge, Mass.: The Belknap Press of Harvard University Press, Copyright 1951, 1955, 1979, 1983 by the President and Fellows of Harvard College.

1. "Aristotle lumped together with what we now call metaphor other transfers to which nowadays other names are given: the transfers now called synechdoche and

metonymy," writes Winifred Nowottny. "But it is useful to begin with his definition, simply because it does lay emphasis on transference of name and by doing so directs attention to the linguistic aspect of metaphor (as distinct from the mental act of perceiving analogy)" (1965, 49–50).

2. Joseph Smith's formulation of the "symbolic mother" is useful to this discussion, as it partially mediates the two positions I have been outlining—the mother as purely semiotic and the mother as an aspect of culture. In *Arguing With Lacan* (from a Lacanian point of view), Smith describes a symbolic mother who has "all along introduced language and mediated being in the place of the Other to the father. It is she whose nonnarcissistic mode of being in the world points the child toward the father and a future apart from herself" (1991, 110).

> The mother is the first to be in the place of the Other. It is she who initially mediates lack, limit, finitude, language, and the world. . . . But the father, as the main other of the mother/infant unity, comes to be the symbol of all the factors challenging symbiotic unity and defensive denial of separateness and limit in the preoedipal dual relationship with the mother. (100)

It seems important that Smith recognizes that the mother as well as the father mediates entry into the symbolic order; however, I take issue with his deeply Lacanian belief that "the symbolized mother is the absent mother. The world that opens up with the image, the signifier, the chain of signifiers, begins as an effort to fill in a lack" (102).

3. Margaret Homans (1983) discusses some of these same poems and the use of metaphor in them with very different results. For Homans, metaphor is the ultimate patriarchal trope, "since the bridges built by the structure of metaphor show how romantic love is supposed to work. That is, metaphor gains its effects through coupling unlikely pairs and subordinating one term to another" (117). Consequently, in the poems that privilege the gaze she sees at work something more like metonymy, a "rhetoric of sameness . . . in which each figure could be said to be the name of the other" (124); thus "the touch and direct vision possible at or after death in these poems represents a different structuring of language by metonymic contiguity rather than by difference or absence; they model a less dualistic language" (125); this is ultimately "a language where signified and signifier are becoming one" (128). Nonetheless, when she notes that "the speech that crosses the boundary between life and death is a language in which the physical properties of the sign are as important as what it signifies: at the end of the search for the source of speech there is a kiss," that "the act of communication is itself the love" (127), she and I are observing the very same phenomena, no matter how different the conclusions we draw.

4. In poem 323, Dickinson associates Orient with the dawn:

> As if I asked the Orient
> Had it for me a Morn—
> And it should lift it's purple Dikes,
> And shatter me with Dawn!

In poem 1048 it is associated with the exotic or fabulous: "But like an Oriental Tale / To others, fabulous—"; in poem 1526, with heresy: "His oriental heresies / Exhilirate the Bee / . . . filling all the Earth and Air / With gay apostasy."

5. Thank you to Kim Hosman, whose years spent in the Connecticut Valley brought her memories not only of river floods but of notch marks on church walls recording the dates of floods long ago.

Knowing All the Way Down to Fire

Elaine A. Jahner

Native American women's poetry often appeals to readers with a tenacity that does not, however, cancel the insecurity that many experience over how to think about features of it that derive from unfamiliar cultural histories. This is often the case even for other Native Americans because there are so many different and contrasting indigenous cultures. But precisely because of the many discursive challenges that writers and readers have to confront if the poetry is to communicate beyond an immediate locale and audience, Native American women's poetry provides an exemplary array of different metaphoric mediations among cultures. We critics need better descriptive categories in order to show the working of metaphors that establish a cognitive middle ground between cultures, thus enabling metaphoric signification to move between the monocultural and multicultural, the personal and communal, the traditional and the innovative. Any analysis of those metaphors that negotiate the discursive conditions of more than one culture involves the critic in still another mode of mediation, that which takes place between poetic and theoretical language, so that the critical narrative becomes a model and summation of the entire range of different negotiations, transferals, and translations.

Knowing the difficulties of any kind of mediation or translation, we bring our best skills and attention to the effort, only to grow more aware of the limitations of the mediational strategies within our various discursive and disciplinary formations. In cross cultural criticism we try to use our skills to minimize the "cross fire of signals" whose dissonance, as Joy Harjo tells us, is as dangerous as love and as inescapably relational.

> I, too, try to fly but get caught in the cross fire of signals
>   and my spirit drops back down to earth.
> I am lost; I am looking for you
>   who can help me walk this thin line between the breathing
>   and the dead.
>   ("We Must Call A Meeting" 1990, 9)

As I examine the work of two Native American women poets, Joy Harjo and Linda Hogan,[1] I want to place that critical exploration within the broader context of various cultural practices that the global situation requires of us as women who want to respond rather than repress, translate rather than assimilate. I also want to advance my belief that Harjo's and Hogan's poems reveal metaphoric strategies that help us understand communication in all those social contexts where individuals routinely negotiate the terms of more than one culture. Mass global movements of people and ideas are resulting in the development of perceptual and interactional strategies so new that we can as yet barely recognize them, even though they are often in a direct line of descent from ancient cultures. In order to give coherence to my advancement of this complex agenda, I need to begin by addressing some general questions of cultural analysis in relation to a metaphoric process that is fundamental to linguistic perception.

At issue is how to employ contextualizing information in the development of reading strategies that reveal cultural determinants within metaphoric meaning while avoiding the critical domination that refuses to recognize elements of what is newly emergent, possibly even transgressive of older cultural categories. Recently developed psychoanalytic approaches to metaphoric functioning present alternatives to crude authoritarian imposition of cultural reference onto metaphoric terms; I want to explore the cognitive implications of psycholinguistic approaches to metaphor within the practice of cross-cultural criticism.

Norman N. Holland has cogently summarized how psychoanalytic ideas that are now part of our habitual approach to literature have effectively reshaped our expectations as readers, whether or not we are thinking in specifically psychoanalytic terms. What he wrote some years ago has proven to be a good indicator of increasingly insistent critical preoccupations. Because his summary includes reference to cognitive psychology, he also suggests some methodological parameters for any comprehensive study of metaphors of cross-cultural transfer. He notes that we now habitually

> transact literature along two of the great axes of human experience, the line of time and the boundary between self and other. Further, the literary transaction understood in the psychoanalytic way has the same shape as other acts of perception, particularly linguistic perception, as revealed by modern psycholinguistics and cognitive psychology. That is, we perceive through a preexisting schema. What we perceive is our own self-generated schema plus the differences between that schema and what comes in from outer reality. (Holland 1978, 22)

All the preexisting schemata that shape perception can be fragmented or augmented by splitting that occurs when people live culturally divided lives.

Whether we concentrate on the advantages or on the problems of a way of living that always negotiates more than one cultural style, we know that gender as a part of culture has a formative role in the development of perceptual schema. Driven by the need to theorize gender dynamics in ways that can lead to social action, feminists have productively situated much of their theory at that psycholinguistic threshold where instinctual drives meet the structuring force of symbolic reference and shape our perceptual and cognitive frames.[2] I think in particular of Julia Kristeva, whose continuing writing details the semiotic evidence of affect as it augments semantic meaning. She has greatly expanded our descriptive adequacy as we move from the general human foundations of psychoanalytic theory to those levels where specific historical and cultural significations have determining force. Her writing has incorporated more and more historical and cultural analysis as she pursues the question of how poetic language is coimplicated with all the instinctual drives that can hold semantic meaning in bondage or give joyous musical momentum to its signifying energies. And within this awareness of multiple interrelated dynamics lies the metaphoric tale that I want to trace in relation to the poetry of two Native American women. We can use foundational psycholinguistic theory like Kristeva's to facilitate an interpretive dynamic that depends on an awareness of metaphoric instrumentality as achieving a trajectory of signification which originates with primary affects and gathers traces of multiple historical and cultural specifications (the whole realm of the cognitive) along the way toward the stasis that poetic utterance eventually grants. Kristeva's theory allows the cognitive its constitutive place within the transferals that metaphor achieves and therefore within the critical narrative that maps those transferals so that we can all be held to the kind of accountability that different human communities require in order to establish the grounds for good faith exchanges and pedagogical integrity. This is a global agenda. But in order to advance it, we have to begin by examining it in its local origins.

Joy Harjo commented on her sense of this global agenda in her interview with the Italian feminist Laura Coltelli; and Harjo used the feminist community to illustrate her belief that we need to note the disjunctions as well as the conjunctions within our human networks:

> I know I walk in and out of several worlds everyday. Some overlap, some never will, or at least not as harmoniously. The word "feminism" doesn't carry over to the tribal world, but a concept mirroring similar meanings would. Let's see, what would it then be called—empowerment, some kind of empowerment. (Coltelli 1990, 60)[3]

As we all walk in and out of our several worlds, we stand at the edges of meanings and watch their mirror effects. Metaphor turns the mirrored meanings into the light show that is poetry; and the boundaries of our several worlds challenge our critical concepts. There is urgency to our attempts at greater critical adequacy because the misunderstandings that arise from our lack of knowledge about how to communicate as we daily walk in and out of our several worlds are dangerous. Contemporary political conflicts are teaching us that we must stand watch for changing meaning and renewed language; or as Joy Harjo says:

> We all watch for fire
>> for all the fallen dead to return
> and teach us a language so terrible
>>> it could resurrect us all.
>
> (18)

Walking the fire line that Hogan and Harjo show us, we can also note how each woman has developed contrasting techniques for incorporating distinctive cultural references into her work, thereby using the cognitive referential dimension of metaphorical meaning as a way to mediate between cultures. Sometimes, as in Harjo's use of Deer Woman references, cultural history establishes a connotative field whose specification dictates that we begin the critical narrative with cultural information in order, then, to trace how this level of reference extends the cultural range of metaphoric meaning through metonymic transfers that are part of an ancient tradition. References to Deer Woman, though, are more than just the evocation of a known legend with all its cultural resonances. Harjo also uses the legendary reference to point to other processes that are both new and individual. At this level of comparative analysis, we can observe two other features of cross-cultural metaphoric action. The image of the deer can reveal how basic psychological dynamics achieve alternative imagistic configurations within different cultures and how the resulting cultural cathexes configure processes guiding individual development. Then, finally, the image of the deer stands for a process whereby outsiders grasp some, but not all, of what is happening in a work of art. Reader and writer are linked in an ongoing dynamic of cultural and individual transfers that shape and control the critical narrative mediating the process.

Linda Hogan's central metaphors can illustrate a rather different use of cultural history. In Hogan's poetry, the Chickasaw tribal history of displacement from an original homeland coexists with her awareness that "we still travel together, so far / the sound is all that can find us" (1979, 9). Memory harks back to whatever can "find" the one who seeks evidence of continuity still persisting at some generally unperceived phenomenal level. The cultural and the individual searches combine to motivate a metaphoric dynamic that depends on a few central images drawn from nature as metaphoric vehicles that function to turn the phenomenal world into a text that speaks of what once was. Hogan consistently relies on imagery drawn from nature and from science. For example, something so basic as the conceptual dimension of sound becomes the connecting substance that operates across historical loss. But if we can all grasp the referential range of her specific metaphoric terms without any research into ethnohistory, we do not all necessarily understand how tribal history can affect the individual as an inescapable need to try to express the perceived continuity extending from geologic to historical time. Yet this is the need that motivates the intricate metaphoric patterning that makes Hogan's book title *Savings* into a statement of poetic purpose.

My assertions about how metaphor works to reveal cultures to each other in the very process of helping the individual poet find herself within a multicultural world can be verified only in relation to specific poems, so I want to illustrate with comparable poems from each poet so that the similarities underline the differences that characterize the two strategies I want to highlight. I also want to indicate how the featured metaphoric patterns represent important techniques and preoccupations within each woman's poetics. Harjo, of course, does not always depend on the kind of cultural reference that I describe here, and Hogan occasionally departs from the uses of natural imagery that I detail. My purpose is not to try for a complete picture of the individual poet's work. Rather, I want to suggest different possibilities for cross-cultural study of metaphor in general, and by engaging in descriptive analysis of two kinds of cross-cultural strategies, I want to encourage global comparative research.

Joy Harjo's *In Mad Love and War* is divided into two sections: the first is called "The Wars" and the second is "Mad Love." Each section begins with a poem about Deer Woman, "the myth slipped down through dreamtime. . . . The deer who crossed through knots of a curse to find us" (1990, 6). The "Mad Love" section of the book has as its epigraph lines that should remain part of any study of Harjo's deer poems: "And if I go / into the wild sweet of your eyes / will I know more / of this burning country I love?" (1990, 27).

"Deer Ghost"
1.
I hear a deer outside; her glass voice of the invisible
calls my heart to stand up and weep in this fragile city.
The season changed once more, as if my childhood
was forced from me, stolen during the dream of the lion
fleeing the old-style houses my people used to make of mud
and straw to mother the source of burning. The skeleton
of stars encircling this misty world stares through the roof;
there is no hiding any more, and mystery is a skin that will never

quite fit. This is a night ghosts wander, and in this place
they are as nameless as the nightmare the muscles in my
left hand remember.

2.

I have failed once more and let the fire go out. I misunderstood
and left my world on your musk angel wings. Your fire scorched
my lips, but it was sweet, a bitter poetry. I can taste you
now as I squat on the earth floor of this home I abandoned
for you. On this street named for a warrior people, a street
named after bravery, I am lighting the fire that crawls from my spine
to the gods with a coal from my sister's flame. This is what names
me in the ways of my people, who have called me back.
The deer knows what it is doing wandering the streets of this
city; it has never forgotten the songs.

3.

I don't care what you say. This deer is no imaginary tale
I have created to fill this house because you left me.
There is more to this world than I have ever let on
to you, or anyone.

(1990, 29)

The first stanza of "Deer Ghost" immediately establishes the poem's uncanny tonality by linking the image of the deer with the "glass voice of the invisible" and with mystery so intimate that it is the "skin that will never quite fit." Less immediately apparent is the way the house of self and language in the city of fire is a metaphoric figuration of intersubjectivity; but other poems allow us to trace basic figures of shelter all the way back to their mythic blueprint in "the old-style houses my people used to make of mud / and straw to mother the source of burning." In Harjo's poetic city, the self as shelter can enable and endure radical, pluralizing intersubjectivity, and the deer as a traditional legendary image helps us understand some of the psychological dynamics that come into the poem through the cultural associations surrounding the image of the deer. These associations alone, however, do not account for the impact of the poem. That is a much more subtle and individual matter bound up with all that is implied by the verse beginning the second stanza: "I have failed once more and let the fire go out." The loved one to whom the poem is addressed has her own fire that scorches the lips, and "the bitter poetry" of otherness compels the poet to return to shelter and light the traditional fire "that crawls from my spine / to the gods with a coal from my sister's flame" because "[t]his is what names / me in the ways of my people, who have called me back."

Fire and passion are so inevitably bound in popular imagination that a reader uncritically accepts that obvious association, especially since the poem is addressed to a loved one. But references to the deer interrupt the slippage along well-known associative paths and add cognitive features deriving from the cultural memory of an indigenous nation that kept its sacred fire burning even as it was relocated away from its hereditary homeland. The image of the deer has features of meaning that only the historical legend can reveal. As the poet tells us, "The deer knows what it is doing wandering the streets of this / city; it has never forgotten the songs."

Because the deer who never forgets the songs is a familiar figure in Harjo's poetry and beyond it in the oral traditions of many Native American peoples, we can begin a first stage explication of her mediations by examining the oral traditions.[4] Deer Women stories are among the most enduring legends in the Great Plains. In most tales, deer assume the form of women and seduce men, who are then caught in a passion that can find no appropriate outlet since it draws them to a being they can never possess. Some stories tell about how only the very strongest of these men can be cured. Other tales end in death for men who cannot sustain the call of Deer Woman. In addition, there are rare tales about encounters between women and deer spirits. Comparing the two kinds of stories, we can see how Deer Woman sets up distinctions that divide along the lines of gender. Women have quite different experiences from men when they meet her. Generally an encounter leaves the woman with amazing artistic talent, and stories are sometimes quite clear about the connection between art and redirected sexual energies. These women also intensify their bonds with other women. Deer sirens from the woods alert everyone that the uncanny introjected is a powerful force, capable of destructuring and restructuring all of our libidinal energies and of unleashing the creativity of all those they call.

Deer Woman frames the experience of the uncanny, gives it cultural expression by giving it a narrative frame and a legendary path to pursue through history. Deer Woman is a mediator, and she achieves some of the basic transferals and translations that we need to appreciate how other key metaphors function in Harjo's poetry. Yet she never gives away all of her secrets. She just sets up the mirror play of possibilities as we compare cultural understandings. Therefore, this pattern of reference also works to define the critical task as one that sets forth the cognitive detailing needed to establish appreciation for alternative semiotic processes without pretense of informational mastery over another's way of experiencing what we only partially understand. At this stage of analysis, we can switch to Kristeva's "semiology of the uncanny," which expands and reinterprets Freudian insights. If we can follow the trail of the uncanny that Kristeva marks, then we can compare that path with the one Deer Woman treads. Both the differences and the similarities point toward psycholinguistic foundations for cultural studies and the place of metaphoric mediations within such studies.

In a sentence that could act as a summation of all the stories and poems about Deer Woman, Kristeva tells us: "To worry or to smile, such is the choice when we are assailed by the strange; our decision depends on how familiar we are with our own ghosts" (1991, 191).[5] Reading Kristeva's analysis of the uncanny from the perspective of Harjo's Deer Woman in the streets of the city of self and language, we can see how Freud and Kristeva after him have sought language within European conceptual frameworks to represent dynamics that Deer Woman dramatizes in cultures where she is a living narrative presence. The critic who stands between these two perspectives is transposing over and over again, back and forth from the key of psychoanalysis and semiotics to the key of legend—back and forth from cognitive experience to conceptual language—back and forth from Euro-American cultural history to cultures whose origins and mainsprings are outside these histories, even though wars, colonization, and domination have introduced terrifying tensions into the relational contexts that link us all. Translation and transposition teach us as much about what does not cross over as they do about how to transfer.

Kristeva's purposes for studying the semiology of the uncanny are certainly consistent with the goals of studies like this one.

> It is through unraveling transference—the major dynamics of otherness, of love/hatred for the other, of the foreign component of our psyche—that, on the basis of the other, I become reconciled with my own otherness-foreignness, that I play on it and live by it. Psychoanalysis is then experienced as a journey into the strangeness of the other and of oneself, toward an ethics of respect for the irreconcilable. (1991, 182)

But in order to apply Kristeva's analysis to another culture, we also have to be ready to alter and expand her focus somewhat. She addresses the experience of the uncanny throughout her many books, but it is particularly central to the arguments pursued in *Strangers to Ourselves* (1991). This recent work, as the American book jacket tells us, "examines estrangement from self, country and mother tongue." The history she uses to examine the construction of categories of otherness is European, a fact that emphasizes the need for comparative work. At the end of *Strangers to Ourselves,* Kristeva attempts the first stages of a semiology of the uncanny.

Kristeva begins her narrative of otherness on grounds that are now as familiar to us as the first motifs of an often told fairy tale. Once upon a time, "the archaic, narcissistic self, not yet demarcated by the outside world," began to project outward what is dangerous to the self. That projection can return as the malevolent other. "Such malevolent powers would amount to a weaving together of the symbolic and the organic—perhaps drive itself, on the border of the psyche and biology, overriding the breaking imposed by organic homeostasis" (1991, 185).

Then the familiar tale takes some unforeseen turns. The link between anguish and the uncanny constitutes a crossroads. It can lead to psychotic symptoms and fearful representations, or it can serve to achieve an opening toward the new. The second option, the opening toward the new, almost an afterthought for Freud, is Kristeva's point of emphasis. She can then use this possibility as a way to observe the beneficent effects of the uncanny in literature and in culture. As she makes this move away from the controlling other, she also opens her psycholinguistic theoretical frames to more productive political analysis, because she shows a first-stage framing of an ethics of equality that removes the interiorized other from a position of domination and establishes the psychological foundations for mutuality and equality.

> The clash with the other, the identification of the self with that good or bad other that transgresses the fragile boundaries of the uncertain self, would thus be at the source of an uncanny strangeness whose excessive features, as represented in literature, cannot hide its permanent presence in "normal" psychical dynamics. (Kristeva 1991, 188–89)

The uncanny is always excessive. It burns like fire. And we all know its existence within ourselves. But whether the fire harms or helps depends on the moment at the crossroads when we look at what the uncanny projects and view it either as a demonic or a beneficent guide. Kristeva would have us believe that the confrontation at the crossroads has urgent cultural implications for us all because the projected demonic uncanny easily takes on the face and form of anyone we deem strange, and when we try to banish the demon, we tragically turn against those in our midst whose meanings should mirror our own and thereby resist the aspect of ourselves that can lead us out of our narcissistic prisons in amazed wonder at all we can hope to encounter. Kristeva's simple but socially unrealized point is that if we recognize the uncanny in ourselves, we can also respond to strangers in our midst with the recognition that arises from mutual need.

Finally, we can conclude our rapid summary in a way that lets us return to Deer Woman in the streets of Harjo's poetic city. The paths from affect to representation to literature that Kristeva points out are semiotically marked trails letting us go from abstract, psycholinguistic conceptualizations to imagistically concrete forms in order to understand how "the sense of strangeness is a mainspring for identification with the other, by working out its depersonalizing impact by means of astonishment" (1991, 189).

The Deer Woman legend charts the same path. Its different cultural specificity, however, shifts aspects of how the self confronts otherness. The most basic and easily understood differences all derive from the fact that the legend provides a communally transmitted means for cultures to accept what is meant by the last verse, "[t]here is more to this world than I have ever let on / to you, or anyone." All the mystery for which Deer Woman stands acts as an ongoing counterbalance for the fact that "In this language there are no words for how the real world / collapses" (1990, 5). The legend reflects how cultures have found ways to cope with collapses of reason and structure. It carries these ancient encounters with mystery into the possibilities of cross-cultural interactional dynamics.

Harjo's culturally distinct cognitive and relational style, brought into the poem by reference to the legend, shows how metaphoric mediations between cultures can depend upon a history of represented interactional dynamics that safeguard options within psycholinguistic parameters. Because mythic metaphors represent primary negotiations between affect and symbol, their function is to convey an affective heritage in tandem with a linguistic one; and they reveal how affect can shift poetic significations ranging from rhythm to discursive structures. Critical commentary on poems using this strategy requires presentation of cultural information that shows how any given mythic reference establishes metonymic transfers that function as a traditional basis from which to move toward what is new. Therefore, registering the signifying energy of any living tradition is a process that begins with cultural specification only to use what is thus understood to chart the path of metaphoric trajectories within which mythic nominations acquire more and more significance in the particular textual and intertextual world of a poem. Harjo characterizes this metaphoric process as a journey.

> I no longer see the poem as an ending point, perhaps more the end of a journey, an often long journey that can begin years earlier, say with the blur of the memory of the sun on someone's cheek, a certain smell, an ache, and will culminate years later in a poem, sifted through a point, a lake in my heart through which language must come. That's what I work with, with my students at the university, opening that place within them of original language, which I believe must be in everyone, but not everyone can reach it. (Coltelli 1990, 68)

Harjo's poetry, always "original language," teaches that the place of that language, that fire, is a shelter enabling the poet to endure openness toward others and intersubjectivity. The creating self can use language to build imagined shelter only after abjection and rejection, all the painful, psychological coordinates of love's singling out, gathering in, and sending forth have been given their positive valences and turned inside out, as ability to release others into their own freedom.

In its complex intertextual existence, the Deer Woman narrative also sets up a gender-specific play of difference within a dynamic that has already been marked as culture bound. Deer Woman gave sanction to women's independence. (Reading Louise Erdrich's novels *Tracks* [1988] and *Love Medicine* [1984b] from this perspective proves illuminating.) If one marks the differences at work within the Deer Woman narrative traditions in terms of inside/outside (wilderness/inhabited space); male/female; and cultural insider/cultural outsider, then the resulting combinatory variables let us trace the impact of Deer Woman's legendary actions across several different conceptual registers. If she catalyzes encounters with what is outside the sphere of the ordinary, she also structures that encounter with an imagistic fullness that sets up relations appropriate to different subjective positionings. She represents a culturally distinct cognitive style that orchestrates gender dynamics along with those of insider and outsider.

My analysis of metaphoric configurations within Harjo's poetry suggests the subtle but precise permutations of signification that occur through historical markings within metaphoric significance. I would not want to suggest that every legendary reference found within Native American women's poetry or novels has such historical resonances with psycholinguistic and therefore cognitive import. Many do. History, though, can shape metaphor through means that affect cognition without depending on psycholinguistic variations. Linda Hogan's work illustrates an approach to historical understanding that leads to other kinds of choices of central metaphors with different cognitive import.

Fishing

Stones go nowhere
while the river rushes them
dark with rain.
Fish are pulled out of their lives
by red-armed women on the banks
of vertigo.

What is living
but to grow smaller,
undress another skin
or scale
away rough edges
the way rivers cut mountains
down to heart.

We already know the history of sand,
and how days pass.
We know water and air
trying to break the spirit of stone.

We know our teeth grinding down
to their pith.

We know flint
all the way down to fire.
Go nowhere, be the fire.
Wait here for a nibble, you fishwomen,
stand where light is pared to a spark.
Be dust
growing to life.

(1988, 22)

Hogan's need for access to cultural memories was first experienced as devastating, irremediable loss. Her Chickasaw heritage first came into her life as the "secret" of "never having a home" (1978, 17). Like the Creek nation to which Harjo belongs, the Chickasaws were forcibly removed from their ancestral territory in the American Southeast to the plains of Oklahoma. They endured "the long walk" over hundreds of miles to new homes in a region drastically different from what they had known earlier.

Chickasaw
chikkih asachi, which means
they left as a tribe not a great while ago.
They are always leaving, those people

(1978, 27)

By confronting the negativity of loss, of not having a home, Hogan learns to see the negative as absence and therefore as sign of a former presence. Absence turns the world into a text that speaks what once was, and the poet listens to learn that

the wind in leaves
feeds fire
gives you dreams
and words
to move your lives.

(1981, 15)

Listening lets the poet register a call to a self that is home. As we saw in Harjo's poems, the fire of home is the fire of life, and that awareness lets the poet enter the significance of the historical past as she learns how it has shaped her subjective consciousness. There is more to history, though, than what we usually find in books, and Hogan's historical references are far more inclusive than the temporal frames of historiographic narrative can ordinarily accommodate. The poem "Fishing" tells us, "We already know the history of sand," and "We know flint / all the way down to fire." Furthermore, we can "be the fire." We too are part of the physical world; therefore, our knowing opens us to dimensions of existence that let us make hitherto unknown connections whereby poetic language can echo within loss, becoming both its emblem and sublimated object. The imagery that Hogan draws from physics and geology flows from this conjunction between personal need, cultural experience, and the psycholinguistic transferals that imbue universal images with motives arising from historical knowledge.

Hogan asks us to think of a translation process even more basic than that which occurs between cultures. It involves listening to the life that is within all form, including geological form, so that the text that form itself is can tell the story within which the ethnohistorical specifics of any one person's experiences are a subtext. This subtext is important and indispensable but always just a part of the global telling that sustains all our memories of loss by linking them to the physicist's knowledge that cosmic matter is transformed, not lost, as our universe evolves. The text of form records "The Truth of the Matter." Hogan's poem with that title tells us that

> Stars go on forever
> about their lives.
> Thank heaven,
> . . . .
> emptiness admits it wants to steal your breath
> but didn't I know it all along,
> hearing those stars chatting
> with their brothers, the stones,
> and telling the truth.
>
> (1988, 47)

The poet attunes her listening to "the truth of the matter," and her task becomes one of registering the distinctions among different voices in the cosmic chorus. She has to recognize the sameness as well as the otherness in the voices she hears so as to achieve imagistic specification that is also translation and transferal.

> the other voices speak
> and they are mine
> and they are not mine
> and I hear them

> and I don't,
> and even police can't stop earth telling
>
> (1988, 46)

As she listens and transfers what she hears into the sounds and rhythms of poetic language, Hogan knows that translation from one kind of telling to another is an enabling prelude to other kinds of cross-cultural communication precisely because it allows the conditions of survival for different peoples and cultures and thereby sets up the relational terms for communication among all survivors. Translation among forms is fundamentally educative because it teaches us what it is to know something "all the way down to fire." Even this phrase, which I am borrowing to sum up the substance and purpose of this entire critical transpositional exercise, is based on the extended, slow temporality and the transformative force of geological life that women know by analogy to their somatic existence. Women, listening to their bodies, are attuned to the slow processes of dust growing to the spark of life. From this somatic knowing to hearing is already a synesthetic transfer. Our bodies teach the attentiveness that is a prelude to hearing. And from their listening, the women speak. Phonic substance gets transformed to phonemic significance. Sound breaches the divide between individuals and between past and present. It is inherent in all form. It is an image of what endures beyond transformation in order to emerge as originary sign of the process that melds endurance into meaning.

> Something lives in everything
> In stone
> metal becomes a bell
> and takes hold of silence
>
> (1983, 60)

Sound is evidence of ultimate anteriority. For Hogan the origin of the universe, the big bang, becomes guarantee of connection with her own culture in spite of exile and losses because it is evidence that sound ultimately connects all times and places. This scientific understanding serves as the foundation for her metaphoric uses of sound to recover the cultural past through her own listening. Laura Coltelli also interviewed Hogan. Statements from that interview point directly to the importance of sound in the dynamic of transfers that constitute Hogan's complex poetic agenda.

> Everything speaks. I have a friend, Flying Clouds, who one time said, "Some people are such good listeners the trees lean toward them to tell their secrets." I think that's true. When I wrote that poem ["Blessing"] I thought about my

family that we were the last in our own blood group, the last Indian people—
which wasn't true at all—but at the time I thought of Indian people as vanish-
ing and that our stories and histories were disappearing. In some ways I got
that idea from public education, from white education. They want us to
believe we don't exist. I realize now that the stories are eternal. They will go on
as long as there are people to speak them. And the people will always be there.
The people will listen to the world and translate it into a human tongue. That
is the job of the poet. (Coltelli 1990, 72)

With this description of listening, Hogan indicates how and why she rearranges
our commonplace dialogical priorities giving the place of privilege to listening
rather than to speech. "What do we have left / except the mirage of sound?"
(1983, 9). Listening is radically preliminary to responsive speech because it is the
only act that can lead speech back to narrative origins; it is an act of receptive
somatic interiorization that precedes exteriorizing speech and authorizes the
speaker. It is how we come to know something "all the way down to fire."

By making the conceptual dimensions of sound into a basic metaphoric vehi-
cle, Hogan extends the temporality of her poems and slows its pace to the near
stasis of geological time. Within the minimal temporal progression of Hogan's
poems, we can observe as action what would appear to be static if observed at
our ordinary perceptual tempo, and we learn to ask "[w]hat is living / but to grow
smaller?" Even more fundamental is the way we endure our living to "the way
rivers cut mountains / down to heart."

Several different imagistic features of the cosmologically bound life process
that Hogan listens for and fights to sustain are present in the poem "The Sand
Roses." With that poem we can follow how listening to voices audible only
through Hogan's slow temporality of exile becomes a cross-cultural dynamic. She
shows transfers based on listening that take her from culture to culture, from
Crazy Horse to Nijinski, through a hearing that occurs at a level created and
expressed by the poem. Her poem begins with a series of synesthetic transferals
that connect Hogan's metaphors of temporal transfer. The poet listening achieves
such exquisite attentiveness that she can hear flowers forming:

> as once I heard
> invisible hooves of elk
> . . . .
> and heard the breastplate of Crazy Horse,
> a man who listened to stones
>
> (1985, 61)

Gradually the reference to the stone that Crazy Horse carried with him becomes
an inclusive one, linking different persons in many lands before leading the

poet inward and backward through time to "the ancient ones that burn inside us." In this poem we can see again how "thin flesh" is a moving boundary between different life forms whose development through time is a continuing transformation of everything "born of nothing" light years ago.

> It was on his breast,
> that song
> that bone plate
> that thin flesh
> over lungs and heart, on skin
> moving across the land,
> the song of all people in a stone
> he wore beneath his arm.
>
> Beyond time,
> beyond space
> Nijinski heard that stone
> and danced his body into the shape
> of Guernica and war.
> Who didn't know
> gods live in stone and in our bodies,
> that inside each other's skin
> we hear voices
> in the solar plexus
> the heart
> the ancient ones that burn inside us
> rising up from nothing
> in the dark fields of ourselves
> Like roses

(1985, 61)

Within the "dark fields of ourselves" we hear the voices of "the ancient ones that burn inside us," and what we hear may have already been transfered across cultural boundaries, just as Nijinski heard Crazy Horse's message and danced in magnificent response. In Hogan's poetry listening anneals loss, lets what was lost live again in new forms. Thus any evidence of form can be a starting point for a translation process that moves from culture to culture, filling in the details that once belonged to a concrete but transitory historical realization of form. Yet, if Hogan's poetics of transferal establish a coalition able to gather in members from everywhere and all times, it never assimilates the differences. The women speak in their own tongues; they wear the costumes of their own nations. Crazy Horse has his personal story, as do Picasso and Nijinski. The poet asks us to be true to each story and what it can bring into her poems where sound establishes relationships among the stories.

Knowing all the way down to fire is different from feeling or intuiting all the way down to fire. Knowing implies cognitive and conceptual determinations that Hogan's metaphors of fire never destroy. The sound that survives fire is the raw material for a speaking that continues the many stories of people in different nations. The cognitive force implied by knowing is of particular importance when the histories in question incorporate the endangered stories of exiles and the survivors of genocide.

Cognitive Style and Poetic Metaphor

Hogan's cognitive transferals bring us back to the requirements and possibilities of the critical narrative. Poetry invokes and evokes. Criticism specifies and achieves supplemental translations. The critical narrative that begins in cautious and informed response to poetry has to negotiate carefully its points of transfer from imagistic to conceptual registers, from the syntax of poetic form to the logical structures of critical narrative, from the markings of subjective agency to cultural determinant. If the poetry crosses in and out of different cultural worlds, critics also have to traverse more than one cognitive territory, mapping the semiotic formations we discover in each. Within the poetic territories we explore, some semiotic formations arise from the workings of gender, some from the influence of culture, and many from interactions between gender and culture that can only be understood with respect to definite times and places.

Our mappings of the cognitive territories within which poets situate themselves have all the risks of our political situation. Even if the statements we make do not have particular political reference, our way of structuring the cognitive dimensions of our argument is implicitly bound to cultural politics. That is why I want to safeguard the hesitations that are an honest element in cross-cultural responses to poetry, just as I want alternatively to stress the determinations imposed by ethnohistorical reference within the trajectory of metaphorical signification. This weaving between critical hesitation and authority uses the exclusivity of pragmatic specification to inaugurate a relational responsiveness within which hesitation marks the moment of recognition. Gayatri Chakravorty Spivak further describes what is at stake as we explore the dimensions of the cognitive middle ground between image and concept that metaphor allows us to negotiate. In "Explanation and Culture: Marginalia," Spivak turns her formidably discerning ability toward the "ferocious apartheid" that opposes the literalist language of the conceptualism of pure theory to the "entrenched privatism" of many approaches to metaphor. Privatism drives metaphor out of political play by claiming a special status for metaphor that either holds it so rigidly to conceptual standards that it can never challenge their epistemological limits or assigns it a radical freeplay of signification that has only the contrived links of artifice to bring poetic significance into pragmatic relationships with our conceptual frames.

Using examples from Giambattista Vico and Wallace Stevens, Spivak deconstructs the "marginalization between metaphor and concept" to show

> not only that no pure theory of metaphor is possible, because any pre-metaphoric base of discussion must already assume the distinction between theory and metaphor; but also that no priority, by the same token, can be given to metaphor, since every metaphor is contaminated and constituted by its conceptual justification. If neither metaphor nor concept is given priority (or both are), the passage of poetry above could be taught as a *serious* objection to the privileging of theory that takes place when humanists gather to discuss "cultural explanations." (Spivak 1987, 115)

Spivak's examples are meant to emphasize "the conceptuality of poetic language and the metaphoricity of historical language *to similar pedagogical ends*" (Spivak 1987, 117), all of them requiring the mutuality of the interpreting relationship to which poetry like Harjo's and Hogan's issues an invitation to feminists.

The cognitive middle ground, strategically established through metaphoric mediations like the ones I have been describing, allows us a way out of the apartheid and politically neutralizing views that Spivak deplores because it frames an analytic stance that engages socially contingent conceptual meaning through the metonymic transfers that any culture necessarily sets in play. Culture functions less as definition (the semantic register) than as associative and interactive entailment (the cognitive register). Culture sets up interactional expectations; it does not define the outcomes of interactions. When metaphors cross cultural boundaries, they carry their original cognitive determinations and potentialities while they add to them the weight of another culture's significations, and the combinations push both sets of signifying features toward new interrelationships. In poetry, the interweaving of different meaning traces is even more intricate than in other discursive formations because the poetic voice gathers more of its force from desire.

Poetry has a unique place in cultural analysis, not because of its autotelic character but because of its desiring drive toward the revelation and innovation that has to distinguish whose history is being gathered into the momentum. Poetry's metaphoric impetus is toward limits of all kinds in order to reach beyond them; but as it reveals the limits of culture, it also emphasizes the originary energy channeled through these limits:

> I am an arrow, painted
>   with lighting
> to seek the way to the name of the enemy,
>   but the arrow has now created
> its own language.
>
>   (1990, 9)

Once when I tried to replay this argument for an anthropologist, he interrupted my description of how basic cultural metaphors establish a process of analogical entailment and he exclaimed: "But that is the definition of culture!" He was right, of course. The tropological resources that "define" any culture function in a multicultural world as epistemological and poetic radicals, basic starting points for extensions of cultural knowing. But that is only part of their task in cross-cultural discursive formations. They also launch moves away from what any one culture defines and alternatively back to what cultures have preserved for those exiled from them. That too may just be what culture does; but this intercultural dynamic has not been given much place in our critical narratives about the workings of culture within literary forms. Poets have been better than ethnologists or cultural historians at showing us how metaphors can usher their users in and out of worlds and ways of knowing. Poetry that springs from this back-and-forth movement orchestrates a unique metaphoric dynamic depending sometimes on the stability of determined reference, sometimes on the energy of destabilized determinations.

In the process of becoming more adept at noting cultural determinants as well as innovative departures from them, we will have taken important steps toward teaching about metaphor's most basic transpositional operations. In cross-cultural contexts, we linger over basic narrative positioning because it represents the most politically sensitive aspect of our work. We do not want our critical narratives to impose ever more clever but inappropriate determinisms; nor do we want the whole enterprise to hover in well-meaning suspension among optional empathetic responses with minimal institutional efficacy. Bringing the analysis of cognitive style into a working relationship with thinking about metaphor and culture helps us deflect the institutionalized will to power by confronting it with its own social contingency and the metaphoric foundations of all human cognition. Those central metaphors that I am calling the metaphors of cultural transfer always bind an associational network that is also a semiotic guide to fundamental cultural dynamics. Some metaphors of transfer come straight from myth or legend. Deer Woman is an intriguing example. Others, like the ethnohistorical significations of loss as they are bound to images in Hogan's poetry, require more indirect analytic effort. Nevertheless, Hogan's use of poetry to place images that spring from a radically expanded temporality is as characteristic a cultural task as anything that the mythic figure of Deer Woman can subsume.

The awareness of need for women's empowerment that is Harjo's Native American endorsement of the feminist movement intensifies the need to give poetic realization to relational networks that can go beyond exile to transformation and to renewed recognition of commonalities and differences. In the last paragraph of her historical novel *Mean Spirit* (1990), Hogan identifies a characteristic moment of history that shaped a whole range of cognitive presuppositions at work among survivors within cultures where a history of genocide always exerts determinate force within personal histories:

> They looked back once and saw it all rising up in the reddened sky, the house, the barn, the broken string of lights, the life they had lived, nothing more than a distant burning. No one spoke. But they were alive. They carried generations along with them, into the prairie and through it, to places where no road had been cut before them. They traveled past houses that were like caves of light in the black world. The night was on fire with their pasts and they were alive.

The poets Harjo and Hogan are alive too; and so are the cultures in which their central metaphors originate. The critical narrative recognizes the cultural life through ethnohistorical specification, but it also has to safeguard a place for the individual who reaches irrepressibly toward the future. Highlighting the creativity of women who are poets gives us amazed pause. Hesitation has its moment in our response and in our critical language.

NOTES

1. A member of the Creek nation, Joy Harjo was born in Tulsa, Oklahoma, in 1951. She has taught Native American literature and creative writing at many different universities and colleges and is currently teaching at the University of Arizona in Tucson. Her best-known publications include two collections of poems, *She Had Some Horses* (1983) and *In Mad Love and War* (1990). *Secrets from the Center of the World* (1989) is a book of poetic prose responses to photographs by Stephen Strom.

Linda Hogan is a member of the Chickasaw nation. She was born in Denver, but she grew up in Gene Autry, Oklahoma. She received a master's degree in English and creative writing from the University of Colorado, where she now teaches creative writing and American Indian literature. She also taught at the University of Minnesota, and she has been poet-in-residence for the Oklahoma and the Colorado Arts Councils. Her first book of poetry was *Calling Myself Home* (1978). Her other collections of poems include *Daughters, I Love You* (1981), *Eclipse* (1983), *Seeing through the Sun* (1985), and *Savings* (1988). She has also published a novel, *Mean Spirit* (1990).

2. For a recent article that addresses contemporary feminist theory and its relationship to the criticism of poetry, see Linda A. Taylor's " 'A Seizure of Voice': Language Innovation

and a Feminist Poetics in the Works of Kathleen Fraser." Taylor recognizes her indebtedness to the critical work of Marianne DeKoven and quotes DeKoven in a way that is relevent to this article. "The fact that one hardly ever sees [women]writers . . . mentioned in print except by one another is particularly surprising given the widespread interest among feminist critics in 'French theory,' which emphasizes precisely the kinds of formal dislocations these writers employ" (1992, 337).

See also Chaviva Hošek and Patricia Parker's *Lyric Poetry* (1985), a collection of essays addressing relationships between theory and poetry. Jonathan Arac's "Afterword: Lyric Poetry and the Bounds of New Criticism" provocatively frames questions about the current emphasis on literary language and our professional habits of comparison as they are based on institutional teaching of canonical literature. He reminds us that intertextuality has had limited application to the study of poetry because it is assumed to be canonical intertextuality. He also reminds us that "intertextual reading prods into consciousness cultural traces that we wish—in some happier time—could remain unconscious but that we know now would not otherwise exist at all" (1985, 349). The minimal representation of feminist positions is notable in this collection of essays designed to provoke new agendas of poetry.

3. Laura Coltelli's *Winged Words: American Indian Writers Speak* (1990) also includes interviews with Paula Gunn Allen, Louise Erdrich, Wendy Rose, Leslie Marmon Silko, and several male writers.

4. For a representative transcription of an oral tale from the Great Plains, see Ella Deloria's *Dakota Texts* (1932). For examples of literary uses of the traditional tale, see the chapter entitled "Crown of Thorns" in Louise Erdrich's *Love Medicine* (1984b). Erdrich has a poem about Deer Woman in *Jacklight* (1984a). Paula Gunn Allen has written a short story, "Deer Woman," that is set in Oklahoma (1991).

5. In *Black Sun* Kristeva sketches the therapeutic role she sees for literature:

the line of questioning that I shall pursue could be summed up as follows: aesthetic and particularly literary creation, and also religious discourse in its imaginary, fictional essence, set forth a device whose prosodic economy, interaction of characters, and implicit symbolism constitute a very faithful semiological representation of the subject's battle with symbolic collapse. Such a literary representation is not an *elaboration* in the sense of "becoming aware" of the inter- and intrapsychic causes of moral suffering; that is where it diverges from the psychoanalytic course, which aims at dissolving this symptom. Nevertheless the literary (and religious) representation possesses a real and imaginary effectiveness that comes closer to catharsis than to elaboration; it is a therapeutic device used in all societies throughout the ages. If psychoanalysts think they are more efficacious, notably through strengthening the subject's cognitive possibilities, they also owe it to themselves to enrich their practice by paying greater attention to these sublimatory solutions to our crises, in order to be lucid counterdepressants rather than neutralizing antidepressants. (1989, 24–25)

"An Utterance More Pure Than Word": Gender and the Corrido Tradition in Two Contemporary Chicano Poems

Teresa McKenna

me encorporé a las filas por
  una mujer bonita
Soy soldado de la levita, de esos
  de las filas del movimiento
                Juan Gómez-Quiñones, "The Ballad of Billy Rivera"

I come from a long line of eloquent illiterates
whose history reveals what words don't say.
Our anger is our way of speaking,
the gesture is an utterance more pure than word.
           (Lorna Dee Cervantes, "Visions of Mexico while at a
           Writing Symposium in Port Townsend, Washington")

The corrido tradition has long been constructed by primarily male Chicano scholars as a male-dominated genre that takes as its root a narrative of Chicano/Mexicano history centered on social conflict. As Américo Paredes has studied this narrative ballad form, the poem originates from the conflict arising out of the encroachment of Anglo Americans into the South Texas valley in the latter half of the nineteenth century, and the response of the resident Spanish/Mexican population that had established its presence in that territory since the Spanish settlement in the eighteenth century.

Since the publication of Paredes's classic study of "The Ballad of Gregorio Cortez," *With His Pistol in His Hand: A Border Ballad and Its Hero* (1958), this narrative song has achieved a metonymy with the corrido form itself for many Chicano scholars. The master story relates the exploits of Gregorio Cortez, a man who is accused of horse stealing by an Anglo American sheriff and who, because of a misapprehension of language, engages in an altercation with the law resulting in the wounding of Cortez's brother and the death of the sheriff. This leads Cortez to dash across half the state of Texas to the border with Mexico, where he gives himself up to authorities because of reprisals that have been taken against his family and community. The social narrative is encapsulated in Cortez's stance of defending himself, "con su pistola en la mano" (with his pistol in his hand), a phrase that frequently punctuates the ballad verses. The generic corrido, as studied by Paredes 1958, 1964, 1976; and later by Limón 1983, 1986b, 1992; R. Saldívar 1990; J.D. Saldívar 1991; McDowell 1972, 1981; Herrera-Sobek 1990; and others, is a heroic tradition with close ties to the epic and to Spanish romantic forms. It is also, in their opinion, particularly in the master story about Cortez, a quintessentially Mexicano/Chicano genre because it narrates the broad dimensions of Mexicano/Chicano history as a story of conquest and resistance to geopolitical and cultural domination.

In both Limón's and Ramón Saldívar's analysis, the corrido functions as a poetic and narrative influence on the development of Chicano literature. They construct a history out of the corrido narrative and take this to stand for a much larger and more complex set of historical circumstances that they project fall into this paradigmatic story.[1] The corrido narrative, told not only through the "Ballad of Gregorio Cortez" but also through similar heroic songs about social resistors, centers on the exploits of men who take the burden of action on their shoulders and fight against all odds in order to resist political or cultural annihilation. This story, it has been argued, resonates in contemporary Chicanos' fight to maintain political and cultural autonomy in their twentieth-century battles to deflect assaults on their own community's economic, cultural, and political integrity.

Using Victor Turner's (1974) formulation of the social drama, Limón (1986b, 1992) argues that in "greater Mexican history" there are at least two phases to this master story, which he identifies as integrated social dramas. The periods coincide with the years 1890–1930 (that time of cultural conflict following the Mexican American War and the Mexican Revolution), and 1966–1972 (the era of the development of the Chicano Movement in the United States, beginning with the United Farmworkers' struggle and ending with the flowering of the Chicano student movement on college campuses). Limón articulates a master narrative of social and poetic influence based not only on the historical playing out of events, but also on the intellectual influence of Chicano scholar Américo Paredes and his classic study of the border corrido as well as his role in the construction of a prototypical Chicano "history" (Limón 1986c, 1992). By melding together the Turnerian social drama and its foundation on processual events, with an equal emphasis on Bloomian anxiety-of-influence theory, Limón fleshes out a provocative argument uncovering both the connections between the corrido narrative and Chicano scholarship, and the extent to which both of these are rooted in patriarchal tradition (1986b, 1986c, 1992).[2]

The strength and influence of the master story of cultural conflict, as Limón cautions, remains essentially male, despite efforts by scholars to account for a female presence in the corrido narrative through a reading of the story's gaps. The resonances of a female voice are never accounted for fully or explained in dialectical relationship to the dominant song of the male singer, in male-centered chronotopes of performance and, of course, in the process of the construction of the history itself. The female is reduced to archetype (Herrera-Sobek 1990), or to androgynous possibility in her absence from the narrative (Limón 1992).[3]

By noting how the corrido narrative has been constructed as a border ballad, as well as focusing upon the evolution of the corrido form in contemporary Chicano narrative poetics, we can more clearly understand the transformative role that female subjectivity plays in the development of Chicano narrative poetic form. Particularly with the development of the Chicano Movement and the flowering of Chicano poetry in the latter half of the twentieth century, both male and female poets find significance in the ballad narratives and appropriate aspects of the corrido into their poetic form. Juan Gómez-Quiñones's "The Ballad of Billy Rivera" (1974) and Lorna Dee Cervantes's "Visions of Mexico while at a Writing Symposium in Port Townsend, Washington" (1981) are fruitful examples of the legacy of this tradition; they also represent significant benchmarks of its dissolution.

Here I would like to isolate two areas of comparison in these poems that underscore the different appropriations of the ballad narrative by these contemporary Chicano poets, and to explore how these areas intersect with the use of gendered narrative voice. In both instances, I will argue, the poets reject the efficacy of the Chicano master narrative as constructed in much of Chicano scholarship. They attempt to nullify the hold of patriarchal propositions about history, culture, and politics by altering the male-centered voice of the corrido. Their multivocalic play with the corrido form undermines the exclusionary effect of a history told without women, and which is inadequate to speak for the multidimensioned politics of the later twentieth century. First I will examine what constitutes tradition, both narratively and philosophically, for Juan Gómez-Quiñones and Lorna Dee Cervantes; second, I will consider the force of narrative event and spatial placement of the political sphere within the text—that is, land, home, creative space, all of which constitute that which is contested politically. For these Chicano writers this latter aspect has been homogenized into a dialogue regarding "Mexico," the border and the figural implications of this sociopsycho-political region. By manipulating gendered narrative voice, these two writers challenge and ultimately subvert the terms of the master narrative of Chicano/Mexicano history as constructed over time. To a greater extent in "Visions" than in "Billy Rivera," the force of narrative is rejuvenated within the subversive speaking voice of a female subject.

"The Ballad of Billy Rivera"

"The Ballad of Billy Rivera" opens Juan Gómez-Quiñones's volume *5th and Grande Vista: Poems 1960–1973* (1974). Gómez-Quiñones, Chicano historian, poet, and cultural critic, has been a long-standing figure in the Chicano Movement and a leader in the development of the discipline of Chicano Studies. This book of poetry not only chronicles his personal experience but also reflects his reconsideration of the future of Chicano politics. We are alerted to this fact by the addition of the following epigraph, included on the cover and title page of the collection: "Austin {TEXAS}, primera frontera Spring 1973." Long before border consciousness and border studies had become popular with Chicano critics, Gómez-Quiñones acknowledges the sociopolitical importance of borderness. The "primera frontera" (first border) suggests psychopolitical borders that are yet to be encountered. The phrase underscores the border as an ongoing process, a figure for the personal and historical commentary that will be reflected in the collection's poems. As we will see, the intersection of personal history and politics is central to this poem.

In his extended analysis of the influence of the corrido protopoem on "Billy Rivera," Limón has argued persuasively about Gómez-Quiñones's oscillation between the tradition of the narrative posed by the male corrido tradition and song, and the unfolding political historical narrative of Chicano politics at the height of the Chicano student movement of the late 1960s and early 1970s (Limón 1992). It is clear that Gómez-Quiñones not only operates within Mexican male belles lettres and oral folk narrative tradition, but he also negotiates the Western cultural legacy espoused by writers such as Whitman and T.S. Eliot. Gómez-Quiñones's poem moves complexly and intertextually within several embedded, inherited narrative strains.

There is no doubt that the corrido as a heroic tradition and canto (song) in its generic sense is at the center of this poem. Concomitantly, Eliot and his particular brand of modernism are equally at the core of his text.[4] In the first stanza of the prologue, "Canto al trabajador" (Song to the worker), we are told: "todos los meses son crueles / para ellos de las manos esculpidas" ("All the months are cruel for those with calloused hands") (Gómez-Quiñones 1974, 7). The speaker alters the famous lines from *The Waste Land* to underscore the difference between the ennui of the upper class and the despair of the worker (Tovar 1975). Clearly then there are at least two poles of tradition against which the speaker of the poem reacts: high modernism and working-class ideology. They constitute a central tension and unfolding contradiction within the poem that are further complicated by the poet's recurrent reformulation of the Chicano Indianist ideology invoked by references to Alurista's poetics. In the larger sense, this sets out a discourse about "history" and also about the speaker's "historicity," that is, the possibility that one can reconstitute the past in an authentic and a politically viable way to inform the present and the future. Cortez's heroic stance, "With His Pistol in his Hand," becomes a problematic legacy for this poet's ambivalent and shifting political and poetic ideologies. For Gómez-Quiñones, history, time, and space become the arenas for exposing these contradictions. The speaker pivots between several spheres of influence. At one time the speaker asserts the possibility of the efficacy of struggle as described in the story of conflict represented in the corrido tradition, and at other times he despairs of action having meaning. In many ways, his oscillation parallels that of Eliot, who, throughout his work, asserted meaning and tradition and yet despaired of them. Through a multiplicity of embedded narrative strains, the speaker calls into question time and, by extension, the progression of history. This is no clear restatement of "With His Pistol in his Hand"; it is a questioning of what constitutes that pistol, in what historical context, whether it exists, and can it fire anymore?

I will forgo an extended explication of this complex poem, especially since Limón has furnished us with a detailed and insightful interpretation in his *Border Ballads, Chicano Poems* (1992). Suffice it to say that we see a poetic mode of competing rhetorics—Indianist, modernist, religious, nihilist, traditional—that will sustain the speaker's oscillation between the assertion of meaning and despair of the void. And it becomes clear that in an attendant strategy the speaker dramatizes this vacillation. The key concept here is *drama,* as the poet introduces two moments in which the historical process in question is made explicit. These minidramas (which appear to correspond to Limón's typology of the stages of the Chicano social drama) take place in stanzas 11 and 12 and refer to the Chicano student Movement and the Mexican Revolution respectively. They are juxtaposed and presage the philosophical, creative, political space the speaker will occupy at the end of the poem. In other words, these dramas make explicit the indeterminacy of the poet's position.

This ambiguous space is most clearly reflected in the speaker's efforts to incorporate the feminine into his sociopolitical dilemma. In one of the scenes concerning the Chicano Movement, the speaker reverses the stereotypic drama, chronicled in Mexican popular song, in which the romantic love for a woman gives rise to spontaneous violence that validates male superiority. Rather, the male chooses to fight a different kind of battle. Here the woman becomes transformed into the Chicano Movement itself:

> Que lejos estoy del pueblo donde nací
> México lindo y querido
> porque no morir
> Por una mujer casada
>   loco y apasionado

ando en el movimiento
has dejado sólo amargos sentimientos
me encorporé a las filas por
    una mujer bonita
Soy soldado de levita, de esos
de las filas del movimiento

                        (14)

I am so far from the town where I was born
Beautiful and beloved Mexico
Why not die
for a married woman
    crazy and passionate
I am in the movement
You have left only bitter sentiments
I will join the troops for
a beautiful woman
I am a soldier, one of those troops
    of the movement

                        (translation mine)

The stanza begins with iteration of lines from a Mexican romantic song of the early twentieth century.[5] Woman, "la mujer," is introduced as an object of patriarchal contestation in the song. Yet, a reversal of sorts occurs. In the subjectivity of the speaker, woman becomes "Mexico" and all it connotes for Chicanos, especially as the nationalist catalyst for political engagement. As I will argue later, this identification of woman with Mexico is a point of radical departure for Cervantes who, in her poem's narrative, obliterates the objectification of Mexican women that underlies this type of political rhetoric.

The competing rhetorics of the narration indicate that the speaker in "Billy Rivera" recognizes that a singular narrative such as Cortez's heroic run for the border and armed resistance gets lost in a vacillation of space and time. The Chicano poet can no longer rely on a single-voiced narrative representation of what increasingly emerges as a heteroglossic, transnational, gendered, and class-differentiated history. Crucial to this disaffection with the traditional historical master story is the speaker's frustrated attempt to deal with gendered subjectivity. The speaker conducts an active dialogue with several voices that at times are present or even foregrounded, at times are implied, and at times remain mere echoes. The voice of the contemporary Chicano Movement enters into the drama:

later.
you never saw so many fucken pigs.
We left LA around 1 in the morning
3 meetins, usual shit and a demonstration tomorrow.

(13)

The parallel historical moment takes place during the Mexican Revolution at the famous battle of Celaya, well sung in corrido form. An unidentified voice relates the scene:

He saw the dust become the troop
        gritó, tomen las alturas al otro lado del río
tuvo tiempo de recordar cuando
        habían desfilado por las calles de la capital
hace tres días los vecinos de Sencillo
        had made barbacoa, hung streamers, shouted
Viva Villa.

(14)

He shouted, take the heights on the other side of the river
he had time to remember when
they had filed through the streets of the capital
It's been three days since the people in Sencillo . . .

(translation mine)

In these dramatic scenes, competing voices move in shifting dominant/ nondominant relationship to each other. Furthermore, the frequent use of direct address ("Sabes," "¿Sabes qué?") complicates the issue and is key to understanding this disjunctive conversation. Who is it that the speaker is trying to persuade, to draw into recollection, to make one with himself? That addressee alternates, I submit, between the male-gendered historical "we" to whom "so many fucken pigs" would be an important public communal memory to recollect (since the dominant narrative of the Chicano student Movement was that it was led and principally conducted by males), and the private "we" to whom memories of "menudo" and "barbacoa en Sencillo" would carry the force of familial recognition (females are traditionally associated with domestic space, in which food is central).[6] In the final lines of the poem there are many memories and historical moments that compete for dominance. The poet-speaker is in a dialogue in which the reconstitution of history (personal/public) is at stake. In this argument, the power of narrative song to forge and sustain that recollection is pitted against the forces of forgetfulness and loss that threaten to dissipate it. Despite references to corridos, popular song, and the domestic sphere, the unspoken voice of the female is always peripheral to this conversation or absent altogether. This voice is unattainable and unincorporable, given the entrenched male voice in this poem. Tradition governs Gómez-Quiñones's poem from its roots in Mexican oral culture, belles lettres, and Western literary modes.

Despite the masculine focus, it is clear that the Chicana feminine does enter into this text, albeit as a rhetorical feminine, one that has been constructed by Mexican male culture, male balladeers, Chicano culture, and male poets. While problematic, this rhetorical presence does emerge in the narrative at key times. The references begin in stanza 4 where the feminine appears as the lioness giving birth to her cubs, as the movement of the tortoise in her shell:

> La leona parrió, La concha se movió
>   entre gritos de rabia se pelió
>   abandonados de los dioses
>   el que no luchó lo apedraron
>   la muerte cobró su día
>   en esos meses cuando se acabó el mundo
>   pueblo de cantares y guerreros
> Ay Tenochtitlán, sobrevivimos.
>
> (11)

> The lioness gave birth, the tortoise moved
>   between shouts of rage it was fought
>   abandoned by the gods
>   he who did not fight, was stoned
>   death won the day
>   in those months when the world ended
>   people of singers and warriors
> Oh Tenochtitlán, we survive.
>
> (translation mine)

These lines are bracketed by the preceding stanza, which speaks of the Chicano farmworkers' strike, and the following stanza which refers to the abandonment by the gods. The world that is dying is linked imagistically to the powerful force of singers and warriors. These two imagistic poles, birth/political action or song/battle, are brought together to heave forward the acclamation of the last line: "Ay Tenochtitlán, sobrevivimos." Thus, the feminine as constructed here forms the core dialectic of survival. Furthermore, in the next stanza's references to Alurista's reinterpretation of the male-constructed "Chingada" and "La Llorona" female symbologies, Gómez-Quiñones achieves a syncretic representation that brings together feminine life force, God, and the creative power of struggle:[7]

Por las calles de mi pueblo
llaman los antiguos dioses
lloran por su pueblo
llamas en brote

(12)

Through the streets of my village
the ancient gods call
they cry for their people
budding flames

(translation mine)

The call of the ancient gods, here likened to La Llorona's search for her lost children of Mexico, suggests that Chicano history is characterized by a lack of the feminine, by the loss of mother. And at the end of the poem, Gómez-Quiñones underscores the need for the transformative image of the feminine creative force of poetry and song through allusion to "flor y canto," flower and song, the Aztec dialectic of creativity:

AZTLÁN, ha de ser tierra de rosas.
tierra de un pueblo de rosas.
· · · · · · · · · · · · · · · · · · ·
Roses are Rosas.

(17)

AZTLAN, should be a land of roses.
land of a people of roses.
· · · · · · · · · · · · · · · · · ·
Roses are Rosas.

Alurista's construction of this principle is invoked here: "peace exhaled by flowers in midafternoon / . . . eternal transformation / never dead and gone: only absent flowersong" (Alurista et al. 40, 1976). The insistent voice of the feminine ("Rosas") is incorporated into flowers and song, which becomes the creative power to transform the poet. But it is still a male-constituted alternative, and it is a convenient vehicle for cultural and political rescue. That the speaker in "Billy Rivera" gestures toward the necessity to incorporate the feminine is part of his departure from the male-dominated corrido master poem. Yet the result still reflects the weakness of that song to serve a fully gendered Chicano/a narrative history.

"Visions of Mexico while at a Writing Symposium in Port Townsend, Washington"

Whereas the speaking voice in "Billy Rivera" mediates between Mexican/ Chicano and European male traditions, the speaking voice in Cervantes's "Visions of Mexico" operates self-consciously outside of and counter to patriarchal tradition. Cervantes at once constructs her speaking voice out of her own experience and incorporates the communal by elaborating a personal/political discourse based on radically different demarcations of space and time. It can be argued that Cervantes forges a female tradition that counters the phallocentric when she reaches back to uncover the legacy of her grandmother and mother. The story she elaborates upon revolves around rejection of dependency on males and, conversely, on an affirmation of female agency. She constructs an oppositional history to that which binds the speaker in "Billy Rivera."

In "Lots II: Herself," one of the first poems in *Emplumada* (1981), Cervantes articulates this rejection of phallocentric tradition and affirms her own agency in the construction of self:

> I picked myself up   ignoring
> whoever I was   slowly
> noticing for the first time my body's stench
> I made a list in my head
> of all the names who could help me
> and then   meticulously   I scratched
> each one
>
> > *they won't hear me burning*
> > *inside of myself*
>
> my used skin glistened
> my first diamond

(9)[8]

The silence of her developing subjectivity becomes a strategy as she sheds traditions, like the feathers of birds who molt in the spring, an image that becomes overdetermined in her poetry. That her speaking voice is highly idiosyncratic and self-located forms one of the major departures from the narrative corrido tradition. As Ramón Saldívar notes, "[T]he corrido focuses on those events of immediate significance to the corrido community that are capable of producing a heightened, reflexive awareness of the mutual values and orientations of the collective" (1990, 32). That a homogenized collective and interpretive audience exists or existed is the assumption here. Most critics have understood that a large segment of the Chicano/Mexicano population (including women) knows corridos, that they form a recognizable consciousness in the development of Chicano/Mexicano ideology on this side of the border. Yet, ascribing figural status to the Texas border corrido narrative has elided differences in regional cultural production. This is not to mention the gloss over gender and class elements of an extremely heterogeneous population. This elision has resulted in an essentializing of Chicano collectivity for which the corrido, particularly in its Texas border form, has been constructed as a core narrative form. In this collectivity, female subjectivity has been invisible.

Annette Kolodny cautions against this type of essentializing in her critique of the Bloomian account of tradition:

> What is left out of account, however, is the fact that whether we speak of poets and critics "reading" texts or writers "reading" (and thereby recording for us) the world, we are calling attention to interpretive strategies that are learned, historically determined, and thereby necessarily gender-inflected. . . . Bloom assumes a community of readers (and, thereby, critics) who know that same "whole system of texts" within which the specific poet at hand has enacted his misprision. (1985, 47)

Chicano scholars and critics have assumed a similar homogenizing force of tradition and collective will and have rarely questioned its gender-inflected elements. Even in Gómez-Quiñones's "Billy Rivera," with its gestures toward incorporating the feminine, the male corrido hero is taken to stand for the oppressed community in general. Although Billy Rivera is a type of hero manqué, whose absence in the narrative calls into question the validity of the corrido form, his story is meant to be taken as our story, whether we are male or female, vaqueros in Texas, cannery workers in California, or foundry workers in Chicago. Saldívar assumes a similar totalizing identification when he finds that "[b]ecause of the narrative objectivity of the corrido's transpersonal point of view, only the narrative product, not the poetic producer, appears" (1990, 35–36). He elaborates on this idea in the following:

> In the same way, in the corrido, a product of an integrated community sharing a working-class world view and values, there is no place for the idiosyncratic, for an individual perspective that stands totally outside of communal concerns. No individual life, even that of the hero, may be regarded as uniquely different

from the fate of the community as a whole. Gregorio Cortez stands, conse-
quently, not as an individual but as an epic construction of the society that
constitutes him. His fate cannot be disconnected from communal fate. (36)

At issue here is the notion of the communal and how it has become a highly
textualized construction that evades gender, class, and regional dimensions. For if
Cortez's story dominates a certain form of classic ballad corrido, there are nu-
merous others in which the "hero" is not so communally constituted. These
corridos proceed out of distinct sociohistorical circumstances that reflect the
heterogeneity of Chicano historical events. We must not forget the strains of
corrido narrative that deal with migration and that are prominent in diverse
regions of the United States. For example, one strain deals with the migrant
worker who travels north to avoid the bloodshed of the Mexican Revolution, to
find work and survival. The "Corrido del Deportado" is representative of this
genre and, I submit, is more closely tied to the types of constructions of history
that are useful for both Gómez-Quiñones and Cervantes.[9] In this corrido, the
narrative voice is individualized. He tells his own story, and by doing so inserts
himself into the narrative product as agent and poetic producer.

Because the producer is traditionally assumed to be male, the only way a
woman can appropriate the corrido form is to seize the narrative voice back, to
subvert the homogenizing and dominant male narrative by claiming control of
the narrative herself. By interjecting herself as "speaking voice" into the historical
narrative story that recounts male heroic exploits, she makes her perception and
experience subject of a new narrative construction and becomes its poetic pro-
ducer. The manipulation of narrative voice interrupts the master corrido narra-
tive (as it has been traditionally produced and analyzed) and calls reflexive atten-
tion to an aspect of cultural conflict not usually addressed by the corrido—gender
and its role in the reconstruction of Chicano/Mexicano historical narrative. In
this way, the woman poet claims interpretive power.

Unlike Gómez-Quiñones, Cervantes responds to no prior poem, nor does she
refer to historical events in Mexico or the United States. The poems in her
collection forge her own unique history, her own tradition, and the authority of
her narrating voice. She builds an idiosyncratic, personal, and political discursive
voice that comments publicly on gender-inflected events.[10] The master story of
"With His Pistol in His Hand" does not appear in "Visions of Mexico," but the
migrant story with all of its vacillation between the nostalgic pull of the Mexican
homeland and the need for economic survival up north resonates in the narrated
events of the poem.

As in Gómez-Quiñones's poem, the symbolic site of "Mexico" is key to un-
raveling the constantly shifting meanings and representations of political action
for Chicanos and Chicanas. In "Oaxaca, 1974," the poem that precedes "Vi-

sions" in the collection, Cervantes sets out the problematic nature of this site of geographical and cultural origin:

> México,
> I look for you all day in the streets of Oaxaca.
> The children run to me, laughing,
> spinning me blind and silly.
> They call to me in words of another language.
> My brown body searches the streets
> for the dye that will color my thoughts.
>
> But México gags,
> ¡Esputa!
> on this bland pochaseed.
>
> (1981, 44)

The constant return south (Mexico) and migration north (United States) constitutes a story of competing languages, cultural identities, races, and genders. Thus the reader who turns to "Visions" has been prepared for the overdetermined symbolic locations that frame this gendered representation of the master narrative of migration.[11] The poem is divided into two locations (Mexico and Port Townsend, Washington), which offer competing perspectives on what is the defining place of Mexico in the narrator's subjectivity: "When I'm that far south, the old words / molt off my skin, the feathers of all my nervousness."

The reference to feathers and molting recalls the allusions to birds and locations that form a narrative strain in Cervantes's collection. This first line also recalls one of the collection's cornerstone poems, "Beneath the Shadow of the Freeway," in which the speaker alternates between two female traditions—that of "Mama, the Swift Knight, Fearless Warrior. / Mama wanted to be Princess instead" and that of "Grandma, our innocent Queen." The speaker cannot decide between them. She becomes "Scribe: Translator of Foreign Mail" (11). But it is to her grandmother that she eventually turns, because of the old woman's connection to the rhythms of the animals and the natural ordering of events:

> Before rain I notice seagulls.
> They walk in flocks,
> cautious across lawns: splayed toes,
> indecisive beaks. Grandma says
> seagulls mean storm.
>
> (11)

The birds offer clues about how to negotiate patriarchal culture. They do not "leave their families / borrachando." Given the patriarchal social structures that enslave women, and taking her cue from her grandmother, the speaker opts for the ways of birds and for their self-sufficiency:

> She believes in myths and birds.
> She trusts only what she builds
> with her own hands.
>
> (12)

Mexico is not the location of her speaking authority. Place has been distorted by the patriarchal and historical circumstances of women living in Chicano/Mexicano society. The freeway (symbol of destructive urban sprawl) that dissects their barrio becomes a fitting metaphor for the uselessness of traditional locators of space to provide coherence for these women's stories. It is the flight of birds in migration, the rhythms of discourse emerging out of a female subjectivity, that finally frees the narrating voice to speak:

> Back. The freeway is across the street.
> It's summer now. Every night I sleep with a gentle man
> to the hymn of mockingbirds,
>
> and in time, I plant geraniums.
> I tie up my hair into loose braids,
> and trust only what I have built
> with my own hands.
>
> (14)

The image of the freeway forms the backdrop to the speaker's shifting locations of self in both Mexico and Port Townsend, Washington. The "old words" are embedded in a narrative of patriarchal tradition against which the speaker has been defining herself throughout the collection. Thus, Mexico becomes the site for the speaker's gender-inflected contradiction within Chicano historical narrative.

The Mexico of "Visions" is the one constructed in Chicano Movement rhetoric. In the first stanza, it is a discourse into which the speaker inserts herself, although she belongs only through vicarious activity:

> My own words somersault naturally as my name,
> joyous among all those meadows: Michoacán,
> Vera Cruz, Tenochtitlán, Oaxaca . . .
> Pueblos green on the low hills

> where men slap handballs below acres of maíz.
> I watch and understand.
>
> (45)

In this positioning of her subjectivity, the poet/speaker learns from a juxtaposition of placement—the Chicana from the north becomes translated into the adobe huts of the meso-American Indians: "Alone with the women in the adobe, I watch men, / their taut faces holding in all their youth" (45). From this placement the speaker begins to understand the dimensions of physical survival that are at the center of Indian life:

> This far south we are governed by the law
> of the next whole meal. We work
> and watch seabirds elbow their wings
> in migratory ways, those mispronouncing gulls
> coming south
> to refuge or gameland.
>
> (45)

The speaker is one of these migratory birds who has come south to locate her subjectivity in discourses of culture and survival long storied by Chicano patriarchal tradition. But she is acutely aware of the difference between her status and that of an Indian past, present, or future. Hers is a distinct historical circumstance that distances her from Mexico, space of source and refuge. Her survival is located in the North, where the discourses of gender and economics are radically different and for which a new discourse must be found. The second stanza reflects the speaker's cognizance of her transitory position:

> I don't want to pretend I know more
> and can speak all the names. I can't.
> My sense of this land can only ripple through my veins
> like the chant of an epic corrido.
> I come from a long line of eloquent illiterates
> whose history reveals what words don't say.
>
> (45)

The epic corrido is an echo that gives a sense of the land that she can appropriate only through the obfuscating barriers of time and space.[12]

What resonates within the speaker is the stance of active resistance to domination which forms the core of the corrido narrative. Yet, as I have indicated, the story as it has traditionally been told excludes feminine-gendered elements of that resistance. The male-dominated story has become a type of sanctioned official Chicano rhetoric against which she must place herself as a poet. Consequently, at the same time that ぃ acknowledges her connection to the stance of resistance, she also underscores her distance from the story. The speaker asserts her inefficacy in traditional narrative terms, but she affirms her speaking voice in her refusal to let an inappropriate language speak for her. In the construction of Mexican narrative, she comes from a long line of illiterates, since the corrido has historically been an oral form. Yet illiteracy for Cervantes becomes an overdetermined figure for the poet's struggle to forge a language suitable for her singular speaking voice. Her history is not revealed by known words, that is, by the stories of Mexican cultural survival, particularly those uttered by a traditional patriarchal Mexican society that keeps women in the adobe and men in the fields. She declares a feminist voice born out of anger and fed by the circumstances of raw urban life in the North:

> Our anger is our way of speaking,
> the gesture is an utterance more pure than word.
> We are not animals
> but our senses are keen and our reflexes,
> accurate punctuation.
> All the knifings in a single night, low-voiced
> scufflings, sirens, gunnings . . .
> We hear them
> and the poet within us bays.
>
> (46)

The poet's migration south to Mexico has symbolically relocated her more firmly in her unique space as Chicana and poet. The motivating principle for the articulation of her narrating voice is found not in any geopolitical space but in the liberating power of her anger as a woman. Audre Lorde has written that

> [e]very woman has a well-stocked arsenal of anger potentially useful against those oppressions, personal and institutional, which brought that anger into being. Focused with precision it can become a powerful source of energy serving progress and change.
> . . . [A]nger expressed and translated into action in the service of our vision and our future is a liberating and strengthening act of clarification, for it is in the painful process of this translation that we identify who are our allies with whom we have grave differences, and who are our genuine enemies. (1984, 127)

In part two of "Visions," the action shifts to the North, and it is here that the speaker qualifies her anger. No longer is anger defined by reaction to cultural domination that ignores gender oppression. The speaker moves from the sense of violence and injustice garnered on the streets of the barrio to a situation involving male/female domination. The speaker situates us in a bar in Port Townsend, Washington, where a minidrama will underscore the root of her discursive displacement in the Chicano narrative paradigm handed down to her through tradition: "I don't belong this far north. / The uncomfortable birds gawk at me. / They hem and haw from their borders in the sky" (Cervantes 1981, 46).

Again the contradiction lies in the representation of "Mexico" as the nation has been symbolically constructed in the master narrative as woman (the violated "chingada" who carries the responsibility for the loss of land and culture, that is, for the entire conquest itself). In this bar in Port Townsend, "Mexico/woman" is narrated by others in the group as an embarrassing cartoonlike figure:

> I heard them say: México is a stumbling comedy.
> A loose-legged Cantinflas woman
> acting with Pancho Villa drunkenness.
>
> (46)

In one sweep of stereotypes, the story of Mexican/Chicano history has been devalued into a "comedy" in which Mexico/woman assumes the role of the legendary Cantinflas, who cannot keep his pants up on his waist. Even the heroic character of the Mexican Revolution is discredited, as Francisco Villa is recalled not for his exploits against the dictatorships of Porfirio Diaz and Victoriano Huerta but for "drunkenness" and social ineptitude. It has been widely reported that Villa did not drink. Thus, the stereotype is grounded not merely in distortion but in falsehood. Significant to this disparagement is how "Mexico" becomes an androgynous figure encompassing all the worst stereotypes of both genders. The speaker sets herself in opposition to this appropriation of gender and political rhetoric by deconstructing a minidrama that takes place in the bar:[13]

> Last night at the tavern
> this was all confirmed
> in a painting of a woman: her glowing
> silk skin, a halo
> extending from her golden coiffure
> while around her, dark-skinned men with Jap slant eyes
> were drooling in a caricature of machismo.
> Below it, at the bar, two Chicanas
> hung at their beers. They had painted black
> birds that dipped beneath their eyelids.
> They were still as foam while the men

fiddled with their asses, absently;
the bubbles of their teased hair snapped
open in the forced wind of the beating fan.

(46)

In this scene several representations of women are brought into contradiction. The painting of the blonde that dominates the bar is juxtaposed to the syncretic and androgynous "Mexico/woman" section that precedes it. Both present negative views of women reduced to symbol and object. The men sit under the icon at the bar "drooling in a caricature of machismo." But theirs is not the sole conspiracy to appropriate women. The speaker's subjectivity equally takes into account the lumpen passivity of the females in this scene, who allow themselves to be fondled "absently" while their unique life spirit is trapped like "painted black birds beneath their eyelids." Birds that connote for the speaker the power of discourse to re-create self are here disempowered and reduced to decoration. Given the paucity of the story she recounts here, the speaker is left to assert her own subjective voice to counteract the inherited social, gendered structures that have been handed down through a decadent Mexicano/Chicano historical narrative plot.

When in "Billy Rivera" the speaker inverts the popular romantic imagery of violence committed for "una mujer casada" and turns it into violence for the loftier goals of the Chicano Movement, it is still the plot of the objectified beautiful woman that serves as symbolic catalyst to male agency. But the speaker-poet in "Visions" refuses the plot altogether. Events have little authority when they become subject to the speaking voice of the narrating "I." "As she shifts the narrative lens by which facts become events in a story," Joanne Frye suggests, "the narrator protagonist changes the very nature of the 'event'—its meaning, its place in a causal pattern, its temporal significance. When she shapes her story according to a female experiential perspective, even the events acquire new definition" (1986, 57).

In "Visions," place and event are reconstructed and subverted within a developing narrating voice. Neither Mexico nor Port Townsend, Washington, are destinations or locators of meaning for this speaker. Rather, it is in the interstices of these points of "vision" that she garners the power of her subversive creative agency. For the speaker in "Billy Rivera," Mexico as it has been constructed in corrido and popular song also is not adequate to his ambivalent cultural and political placement in the United States. For this reason, East Los Angeles becomes a site for refuge and cultural reparation in that poem, although the speaker does not succumb to the romanticism of this reflection. Billy Rivera, who has been absent from the narrative altogether and whose life has no political significance, dies without having achieved his own narrative agency. He is to be buried at a specific place—"1724 E. Florence Avenue"—which belies any symbolic space of cultural and political rescue. But East Los Angeles still exists as a space for event and subsequently for the reconstitution of the narrative of Chicano history.[14] For Cervantes, neither Mexico nor Washington offers a site for agency. Like the migrating birds of her narrative progression, she achieves agency through the process of the construction of her own female subjective voice:

> there are songs in my head I could sing you
> songs that could drone away
> all the Mariachi bands you thought you ever heard
> songs that could tell you what I know
> or have learned from my people
> but for that   I need words
> simple black nymphs between white sheets of paper
> obedient words   obligatory words   words I steal
> in the dark when no one can hear me
>
> as pain sends seabirds south from the cold
> I come north
> to gather my feathers
> for quills

(47)

The speaker refuses the romantic or politically limited refuge of "Mexico" as it has been constructed by the male narrative songs of the corridos or popular culture. She is a scavenger of words who constructs her subjectivity out of the detritus of the cultural melange of sociosexual arrangements that threaten to define her.

One could explore the problems with this position in Alicia Ostriker's terms— that is, by confirming her assertion that "women have always tried to steal the language" and that we probably could never "break out" of the prison of male-dominated discourse (1985, 315). Or we could question Cervantes's poetic process through Audre Lorde's dictum that "[T]he Master's Tools will Never Dismantle the Master's House" (1984, 110). Instead, I would suggest that Cervantes is affirming that the power of the female "I" resides in her ability to live in multivocal borders of language and consciousness. Her narrating "I" both deconstructs the phallocentric hold of history and, in an opposite action, reconstructs a self-located concentric discourse out of an evolving self-defining sociosymbolic system. The first action rests on a refusal of the dominant male Chicano historical narrative, which positions itself within a notion of cultural conflict tied to specific borders, geopolitical territories, and male-gendered space. The second action underscores an elaboration of personal/political poetics. This speaker deliberately refuses to go south for respite during the cold; she hunts up north for the feathers that she transforms into the medium of her self-creation— her quills. She claims an interpretive power over her own experience, and by doing so she resists the silencing of the female voice as it has been historically determined. Here she seizes the opportunity to develop new capacities for representation so as to reground and restore agency within female subjectivity.

These final stanzas of "Visions" juxtapose the processes of creation in oral and written discourses. There are "songs" she "could sing" that "could drone away" all traditional male songs. The conditional verb tense in these lines not only indicates probability, it also points to potential action. Yet, the conjunction "but" in line 6 indicates opposition to the intention to speak in this manner: "for that I need words / simple black nymphs between white sheets of paper." She needs language, a discourse born out of subversive activity: "obedient words obligatory words words I steal." These are words that function between discourses, the oral and the written. They are found between "white sheets of paper," but they also represent the contradiction of silent song: "in the dark when no one can hear me" (47). Marta Sánchez argues that the sexual innuendos in "nymphs" and "sheets" "reinforce the theme of desire to give birth to the poet's songs" (1985, 102). And further she asserts that "nymphs" refers to the Greek goddesses of the forest. Given Cervantes's use of ornithological images in her poems, I suggest that "nymphs" also refers to the word's definition as an insect (usually a genus of butterfly) that is at the stage of metamorphosis. In this sense, the speaker's "stealing" of language is a process. The words that indicate obedience and obligation to a tradition are in the process of becoming a new form, one that can be seen (written) and heard (oral). Hers is a different discourse in the making that forges a new literacy to counteract the long line of "illiterates." This new form takes the gesture of anger (introduced in stanza 2) as the initial move toward a subjective speaking voice, a female consciousness and agency:

> As pain sends seabirds south from the cold
> I come north
> to gather my feathers
> for quills.[15]

(47)

The corrido refrain, "With his pistol in his hand," is revisioned by both Gómez-Quiñones and Cervantes as the intellectual's pen or quill that has the power to articulate the ambiguities of their own historical circumstances. These are intellectuals who position themselves through very different constructions of their own historical, narrative traditions. For both, history and the narration of it prove problematic. There are no heroic acts or land to claim as source and home for Chicanos or Chicanas whose survival rests on the ability to articulate their constantly changing processes of their own subjective creative agency. The chants of the epic corrido "ripple through their veins" as a catalytic memory that ties them to their given sites of difference of their gender-inflected subjectivities. They continue to tell stories, not as prisoners of history, but rather as multivocal agents of the historical process itself. This truly is the dialectics of political survival of a people hovering in the psychosexual borderlands of a shifting and changing historical saga.

In the title poem to *Emplumada,* Cervantes points to the dialectical indeterminacy of this gendered historical narrative imperative. The female speaking voice "contains the wind"; it has interrupted and subverted the expectations of history and historicity itself.

> —this
> she thinks of, watching the branch of peaches
> daring their ways above the fence, and further,
> two hummingbirds, hovering, stuck to each other,
> arcing their bodies in grim determination
> to find what is good, what is
> given them to find. These are warriors
>
> distancing themselves from history.
> They find peace
> in the way they contain the wind
> and are gone.

(66)

Notes

1. Following closely upon Jose Limón's argument in "The Rise, Fall, and 'Revival' of the Mexican-American Corrido: A Review Essay" (1983, 2:202–7), Ramón Saldívar maps out in close detail the sociohistorical and political milieu of nineteenth-century history of South Texas. He relates a story about the movement out of a primarily agricultural and ranching economy into the social and economic displacements of advancing capitalism. He explains the corrido form as a response to this complex social upheaval (Saldívar 1990).

2. Limón's arguments about the ephebe scholars of Américo Paredes are indeed provocative. By using Bloomian anxiety of influence theory, he underscores the largely patriarchal tradition of Chicano scholarship itself. Consequently, women are not only eclipsed in the historical construction of Chicano history, they are made invisible in the male tradition of Chicano scholarship as well, despite their productive and significant contributions to Chicano Studies.

3. One notes the obvious phallic figural implications of "la pistola" (gun) in this patriarchal narrative form. The stance of the male, "defendiendo su derecho, con su pistola

en la mano" (defending his rights with his pistol in his hand), has been taken to be a gesture appropriate for a people who are oppressed and whose rights have been transgressed. Yet, by implication, the "people" retain a male-centered identity in which the female is absent as an agent of her own defense, or even as a constituent member of that communal group. Ironically, the pistol that defends the culture is also the vehicle, figurally, for female absence, or what might by extension be construed as cultural death for women.

4. Marjorie Perloff persuasively argues that Anglo-American poetry follows from a tradition more closely linked to Rimbaud than to Eliot (1981). That the former is tied to an antisymbolist mode and the latter to symbolist tradition is clear, although she does not expand significantly upon the intersection of those two poetic strains. In each a form of poetic indeterminacy plays itself out not only in theme but also, for the followers of Rimbaud, in form: "but there is a big difference between the reference to indeterminacy and the creation of indeterminate forms" (Perloff 1981, 22). For all the complexity of his poetry, Eliot, she reminds us, creates a coherent discourse. I agree with Perloff that his indeterminacy is one of content and not of form. In my argument, I am referring to Eliot's thematic "undecidability," a term that Perloff borrows from Todorov. Juan Gómez-Quiñones is drawn to this vacillation in Eliot, but he moves beyond it into a fragmentation of his discourse that is more closely allied to the tradition mapped out by Perloff as coming from Rimbaud. Gómez-Quiñones not only plays intertextually with a number of traditions and vacillates between them, but his poem is also marked by syntactic shifts, unclear referents, and jarring movements between historical moments and spatial locations. He presents a uniquely indeterminate disjunctive form that reflects the political and poetic dilemma of his Chicano sensibility. For my purposes, indeterminacy in "The Ballad of Billy Rivera" lies in an intersection between content and form that comprises a particular Chicano response to being caught between traditions and between political borders.

5. The shaping of the Mexican nationalist consciousness through this reference to the famous Mexican singer Jorge Negrete and the golden age of Mexican popular nationalistic song is critical, as the poet questions his consciousness and deliberates about what must be sacrificed, died for, contested.

6. Jose Limón argues that the woman's voice emerges as the speaker moves toward an acceptance of the "people" as an androgynous entity:

> Within the terms of his culture, yet without delimiting an "image" of "woman," this poet departs from the patriarchal, confrontational terms of conventional male heroes to articulate an entirely different heroic modality: the strength of nurturing concern, of the androgynously defined persistence of life. Honor, virtue, and strength are not epitomized solely by the man with his pistol in his hand; these heroic qualities are everywhere found in the living, persisting idiom of our *people*, articulated in androgynous symbols of food, family, marriages and roses. (1992, 147)

Although I agree that this section of the poem marks the speaker's search for a female subjectivity, I am not convinced that the poet succeeds. In this poem, the Chicano people are faced with traditions that are insufficient to meet their experience. And they are fractured by splits in gendered subjectivities. The resonance of the feminine persists, but it does not emerge with power.

7. The disparaging implications of the representation of the female as "La Malinche" (the Indian woman who translated for Cortez and bore his son), the betrayer of her people in whose body is inscribed the rape of Mexico, has been well documented (see Del Castillo 1977; Paz 1961; Franco 1989). Similarly, the ambivalent legacy of the legend of "La Llorona" (the woman who has lost, or killed, her children and who walks the streets at night crying and wailing for their return) has also been well studied (see Limón 1986c; Anzaldúa 1987). The following lines in Gómez-Quiñones's poem allude to Alurista's two poems, "Sombras Antiguas" (Alurista et al. 1976) and "Must Be the Season of the Witch" (Alurista 1971).

8. The speaker in this poem seems to reject all tradition, phallocentric and otherwise. Reading this poem as a counterpart to the poem that preceeds it in the collection, I would suggest that phallocentric tradition is the target of the rejection. The titles of these poems that face each other on the pages of the volume are "Lots: I The Ally" and "Lots: II Herself." "The Ally" recounts a rape, an event that signals the subject's refusal to be silent given the threat of violation and death. "Herself" presents the subject's metamorphosis, which grows out of the last lines of the first poem: "She would live, / Arrogantly, / having wrestled / her death / and won" (Cervantes 1981, 8). Clearly, the opposition of the speaker's subject position in both poems is directed against the patriarchy.

9. Marta Sánchez notes the images of migration that pervade her poetry. She does not, however, draw a correlation between the precursor corrido of migration and Cervantes's play with that narrative tradition in "Visions" (Sánchez 1985). We should note that although Gregorio Cortez speaks in the ballad, his limited dialogue is recounted by the corridista or balladeer. He does not tell his own story in a sustained manner in the song.

10. Cervantes neither incorporates nor acknowledges as precursor any events that form a collective inherited past. Neither the Mexican Revolution (1910) nor the Chicano Moratorium (1970) are aspects of her story or history. Yet, Cervantes does record certain events in her poems that become watershed moments for her construction of history and consciousness. We should note that the title of the poem is pointedly specific, giving the location and function of the event to be narrated. The setting of geographical and historical context is at once collective (Mexico representing here the mythical place of origin) and personal (a writing symposium becomes the place where the narrative of origin and placement for the speaker will be contested). And finally, we are given Port Townsend, Washington, an extreme point "north from Mexico" (to use historian Carey Mcwilliams's phrase [1968]) where the contradictions of story and history will be deconstructed in the perceiving consciousness of the poet.

11. In her reading of "Visions," Marta Sánchez argues that the speaker in the first section of the poem romantizes Mexico. She chides the speaker for not "taking issue, directly or indirectly, with a social structure implied by inequality such as poverty" (Sánchez 1985, 99). I disagree. Mexico is presented as a conflictual site and metaphor for absent or lost history in many of Cervantes's poems. The speaker in "Visions" translates herself back in time to an Indian past that has been constructed in Chicano Movement (especially Indianist) rhetoric as the place of origin. She tries to become part of that rhetorical story, but she only observes her disjunction from it. What should be claimed as her patrimony, given the construction of the past in Chicano Movement rhetoric, is incom-

patible with her Chicana subjectivity. The next stanza confirms the rejection of this pa-
trimony: "I don't want to pretend I know more / and can speak the names. I can't"
(Cervantes 1981, 45).

12. Sánchez correctly points out that "[L]ike any Chicana who writes, Cervantes is
alienated from the corrido, with its gestural elements" (1985, 99). Yet, I disagree with
Sánchez's conclusion that Cervantes functions as the corridista, the person who recites or
sings the corrido: "Like the corridista, she too is more a vehicle for the experiences of
others than a composer-creator of personal experience" (100). "Visions" is a poem about
personal experience raised to the collective level. Events that take place in the bar con-
stitute a scene of contestation that will provoke the speaker to sing an altered song. She is a
balladeer, the creator and producer of the medium and the song.

13. The corrido as a narrative poem usually focuses on narration of lived events that
call into question existing power relations. Both "Billy Rivera" and "Visions" retain this
focus on narrated events, an aspect of the corrido form that survives the contestation of the
story being told. The dramas discussed in both poems underscore the persistence of the
corrido form, as well as its subversion.

14. The poem paradoxically ends with the announcement of Billy Rivera's wake, or his
ritualistic passage into death or history. Yet, his death in 1958 can be read as a beginning
for the poet. 1958 harks back to other significant historical dates with which it is linked:
1848 (Treaty of Guadalupe Hidalgo), 1968 (East Los Angeles walkouts, massacre of
Tlateloco in Mexico City). The year 1958 stands alone in its obscurity, in its nonheroic
passivity. Ironically, "The Ballad of Billy Rivera" is written in the late 1960s and early
1970s, and so the final drama of the poetic narrative does not end in the present, but in
some intermediate space that lies outside of the master stories against which the speaker
has been competing. Yet, as a consequence of its indeterminacy, this drama constitutes the
beginning and end of narrative song. The absent Billy Rivera is an incarnation of that
dialectic. The speaker reconstitutes his death as a beginning; his story ("Sabes que Billy
o.d. . .") and song of life continue although even as he is invoked in the present, he is
relegated to the past. Yet, ironically he embodies the future.

15. Marta Sánchez helpfully notes that the feather imagery refers to the Aztec image of
the feathered serpent (Quetzalcoatl), "a pre-Columbian god who represented the union of
quetzal or 'bird' (feathers) and coatl or 'snake' (earth), a union joining flight and land. The
unifying of two extremes in the mythic bird suggests that Cervantes wants to resolve
tensions between poetry and community, oral and written, high and low, north and south"
(1985, 103).

The Feminist Poetics of Aemilia Lanyer's "Salve Deus Rex Judaeorum"

Janel Mueller

Vouchsafe to view that which is seldome seene,
A Womans writing of divinest things . . .
—Aemilia Lanyer, "To the Queenes most Excellent Majestie" (Anne
of Denmark)

The year 1611 saw the publication, in London, of the first volume of poetry in English written by a woman: *Salve Deus Rex Judaeorum*. Its title page identified the poet as "Mistris Aemilia Lanyer, Wife to Captaine Alfonso Lanyer, Servant to the Kings Majestie." In the expatiating fashion of the time, the title page also highlighted the following portions of the volume's title poem: "1 The Passion of Christ. 2 Eves Apologie in defence of Women. 3 The Teares of the Daughters of Jerusalem. 4 The Salutation and Sorrow of the Virgine Marie," while lumping together its shorter poems as "divers other things not unfit to be read" (title page of *Salve Deus*, reproduced in [Lanyer] 1993, 1). Who was Aemilia Lanyer, and what was she doing in her "Salve Deus Rex Judaeorum," thus characterized? Questions like these are no merely naive voicings of curiosity. They have proven useful as starting points for interpretation all along the discontinuous time line that charts the history of women's authorship in the West. In historical criticism sensitive to the category of gender, it is now regularly accepted that the exercise of authorship—by women no less than by men—requires some empowering sense of authorization, of authority, to write and publish (e.g., Davis 1980; Gubar 1981; Waller 1985). As applied to Lanyer and her volume, such questions engage the interplay of her social identity with the poetic identity of her work, on the assumption that the two are mutually self-constituting in ways that can be traced—to at least some degree—from recoverable features of text and context.[1]

Who was Aemilia Lanyer? She was born in London in 1569 as Aemilia Bassano, the second of two daughters of a common-law marriage between an otherwise unknown Margaret Johnson and Baptist Bassano, one of Queen Elizabeth's musicians. The Bassanos were a Venetian Jewish family of musicians who had Christianized and relocated at the court of England, as members of the King's Musick, on the invitation of Henry VIII (Prior 1983). Although Aemilia was only seven when her father died, income from some London properties provided her mother, her sister, and herself with a livable maintenance (Woods 1993, xv–xvii). As indicated in her later verse epistles, the growing girl Aemilia also retained her court connections—which she redraws poetically as an illustrious society comprised solely of females (see Lewalski 1993). The first dedicatory epistle to the *Salve Deus* volume wistfully reflects on that vanished time when "great *Elizaes* favour blest my youth" ([Lanyer] 1993, 8). Another salutes Susan Bertie, countess of Kent, as "the Mistris of my youth, / The noble guide of my ungovern'd dayes" ([Lanyer] 1993, 18), thus signaling her adolescent formation under the then widespread practice of being sent from one's family to be trained up in service in an aristocratic household (Houlbrooke 1984, 147; Laslett 1984, 13). Lanyer significantly credits the countess's own capacity for moral governance to her mother's influence: "By your most famous Mother so directed, / That noble Dutchesse, who liv'd unsubjected" ([Lanyer] 1993, 19). Susan's mother was Catherine Bertie, duchess of Suffolk, an outspoken Protestant who went into voluntary exile under Mary Tudor, taking her children with her. The duchess had married her former steward, Richard Bertie, in an earlier notable act of self-assertion (and one often proposed as a source-idea for the tragic heroine of John Webster's *Duchess of Malfi*, staged ca. 1614, published in 1624).

In 1587, when Aemilia was eighteen, her mother died. Close to this time the orphaned girl became the mistress of a high-ranking court official, the lord chamberlain, who was also Queen Elizabeth's first cousin. Henry Carey, Lord Hunsdon, was forty-five years older than Aemilia. When she showed signs of pregnancy in 1592, Hunsdon arranged for her to marry Alphonso Lanyer or Lanier, a court musician like her father, and a descendant of an expatriate French Huguenot family from Rouen. There are baptismal records for two children in early 1593—a son, Henry, presumably named after Hunsdon, and in late 1598 a daughter, Odillya, who died in infancy. Notes kept by the astrologer Simon Forman, whom Aemilia consulted on several occasions, additionally record the Lanyers' anxieties over their declining fortunes between 1597 and 1599 (Rowse 1978, 9–17; Woods 1993, xviii–xxv). Alphonso received some income from a patent granted him by King James in 1604, and Aemilia, again on the testimony of her poetry, spent some time before 1609 at Cookeham, a royal estate, in cherished intimacy with Margaret Clifford, countess of Cumberland, and her daughter, Anne, soon to become countess of Dorset by marriage (see Lewalski 1991, 1992).

Nothing else is known of the intervening years before Aemilia published *Salve Deus Rex Judaeorum* in 1611. Particularly unfortunate is the lack of any clue in the scanty biographical record for dating the intensity of religious feeling to which the long title poem of this collection bears witness. However, inferential connections have been drawn between its other contents and the Lanyers' financial situation. Judging from various arrangements of its dedicatory verse epistles to highborn ladies and from presentational inscriptions in nine extant copies, wife and husband both used *Salve Deus* as an instrument to solicit patronage (Rowse 1978, 11–16; Greer et al. 1988, 44–46). Alphonso, however, would die shortly, in 1613. Aemilia's widowed years remain shrouded in anonymity and authorial silence, although records of intermittent lawsuits bespeak her self-reliance in, briefly, founding a school "to teach and educate the children of divers persons of worth and understanding" and otherwise maneuvering to secure her financial rights. Her struggles eased somewhat when her son Henry reached his majority, married, and started a family. When she died at seventy-six in 1645, Lanyer left an inheritance to two teenage grandchildren, Mary and Henry, whom she apparently helped to raise (Woods in [Lanyer] 1993, xxviii–xxx).

So much, then, for a basic answer to the question, Who was Aemilia Lanyer? But a no less basic answer is called for when this question is denied the privilege of historicist interest on which I build in the bulk of my discussion here. The present-day context for asking Who was Aemilia Lanyer? is the happy phenomenon of numbers of women writing poetry that is rich, outrageous, and originary because it is increasingly unfettered and self-assured. Given a contemporary twist by a late twentieth-century and presumably postmodernist reader, the question might run as follows: Who was Aemilia Lanyer, that we should care about her poetry after almost four hundred years? As Lanyer's advocate I would concede at once the datedness of key aspects of her outlook. She believes that the feminine and the masculine are essential, innate features of two sexes. She also makes universalist assumptions about God's purposes, both in creating persons whose common humanity is marked by sexual difference and in holding them accountable by a single moral standard for their actions in what simply is the course of history. Our current tactics as feminists no less than our theories disparage notions that human nature has significantly differentiated traits outside of culture and thus emphasize gender rather than sex as the reciprocal social production and acquisition of a given sexed subject. Relativistic and deterministic implications afford us little basis for moral judgments, which we reach nonetheless on other terms: our ideological commitments, our best attempts at reasoning, our emotional responses. Emphasizing cultural embeddedness, we formulate our political, critical, and poetic projects accordingly. But, I would urge, Lanyer does exactly the same, even though her notion of culture is Christian world history and her understanding of embeddedness finds two sexes locked in a domination-subordination relationship that shows everywhere as a given of social organization. Lanyer proves every bit our contemporary, moreover, in her resolve to find and articulate transformative possibilities in gender relations that will carry their own secure imperative for actualization. For this purpose, which is to say oddly from a contemporary point of view, she looks to the figure of Christ in history— to divinity humanized or humanity divinized—as she reads the record of Scripture with wholly unconventional eyes. The mystery that explodes into a demonstrated truth in her poem "Salve Deus Rex Judaeorum" is Lanyer's understanding of Christ's incarnation: she views it in light of the Crucifixion as a public, historical action taken by men alone; this vindicates, once and for all, female nature and feminine values, and it authorizes gender equality ever after. In her handling, universalism and essentialism empower a feminism that proves rich, outrageous, and originary by any present-day standard. Beyond the inherent interest that I hope to verify for Lanyer's poem, an object lesson emerges for contemporary readers: our best wisdom, our most sophisticated and influential theories, are no sine qua non for a feminist poetics. Hers is a striking case in point.

Present-day feminist scholarship has another pressing need: an eventual set of useful generalizations about the conditions that empowered female authorship in preindustrial and pre-Enlightenment Europe. I want to shift from individual biography to a cross-cultural and transhistorical perspective in order to note certain suggestive structural similarities between Lanyer's situation and that of Christine de Pizan, the first professional woman of letters in France, despite a divide of two centuries. These structural similarities include expatriate family origins, youthful formation in the inner circle of a major court in close contact with persons of the highest rank, marriage unconstrained by the full force of conventional wifely subordination and dependency relations, and an extended period of finding a living for themselves and their children. They also bear on the second question—about the specially highlighted portions of the title poem of Lanyer's volume—which I began by asking.

In 1369 at the age of four, Christine was brought from Venice with the rest of her immediate family to the court of France by her father, King Charles V's astrologer. Happily married at the age of fifteen to Etienne du Chastel, a court notary ten years her senior, at twenty-five she witnessed within a few short months her father's death and her husband's death, leaving her to provide for her three young children and her mother. Converting her grief for her husband into lyric artistry, Christine declined to remarry. Instead she undertook to make a name for herself, first as a versatile and accomplished poet, later as an author of prose works, who won powerful patrons and a position of her own at court (Richards 1982, ix–xx; Quilligan 1991, 1–2).

Circumstantial differences aside, a first key homology in Pizan's and Lanyer's accession to authorship is the double unconventionality of their upbringings. On the one hand, both were educated to a standard of courtly cultivation well above their own rank; on the other, both were less than ordinarily bound by social ties and traditional processes of acculturation due to their families' recent relocation out of an ancestral milieu. Again, discounting differences in their marital histories, it seems clear that childbearing spurred both Pizan and Lanyer to assert their own agency as literary creators and self-providers. Most significantly of all, however, for my purposes, the twofold anomaly of Pizan's and Lanyer's social situations—as insiders to court circles but outsiders in rank and ethnic descent—positioned them to experience and judge critically the constraints then in effect on female roles in their respective adoptive cultures. Both women, then, had "the best of both worlds"—the empowerment of membership without the usual quotient of constraints, the observational vantage of the outsider without the usual marginalization. The next step—prudential in both cases, but surely not only that—was authorship, and authorship in an otherwise unprecedented feminist vein. By calling both *feminist* I mean that they explicitly confront misogyny and the injustices of male domination and prerogative in their writings, working to counter these with alternative, women-centered constructions.[2] Entering the category of authorship at what, for each, was the present stage of the so-called *querelle de femmes* or controversy about women, Pizan and Lanyer respectively engage as revisionists with literary vogues made current by male writers.

A quantity of recent discussion has documented the extent to which the clashes and aftershocks of the centuries-long, Europe-wide controversy about women served as crucial stimuli for female authorship across several generations and national boundaries (Kelly 1984, 65–109; Henderson and McManus 1985, 3–184; Shepherd 1985, 9–23; Jones 1990, 1–35). Virtually every explanation of how premodern women came to be authors insists on the importance of this controversy. It picks up in 1399 with Pizan's own instigation of the so-called quarrel of the *Romance of the Rose* by attacking this central love allegory for its general immorality and its particular slanders of women (Richards 1982, xxi–xlvi). In Pizan's own reclamation project the central targets were secular works of high repute—Jean de Meun's continuation of the *Roman de la rose*, Boccaccio's *De mulieribus claris* (On illustrious women)—which kept in circulation the debased coinage of patristic misogyny long since issued by Tertullian and St. Jerome. In English poetry these antifeminist materials are familiar as the readings that infuriate the Wife of Bath against her scholar-husband, as she vividly relates in her prologue in Chaucer's *Canterbury Tales* (1386–1400).

Preeminently among Pizan's works, her prose *Livre de la cité des dames* or *Book of the City of Ladies* ([1405] 1982) vindicates women's claims to respect and fame by rewriting the tales of their achievements—in the domains of public and cultural life, family relations, and religious sainthood—that have been at best equivocally set down by male authors in secular and ecclesiastical sources. Analogously, Lanyer's *Salve Deus Rex Judaeorum*, an assemblage of shorter poems and two prose pieces around an extended narrative poem on the last events in the life of Christ that gives the volume its title, undertakes to merge the secular genre of verse panegyric addressed to highborn personages—in this case, all females—with the sacred genre of devotional meditation on biblical subjects in verse. Lanyer's increasingly manifest purpose in this generic merger is to articulate the connections she discerns to hold in the biblical record between the incarnational theology of Christianity and disclosive truth in speech and action, public as well as private. In her view, these historically concrete connections invest femininity not only with superiority to masculinity but also with mandates for personal and social autonomy that give women special access to godlikeness. Limitations of space make it unfeasible for me to discuss Lanyer's epistles to noble ladies; however, as I indicated above, these have already drawn some extended critical attention. By comparison, "Salve Deus Rex Judaeorum" has received only selective treatment (Beilin 1987, 191, 193–99; McGrath 1991). Concentrating on this title poem, I will be arguing the boldness and cogency of Lanyer's feminist theology, language theory, and social theory as well as the expressiveness of the poetic system of equivalences and exchanges by which she connects the feminine and the divine.

To position what may seem, prima facie, my somewhat improbable argument for Lanyer as the early seventeenth-century English creator of a fully cognizant feminist poetics, I return to considerations of context, now in order to individuate her and her work further as subjects of interpretation. While spirited protest against the wholesale denigration of women's bodies and moral character makes for the most immediately arresting and memorable passages in both Pizan and Lanyer, differences in literary forms and the specific inflections of their feminism prove at least as significant as the similarities in their situations and their writings. These differences arise as functions of the discrete historical and local circumstances of the controversy about women that led them, respectively, to write. Lanyer declares as much of her *Salve Deus* in "To the Vertuous Reader":

I have written this small volume, or little booke, for the generall use of all virtuous Ladies and Gentlewomen of this kingdome; and in commendation of some particular persons of our owne sexe, such as for the most part, are . . . well knowne to my selfe, and others. . . . And this have I done, to make knowne to the world, that all women deserve not to be blamed though some forgetting they are women themselves, . . . fall into so great an errour, as to speak unadvisedly against the rest of their sexe; which if it be true, I . . . could wish . . . they would referre such points of folly, to be practised by evill disposed men, who forgetting they were borne of women, nourished of women, and that if it were not by the means of women, they would be quite extinguished out of the world, . . . doe like Vipers deface the wombes wherein they were bred, only to give way and utterance to their want of discretion and goodnesse. Such as these, were they that dishonoured Christ . . . putting [him] to shamefull death. . . . It pleased our Lord and Saviour Jesus Christ, . . . to be begotten of a woman, borne of a woman, nourished of a woman, obedient to a woman; and that he healed women, pardoned women, comforted women: yea, even when he was in his greatest agonie and bloodie sweat, going to be crucified, and also in the last houre of his death, tooke care to dispose of a woman: after his resurrection, appeared first to a woman, sent a woman to declare his most glorious resurrection to the rest of his Disciples. . . . All which is sufficient to inforce all good Christians and honourable minded men to speak reverently of our sexe, and especially of all virtuous and good women. To the modest sensures of both which, I refer these my imperfect indeavours, knowing that . . . they will rather, cherish, nourish, and increase the least sparke of virtue where they find it, by their favourable and best interpretations, than quench it by wrong constructions. ([Lanyer] 1993, 48–50)

In marked contrast to Pizan, Lanyer locates her own project of defending her female sex squarely in the domain of religious poetry and, beyond that, in a specifically scriptural subject—here, the last events of Christ's life. There are several recoverable reasons for such a choice in a London vernacular publication of 1611. First, in the interval between flare-ups in 1588–97 and 1615–37, the English controversy about women saw a relatively quiescent phase with regard, at least, to the circulation of antifeminist themes in satirical tracts or polemical diatribes (Henderson and McManus 1985, 14–19). Lanyer had no immediately pressing motive to engage in prose controversy from a feminist position. "To the Vertuous Reader" shows her much more concerned with the bad effects of *both* sexes' speaking ill of women, which undermines not merely women's reputations for virtue but their very capacity and incentive to be virtuous.

While lauding the exemplary virtues of Margaret Clifford, countess of Cumberland, in a framing section near the opening of "Salve Deus," Lanyer addresses what she represents as a pressing contemporary problem—how female moral agency is represented in recent English secular poetry and drama. She decries portrayals of Lucrece, Cleopatra, Rosamund, and Matilda, alluding perhaps to Shakespeare's *Rape of Lucrece* (1594) and to *Antony and Cleopatra* (1606–7), or to Samuel Daniel's *Cleopatra* (1593) and *Complaint of Rosamond* (1592), as well as to Michael Drayton's *Matilda* (1594). The framing section that concludes "Salve Deus" with another celebration of the countess of Cumberland's active virtue returns to the figure of Cleopatra, detailing the fickleness, adultery, cowardice, and treachery of this "blacke Egyptian" as an egregious instance of a woman's loss of moral direction ([Lanyer] 1993, 60, 111–12). Lanyer's preoccupation with Cleopatra testifies to a conspicuous development in London stage plays that drama historians regularly note (e.g., Rose 1988, 95). This is the quite sudden emergence, from a virtual void, of women with the full stature of evil-doing tragic protagonists like Alice Arden in *Arden of Faversham* (1591), Anne Frankford in Thomas Heywood's *A Woman Killed with Kindness* (1603), and Shakespeare's Lady Macbeth (1606). As Lanyer acutely saw, the moment was ripe for intervening in the discursive construction of women by male authors as (im)moral subjects: it was time to counterclaim for them as gender-specific exemplars of virtue.[3]

At just this time, moreover, calls were sounding for a redirection of poetic energies from secular love to sacred subjects. Probably the best known of these are George Herbert's two sonnets, "My God, where is that ancient heat towards thee" and "Sure Lord, there is enough in thee," sent to his mother as a New Year's gift in 1610 (1974, 205). Scriptural subjects, specifically, received fresh validation in the year that Lanyer published *Salve Deus*. The team of scholars who had been working since 1606 under royal mandate to verify the accuracy of the text of the entire English Bible against its sources in the original languages published their Authorized (or King James) Version in 1611, with an epistle dedicatory offering it "to your MAIESTIE, not onely as to our King and Soveraigne, but as to the principall moover and Author of the Worke: . . . it being brought unto such a conclusion, as that we have great hope that the Church of England shall reape good fruit thereby" (Pollard 1911, fol. A2v). Court culture, humanist scholarship, and vernacular biblicism all intersect in this milestone event. To lodge a timely challenge to invidious constructions of her sex, onstage and off, by male poets and by her society more broadly, Lanyer considered it necessary not just to contradict standing portrayals or to celebrate living women but to develop a new poetic ontology for figuring femininity as worthy, true, and good. This ontology would ground itself in a portrayal of a maligned, about-to-be-murdered Jesus of Nazareth that quite closely follows scriptural sources. It would proceed, however, on Lanyer's own authority to figure women and women alone as capable of rightly recognizing and receiving the incarnate divine Word.

Recent work devoted to Lanyer's poetic development and practice has focused on the two patronesses with whom she represents herself as being most intimate—Margaret Clifford, countess of Cumberland, and her only child, Anne Clifford, countess of Dorset—and especially on Lanyer's affectively charged, utopian depiction of her relations with the Cliffords as the source of her personal no less than her poetic raison d'être in "A Description of Cooke-ham," written about a year before *Salve Deus Rex Judaeorum* appeared (Lewalski 1985, 1991, 1993; Woods in [Lanyer] 1993).[4] Nowhere, moreover, does Lanyer say anything explicit about how she positioned herself and her work with respect to contemporary male poets. Yet this question is too significant to leave dangling from lack of direct testimony, for the very reasons that have promoted the advent of gender studies in the second wave of twentieth-century academic feminism. No less than the relational categories of femininity and masculinity, women's writing has historically been undertaken and maintained in dynamic relation to men's writing. Differences only register as such, as making a difference, by means of interpretive methods that operate comparatively across both bodies of textual practices (see Greene and Kahn 1985; Scott 1986; Newton 1989; Porter 1990).

Regarding Lanyer's literary relations with male poets, there has been the lone opinion voiced by her only modern editor until Susanne Woods, whose edition of Lanyer's poetry appeared in 1993. A.L. Rowse—better known as a social than as a literary historian—placed Lanyer "in versification . . . close to Samuel Daniel, and this is natural, for he belonged to the circle of which she became a member. Margaret, Countess of Cumberland was a patroness, with her daughter, Lady Anne Clifford. . . . Daniel was tutor to the daughter" (Rowse in [Lanyer] 1978, 18).[5] Rowse does not elaborate. He may have been referring to Daniel's reworking of his four-book historical poem in rime royal, the *Civil Wars between the two Houses of York and Lancaster* (1595); an eight-book version in ottava rima appeared under the same title in 1609. Lanyer's "Salve Deus" is likewise in ottava rima.

But in other salient respects Lanyer's compositional practices run counter to Daniel's. For example, in his *Defence of Rime* (published 1602) he prided himself on strictly avoiding so-called feminine line endings—final unstressed syllables— especially when rhymed as a pair with a masculine line ending but even, as he insists, in a rhymed pair of their own. Daniel thought feminine endings appropriate only to song lyrics, not to serious narrative poetry:

> To me this change of number in a Poem of one nature sits not so wel, as to mixe uncertainly, feminine Rymes with masculine, which, ever since I was warned of that deformitie by my kinde friend and countriman Maister Hugh Samford, I have alwayes so avoyded it, as there are not above two couplettes in that kinde in all my Poem of the Civill warres: and I would willingly if I coulde, have altered it in all the rest, holding feminine Rymes to be fittest for Ditties, and either to be set certaine [i.e., recast as masculine rhymes], or else by themselves. (Daniel 1950, 156–57)

Lanyer's verses abound in feminine endings across a variety of stanzaic forms in her *Salve Deus* volume. In larger matters of composition Lanyer also sets herself against Daniel, not only in what I take above as her aspersions on his tragedy *Cleopatra* and his *Complaint of Rosamond* with their sustained studies of the psychologies of adulterous women, but in a still more fundamental determinant. Lanyer's major poem is religious; all of Daniel's major poems are on secular subjects.[6]

Although I make no pretense of offering a last word or even a complete treatment of a barely opened question, my own sense of a suggestive antitype in contemporary male-authored poetry for the title poem of Lanyer's volume is Giles Fletcher's *Christs Victorie and Triumph in Heaven, and Earth, over and after Death* (1610). His four-part poem in 265 ottava rima stanzas (with the variant of concluding alexandrines) is framed at its head by prose epistles to the dedicatee, the scholar-cleric Thomas Neville, and "To the Reader"; these articulate Fletcher's resolve to redeem the poet's role in the commonwealth by writing verse on a high biblical subject in the line of named illustrious antecedents, climaxing in King James himself. To these are added verses commending the poet and the poem by Giles's brother and fellow poet, Phineas Fletcher, and by Sir Francis Nethersole. The last eight stanzas of *Christs Victorie and Triumph* close the frame by entrusting the work to the approbation of King James, hailed for bringing to Britain an earthly peace and beatitude that are an extension of Heaven's, and then by folding this poem's final religious allegory into that of a poem by Phineas on "faire Egliset," the Church of England. By comparison, "Salve Deus Rex Judaeorum," in sixty ottava rima stanzas subdivided by marginal rubrics, is framed by opening and concluding celebrations of the surpassing virtues of the closest noble associates of Lanyer's present adult life: the Cliffords, mother and daughter. Nearly simultaneous publication, closely similar verse form, framing pieces that set this scripturally based poetry within a context of relations to influential patrons (including royalty), and commitment to an affective, strongly rhetorical rehearsal of the climactic events in Christ's life comprise the fundamental resemblances between Fletcher's and Lanyer's poems.

Nevertheless, suggestive differences once again mark Lanyer's feminist poetics. *Christs Victorie and Triumph* has prominent allegorical dimensions that are altogether absent from "Salve Deus Rex Judaeorum." In allegory and only in allegory does Fletcher make place for female personages in sacred story: the sisters Justice and Mercy of the first part, who roundly dispute in a heavenly council what dealings fallen, perverse man shall receive at God's hand; the sensual and seductive Panglorie or Pangloretta, who tempts Jesus in the second part. When Fletcher begins to versify biblical material in the third part of his poem, all the persons are male. Tracing the events from the evening before the Crucifixion to the entombment of Jesus's body, Fletcher heightens devotional affect with prolonged evocations of the contrasting psychologies of the betrayer Judas and the loyal, grief-stricken Joseph of Arimathea, but otherwise works his gospel narrative into a formal rhetorical structure of enumerated topoi (parts, means, effects) signaled by marginal rubrics.

Lanyer's "Salve Deus" differs strongly in most of these respects from Fletcher's poem. She discards virtually all allegory—telescoping the debate between Mercy and Justice, for example, into a single stanza while more nearly approximating his penchant for embellishment in her set piece on night as the time when the devil looses evils in the world ([Lanyer] 1993, 75–76). Most importantly, her own narrative hews steadily and, for the most part, literally to the composite account in the Gospels, beginning with Christ's agony in Gethsemane and ending with his expiration on the cross. (The exception to her biblical literalism is "Eves Apologie," which elaborates the message that Pilate's wife is recorded as sending to her husband in Matthew 27:19.) Thus Scripture is in much firmer ascendancy in Lanyer's poem than in Fletcher's.

Not only is there this difference within similarity; Lanyer too is drawn to study contrasting psychologies for devotional affect. Unlike Fletcher, however, with her an emphasis on spiritual and emotional valence entails that female figures will assume prominence as actual historical personages from the Gospels, not personified abstractions from allegory. At the center of Lanyer's "Salve Deus" is a highly wrought narration of Jesus' suffering and abasement, with inset episodes that repeatedly foreground women: Pilate's wife, the women of Jerusalem, Jesus' mother Mary. That these episodes are crucial to the design of Lanyer's poem shows in the numbered rubrics of her title page. In each case, women find means of registering their resistance to the deadly course of action that the male figures are in the process of enforcing as criminal justice. Moreover, what the men treat as criminal justice, the women perceive as the gravest possible injustice to one who has confounded masculine power and authority by acting and speaking in ways that the women instantly comprehend and recognize as their own. Lanyer's steadily maintained social milieu endows her characters and imagery with the concrete specificity of a seventeenth-century Dutch genre painting.

A marginal *incipit* opposite stanza 42 of "Salve Deus" signals the onset of the poem's central narration: "Here begins the Passion of Christ" ([Lanyer] 1993, 65). Lanyer employs the in medias res opening that had become standard in Renaissance poetic narratives on lofty subjects, secular or sacred. With this she conjoins a skillful use of temporal and spatial setting for emotive heightening, a convention shared with such Ovidian poetic narratives as Shakespeare's *Lucrece*, Daniel's *Rosamond*, and Drayton's *Matilda*. It is deep night in the garden of Gethsemane on the Mount of Olives. Jesus is alone with his fears and forebodings. Behind him is his Last Supper; ahead lies his betrayal by Judas and his forcible seizure by the soldiers of the high priest Caiaphas. The garden's atmospheric darkness is liminal—a space no longer of private life, like the upper room where he has just shared a meal with his twelve disciples, but not quite yet a public space of arrest, interrogation, and judicial sentencing. In this liminal setting, Lanyer's narration follows the gospel story closely while furthering her systematic portrayal of a Christ who is not understood through any species of private or public relationships with other men. Peter, James, and John, his favor-

ite disciples, whom he entreats to keep him company while he prays, fall into a
sleep that Lanyer feelingly equates with spiritual blindness. They

> could not watch one houre for love of thee,
> Even those three Friends, which on thy Grace depends,
> Yet shut those Eies that should their Maker see;
> What colour, what excuse, or what amends?
>
> ([Lanyer] 1993, 69)

Immediately thereafter, Judas leads Christ's enemies to him and betrays him in a
far graver perversion of intimacy:

> A trothlesse traytor, and a mortall foe,
> With fained kindnesse seekes thee to imbrace;
>   And gives a kisse, whereby he may deceive thee,
>   That in the hands of Sinners he might leave thee.
>
> (72)

But, as brought out through Lanyer's continuous emotional coloration of her
narrative, the public action of arresting Christ also proceeds in total in-
comprehension and misprision of its subject:

> Now muster forth with Swords, with Staves, with Bils,
> High Priests and Scribes, and Elders of the Land,
> Seeking by force to have their wicked Wils,
> . . . .
> And who they seeke, thou gently doest demand;
>   This didst thou Lord, t'amaze these Fooles the more,
>   T'inquire of that, thou knew'st so well before.
>   . . . .
> His name they sought, and found, yet could not know
> *Jesus* of Nazareth.
>
> (73)

Incomprehension darkens into willful misconstrual and perjury as Christ is
brought before Caiaphas to be formally examined. Lanyer's narration tracks the
gradation from abuses of language to abuses of justice that repeatedly leaves her
Christ with the option, only, of keeping silent. "They tell his Words, though farre
from his intent, / And what his Speeches were, not what he meant" (79). In
responding to repeated encounters with men who both coerce and misjudge
him—a pattern intensified in his dealings with Caiaphas, Pilate, and Herod as the

legal process runs its course—Lanyer's Christ exhibits perfect quiescence in both demeanor and language.

> The people wonder how he can forbeare,
> And these great wrongs so patiently can take;
> But yet he answers not.
>
> (80)

> Three times thou ask'st, What evill hath he done?
> And saist, thou find'st in him no cause of death,
> Yet wilt thou chasten Gods beloved Sonne,
> Although to thee no word of ill he saith.
>
> (88)

> Yet neither thy sterne browe, nor his great place,
> Can draw an answer from the Holy One:
> His false accusers, nor his great disgrace,
> Nor *Herods* scoffes; to him they are all one:
> He neither cares, nor feares his owne ill case.
>
> (89)

On those rare occasions when Lanyer's Christ has anything at all to say, the speech that befits his behavior is correspondingly sparing, yet always transparent—and true in the strongest sense of truth, self-identity. Every sentence that Lanyer's scripturally styled Christ utters under interrogation packs a characteristic semantic and spiritual force, registering profound self-disclosure in tautology or near-tautology: "I am he," "Thou hast said it."

> For when he spake to this accursed crew,
> And mildely made them know that it was he:
> Presents himselfe, that they might take a view;
> And what they doubted they might cleerely see;
> Nay more, to re-assure that it was true,
> He said: I say unto you, I am hee.
>
> (74)

> He held his peace, yet knew they said not true,
> No answere would his holy wisdome make,
>   Till he was charged in his glorious name,
>   Whose pleasure 'twas he should endure this shame.
>   . . . .
> Beeing charged deeply by his powrefull name,
>   To tell if Christ the Sonne of God he be,
>   Who for our sinnes must die, to set us free.
>
> (81)

> To thee O *Caiphas* doth he answere give,
> That thou hast said, what thou desir'st to know,
> . . . .
> He speaketh truth, but thou wilt not beleeve,
> Nor canst thou apprehend it to be so:
>> Though he express his Glory unto thee,
>> Thy Owly eies are blind, and cannot see.
>
> (82)

Where, moreover, Lanyer's Christ proves incomprehensible to the men about him, to her as commentator he remains so continuously readable that she is able to specify the virtues that ground his speech and behavior at each point: "Here faire Obedience shined in his breast, / And did suppresse all feare of future paine"; "His paths are Peace, with none he holdes Debate, / His Patience stands upon so sure a ground" (74, 77). One rhetorical and poetic high point takes the form of a bold stanzaic enjambment in which Lanyer asserts herself authorially by interrupting the lying enemies of Christ in Caiaphas's hall. These men call Christ a blasphemer, but she can name him truly. And so she does, inserting her catalog of ascriptions into a sentence that had begun as a description of the men's perjury:

> High Priests and Elders, People great and small,
> With all reprochfull words about him throng:
>> False Witnesses are now call'd in apace,
>> Whose trotheless tongues must make pale death imbrace
>
> The beauty of the World, Heavens chiefest Glory;
> The mirrour of Martyrs, Crowne of holy Saints;
> Love of th'Almighty, blessed Angels story;
> Water of Life, which none that drinks it, faints;
> Guide of the Just, where all our Light we borrow;
> Mercy of Mercies; Hearer of Complaints;
>> Triumpher over Death; Ransomer of Sinne;
>> Falsely accused: now his paines begin.
>
> (79)

As the foregoing quotation clearly indicates, there is nothing explicitly feminist about this poetically striking juncture in Lanyer's narration of the passion of Christ. Yet here and elsewhere for considerable stretches Lanyer skillfully predisposes her story, description, and commentary to feminist implications. These implications become remarkably and fully explicit when Pilate's wife breaks in upon her husband to remonstrate with him in "Eves Apologie," the second of the subdivisions highlighted on the poem's title page. I want to work toward a concluding discussion of "Eves Apologie" by tracing the diverse, local feminist predispositions that lead into and away from its unique outspokenness in other parts of Lanyer's "Salve Deus."

Perhaps the most obvious of these predispositions—certainly the first to become conspicuous in the poem—is the pattern of fundamental misprision exhibited by all of the males in the story, friends and foes alike, while the female poet unfailingly understands what and who Jesus is. Although the conventional epic guise of an omniscient narrator serves as her vehicle for expressing this understanding, deeper ideological implications remain untouched by this identification of poetic means. As now amply documented in a range of studies focused on the social construction of femininity in sixteenth- and earlier seventeenth-century England (e.g., Kelso 1956; Hull 1982; Woodbridge 1984; Hannay 1985; Beilin 1987), it appears scarcely less obvious that Lanyer understands her Christ because he is thoroughly feminized in demeanor and language according to the period norms set out in conduct books and doctrinal tracts, especially those of the late Elizabethan and Jacobean Puritan divines—John Dod and Robert Cleaver, William Perkins, William Whateley—who were actively publishing as Lanyer wrote. Her Christ, like the ideal woman of the Puritan manuals, is silent except when induced to speak, and modest and taciturn when he does; he is gentle, mild, peaceable, and submissive to higher male authorities.[7]

Not only does Lanyer herself appear to understand the traits of her Christ's character from familiarity with them as the virtues that women were to acquire and manifest as defining their femininity. She also conducts two psychological studies—of the women of Jerusalem, of Christ's mother Mary—in which she writes the same process of understanding into her narration of the ostensibly historical events of "Salve Deus." These women empathize with Christ through their shared affinities in demeanor, language, and feeling. Because his social identity resonates with their own, they, like Lanyer, can comprehend him inwardly. And again, on the evidence of the numbered subsections of her title page, Lanyer highlighted these instances of reciprocal recognition as "The Teares of the Daughters of Jerusalem" and "The Salutation and Sorrow of the Virgine Marie." They are highlighted accordingly in the body of the poem, where schematic gender opposition first links the women with Christ in action and utterance and then sets them as a group over against the other males. In a transitional stanza between these two highlighted sections, Lanyer's pointed phrases exemplify what I am terming the feminist predisposition of her commentary:

> When spightfull men with torments did oppresse
> Th'afflicted body of this innocent Dove,
> Poore women seeing how much they did transgresse,
> By teares, by sighes, by cries intreat, nay prove,

> What may be done among the thickest presse,
> They labour still these tyrants hearts to move;
>   In pitie and compassion to forbeare
>   Their whipping, spurning, tearing of his haire.
>
> (94)

Thus as Christ sets out toward Calvary, bearing his cross on his scourged and bleeding shoulders, the executioners and their hangers-on "thinke he answer'd for some great transgression, / Beeing in such odious sort condemn'd to die," while the women bystanders see that "his own profession / Was virtue, patience, grace, love, piety." They weep aloud for Christ as he passes; he in turn pauses and speaks to them consolingly. Lanyer's reiterated identical nouns—grace, love— affirm the spiritual and ethical oneness of the suffering women with the suffering Christ:

> Thrice happy women that obtaind such grace
> From him whose worth the world could not containe;
> Immediately to turne about his face,
> As not remembring his great griefe and paine,
> To comfort you, whose teares powr'd forth apace
> ·
>   Your cries inforced mercie, grace, and love
>   From him, whom greatest Princes could not moove.
>
> (93)

Although the women of Jerusalem are powerless to alter the outcome of the procession to Calvary, Lanyer nevertheless grants them a clear moral victory by poetic means, as the sound and significance of the men's cries are supplanted by those of the women's cries by stanza's end:

> First went the Crier with open mouth proclayming
> The heavy sentence of Iniquitie,
> The Hangman next, by his base office clayming
> His right in Hell, where sinners never die;
> Carrying the nayles, the people still blaspheming
> Their maker, using all impiety;
>   The Thieves attending him on either side,
>   The Serjeants watching, while the women cri'd.
>
> (92–93)

Lanyer's section on the salutation and sorrow of the Virgin Mary works a comparable but far more complex and subtle transmutation of tones and themes. The narrative point of departure is a scriptural given, a grief near despair.

> How canst thou choose (faire Virgin) then but mourne,
> When this sweet of-spring of thy body dies,
> When thy faire eies beholds his bodie torne,
> . . . .
> Bleeding and fainting in such wondrous sort,
> As scarce his feeble limbes can him support.
>
> (99–100)

Lanyer's local poetic objective is to convert this extremity of evil to an assurance of blessedness that the suffering mother will register as immediately and experientially as she does her present grief. To begin this process Lanyer reminds Mary of the greeting pronounced by the angel of the Annunciation and elaborates its significance:

> He thus beganne, Haile *Mary* full of grace,
> Thou freely art beloved of the Lord,
> He is with thee, behold thy happy case;
>
> (96)

> That thou a blessed Virgin shouldst remaine,
> Yea that the Holy Ghost should come on thee
> A maiden Mother, subject to no paine,
> For highest powre should overshadow thee:
> Could thy faire eyes from teares of joy refraine,
> When God look'd downe upon thy poore degree?
> Making thee Servant, Mother, Wife, and Nurse
> To Heavens bright King, that freed us from the curse.
>
> (97–98)

Key to this passage and to Lanyer's broader authority as a religious poet in "Salve Deus" is the salutation as a locution. A rarely employed poetic resource in her contemporary English but a salient feature of spoken dialogue in half a dozen important gospel episodes,[8] the salutation begins with a special, reverential word of greeting, then adds the addressee's name and significant attributes. Its structure here is "Haile *Mary* full of grace, . . . Servant, Mother, Wife, and Nurse / To Heavens bright King, that freed us from the curse." In Lanyer's poetic, not only does knowing aright bespeak naming aright, but naming and knowing cast in the form of a salutation bespeak a direct, intimate encounter with another person that authorizes the salutation itself. The salutation thus comes to figure as the linguistic hallmark of Lanyer's poetics of femininity—a speech act uniquely expressive of the capacity to apprehend truth that distinguishes women and the feminized Christ. Lanyer's treatment of Mary in this final highlighted subsection of the poem insists on her uniqueness in assuming just those womanly roles of "Servant, Mother, Wife, and Nurse" that enabled Christ to incarnate his corresponding ones as "Her Sonne, her Husband, Father, Saviour, King, / Whose death killd Death, and tooke away his sting" (98, 95). If Mary can sustain her sense of the blessedness of her agency in relation to Christ as specified in the roles foretold by this angel of the Annunciation, even her present sorrow can be turned into acceptance of Christ's death as a necessary means to the "good" of human redemption. Two remarkable stanzas narrate Mary's achievement of this delicate spiritual and emotional modulation as she reflects on Christ's gender roles while performing her own:

> His woefull Mother wayting on her Sonne,
> All comfortlesse in depth of sorow drowned;
> Her griefes extreame, although but new begun,
> To see his bleeding body oft she swouned;
> How could she choose but thinke her selfe undone,
> He dying, with whose glory shee was crowned?
>   None ever lost so great a losse as shee,
>   Beeing Sonne, and Father of Eternitie.
>
> Her tears did wash away his pretious blood,
> That sinners might not tread it under feet
> To worship him, and that [,] it did her good
> Upon her knees, although in open street,
> Knowing he was the Jesse floure and bud,
> That must be gath'red when it smell'd most sweet:
>   Her Sonne, her Husband, Father, Saviour, King,
>   Whose death killd Death, and tooke away his sting.
>
>   (94–95)

Lanyer's prose postscript to her volume partially elucidates the vital connotations she attached to the biblical salutation as she lays out her first and only explanation of her title:

Gentle Reader, if thou desire to be resolved, why I give this Title, *Salve Deus Rex Judaeorum*, know for certaine: that it was delivered unto me in sleepe many yeares before I had any intent to write in this maner, and was quite out of my memory, untill I had written the Passion of Christ, when immediately it came into my remembrance, . . . and thinking it a significant token, that I was appointed to performe this Worke, I gave the very same words I received in sleepe as the fittest Title I could devise for this Booke. (139)

Further elucidation comes at the recurrent junctures where Lanyer as omniscient narrator and commentator reproves Christ's enemies for hailing him by name yet knowing him not at all. Thus she writes of the high priests and scribes who arrest him:

> His name they sought, and found, yet could not know
> *Jesus* of Nazareth . . .
> When Heavenly Wisdome did descend so lowe
> To speake to them: . . .
>   Nay, though he said unto them, I am he,
>   They could not know him, whom their eyes did see.
>
> (73)

And thus she writes, more scathingly, of Christ's interrogation by Caiaphas, who charges him once "in his glorious name" to tell "Whose pleasure 'twas he should endure this shame" and again "by his powrefull name, / To tell if Christ the Sonne of God he be, / Who for our sinnes must die, to set us free." Lanyer's Christ returns to Caiaphas the truth of Caiaphas's own linguistic formulation:

> Then with so mild a Majestie he spake,
> As they might easly know from whence he came,
> . . . .
> To thee O *Caiphas* doth he answere give,
> That thou hast said, what thou desir'st to know.
>
> (81–82)

But these words of truth are rejected as blasphemy, and the Word of Truth as a blasphemer. Caiaphas pronounces a sentence of death for blasphemy against this same "Christ the Sonne of God . . . Who for our sinnes must die, to set us free" and sends him to Pilate for its ratification. The soldiers who crucify Christ mock him with a crown of thorns, a reed for a scepter, and the salutation, "Haile king of the Jewes"—in the Latin of the Vulgate, "*Salve Rex Judaeorum.*" Above his head his cross eventually bears a caption—"This is Jesus the king of the Jewes" (Matthew 27:37) or simply "The king of the Jewes" (Mark 15:26, John 19:19)— which the high priests futilely try to have altered to read: "He said, I am King of the Jewes" (John 19:21 in Pollard 1911). These multiplied misprisions that yet vindicate salutation as an acknowledgment of incarnate divinity inscribe the core of Lanyer's poetic and supply the narrative crux of her poem. *Salve Deus Rex Judaeorum.* Hail, God, the king of the Jews. Lanyer's title both opposes and embraces the truth of the gospel narrative that had been uttered uncomprehendingly, as a verbal gesture of mockery, by the soldiers who crucified Christ. By her addition of just one word in apposition, *Deus*, she makes fully explicit her expression of personal faith in the divinity of one whom the Jews (the people of her own descent on her father's family's side) did not recognize as their king. She does so recognize him, and she salutes him as such.

However, the intricacies that register in "The Salutation and Sorrows of the Virgine Marie" and in the mystique—if I may so call it—of salutation in Lanyer's religious poetics may seem far removed from the feminist predispositions and feminist poetics that I claim for her text. Briefly, it may look in this historical narrative of a political and social world as if Christ and the women are the losers, and that the grieving Mary, no less than the women of Jerusalem, must content themselves with either an inward or an otherworldly assurance that this feminized Christ will be victorious over masculinist evil and violence. Despite a sensitive and often perceptive discussion of "Salve Deus," Elaine Beilin comes to adopt this line. As she puts it, "I would not agree . . . that Lanyer was a feminist, because her advocacy for women begins with spiritual power and ends with poetry; and in fact, she assumes that men control society, art, and the worldly destiny of women, including herself" (Beilin 1987, 320). But I in turn cannot agree with Beilin. I read Lanyer's portrayal of the spiritual power of femininity— of Christ and the women—in "Salve Deus" as having extreme revisionary implications for men's control of society, art, and the worldly destiny of women. My reading, apart from the overt declarations of "Eves Apologie" that still await discussion, goes like this.

Lanyer vindicates femininity to male critics and the misogynists of both sexes, whom she deplores in her preface, "To the Vertuous Reader," not merely by portraying the closeness of Christ and actual good women. She historicizes her retracing of the gospel account of the passion. This poetic narrative devolves in a space that is social and political, through and through. Its implications and those of the authorial commentary are social and political as well. More specifically, Lanyer uses her portrayals of Christ and actual good women to trace the impact of feminine or feminized virtue on the masculine side of a range of standing dichotomies that mark conceptions of social and political relations: public/ private, mind/body, culture/nature, reason/passion. As narrated, the superiority of feminine virtue is constantly confirmed as it makes its impact in the masculine domain. Christ leaves the privateness of the upper room and the garden to engage the public proceedings of the soldiers, Caiaphas, Pilate, Herod, which the women likewise engage on his behalf. The connection between Christ and the women proves the more effective in that these figures together demonstrate, through what they are made to suffer, the problematic reciprocal relation between political submission and sexual subordination, and they do so more tellingly than almost any other rare sixteenth- and seventeenth-century text that in any way critiques this relation as a problem.[9] The net impact of Christ and the women in the narrative is to leave Jerusalem's public life and its intersecting political and priestly jurisdictions exposed as a sham of justice, as corruption, malignity, and violence.

Similarly, as my account of highlighted sections in "Salve Deus" has already suggested, Lanyer represents the bodies of Christ and the women as more legible expressions of understanding and morality—the qualities that supposedly make for the mind's superiority—than are the minds of the male figures of authority. "Here insolent Boldnesse checkt by Love and Grace, / Retires, and falls before our Makers face" (73).

> Her teares did wash away his pretious blood,
> That sinners might not tread it under feet
> and that[,] it did her good
> Upon her knees, although in open street,
> Knowing he . . .
> . . . must be gather'd.
>
> (95)

In one of several characteristically gendered contrasts, Lanyer authorially reprehends Pilate as he confirms Caiaphas's sentence on Christ. "Art thou a Judge?" she begins.

> The death of Christ wilt thou consent unto,
> Finding no cause, no reason, nor no ground?
> Shall he be scourg'd, and crucified too?
> And must his miseries by thy meanes abound?
>
> (88)

Lanyer's Pilate also becomes a prominent locus in the poem for the working out of culture/nature and reason/passion dichotomies that redound to the discredit of male domination. In a stanza that includes both pairs of binaries in its imagery, she demands of him:

> Canst thou be innocent, that gainst all right,
> Wilt yeeld to what thy conscience doth withstand?
> Beeing a man of knowledge, powre, and might,
> To let the wicked carrie such a hand,
> Before thy face to blindfold Heav'ns bright light,
> And thou to yeeld to what they did demand?
> Washing thy hands, thy conscience cannot cleare,
> But to all worlds this staine must needs appeare.
>
> (91)

Although unanswered, these questions put to Pilate are far from merely rhetorical or, in Beilin's terms, a manifestation—in poetry only—of a woman's spiritual power. The sun attests to the innocence of the Son, as a later passage on "The terror of all creatures at that instant when Christ died" will confirm in its evocation of earthquake and other cataclysms—"The Sunne grew darke, and scorn'd to give them light, / Who durst ecclipse a glory farre more bright" (102). Pilate's handwashing is a sorry irrelevance to the stain of bloodguilt incurred through his complicity in putting to death not merely an innocent victim but divinity incarnate. In the aftermath of Christ's Crucifixion read as history, culture must look to a morally cognizant (and to that extent a feminized) nature for moral refounding.

Which is to say that men must look to women for the refounding of existing political and social relations. Exactly thus runs the argument advanced by Pilate's wife in "Eves Apologie" (meaning defense—the sense is clearly that of apologia). Lanyer draws the warrant for a spirited portrayal of this figure from the passing notice accorded her in a single biblical verse, Matthew 27:19: "When he [Pilate] was set downe on the Judgement seate, his wife sent unto him, saying, Have thou nothing to doe with that just man [Jesus]: for I have suffered many things this day in a dreame, because of him" (Pollard 1911). In keeping with Lanyer's generic representation of femininity as spiritually superior, Pilate's wife's first utterance discloses her true understanding and faith: "Heare the words of thy most worthy wife, / Who sends to thee, to beg her Saviours life. / . . . / Open thine eies, that thou the truth mai'st see, / . . . / Condemne not him that must thy Saviour be." But she just as directly adds the most ominous pragmatic warning she can give Pilate, one based on the status quo of gender politics: "Let not us Women glory in Mens fall, / Who had power given to over-rule us all" (84). Lanyer's figure begins from a bond to scriptural authority as absolute as Lanyer's own to the Gospels: she acknowledges that men got power over women from the Fall of Adam and Eve. But she goes on to argue that the Gospel as history shatters that power. If men commit the far worse sin of killing Christ, their doing so sets women free from men's rule.[10]

Here Pilate's wife exposes her own author's historicity. With a return to origins that demonstrates typical period procedure for tracing the cause or rationale of current practices, she reflects analytically—which for her and Lanyer means comparatively—on the Fall as narrated in Genesis. She details several considerations and lines of reasoning that work in Eve's favor. First, the serpent lied to Eve only; hence she was deceived into sinning, but Adam was not.

> she (poore soule) by cunning was deceav'd,
> No hurt therein her harmelesse Heart intended:
> For she alleadg'd Gods word . . . that they should die. . . .
>
> But surely *Adam* can not be excusde,

. . . .
Being Lord of all, the greater was his shame:
Although the Serpents craft had her abusde,
Gods holy word ought all his actions frame.

(85)

The allusion to "Gods holy word" refers to the prohibition against eating the fruit of the tree of knowledge of good and evil that God gave to Adam before Eve was created (Genesis 3:16–18). There is no explicit indication in scripture that the prohibition was ever transmitted to Eve. This is Pilate's wife's second consideration on Eve's behalf.

The perfect'st man that ever breath'd on earth
. . . From Gods mouth receiv'd that strait command,
The breach whereof he knew was present death:

Not *Eve*. . . .
He never sought her weakenesse to reprove,
With those sharpe words, which he of God did heare.

(85–86)

In the third place, Pilate's wife finds Eve's psychology in sinning far more admirable than Adam's.

We know right well he did discretion lacke,
Beeing not perswaded thereunto at all;
If *Eve* did erre, it was for knowledge sake,

. . . .
Yet Men will boast of Knowledge, which he tooke
From *Eves* faire hande, as from a learned Booke.

(85–86)

Finally, Pilate's wife reasons from Adam's priority in creation to his probable role as source of evil: "If any Evill did in her remaine, / Beeing made of him, he was the ground of all" (86). Her logic infers that an original creature is an originary one also in the case of woman's nature—if not, what is the primacy that is taken to ground male superiority? It will be clear here without further comment how Lanyer lines up the fundamental binaries of culture/nature and reason/passion in this fourfold apologia so that Pilate's wife personifies femininity triumphant in masculine terms.

Lanyer's possible antecedents for this passage make a fascinating if necessarily inconclusive subject. So little is known about her education and contacts—for example, whether she might somehow have had knowledge of the disputation conducted in 1451–53 in an exchange of Latin letters between Ludovico Foscarini, a Venetian doctor of canon law, civil law, and medicine, and the learned Veronese noblewoman Isotta Nogarola on the subject "Of the Equal or Unequal Sin of Adam and Eve." Nogarola argues that Eve's sin was unequal in being less than Adam's, on three counts. First, Eve sinned through ignorance and inconstancy while Adam sinned through a prideful desire for God-like moral knowledge. Second, in delivering the prohibition, God made Adam responsible for himself and Eve, but Adam did not restrain Eve, hence his guilt was greater. Third, God gave Eve a lesser punishment than Adam: she would bear children in pain, but he was condemned to labor and to death.

Nogarola also rebuts Foscarini's argument that Eve's sin was unequal in being greater than Adam's, again on three counts, in which she undertakes to reconfirm that Adam's sin was greater. To Foscarini's charge that Eve sinned more than Adam by setting him an evil precedent and being, in Aristotle's formulation in the *Posterior Analytics*, "That on account of which any thing exists is that thing and more greatly so" (King and Rabil 1983, 62), Nogarola responds that Adam's inherent superiority—as God's original creation, as the one to whom dominion over the earth was given—enabled him to resist Eve, and he is responsible for not doing so. To Foscarini's second charge, that Eve's sin was greater than Adam's because she, as an inferior creature, aspired to divinity equally with the superior creature Adam, Nogarola answers shortly with the principle that guilt is never increased by inferiority or weakness but rather the opposite: "In many people it is seen that he who knows less sins less, like a boy who sins less than an old man or a peasant less than a noble" (King and Rabil 1983, 63). Adam is, therefore, more guilty.

To Foscarini's third charge, that Eve's sin was the greater because her punishment was cumulative—she incurred Adam's punishments of death and labor as well as her own of pain in childbirth—Nogarola retorts that, as opposed to inference, the actual wording of God's pronouncements in Scripture makes Adam's sin look clearly worse. God does not mention Eve's sin at all, only Adam's, in listening to his wife and eating of the tree that he was commanded not to touch (Genesis 3:17). Likewise, God phrases Adam's punishment more harshly than Eve's, for he says to Adam but not to her that he is dust and will return to dust (Genesis 3:19). Nogarola stands fast in her determination that Adam is more guilty than Eve. Hereupon Foscarini moves to close their disputation by admonishing her regarding the fallibility and deceitfulness of the female sex and her possible overconfidence in her own powers of argumentation. Most interestingly for future readers of Lanyer's "Salve Deus," he refers to Pilate's superior moral awareness at the time of Christ's passion as a matter on which he and Nogarola could agree and thus resolve their differences:

Though I have spoken, you may not hear. You may spurn and disdain my words. . . . Let us read the history of the passion and the dreams of the wife, the words of Pilate, the washing of hands, the avoidance of judgment, and we shall confess that he understood . . . that the sentence was unjust. These things make it quite clear that the force of my arguments has not been weakened. (King and Rabil 1983, 68)

Whatever may or may not have been known to Lanyer from Nogarola's Veronese-Venetian antecedent, Lanyer unquestionably figures as a feminist innovator within an English vernacular context. Her Pilate's wife prefigures by several years other women authors' analyses of the Fall of Adam and Eve that began to circulate as the English controversy about women entered its earlier seventeenth-century phase with Joseph Swetnam's *Araignment of Lewde, Idle, Froward, and Unconstant Women* ([1615] 1985). Largely a racy series of anecdotes and denunciations, Swetnam's tract drew its fiercest counterfire from his attempts to reason, especially this one:

Who can but say that women sprung from the Devil? Whose heads, hands, and hearts, minds and souls are evil. . . . For women have a thousand ways to entice thee and ten thousand ways to deceive thee. . . . They are ungrateful, perjured, full of fraud, flouting and deceit, unconstant, waspish, toyish, light, sullen, proud, discourteous, and cruel. And yet they were by God created and by nature formed, and therefore by policy and wisdom to be avoided. For good things abused are to be refused. (Swetnam [1615] 1985, 201)

Responding in *A Muzzle for Melastomus*, Rachel Speght exclaims against Swetnam's illogic, "An impious conclusion to infer: that because God created, therefore to be avoided. O intolerable absurdity!" (Speght [1617] 1985, 77) and elsewhere argues to exonerate Eve in terms closely resembling Lanyer's:

We shall find the offence of Adam and Eve almost to parallel: . . . Woman sinned, it is true, by her infidelity in not believing the word of God but giving credit to Satan's fair promises that "she should not die" (Genesis iii.4); but so did the man too. And if Adam had not approved of that deed which Eve had done, and been willing to tread the steps which she had gone, he—being her head—would have reproved her. . . . And he, being better able than the woman to have resisted temptation, because the stronger vessel, was first called to account: to show that to whom much is given, of them much is required. (Speght [1617] 1985, 66)

Later in 1617 Speght is followed by another, tartly self-styled opponent of Swetnam, Esther Sowernam, who in *Esther Hath Hang'd Haman* commends and sharpens Speght's detection of multiple fallacies in Swetnam's gloss on the

Genesis account of the fall (Sowernam [1617] 1985, 91–95). But Sowernam reserves her chief triumph for her exposure of Swetnam's mistaking of an echo of Euripides for a verse of Scripture, "If God had not made them only to be a plague to a man, he would never have called necessary evils." "Out of what scripture, out of what record, can he prove these impious and impudent speeches? . . . If he had cited Euripides for his author, he had had some colour. . . . Thus a pagan writeth profanely, but for a Christian to say that God calleth women 'necessary evils' is most intolerable and shameful to be written and published" (Sowernam [1617] 1985, 94–95).

Not only does Pilate's wife in Lanyer's "Salve Deus" reason her way to a defense of Eve without explicitly presupposing what Nogarola, Speght, and Sowernam all do, that Eve by nature is inferior to Adam; she also takes the controversy about women two steps further—both, as far as I know, completely unprecedented and original. Granting for the purposes of argument that Eve deserved to be subjugated to Adam for having been the first to fall, Pilate's wife challenges Pilate on the relative blameworthiness of the Fall and the Crucifixion, in which, she charges, "you in malice Gods deare Sonne betray":

> Whom, if unjustly you comdemne to die,
> Her sinne was small, to what you doe commit;
> All mortal sinnes that doe for vengeance crie,
> Are not to be compared unto it:
> If many worlds would altogether trie,
> By all their sinnes the wrath of God to get;
>   This sinne of yours, surmounts them all as farre
>   As doth the Sunne, another little starre.
>
> ([Lanyer] 1993, 86–87)

Sardonically invoking the superiority of the sun's light to image the greater male culpability for the Crucifixion in her female eyes, Pilate's wife inverts the culture/nature and reason/passion dichotomies to explicit female advantage once again in Lanyer's poem. The Crucifixion is worse than the Fall because malice is worse than ignorance as the state of mind in which evil is done. Moreover, by the implicit standards of the long-traditional conception of sin as self-murder, killing oneself is far less culpable than killing the son of God. Finally, no woman wants the Crucifixion; only men do. Pilate's wife now spells out to Pilate the implications of the Crucifixion and the Fall for gender relations:

> Then let us have our Libertie againe,
> And challendge to your selves no Sov'raigntie;
> . . . .
> Your fault being greater, why should you disdaine

Our beeing your equals, free from tyranny?

. . . .

This sinne of yours, hath no excuse, nor end.

To which (poore soules) we never gave consent,
Witness thy wife (O *Pilate*) speakes for all.

([Lanyer] 1993, 87)

Foscarini's complacent hunch to the contrary, an intelligent woman of the Renaissance, reflecting on Pilate, Pilate's wife, and Christ's Crucifixion, would not easily find for the superiority of Pilate's moral understanding and thus confirm the subjection of females to males ordained by God after the Fall. These two personages are styled to enforce exactly the opposite finding in Lanyer's feminist poetics, while a fully reasoned claim—no mere call—issues for sexual equality in the aftermath of the Crucifixion. Interestingly, the lack of punctuation marks to enclose reported speech in early seventeenth-century texts makes it impossible to determine whether the last two lines of the foregoing quotation are spoken by Pilate's wife or by Lanyer as omniscient narrator. No less interestingly, an exact determination does not affect the interpretation or the prescient feminism of "Salve Deus Rex Judaeorum" because a brief for an end to male domination, thus historicized, holds for any date subsequent to the Crucifixion and for any nominally Christian place. In this poem Aemilia Lanyer takes more seriously—that is to say, more historically—the radical social and political implications of the new order broached in the gospel narrative of primitive Christianity than would any other English thinker or writer of either sex until a quarter century later, in the midcentury ferment of revolution and interregnum. Even in that later company (see Hobby 1989; Thomas 1958), she and her Pilate's wife sound voices of the utmost present-time urgency and cogency as they lay claim to what has long since remained for women the receding future of gender equality.

Notes

I am deeply grateful to Doug Bruster and to Laurie Shannon, whose careful critiques of an intermediate draft of this essay improved my final version in a number of specifics.

1. For a thoughtful discussion of relevant theory and methodology, see LaCapra 1983, 13–71.

2. Constance Jordan reflects on the pitfalls of possible anachronism but finds it possible to define "the feminism of Renaissance texts" as "a theory of a point of view, by which to justify feminist assumptions of the virtue of women and, conversely, to call into question patriarchal assumptions of their inferiority," which, for its own part, presumes that "a representation of the world from a woman's point of view has validity, and that such a representation entails an understanding of the assumptions held by the various participants in the debate on the woman question" (1990, 6–7).

3. So, too, John Donne appears to have thought at the same date in writing his extravagantly hyperbolical meditative elegies, the two *Anniversaries* (1610–11), on the deceased fifteen-year-old heiress Elizabeth Drury, only child of his patron, the then-prominent courtier-diplomat Sir Robert Drury. Basic aspects of Donne's representation, however, would surely have failed to satisfy Lanyer: his only supremely good woman, the source of all cosmic vitality and value, is a girl who dies of a fever in virginal adolescence.

4. The other major witness to poetic inspiration flowing to Lanyer from a female source is her evocative vision-poem, "The Authors Dreame to the Ladie *Marie*, the Countesse *Dowager of Pembrooke*," which extols the moral, spiritual, and creative power manifested in Mary Sidney's Psalm translations and declares them the "faire impression" that "Seales her pure soule unto the Deitie" ([Lanyer] 1993, 29).

5. This bibliographical situation has changed with the welcome appearance of Susanne Woods's edition of Lanyer's poems (1993). Before Woods's edition, the only modern source for Lanyer's poetry was A. R. Rowse's editor ([Lanyer] 1978 edition), which does not even carry Lanyer's name on its title page. In writing this essay, I have also had the advantage of access to the transcription of the Huntington Library copy of *Salve Deus Rex Judaeorum* that is available for purchase in hard copy from the Brown University Women Writers Project (Lanyer [1611] 1991), although the text circulated in 1988–91 contained many transcription errors.

6. Further discrepancies emerge where Lanyer and Daniel write in the same genre, as they do in both addressing laudatory verse epistles to Anne Clifford and to Lucy, countess of Bedford. Daniel's "To the Lady Anne Clifford," in terza rima set in block form, praises a girl of "tender youth" for her virtuous self-containment in demure silence and stoic circumspection (Daniel 1950, 119–21); Lanyer's "To the Ladie *Anne*, Countesse of Dorcet," in ottava rima stanzas, hails a young woman for a virtue so surpassingly potent that it dissolves social hierarchy and becomes the standard and repository ("steward") of all human worth, not excluding Lanyer's own moral perceptions and the poetry praising Anne that she writes in the light of them ([Lanyer] 1993, 41–47). Daniel's "To the Lady Lucie, Countesse of Bedford," in cross-rhymed iambic pentameter, hails its subject for studiousness in virtue so exalted and retired, and for happiness so perfected, that she is now positioned as arbiter of all the moral efforts and aspirations of her fellow mortals (Daniel 1950, 116–18); in sharp contrast, Lanyer's four stanzas of rime royal addressed "To the Ladie *Lucie*, Countesse of Bedford" envisage her spiritualized erotic intimacy in her heart's loving embrace of Christ ([Lanyer] 1993, 32–33).

7. I am not implying that Lanyer is the first, or even the first female, author in English to feminize a portrayal of Christ. There is a rich earlier meditative tradition to this effect, which Caroline Walker Bynum (1982) has studied for the thirteenth century and which Julian of Norwich applies in chapters 59–61 of her *Showings* (or *Revelations*) *of Divine Love* (ca. 1393) on Jesus as mother, after having unprecedentedly broached a conception of God as mother in chapter 58 (Julian 1978). Lanyer, however, does not feminize her Christ in a medieval fashion as maternal. He has, rather, the cultivated graces and virtuous bearing associated with marriageable women of rank in the Renaissance, a type that Lanyer could draw from life through her familiarity with the Elizabethan court.

8. On the rarity even of poetic usage, see OED, "hail," vb. The angel of the Annunciation greets Mary with "Haile thou that art highly favoured" (Luke 1:28). Judas betrays Christ in the garden with "Haile master" and a kiss (Matthew 26:49). The soldiers who put a crown of thorns on Jesus's head and a reed in his hand shortly before they crucify him mock him with "Haile king of the Jewes" (Matthew 27: 29, Mark 15:18, John 19:3). This exhaustive listing gives the readings of the King James Bible (Pollard 1911).

9. Indeed I would say that a recognition of this problem should qualify a text of any era as feminist, not only in such clear cases as Mary Wollstonecraft's *Vindication of the Rights of Woman* or John Stuart Mill's *On the Subjection of Women*, but also in Elizabeth Cary, Lady Falkland's *Tragedy of Mariam, Fair Queen of Jewry* (published 1613), a work nearly contemporaneous with Lanyer's *Salve Deus*.

10. Laurie Shannon has suggested to me (personal communication) that Lanyer's Jewish background may have enabled her to conceive the agency at issue in the Crucifixion in gendered terms rather than the ethnic ones that were commonplace throughout Christian Europe.

The Powers of Powerlessness: The Courtships of Elizabeth Barrett and Queen Victoria

Margaret Homans

"I love your verses with all my heart, dear Miss Barrett . . . and I love you too": thus Robert Browning opens his famous correspondence with Elizabeth Barrett, one of the most celebrated poets of her day, and soon to become Mrs. Browning (Browning and Browning, 1:3, 10 Jan. 1845).[1] But what can he possibly mean? They have never met; he cannot mean that he loves a Miss Barrett that he knows separately from her poems; indeed, so to declare himself to such a Miss Barrett would be an astonishing indiscretion. Only a supposed identification between the poet and her poems can legitimate Browning's remark, an identification that, as readers of Browning's poems know, Browning himself— champion of what he calls "objective" poetry and master of the dramatic monologue—fastidiously eschewed.[2] Thus his courtship of Miss Barrett begins simultaneously with extravagant praise and with denigration of her as a writer, a combination that persists not only on his side of the correspondence but on hers as well.[3] Each writer gains an advantage over the other through adopting a pose of abject humility, but my first point will be that this apparently gender-neutral strategy has differing resonances for a man's and for a woman writer's authority in Victorian England.

Browning continues, in all his humble arrogance. Once before he nearly visited her, and he felt "close . . . to some world's-wonder in chapel or crypt" (Browning and Browning, 1:3–4). Responding in kind, she professes herself to be "a devout admirer & student of your works" and claims "the humble, low voice, which is so excellent a thing in women," pointedly inserting humility into Lear's description of Cordelia's voice (as "soft, low, and gentle"). In a lighter vein, she also cautions him that had he entered the so-called "crypt," he "might have caught cold" (1:5, 11 Jan. 1845). Thus she mockingly elbows him out of his worshipful pose, by simultaneously declaring herself unworthy of the compliment and pointing out that to compare her to a corpse in a crypt is no compliment at all. But she does this only so as to occupy the pose of worshiper herself.

In this first exchange the writers have begun to discuss the "faults" in Barrett's poems. Browning accuses himself of failure—of failing to find any "faults" and thus of being unable to "do you some little good" "as a loyal fellow-craftsman" (1:3)—thus managing to praise her and disparage himself in the same phrase. In reply, she "begs" to be informed of her faults. Her "fault," which he claims to admire, is an excess that reveals the poet behind the poem: "for an instructed eye loves to see where the brush has dipped twice in a lustrous colour, has lain insistingly along a favorite outline . . . —for these 'too muches' for the everybody's picture are so many helps to the making out the real painter's-picture as he had it in his brain" (1:7, 13 Jan. 1845). That the erotic as well as the poetic is on his mind is suggested by the example he proposes: Titian's Naples Magdalen. This faulty, praiseworthy revelation of the artist behind the work leads Browning to his best-known formulation of their difference: "You speak out, you,—I only make men & women speak," a formulation that confirms Browning's initial and paradoxically derogatory premise that to love her poems is to love her. Her self-revealing insistency, her speaking out from herself, constitutes for Browning her limitation as a poet, able to speak in only one voice, or only to paint the same line again and again. (Moreover, the letter ends with Browning's refusal to admit that she has successfully dismantled his "crypt" figure: he waits for the spring "and my Chapel-sight after all!")

Disguising his criticism—really his condescension—as humble praise (I only make men and women speak), Browning again claims advantage through humility, and Barrett in return does the same. "The fault was clearly with me & not with you" (1:8, 15 Jan. 1845), she begins, faulting herself for misreading his first mention of faults. She accuses herself of being "headlong" both in her misreading of his letter and in her poetry, equating that term with the insistency Browning described. Indeed, she discusses at great length the fault "which many wd call superfluity" (1:9), thus aggressively repeating—in her own insistency in the letter—the fault of which he originally accuses her. She also castigates her poems for a "difference between the thing desired & the thing attained, between the idea in the writer's mind & the εἴδωλον cast off in his work." But this confession of weakness actually defends against Browning's criticism, for she claims a gap between mind and poem in place of too much self-revelation. Moreover, she uses Greek to make this point, and she introduces the term "headlong" with reference to "an Italian master" she had "years ago," thus reminding Browning of the elite and unfeminine education that makes her his intellectual peer, even while humbling herself before his disparagement.

Nonetheless, she closes this section of the letter by defining their difference as a gender difference that is also qualitative: "Then you are 'masculine' to the height—and I, as a woman, have studied some of your gestures of language & intonation wistfully, as a thing beyond me far! & the more admirable for being beyond." This arrangement of low femininity relative to masculine height reverses Browning's stance of worshipfulness, locating Barrett herself as a woman in the position of worshiper.

Reading the early letters, Browning's biographer Betty Miller points out that the two poets "stood, or attempted to stand, in the same, wholly reverential attitude" (1953, 101), and Barrett's recent feminist critics have pointed out, about the correspondence in general, that the two poets "competed in their letters for the lowest place" (Mermin 1989, 133). "Each insisted on being the lesser artist," writes Angela Leighton, and, linking artistic to amatory competition, she shows that, in a set of conventions in which the beloved is raised on a pedestal and the lover abased beneath, "[t]he imagery of heights and depths, in which both were proficient, is clearly an imagery of subtle competition between them to be the lover, not the beloved" (1986, 93–94). While Miller emphasizes that as the correspondence proceeds Barrett eventually gives in, with regret, and "consent[s] . . . to be worshipped" (1953, 101) and argues that in their married life Browning's desire to "obey" his wife had unfortunate consequences for him personally and poetically, more recent critics writing from Barrett's viewpoint tend to argue for the poets' equality. Like Leighton linking art and love in the letters, Laurence Lerner writes: "Some of the Browning letters . . . seem like a contest to claim that each is beneath the other. They argue endlessly . . . about which has gained more from the other. . . . Sometimes they grovel" (n.d., 5). For Dorothy Mermin, the poets' well-matched epistolary humility demonstrates that their relationship is "nonhierarchical" and characterized by "collaboration" and "reciprocity" (1989, 124). Yopie Prins finds that both poets use translation in their epistolary competition to be "secondary," to deny their own primary authorship, and to be "feminized"; and in a beautiful formulation that is essentially in line with Mermin's view, she argues that "they solve the problem of power by re-allocating it between themselves and calling it love" (1991, 436, 444, 445).

Up to this point in my reading of the first few letters it would seem fair to say, following these critics, that a symmetrical and equal relation obtains between Barrett and Browning. That is, their poses of self-abasement are identical. If we were to analyze their similar posturing from the point of view of Browning and his poetry, we might locate various possible sources for the choice of "loving from beneath" as an epistolary strategy. The history of literary forms would emphasize the attractions of the troubadour lyric as a model (see, e.g., Mermin 1989; Lerner n.d.); economic and social history would emphasize the increasing feminization and therefore diminishing status of the male poet and of all poetry during the nineteenth century, owing to its relegation to the female world of drawing rooms and consumer objects, and to the dissociation of poetry from the public world of

masculine economic activity (Psomiades 1991); finally, a theory of literary influ-
ence derived from the work of Harold Bloom would emphasize the secondariness
that, as Leslie Brisman has argued, is the chosen stance of the Victorian poet
(presumed to be male) vis-à-vis the overwhelmingly primary Romantic past.[4]

For example, in Brisman's Bloomian reading, the self-describedly "fallen"
speaker of Browning's "Pauline" elevates her to a celestial height and then ele-
vates Shelley, the "sun treader," Browning's unconquerable precursor, to the
same height. The speaker uses his worship of the celestial Shelley subtly to
displace Shelley, for example by calling him "still" a star—still in the sense of
"everlastingly" but also stilled, stuck, unchanging. The speaker enthusiastically
embraces secondariness as his solution to Shelley's unalterable priority, delighting
in

> "the contented lowness
> With which I gaze on him I keep forever
> Above me; I to rise and rival him?
> Feed his fame rather from my heart's best blood,
> Wither unseen that he may flourish still."
>   (Browning [1833] 1970, lines 554–59)

The speaker renders himself active and Shelley passive by making himself the
agent of Shelley's elevation ("him I keep"). And to be second is always to have
"some better essence" to quest after. Fixing Pauline and Shelley as stilled celestial
ideals, the speaker seizes the initiative and makes from his abjection a position of
power. Moreover, the equation of Shelley and Pauline suggests how Browning
equates poetic secondariness with the sort of erotic self-subordination he per-
forms in the letters to Barrett. Crudely put, he makes Barrett another Pauline, and
perhaps also another Shelley.[5]

This equation and embrace of erotic and poetic secondariness should alert us
that posing as "the lowest" is likely to have gendered meanings. It takes its
meaning in this instance from the speaker's masculinity, as Shelley's rival and
Pauline's lover. Pauline is ultimately subjected to the sort of constitutively mas-
culine agon it has been Harold Bloom's project to elucidate. Barrett's relation to
the poetic past, as well as to present erotic possibilities, is not likely to follow such
a model.[6] A model of literary influence that would explain Barrett and Brown-
ing's posturing in relation to the literary past tells only part of the story, and in
this case may tell the man's story better than it tells the woman's. But even
Barrett's best feminist critics—such as Mermin, Leighton, Prins, and Lerner—are
overlooking such differences (of which they are quite aware when it comes to
reading the poetry) when they see Barrett and Browning performing symmetrical
acts of humility—each worshiping from beneath and desiring to use that position

for subtle advantage—in the correspondence. For Barrett, posing as "the lowest" has different meanings, resonances, and, possibly, sources, and I will focus here on the gendered asymmetry between the two poets without regard for generic distinctions.

Conventions about absolute and hierarchical sex difference clearly operate within Victorian literature. Mermin (1989), Helen Cooper (1988), and others have discussed Barrett's paradoxical relation to a poetic tradition that divides human possibility into silent feminine object and questing male subject. "The Lost Bower" (first published in 1844), a poem in which a young girl penetrates through a wood to an enclosed gardenlike space, only to find on a return trip that it has vanished, is in Mermin's astute reading (1989, 102) a sad account of the impossibility of a girl's being both (male) quester and (female) object of the quest, of a girl's ever reaching beyond the rigid boundary dividing conventional femininity from more active human possibilities.[7] In her quest, the girl-speaker's

> little struggling fingers
> Tore asunder gyve and thong
> Of the brambles which entrapped me, and
> the barrier branches strong.
> (Browning [1844] 1974, stanza 16)

In the letter about being "headlong" Barrett again precariously places herself in that traditionally masculine role: "Headlong I was at first, and headlong I continue—precipitously rushing forward through all manner of nettles & briars instead of keeping the path." Worshiping Browning, impersonating a chivalric troubadour, may likewise constitute for Barrett an attempt to occupy a powerful speaking position in writing, given that Browning uses that pose to such powerful effect. Yet while he can firmly position himself as active, subjective quester in relation to Pauline and Shelley, Barrett's girl-speaker, and perhaps the "headlong" Barrett of the letters as well, can occupy the role of questing subject only fleetingly.

This way of reading the letters through the poems depends on disregarding generic boundaries between high and low forms, and to give Barrett's letters an even fuller reading, we need to include the social and historical text of Victorian Britain as well. In looking at the social aspects of gender asymmetry, I am pursuing, in part, a line of argument Mermin parenthetically advances at the start of her book. Mermin writes that Barrett Browning tends to reuse traditional metaphors in a way that is "disconcertingly literal," and that she does so "most often in amatory protestations of subordination or dependency (flattery when men use them, but painfully close to the social reality of women's lives)" (1989, 6). To extend Mermin's idea into a reading of the letters, it could be said that for Browning to claim abjection is a flattering conceit. As a man, even an obscure and low-born one, his relation to the pose of worshiper is ironic or playful: a superior posing, in effect, as an inferior. For Barrett to claim abjection, however, is doubly ironic, and therefore potentially not ironic at all. As a woman, even a famous and wellborn one, she is an inferior posing as a superior posing as an inferior. Pretending subordination, to reiterate Mermin's parenthesis, is "painfully close to the social reality of women's lives."

Of recent readers of the correspondence, Lerner notes this gender asymmetry the most explicitly. When Browning speaks "from beneath," Lerner writes, his chivalric pose "looks too like a tactical inversion of the real relations of power" between men and women, "a strategy for reconciling women to the facts of gender relations [in marriage], that they are called goddesses by the men because they are going to have to treat the men as gods." For example, when Barrett revises a line from *King Lear* to describe her woman's voice as not only "low" but "humble," she is not just upping the ante in her competition with Browning for the lowest place; she is also suggesting that she understands and yields (as Cordelia did not) to what the cultural script requires of her as a woman.[8] On the whole, Barrett Browning's recent critics have tended not to emphasize the social meanings of seeking "the lowest place," meanings that bear directly on understanding the epistolary and poetic relationship we are tracing here.

It may be helpful to review here the rough outlines of early Victorian sexual ideology. "By the 1830s and 1840s," write Catherine Hall and Leonore Davidoff, "the belief in the natural differences and complementary roles of men and women . . . had become the common sense of the English middle class" (1987, 149). The ideas of "separate spheres" and of "woman's place," they summarize, had come to dominate discussions of sexual difference: the increasing separation of work and home in industrialism, and the rise of middle-class families sufficiently wealthy to mark their status with nonworking wives, meant that sex difference became reified, hypostasized, and hierarchized.[9] For Sarah Ellis women were "relative creatures" whose "proper sphere" was strictly domestic ([1838] 1839, 1:178, 20). Moreover, Ellis writes, recognition of "one important truth" will make for a successful marriage: "it is the superiority of your husband as a man. It is quite possible you may have more talent, with higher attainments . . . but this has nothing whatever to do with your position as a woman, which is, and must be, inferior to his as a man" (1843, 24–25). This view continues to be elaborated and justified throughout the Victorian period. For Ruskin, lecturing in 1864, "each completes the other" and "they are in nothing alike"; "true wifely subjection" is woman's nature and, paradoxically, the aim of her training ([1865] 1907, 58). In 1871 Darwin writes that, thanks to natural selection, "man has ultimately become superior to woman" and that "the present inequality in mental power between the sexes would not be effaced by a . . . course of early training" ([1871] 1983, 1:411).

Moving from generalities about Victorian sexual ideology to the specific case of Barrett may ring false to some readers because of her specialness among Victorian women. How can she, highly educated, writing poetry in her bedroom and visited there by London's literary elite, have been subject to ordinary Victorian sexual ideology? Moreover, when the two poets met, she was famous already, and richer and of higher social status than Browning, who became a celebrity only later in his life. And yet even in these regards, Barrett may have been as typical as she was exceptional. Davidoff and Hall point out that much of the writing of early Victorian ideologues "explored the contradictions between the claims for women's [moral] superiority and their social subordination," and that Ellis's popularity was due in part to "the tension" in her writing "between the notion of women as 'relative creatures' and a celebratory view of their potential power" (1987, 149, 183). If Browning asserts his superiority to Barrett by asserting her superiority to him, then it is indeed part of, not a contradiction of, Victorian sexual ideology that Barrett should be in some ways his superior. The terms in which she achieved her contemporary fame are saturated with "separate spheres" ideology, despite reviewers' admiration for her classical learning. Cooper (1988, 22–25) demonstrates that reviewers singled out for praise her most sentimental poems in preference to more original ones; she is belittled as "our fair author," a "poetess." Her very unusualness as a Victorian woman is what makes her typical; her superiority what subjects her.

That statement, in regard to Victorian gender ideology, is true of Queen Victoria herself as well. When a genuinely successful mid-nineteenth-century woman acts the part of inferior vis-à-vis an embodiment of manliness, her rhetorical act as well as its unpredictable consequences create a resemblance between her and the most important woman in the land, Queen Victoria. Quite possibly Barrett's position not only resembles Victoria's but is also a conscious or unconscious imitation of it, for Victoria's is a stance that, despite drawbacks, promised to balance the claims of personal and rhetorical power with those of domestic or subordinate femininity.

Before going on to discuss Queen Victoria at some length, I wish to pause briefly over questions of method and perspective. What does it mean to present Barrett and Victoria as figures who are at once exceptional and typical Victorian women? And what does that have to do with the argument I have been advancing about Barrett's possibly self-defeating way of assuming the position of "the lowest"?

On the one hand, in focusing on Barrett and on Queen Victoria as distinctive individuals, I am practicing an author-centered criticism, which has the advantage of honoring and, in many cases, of recovering from oblivion the authorial subject, signature, and agency. Nancy Miller points out that these are feminist aims, because "only those who have it can play with not having it" (Miller 1982, 53; and see 1988 more generally); that is, the critique of Western humanism that takes "the death of the author" as its starting point presupposes men's, but not women's, long and comfortable history of publically acknowledged authorship and subjectivity. Women writers of the nineteenth century lack such a history, as Barrett Browning's still semimarginal position in the canon attests. Focusing on her as author, and taking seriously her agency in shaping her literary and personal relations, would seem to make feminist political sense. Still more, although Victoria is hardly an obscure figure, her writing never receives the serious reading that it merits and that I hope to give to some of it here.[10]

On the other hand, this essay is not simply author-centered, for already the presence of Queen Victoria decenters the more narrowly literary emphasis on Barrett. Victoria appears here as an author in her own right; few, however, would claim that her writing belongs in the elevated category "literature" to which Barrett's poetry (if not also her letters) belongs, and she is also a historical construct around whose image much Victorian sexual ideology coalesces. Victoria's presence, and some of the documents used to invoke it, will decenter Barrett's and indeed the "literary" itself as well. The next section of this essay concerns Victoria, so that when we ultimately turn to Barrett's poems about queenship, those poems will seem by turns the focus of this essay and, conversely, just a few among the myriad cultural constructions of Victoria's figure. Indeed, it could be argued that all the texts surveyed here are mere threads in the vast web of nineteenth-century textuality, a web that it has been the project of such intertextual modes of reading as New Historicism and cultural studies to explore. As Jay Clayton and Eric Rothstein (1991) point out, these approaches have as much claim to political progressiveness as does author-centered criticism, which risks ideological blindness. What appears as freedom, agency, and originality may actually be ideologically constructed: instead of "freedom fighters," women writers may merely be "role players in a social dynamic that permitted, perhaps even caused, their rebellion" (Clayton and Rothstein 1991, 11). Moreover, intertextuality resists canon formation, refuses to hierarchize genres, "and insists upon the treatment of all works, not just 'minor' ones, as social products" (17). An intertextual approach is what allows us to read Barrett's letters in the same way we read her poems and to juxtapose Victoria's diaries, street ballads, and Barrett's poems.

Nonetheless, I see Barrett, and Victoria, as more than mere strands in the ideological web, nor do I wish wholly to abandon the notion of poetry's distinctiveness as a genre. In Barrett's case, both author-based and intertextual approaches have legitimate claims on our attention, especially, and paradoxically, when used together. Given the three major books on her discussed in this essay, she is no longer in need of feminist rediscovery. Yet because her position is not quite secure outside the feminist canon, to demote her to appearing as just one thread in the cultural web would do justice neither to her importance nor to her agency as an individual. For these reasons, this essay will present Barrett and Victoria as *primae inter pares* and try to have it both ways.

The need to cross categorical boundaries between women's agency and their ideological subjection, especially as regards exceptional women like Barrett and the queen, becomes clear when we reflect on the oddity of using "Victorian" to describe Victoria herself. While Victoria may have been subject to an ideology over which no individual had control, it is impossible not to think that she had some active hand in shaping the ideology that bears her name.[11] Indeed, Sarah Ellis cites the newly crowned queen at once as the epitome of women's "influence" (by which she means the containment of women within the domestic sphere), not differentiating between Victoria's powers and those of her female subjects, and as unique authorizing agent of that containment. The women of England must "prov[e] to their youthful sovereign, that whatever plan she may think it right to sanction for the moral advancement of her subjects . . . will be . . . faithfully supported in every British home by the female influence prevailing there" ([1838] 1839, 68). Victoria is at once the subjective author of Victorian ideology and an object of its creation, performing original gestures of self-representation that were legible and efficacious, paradoxically, only because they coincided with popular representations already in place.

This balancing act is what Barrett's and Queen Victoria's politics perform as well. Just as their freedom to defy or escape ideology is countered by their inevitable subjection to it, so their unusual political, personal, and poetic powers are balanced by their tendency to give away those powers: a tendency that an intertextual approach, but not an author-based approach, can show us is created by the ideological scripts "that permitted, even caused their rebellion." Victoria and Barrett can construct their own versions of female authority only by means of the ideology of female submission.[12] Just as I wish to see Barrett at once as central figure and as thread in the textual web, I would also argue that it is possible and important to see it both ways about women's power. At once unique and typical, Victoria and Barrett both exert active agency in posing as inferiors and act out an ideological script prepared beyond their control. By the same token, their shared exceptionalness may permit them to exceed ideological strictures, to exert power beyond that permitted to other women, and may simultaneously prove their submission to that ideology. This essay explores the terrain joining these opposed possibilities.

The terms *woman* and *monarch* are virtually mutually exclusive in British history, just as are the terms *woman* and *serious poet*. Adrienne Auslander Munich points out in particular that the idea of "maternal monarchy seems absurd," an outrageous mingling of separate spheres (1987a, 265).[13] And yet, paradoxically, when Victoria came to the throne and Barrett began publishing, these opposed terms also had a certain history of overdetermined connection. Queen Elizabeth provided one paradigm for active female rule. But Anna Jameson had recently attacked Elizabeth for her lack of womanliness—of affection or gentleness. Elizabeth, Jameson wrote, "never forgot the sovereign in the woman, and surely this is no praise" (1834, 2:322). Victoria "disliked [Elizabeth] for her immodesty" (Longford 1964, 31), and she significantly revises Elizabeth's successful practice of adapting female conventions to royal ones. For example, in the first year of her reign Victoria writes in her diary, "[T]he curious old form of pricking the Sheriffs was gone through; and I had to prick them all, with a huge pin" (1912, 1 Feb. 1838, 1:268). The names of the high sheriffs nominated for each county are presented for the monarch's approval on a roll of vellum. "The monarch pierces the appropriate names with the spike of a brass bodkin . . . a custom believed to date from the time of Queen Elizabeth I who was presented with the Sheriff's Roll for her approval one day when she was sewing in the garden and, having no pen with which to make the usual dots against the chosen names, pricked them with her needle" (Hibbert, in Victoria 1985, 30).[14] Elizabeth not only adapted female convention to royal exigency but managed to make sewing immodestly phallic. In Victoria's hands, however, this custom has different meanings. Her diary record of the event focuses on how much she missed the chivalrous protection of her Prime Minister, Lord Melbourne, who was generally at her side during such performances.

The more immediate paradigm of queenship Victoria inherited was that of Caroline, the consort of George IV. Although she was accused of adultery, during the divorce proceedings George IV instituted against her in 1820 the English people were extravagantly on her side. The dispute became "domestic melodrama," and the king's failure to win his case was read as vindicating her honor and virtue. Her supporters appealed to chivalry: "the tenderness and respect with which women were treated in England, it was argued, were the mark of England's advanced state of civilization." "Men [could] prove their manhood" by supporting this "'poor wronged female.' . . . The most prevalent image was of the 'unprotected female' assailed by the might of the crown" (Davidoff and Hall 1987, 151–52). As a consequence, when Victoria inherited the monarchy, despite the vast difference between being queen regnant and queen consort, she inherited most immediately this queenly identification with vulnerable femininity. Thus a woman monarch was not simply a contradiction in terms, but the name of a subjected being, just as "woman poet" meant "poetess," the author of trivial, sentimental verses.

Two broadsheets from the time of Victoria's succession and coronation represent the polarities of that paradox. In one, satirically titled "Petticoats for Ever," two characters, Kitty and Joan, hold a conversation about the "wonders" the new queen will do "all in favour of the women." There will be a Parliament of women (with names like "Mother Mouthalmighty") and an Act passed providing "that all women, married or single, are to have a roving commission, to go where they like, do as they like, and work when they like. . . . and [that they] shall have . . . a gallon of cream of the valley each to drink health to the Queen" (James 1976, 340). The threat posed by female rule is thus defused by comic exaggeration. A second broadsheet, "The Coronation," represents contrastingly the sentimental possibilities of the figure of queen. Celebrating her sincerely on her coronation day, this doggerel inserts Victoria firmly into the female sphere as dutiful daughter ("Tho' Victoria does the sceptre sway, / Her parent may she still obey") and into her female role as genetic link between generations of men: "E'er she resigns all earthly things, / Be mother to a line of Kings" (James 1976, 341). "Queen," in these popular representations, means one extreme or the other: the alarming oxymoron of female rule or merely an ordinary domestic ideal.

For Queen Victoria, as for Barrett, power and powerlessness are intertwined, as the highly public text of her private life in the early part of her reign demonstrates. In the period just before and just after her marriage to Albert in February 1840, five years before the Browning-Barrett correspondence starts, we can see repeated at the level of national politics some of the same issues present in the Browning-Barrett courtship correspondence. Victoria is not figuratively but literally enthroned, literally an object of worship for a nation and not just for an obscure poet. It is she who must propose to Albert, not he to her. Nonetheless, again and again when she attempts to establish her political and also personal power, she can do so only by giving it away, much as Barrett does.

For example, in the spring of 1839, when the Whig Prime Minister Lord Melbourne resigned because his majority in the House of Commons fell to five, to be replaced by the Tories under Sir Robert Peel, a crisis occurred over the question of the queen's Household. The members of the royal Household, with titles like "Ladies of the Bedchamber," had long ago been personal attendants, but they were by now understood to be political appointments and ordinarily changed with a change of administration. Peel wanted Victoria "to demonstrate . . . confidence in [his] government" by replacing her Whig friends with the wives of important Tories (Victoria 1908, 8 May 1839, 1:159).[15] Victoria, however, vehemently protested this protocol. As a new monarch still in her teens, she desired to bolster her own authority and viewed Peel's challenge as "an attempt to see whether she could be led and managed like a child" (Victoria 1908, 9 May 1839, 1:163). Defying Peel would seem a simple demonstration of her sovereignty, but the way in which she defies him ambiguously constricts, not increases, the extent of her power. Victoria is able to confirm her authority as queen—her right, in this case, to retain her chosen Ladies of the Bedchamber—only by asserting that the

Ladies are not political appointments, but only friends, and thus that she herself is not involved in politics, at least when at home. Whereas Peel argues that for her there can be no line between the personal and matters of state, Victoria insists upon a private, female sphere distinct from public politics.

Her defense turns on her mocking insistence that women's political views don't matter: "The Ladies his only support!! What an admission of weakness! . . . Was Sir Robert so weak that *even* the Ladies must be of his opinion?" (1912, 9 May 1839, 2:170, 172); "I should like to know if they mean to give the Ladies seats in Parliament?" (1908, 9 May 1839, 1:163). In her journal she describes the showdown as if it were a dramatic victory for her own firmness, yet her victory paradoxically empties that firmness of political content.

> Soon after this Sir Robert said, "Now, about the Ladies," upon which I said I could *not* give up *any* of my Ladies, and never imagined such a thing; he asked if I meant to retain them all; all, I said; the Mistress of the Robes and the Ladies of the Bedchamber? he asked. I replied all; for he said they were the Wives of the Opponents of the Government. . . . I said that [they] would not interfere, I never talked Politics with them. (1912, 9 May 1839 2:171)

Victoria argues that never before have the Ladies been treated as political appointments. Her analogy is a self-defeating one, however, because previous Ladies of the Bedchamber have attended only queens consort; Victoria is in effect standing firm by demoting her status from Queen to queen consort, from first to second. Peel objected that "I was a Queen Regnant, and that made the difference; not here, I said,—and I maintained my right" (1912, 9 May 1839, 2:171). Her reply "maintain[s her] right" only by shrinking the profile of her power.

Nonetheless, Victoria did win her point, and she may even have contributed to Peel's failure to form a successful government, although he also lacked a majority in Commons. The public "applauded her pluck in standing up for her rights, and admired the 'vein of iron' which ran through her character" (St. Aubyn 1992, 114). Her attempt to proclaim herself apolitical possibly did have political effects. Still, although Melbourne returned to office for two more years, that was to be the end of his rule. It would be difficult to say whether Victoria narrowed her power in the attempt to assert it, or whether she actually gained power by narrowing her claims for it.

While the controversy over her Ladies was going on, Victoria was involved in another controversy, one that Dorothy Thompson (1990) claims was less politically significant than that of the Household, yet it contributed to her decision to marry, which had enormous consequences for the nature of her reign and power. One of her mother's ladies in waiting, Lady Flora Hastings, had apparently become pregnant and was the subject of much vicious gossip in the court, gossip promoted by Victoria, perhaps in part because Lady Flora was associated with Tories, perhaps also because Victoria was not on good terms with her mother, for whom Flora became the scapegoat. Indeed, her mother's relationship with her comptroller, Sir John Conroy, was somewhat too intimate, and Victoria's special nastiness toward Lady Flora may have displaced her resentment of her mother's active sexuality. Victoria blamed the supposed pregnancy on Conroy, whom she terms "the Monster and Demon Incarnate" (1985, 2 Feb. 1839, 42).[16]

The story is a horrible one: Lady Flora was not pregnant but dying of liver cancer, which had swollen her body in a simulacrum of pregnancy. Medical examination proved that Lady Flora was still a virgin. But Victoria wished to be rid of her mother, who insisted on living at court as a chaperone, as if it were Victoria, and not the duchess herself, who ran the risk of sexual impropriety. Victoria resented her mother's authority as well as her sexual independence. Melbourne pointed out to Victoria that, if her mother wouldn't leave until Victoria married, " 'Well, then, there's *that* way of settling it' " (Victoria 1985, 17 April 1839, 42). During this period, Victoria disliked the idea of marriage as an unwanted dilution of her power as monarch.

> For myself, I said, at present *my* feeling was quite against ever marrying. . . . I observed that marrying a subject was making yourself so much their equal. . . . I said I dreaded the thought of marrying; that I was so accustomed to have my own way, that I thought it was 10 to 1 that I shouldn't agree with any body. (1912, 18 April 1839, 2:153–54)

To marry for the sake of freedom from her mother's unwanted control would only substitute for it another form of subordination, probably a greater one, and gain one power only by losing another.

Moreover, responding to Melbourne's suggestion, Victoria terms marriage "a schocking [*sic*] alternative." She understands that marriage means sex as well as not having one's own way. She uses this same term—"schocking"—two months later when she quotes Melbourne discussing Lady Flora's alleged pregnancy (1985, 42, 43, 17 April, 1839; 22 June 1839). This echo links the prospect of marriage with sexual impropriety and suggests that Victoria aligns trading her mother's domination for that of a husband with trading the scandal of a mother's sexuality for the public deployment of her own. She suppresses her mother's authority and sexual autonomy only at the expense of her own authority and sexual autonomy.

Replying to her fear that she would cease to have her own way in marriage, Melbourne says, " 'Oh! but you would have it still' (my own way)" (1912, 18 April 1839, 2:154). The history of Victoria and Albert's relationship is an ambiguous text of sexual and political powers held and given up on both sides, a text that makes use of the confusing, reversible vocabulary of chivalrous worship that informs the Browning-Barrett correspondence. Although Victoria adored Albert and at one point sought for him the title of "King Consort" and a position equal to hers, she insisted on her prerogatives as queen from the start. Before they were married she overruled his desire to choose his own (politically neutral) Household and instead placed close to him Whig candidates of her own choosing. And it was not he but she who proposed, or rather, "[told] Albert of my decision," as she puts it in her journal (1912, 14 Oct. 1839, 2:267). She gave Albert a ring, and he gave her a lock of hair. A broadsheet from the time of their marriage depicts Albert as a "sausage maker" so poor that his abjection feminizes even his sexual potency:

> She says now we are wed,
> I must not dare to tease her,
> But strive both day and night,
> All e'er I can to please her.
> I told her I would do
> For her all I was able,
> And when she had a son,
> I would sit and rock the cradle.
>
> (James 1976, 343)

Victoria proposed to a man she repeatedly describes, using Victorian conventions for describing a beloved woman, as an angel, a beauty, with a cheek like a rose, not only at the beginning of the marriage, but also in a letter of 28 January 1845, five years into her marriage (1908, 2:33).

Other popular responses reflect the conflict between her roles as wife—theoretically, obedient and subjected to her husband—and as monarch, subject to no one. Emphasizing her status as queen regnant, with the same logic of "Petticoats for Ever," a street ballad cited by Thompson (1990, 38) suggests that Victoria will vow to love but not to obey her subject Albert and that this will disrupt society by encouraging other wives to be insubordinate. By contrast, emphasizing the equal and opposite risks of her status as wife, a cartoon titled "Trying it on" (Thompson 1990, 40), which pictures Albert posing admiringly before a mirror wearing the crown of England, expresses the opposite anxiety—that the suspect foreigner Albert, because (as he puts it in the cartoon's text) "vat is yours is mine, now ve *are* married," will be able to take over the monarchy because of his marital role.

Despite such fears that she would be, as a married queen, either too powerful or not powerful enough, she seems to have managed this conflict astutely. By 1844 Victoria can insist that she is a dutiful Victorian wife and that that, paradoxically, is the source of her authority as queen. Newspapers (reporting on the grand ceremonies for the opening of the Royal Stock Exchange) "say *no* Sovereign was *more loved* than I am (I am bold enough to say), and *that,* from our *happy domestic home*—which gives such a good example" (1908, 29 Oct. 1844, 2:27). The next year they purchased and enlarged—though with her income, not his—Osborne House on the Isle of Wight, which was to be the setting for some of their most impressive performances of monarchy as domesticity. She holds her sovereignty by the popularity she accrues by behaving like an ordinary wife: she rules in the only way she can, by giving over her authority. Historians have generally agreed that during his life Albert was the monarchy: Victoria wrote, but Albert dictated. Perhaps this was so, but it may be a triumph of her art of ruling that Victoria understood the image her people wanted, an image taken perhaps too literally and then promulgated by these historians. In 1852 a letter attests that she handles this ideological contradiction deliberately, holding apart yet conjoining the roles of good woman and concerned ruler. Contrasting Albert's fitness for rule to her dislike of it, she writes, "[W]e women are not *made* for governing—and if we are good women we must *dislike* these masculine occupations; but there are times which force one to take *interest* in them . . . and *I* do, of course, *intensely*" (1908, 3 Feb. 1852, 2:362). To succeed by making her people think she was not interested in success may have been a shrewd if self-sacrificing strategy, but the possibility also remains that it was not a strategy at all, merely an instance of Victorian ideology's power over all women.

To sum up: before her marriage, Queen Victoria gave away her power in order to have it, perhaps in the process really giving up more than she intended, but during her marriage she did have her power, by continuing to give it away. And yet, as with the Brownings, if posterity is the final judge of power or its lack, we might have to admit that her strategy, if it was one, was all too successful, just as Barrett's ironic assumption of the role of humble student is all too successful, too easily taken literally. Their triumphs in the loser's art are at once too great and too temporary. Barrett accurately names canonical realities—of her own as well as our day—when she defines Browning's superiority as masculine and her inferiority as feminine. When she finds fault with herself, it is not frivolous posing as it is for Browning—for all his talk of being beneath, they don't discuss *his* faults—but an anticipation of androcentric canon formation. History has remembered Barrett's poetic faults instead of her successes and has evacuated the name Victoria of any political significance: her name identifies an ideological complex but evokes no images of well-used authority. Her most recent biographer, Giles St. Aubyn, gives her more credit than other historians do: "There is hardly a page of the political history of Queen Victoria's reign which does not bear her impress" (1992, 600). Nonetheless, his summation of her later career describes the effect of the whole:

the Queen herself was to blame for the loss of important prerogatives, in spite of the fact that her policy was to preserve them. . . . Nor did the fact that she spent so much of the year six hundred miles from London [in Balmoral] suggest that she played a vital role in the day-to-day business of Government. The impression, of course, was entirely false. The busiest telegraph office in the Kingdom was probably that at Balmoral. But, nevertheless, the Crown's reputation suffered from the delusion that it had virtually ceased to function. (601)

Barrett's volume of 1838 contains two poems on Queen Victoria, "The Young Queen" and "Victoria's Tears." The poems sentimentalize the figure of the eighteen-year-old monarch, who had been crowned only the year before, by describing Victoria weeping for the death of her "wicked uncle" William IV (Thompson 1990, 15) and by exaggerating Victoria's love for and dependence upon her mother, the duchess of Kent.[17] Poems on the queen published in the volume of 1844, however, after Victoria's marriage, focus, as do Victoria's own writings, on the ambiguous relation between her status as wife and her status as queen. Barrett's poem "Crowned and Wedded," printed five days after the royal wedding, insists on the separation between queen and wife and celebrates, for the day, Victoria the woman:

> Let none say, God preserve the queen! but rather, Bless the bride!
> None blow the trump, none bend the knee, none violate the dream
> Wherein no monarch but a wife she to herself may seem.
> Or if ye say, Preserve the queen! oh, breathe it inward low—
> She is a *woman,* and *beloved*! and 'tis enough but so.
> (Browning [1840] 1974, lines 46–50)

Although the poem ends by leveling Victoria's personal happiness with that of her subjects—"The blessings happy PEASANTS have, be thine, O crowned queen!"—the poem nonetheless betrays anxiety about the conflict between wifely subordination and the monarchy's prerogatives. Like the street ballad on her marriage cited above, it has Victoria vowing to love but conspicuously not vowing to obey, and it makes a rhetorical compromise by recrowning her even while her crown is off: "And hold her uncrowned womanhood to be the royal thing" (line 58).

It is not this poem, however, but another more celebrated one in the same volume that most vividly reflects Barrett's identification (whether unconscious, as a prisoner of the same ideology, or conscious, as a strategy) with the sexual politics Victoria made visible, the poem for which Victoria's public image serves as the important intertext. The most popular of the poems in the 1844 volume was "Lady Geraldine's Courtship," a dramatic monologue in the form of a letter written by a lowly but talented poet, Bertram, about his love for Lady Geraldine. Not literally a queen, she is nonetheless connected by birth to the monarchy:

> There's a lady, an earl's daughter,—she is proud and she is noble,
> And she treads the crimson carpet and she breathes the perfumed air,
> And a kingly blood sends glances up, her princely eye to trouble,
> And the shadow of a monarch's crown is softened in her hair.
>
> (Browning [1844] 1974, stanza 2)

This image of a shadowy crown connects Geraldine to Barrett's Victoria by recalling the ambiguous presence and absence of a crown on Victoria's head in "Crowned and Wedded": "And fairer goeth bridal wreath than crown with vernal brows" (line 38). Moreover, Lady Geraldine is so highborn compared to Bertram ("born of English peasants") that she might as well be a queen, and he frequently compares her to one. "Many vassals bow before her as her carriage sweeps their doorways; / She has blessed their little children, as a priest or queen were she" (stanza 6). Bertram adores the "queenly" Geraldine in the manner of Browning's speaker in "Pauline," or in the rhetorical manner of Browning addressing Barrett in the letters: "Oh she walked so high above me, she appeared to my abasement, / In her lovely silken murmur, like an angel clad in wings!" (stanza 5).

One day Bertram overhears an earl's proposal to Geraldine and the disclaimer she makes on refusing him: "Whom I marry shall be noble, / Ay, and wealthy. I shall never blush to think how he was born" (stanza 66). She means this figuratively and refers, cryptically, to Bertram's metaphoric rank and wealth as an artist, but Bertram, misunderstanding her irony, delivers a tirade about her hypocrisy (the two of them have conversed on the the social ills of England), even while declaring his love for her in the familiar rhetoric of high and low ("I would kneel down where I stand" [stanza 79]). Then he faints and has to be carried away by Geraldine's minions. In a conclusion, a third-person narrator completes the story. Bertram receives a visit from Lady Geraldine, who significantly stands while he stays seated. He addresses her in echoes of the opening of "Pauline" ("Pauline, mine own, bend o'er me"): "Vision of a lady! stand there silent, stand there steady!" (Conclusion, stanza 5). But she too adopts the pose of humble worshiper and asks: "Dost thou, Bertram, truly love me? Is no woman far above me / Found more worthy of thy poet-heart than such a one as *I*?" The last stanza has them vying for the pose of the lowest: "on his knee he fell before her, / And she whispered low in triumph" (Conclusion, stanza 11), and what she whispers restates what she said to the earl, elevating Bertram to her own or a higher rank by virtue of his poethood. For both, it is, as in the Browning-Barrett letters, a pose of humbleness that conceals "triumph"; she has won her point, and he has won her.

This poem's recent readers, like those of the letters, have emphasized this apparent symmetry. Mermin, contrasting the poem to the gloomy romances that precede it, sees the poem as wish fulfillment, Barrett's successful fusion of the roles of beloved (object) and of poet (subject) in a woman character (1989, 110–12). Glennis Stephenson stresses, like Mermin, the equality between Bertram and Geraldine, because each one speaks and each worships the other. Pointing out that the title is grammatically ambiguous, she argues that "the roles of lover and beloved are as interchangeable as the positions of narrative subject and object" (1989, 22). And Stephenson extends to class difference her view that Bertram and Geraldine are equals: the poem shows "how unimportant social standing can become once a woman is permitted to feel normal sexual desire" (26). The social divide simply adds an erotic charge to the courtship. Cooper, taking a position opposed to Mermin's and Stephenson's, stresses the poem's ultimate "inability to imagine a woman poet" (1988, 93): Geraldine, she accurately notes, is placed on a pedestal and made the poet's muse. But even Cooper reaches this conclusion from within the poem's own terms and does not address the wider implications of gender difference between Geraldine and Bertram.

Symmetrical as the poem's close appears, however, Barrett echoes the scene of a poet kneeling to a queen a year later in a letter to Browning that helps to expose the asymmetry that underlies Geraldine and Bertram's relationship. She refers humorously to an episode in which Wordsworth, the aged poet laureate, embarrassed himself with an excess of homage. Bewigged and wearing a borrowed ceremonial sword for an audience with the queen, Wordsworth "fell down upon both knees in the superfluity of etiquette, & had to be picked up by two lords in waiting" (Browning and Browning, 1:84, 30 May 1845). (Recall that Bertram, like Wordsworth, has to be picked up by his queen's servants when he faints at her feet.) Despite the bathos of the scene, Barrett continues in a serious vein to praise Wordsworth for honoring the laureateship (an office disparaged by some). She concludes: "And won't the court laurel (such as it is) be all the worthier of *you* for Wordsworth's having worn it first?"[18] His homage to her (Wordsworth's to the queen) leads to her even greater homage to him (Barrett's to Browning). Barrett writes this letter just after a painful exchange in the wake of a letter from Browning, now lost, which scholars think contained a proposal, or at least declarations of his admiration that Barrett was within reason to take for a proposal: an instance, one might say, of his embarrassingly excessive kneeling. Except (and this may be the subtext of both "Lady Geraldine's Courtship" and the letter about Wordsworth) it is the woman who is the more embarrassed: he caddishly makes her look foolish by implying that she imagined the proposal. "Will you not think me very brutal if I tell you I could almost smile at your misapprehension of what I meant to write?" writes Browning, as he goes on to reassert "my real inferiority to you" (Browning and Browning 1969, 74, 24 May 1845).

For a woman to imagine a proposal, even one she says (as Barrett did) she does not want, is to expose desires that Victorian culture's double sexual standard makes it an offense to feel, much less to show. Browning's proposal and its sequels expose the asymmetry between Barrett's and Browning's kneelings: a man whose desire is rebuffed is merely a wounded suitor, but a woman who betrays her desire has compromised her morals. The exceptional case of Victoria, when she proposed to Albert, only made this asymmetry in Victorian sexual ideology all the more visible and justified its further enforcement (for everyone besides her), as the broadsides discussed here indicate. Unlike Victoria only in this regard, but like Barrett, Geraldine cannot propose to the man she loves and can speak her desire for him only in terms so cryptic that she risks being completely misunderstood. That the poem breaks off after the scene of the misunderstanding, and can be completed only by another narrator in a conclusion with a different numerical sequence, may reinforce the sense of social rupture aroused by a woman's attempting to speak her love. It is true (as Mermin and Stephenson optimistically emphasize) that Geraldine takes the active and risky step of visiting Bertram in his room, yet the words she speaks are highly constrained: she can speak only about his desire for her (" 'Dost thou, Bertram, truly love me?' ") and within the fiction of his "vision" of her (" 'Bertram, if I say I love thee, . . . 't is the vision only speaks' "), or repeat her cryptic lines on the nobility of her successful lover, this time making the point easier to grasp (" 'It shall be as I have sworn. / Very rich he is in virtues, very noble—noble certes; / And I shall not blush in knowing that men call him lowly born' "). In her letter a few days after the exchange about his proposal, the one that implicitly links Browning to Wordsworth and Bertram, and herself to the queen and Lady Geraldine (Browning and Browning, 1:74), Barrett admonishes Browning to give up excessive kneeling—perhaps because it might really humiliate, not him, but her.

"Lady Geraldine's Courtship," read in this way through the correspondence and through the text of Victoria's reign, exposes the conflicts between a woman's authority—be it poetic, political, or simply personal—and the position in marriage that Victoria's unique yet typical case made visible to women of her day. The poem, like Barrett's letters, depends on the maintenance of a precarious double irony: Geraldine's posing as the lower, like Barrett's, carries the risk of being taken literally or unironically by the husband who can legally expect her to obey.[19] This point is underscored by the presence of irony as the poem's most conspicuous rhetorical trope, for the meaning of Lady Geraldine's final words depends entirely on the maintenance of ironic doubleness. Bertram can be identified as the object of her desire only if nobility, wealth, and unembarrassing birth are taken figuratively. If these words were taken literally, as Bertram first takes them, they would point to a man who would indeed have license to dominate her. Given Bertram's proclivity to lecture her and his history of deafness to her delicate ironies, it seems unlikely that the irony of Geraldine's position will stay open and continue to give her room to maneuver.

"Lady Geraldine's Courtship" is especially important to the Browning-Barrett relationship because it was this poem that prompted Browning to write to her.[20] The poem appears uncannily to project the real relation between Barrett and Browning, a low-born poet courting a higher-born lady, and Browning may have imagined that Barrett was licensing his addresses in this way. Yet of course there are important differences, among them (despite Mermin's claim, and as Cooper points out) that the lady is not a poet. When he says of Barrett's poems, "you speak out, *you*," damning her with faint praise, if it is this poem he has in mind, he erases the fact that the poem is a work of art, a dramatic monologue spoken by the male poet and not the highborn lady, even while he represents the poem as Barrett's own sincere and even insistent feeling, inviting his addresses. Turning her into her own queen, he overrides her rhetorical acts as a poet, and to make her a queen is thus—as is true of the correspondence generally—to make her at once a superior and a subjected being. Misreading her gives him the masculine advantage, both poetically and erotically.

No reading of the period of Barrett's courtship would be complete without a look at the *Sonnets from the Portuguese,* written in 1846 after the two poets had become happily engaged and just before the wedding. Despite their disagreements about "Lady Geraldine's Courtship," Mermin, Cooper, and Leighton agree that the *Sonnets* unite woman and poet, in that they at once successfully insert a woman's voice into the conventionally male place of speaker in the amatory sonnet tradition and, in evenly distributing the roles of subject and object, represent a "fine balance of literary power" (Leighton 1986, 110) between Browning and Barrett. I concur with these readings, and I would only suggest further that—either as a cause or as a symptom—the *Sonnets'* effectiveness may be related to Barrett's rejection of any queenly associations for herself. Instead, she places "a strange, heavy crown" on Browning's head, a "wreath of sonnets" that renders the beloved "princely and like a king" (Browning [1846] 1974, sonnet 16) and endows him with "sovranty" (sonnet 28). The speaker is "a poor, tired, wandering singer" with no royalty except what he gives her, no elevated position except that to which he "lift[s]" her.[21] At about the same time, Barrett in a letter to Browning facetiously retells an anecdote about Queen Victoria (the last of her allusions to the queen in the correspondence): "I heard once of her most gracious Majesty's throwing a tea cup,—whereupon Albertus Magnus, who is no conjuror, could find nothing better to do than walk out of the room in solemn silence. If I had been he, I should have tied the royal hands, I think" (Browning and Browning, 2:733; 25 May 1846). Thoroughly debunking the myth of the Queen's domestic virtue at the same time that it represents her power as mere bad temper such as any commoner might display (Barrett connects this anecdote to a scene a friend witnessed in which a woman threw a cup and saucer at her husband in a public restaurant), the anecdote dissociates Barrett from any identification with Victoria.

Has Barrett finally seen through the appeal of Victoria's embrace of secondariness, to rid herself of that seductive yet compromising model of female authority? Perhaps, yet Barrett rejects queenly associations in the *Sonnets* only to abase herself all the more entirely, and although Barrett's feminist critics have amply demonstrated that this strategy ultimately works to enhance Barrett's authority as speaker, the *Sonnets* remain for many readers sheer sentimentality of the Hallmark greeting card sort: the gauge of her true inferiority as a poet. What is power (rhetorical or political) without an audience that acknowledges it as such? Literary history has largely joined Browning in representing Barrett as the Lady in a Victorian erotic drama, not as the speaker of her own. Did the queen and Barrett succeed by failing, or fail by succeeding? Either way, feminist readers need not accept posterity's view, but may value instead the richness of these ironies.

NOTES

1. Except in a few instances where I refer to her career as a whole, I will refer to Elizabeth Barrett Browning by her unmarried name, as the writing discussed here dates from before her marriage.

2. For example, Haigwood, drawing on the "Essay on Shelley," finds that Browning identifies his poetry as objective in contrast to Shelley's and Barrett's subjective styles, which Browning disparages: "Browning comes close to suggesting that many of his peers, including his wife, who continue to write in a 'more or less' subjective style are producing merely 'sentiments' according to a 'convention'" (99–100). Mermin, however, takes Browning's remark to Barrett, and further epistolary comments in the same vein, as a sincere compliment and as an expression of his poetic aim to put more of himself into his poems (1989, 122). Karlin points out that Barrett grew tired of hearing from Browning about this identification between herself and her poems, which might suggest that she didn't take it wholly as a compliment (1985, 52). Recent readers of the letters have not seen the extent to which Barrett and Browning belittle each other directly (if subtly), in addition to condemning each other to idealization with their excessive compliments.

3. Readers of the dialogue between the married poets' poems have discovered a comparable range of competitiveness mixed with compliments. See, for example, Munich, who calls the relation of *The Ring and the Book* to *Aurora Leigh* "appropriative and admiring, diminishing while it possesses" (1987b, 75); others who have written on the Brownings' poems to and about each other include Auerbach (1984) and Knoepflmacher (1984). This essay, however, will not reach far enough forward in time to engage with that discussion.

4. Leslie Brisman, graduate seminar, 1974, on Victorian poetry generally and on "Pauline" specifically. For a related argument about "Pauline" using the same passages I cite here, see Brisman 1979.

5. Betty Miller quotes from "Pauline" to describe Browning's desire to be led by Barrett, although she does not link Barrett to Shelley (1953, 116).

6. It was a key project of feminist criticism of the late 1970s to explain why Bloom's "anxiety of influence" could not be generalized to include women poets: see especially Joanne Feit Diehl 1978 as well as Gilbert and Gubar 1979a.

7. Leighton reads the same poem, to my eye less plausibly, as an optimistic account of a girl's success in combining the very roles Mermin says she cannot combine. Mermin and Cooper concur with Leighton in arguing that the later Barrett Browning (of, for example, the *Sonnets from the Portuguese*) does succeed in merging these roles and reversing the loss of "The Lost Bower."

8. I am grateful to Lynn Keller for suggesting this point.

9. Here I differ from Mary Poovey (1988), who sees the Victorian view of the relation between the sexes as complementary rather than hierarchical.

10. Cynthia Huff (1988), almost alone in reading Victoria's diaries as texts (not just for the historical information they impart), writes that the diaries both resemble and differ from those of ordinary Victorian women.

11. Nonetheless, the word *Victorian* is almost always used without reference to the queen. Even the word *Victoria* appears in titles of books such as Richard Stein's *Victoria's Year* (1987) or Peter Gay's *The Bourgeois Experience: From Victoria to Freud* (1984), books that do not discuss the queen herself. I wish to put Victoria back into Victorian.

12. Analogously, Terry Eagleton points out, about both feminism and nationalism, that revolutionary politics tend to require temporary reliance on the very concept being overturned: "Women are not so much fighting for the freedom to be women . . . as for the freedom to be fully human; but that inevitably abstract humanity can be articulated in the here and now only through their womanhood, since this is the place where their humanity is wounded and refused" (1990, 24). For this effect Eagleton uses the term *irony*.

13. Any scholar attempting to work out the interimplication of Queen Victoria's reign and the literature of her period is indebted to Munich's two pioneering essays (1984, 1987a) on representations of Victoria (especially her body) in the context of her essential unrepresentability.

14. Although most quotations from Victoria's letters and journals come from their first published sources, I am indebted to Hibbert's selection for shaping my own. I quote from Hibbert's edition, however, only where he prints hitherto unpublished material.

15. The quarrel between Victoria and Peel was heated by her deliberate misunderstanding: that he intended to replace them all, rather than just those married to Whig ministers. She insisted that it was the same: to change one was as much a violation of her rights as to change them all. For full accounts of the crisis, see Longford 1964, 109–14; St. Aubyn 1992, 110–15.

16. Cecil Woodham-Smith reports that Melbourne told Victoria that Lady Flora was the duchess of Kent's rival (1972, 167).

17. Cooper reads "The Young Queen" as Barrett's identification with the queen: "token women who attain public prominence feel ambivalent about their status" (1988, 44).

18. In fact, Barrett Browning herself, and not Browning, was nominated to be laureate by the Atheneum in 1850, when Wordsworth died; the queen appointed Tennyson.

19. See, again, Eagleton's use of "irony" (1990).

20. Cooper points out that it was specifically Barrett's complimentary mention of his "Bells and Pomegranates" that "won [his] heart" (1988, 90); more generally, Mermin sees Browning imitating Bertram in the style of his first letter (1989, 116).

21. William S. Peterson detects realism behind Barrett's poetic self-abasement: any forty-year-old unmarried woman would be merely reflecting Victorian convention if she viewed herself as unworthy of a suitor (1977, xv). Peterson's comment reinforces my view that the Victorian woman's pose of humility risks being taken literally (whereas a man's does not).

Measured Feet "in Gender-Bender Shoes": The Politics of Poetic Form in Marilyn Hacker's *Love, Death, and the Changing of the Seasons*

Lynn Keller

Poetry in set verse forms has recently enjoyed a revival.[1] Given the highly politicized history of poetic form in this century—especially the battles in the 1960s over the ideological implications of free verse and "open" forms—it is hardly surprising that the advent of the "new formalism" has renewed disputes about the politics of poetic form. To counter the essentialist understandings of poetic form on which such disputes are often based, this essay will examine the "performative" formalism of lesbian feminist Marilyn Hacker. I adopt the term performative from Judith Butler, who uses it to describe acts and gestures that might purport to express the essence of gender identity, but that she sees as signifying on the surface of the body an illusory internal core. These acts of gender reveal not its substance but its fabrication: "That the gendered body is performative suggests that it has no ontological status apart from the various acts which constitute its reality" (Butler 1990b, 336). Hacker, I will argue, takes analogous de-essentializing approaches to gender and to poetic form, thereby undermining myths that formalist verse necessarily embodies a particular (patriarchal) ideology.

The current popularity of formalism appears to some critics as an alarming mirror of the increasing conservatism of American culture.[2] Ira Sadoff argues in a 1990 issue of *American Poetry Review* that "neo-formalists have a social as well as a linguistic agenda. When they link pseudo-populism (the 'general reader') to regular meter, they disguise their nostalgia for moral and linguistic certainty, for a universal . . . and univocal way of conserving culture" (7). While acknowledging that the "masters of received form—Justice, Bishop, Wilbur, Kunitz, and Walcott . . .—articulate form with vision" (7), Sadoff claims that the resurgent neoformalists and their champions tend to separate form from vision. "The dissociation of sound, sense, and intellect . . . reminds us of the danger of . . . appreciating esthetic beauty, formally and thematically, at the cost of the observed, sensory, disturbingly contingent world" (8). Going further, he asserts that the neoformalists' "exaltation of the iamb veils their attempt to privilege prevailing white Anglo-Saxon rhythms and culture"; they are guilty of "cultural imperialism" (8). They sidestep the problem American artists need to confront of "finding a sense of 'relation' between self and other, the inner and outer world, the personal and social worlds" (9).

In presenting the neoformalists as the most egregious examples of a pervasive failure among contemporary American poets to connect themselves with the social world, Sadoff overlooks much feminist poetry, as Adrienne Rich points out in a subsequent issue of *American Poetry Review*. While announcing her agreement with much of Sadoff's essay, Rich observes that it provides a striking demonstration of the invisibility in nonfeminist publications of "the groundswell of feminist and lesbian writing":

> There are, close to home, among feminist, gay and lesbian poets, among poets from the communities of color, a profusion of what Sadoff is seeking: "poems that make engaged, dramatized, and surprising connections between the self and the social world, the moment and history." (Rich 1990, 17)

Yet most feminist poets and critics in the United States, Rich among them, remain wary of received poetic forms. Whether sympathetic with Anglo-American or with French theories of language and representation, feminists have tended to share assumptions like Sadoff's that equate aesthetic choices with political stances; they tend to see in more open or experimental forms greater possibility for subversion of the patriarchal and expression of the feminine. Many doubt the ability of language—here I quote Marianne DeKoven as a representative example—"to represent adequately, through relatively conventional literary forms, the specificity of women's experience" (1989, 75–76). Drawing upon Kristeva and Irigaray, DeKoven argues that writing that fails to obstruct normal reading practices and encourages construction of coherent meaning fails to challenge patriarchal and phallogocentric structures. Even those who do not share DeKoven's insistence on radical experimentation tend to regard the inscription of women's experience as new to our literature and perceive, as Rich does, the "necessity to break from [traditional structures] in recognition of new experience" (Rich 1986a, 181).

Rich herself—member of a generation of poets who in the 1960s came to see regular metrical verse as emotionally or politically repressive, as incapable of capturing authentic experience or individual speech—long ago rejected the "asbestos gloves" of formalism that once shielded her from the burning political issues she needed to address (1979, 40). She continues in her most recent work to deplore the political backwardness of traditional poetic forms. *Time's Power: Poems 1985–1988* contains a "Love Poem" that dismisses the sonnet as inappropriate to politically engaged feminist writing: the beloved woman addressed is a "bristler" with "a warrior's mind," "testing the world / the word," and consequently "to write for you / a pretty sonnet / would be untrue" (1989, 7). The presence of irregular rhyme throughout her love poem suggests Rich is not insisting on abandoning traditional poetics entirely, yet received forms remain in her eyes "untrue" to the gynocentric world her poems attempt to help bring into being.[3]

Marilyn Hacker (born in 1942, thirteen years later than Rich) is a notable exception to the feminist trends I have sketched. Since the publication of her first volume, *Presentation Piece* (1974), she has continued to delight in the technical challenges posed by villanelles, canzoni, crowns of sonnets, sestinas, heroic and tetrameter couplets, and the like. Her poetry during the 1980s has chronicled her life within lesbian communities in New York and France and is committed to many of the same political goals as Rich's. Yet Hacker does not equate prescribed forms with hegemonic ideology. A 1978 interview demonstrates that while Hacker shares Rich's interest in unearthing women's contributions to literary history, she is confident that women can express themselves through the resources of received tradition—which she refuses to see as predominantly masculine:

> Traditional forms . . . aren't in any way inimical to women's poetry, feminist poetry. . . . It is important for women writers to reclaim the tradition, to rediscover and redefine our place in it and lay claim to our considerable contributions, innovations, and inventions. Traditional narrative and lyric forms have been used by women for centuries—even if our professors of Western literature never mentioned Marie de France or Christine de Pisan. The language we use was as much created and invented by women as by men. . . . We've got to reclaim the language, demand acknowledgement of our part in it, and proceed from there. (1980, 22)

Not surprisingly, in a largely admiring review of *Time's Power,* Hacker takes issue with Rich's perspective on the sonnet. She observes that "the echo of the mnemonically compelling iambic pentameter . . . is never really absent from [Rich's] work. This puts that work within, and in relation to or dialogue with, a whole body of narrative and didactic poems in English written in that meter." She therefore questions why Rich had to "bad-mouth a tradition that helped to form her art" in the "Love Poem" quoted above. Objecting to Rich's limiting conception of the sonnet as "pretty," Hacker asks, "Why not a beautiful sonnet, or an ugly, thorny, passionate one?" She expresses doubts whether "Twenty-One Love Poems" (Rich 1978)—"a cycle that, although in free form, has the heft and feel of a sonnet sequence"—could have been written by a poet without Rich's earlier expertise in fixed forms. And, in the context of this particular issue, she laments Rich's influential position: "next year some college junior, some fourth-grade teacher, some bookstore clerk is going to decide that sonnets are 'pretty' and 'untrue' because Adrienne Rich said so. And that's too bad" (1989a, 467).

Hacker's desire to place her own work conspicuously "within, and in relation to or dialogue with," the tradition of iambic pentameter verse, especially the sonnet tradition, is apparent in her 1986 sonnet sequence, *Love, Death, and the Changing of the Seasons*. The book's first epigraph, Shakespeare's sonnet 73, "That time of year thou mayst in me behold," not only anticipates Hacker's speaking as an older lover in a May/January same-sex relationship; it also signals the multitude of links between her cycle of love lyrics and the Petrarchan sonnet tradition, in particular with Shakespeare's sonnets. Not content with merely laying claim to this tradition, however, Hacker is reforming it so that it can represent a contemporary lesbian feminist's experiences in a love relationship and convey her romantic ideals, many of which differ markedly from those of the male lovers/poets who preceded her. Of course, Hacker is hardly the first to reform this evolving tradition in which Shakespeare himself was an innovator; it has been recently reworked by John Berryman, Robert Lowell, James Merrill, and others. Hacker's sequence is distinctive, however, in its self-conscious invocation of Shakespeare's sequence as a central intertext. This foregrounded archaism renders *Love, Death, and the Changing of the Seasons* particularly useful for critical intervention in the debate about the politics of current poetic formalism and in the corollary feminist debate about whether the sonnet form in particular can accommodate a feminine speaking subjectivity or whether it is, as Jan Montefiore has argued, "masculine in conception" (1987, 105).

Expressing her excitement about her new love relationship as well as the sonnet sequence developing from it, Hacker's speaker announces early in the work that she's getting "some / brand-old ideas," an apt phrase for the combination of innovation and conservatism evident in Hacker's formal sequence. Love, death, and aging have preoccupied lyricists for centuries; in choosing to explore her relation to these experiences in a sonnet sequence, Hacker accepts many of the traditions of the egocentric personal lyric, which presumes a recognizable— if, for her, flexibly inclusive—subject using language representationally to address a discrete—if no longer oppositionally defined—other. While many feminist writers resist continuity with the given tradition—as Rich does in her organicist championing of free verse, Hélène Cixous in striving for a new language in *écriture féminine*, Monique Wittig in attempting to "pulverize the old forms and formal conventions" (Wittig 1992, 69)—Hacker accepts a continuity. Yet, Hacker's play with and against the Shakespearean/Petrarchan model reveals that working from the basis of an established tradition (especially from its most popularly known text) also enables a poet to define clear differences from an inherited patriarchal norm, precisely because the poet can diverge from that invoked norm in ways readily discernible to a nonspecialist audience. I contend that the differences Hacker establishes denaturalize gender roles and broaden the identities available to both lover and beloved. Her politically significant play within the tradition, which parodies both the limits of the sonnet form and the limits of gender coherence, enables a multifaceted, performative approach to sexuality and gender that calls into question conventional notions of gender and opens up a range of possibilities for the female subject.

This essay's reading of Hacker's sequence refutes the idea that contemporary formalist writing is necessarily any more co-opted by hegemonic ideology than free verse. Works like hers should help temper current exaggerations of the differences between those writing in received lyric forms and free-verse writers, who often trained in the same academic workshops. Arguments about whether didactic, earnest free verse like Rich's is more political than Hacker's playful exploitation of the artificialities of received conventions of womanhood, gender, and poetic form, may be largely disputes about personal taste. The most significant political division might fall not between the formalists and those writing in open forms, but between those writing personal lyrics, whether in free or set verse, and the experimental politicized avant-gardes (e.g., the Marxist-affiliated Language writers or the materialist feminist experiments of Wittig or the quite different innovations of *écriture féminine*). Thoroughly innovative work—brand-*new* ideas—may well demand a break from the personal lyric mode and from the conventions of logic and representation on which it depends.

Yet Hacker's work confutes a simple opposition between formally experimental and more conventional (formal or free verse) lyric as well. Hacker's formalist verse becomes radically innovative as she pursues the implications of nonorganicist assumptions about form and nonessentialist assumptions about gender. Like recent (also antiorganicist) Language poets, Hacker highlights the ways in which genre and language constitute, rather than reflect, our realities. Clearly, how one approaches one's formalism—for example, whether one regards the repetitions of metered verse as arbitrary or as reflecting "the recurrent structural principles to be found in nature" (Golding 1991, 85)[4]—or, for that matter, how one approaches one's experimentalism, has more potential political significance than the formalism itself.[5]

To the extent that Hacker's epigraph reminds readers of the homoerotic dimension of Shakespeare's sonnets, it undermines any monolithic understanding of the Petrarchan sonnet tradition and of generic traditions more generally. (We recall, for example, that the speaker's beloved need not be a woman, and when the beloved is a woman she need not be fair or chaste.) The more varied a tradition, the more room for diversity within it, and the less restrictive it need be for those claiming a place in its development. In context, then, Hacker's first epigraph alone encourages an expansive view of literary traditions, and of the sonnet tradition in particular, as varied and adaptable.

That all the love relationships—indeed, all the relationships—Hacker portrays in *Love, Death, and the Changing of the Seasons* are between women (or women and girls) radically distinguishes her sequence from the Shakespearean model. Lacanian critics and theorists might argue otherwise: that the gender of the lovers is irrelevant in the sonnet's dynamics. Montefiore, for instance, claims that what is really at stake for the Petrarchan lover-poet (whose poem she sees as structured on the Imaginary I-Thou dyad of mother and prelinguistic infant) is not the success or failure of his courtship but rather "defining his own self through his desire either for the image of his beloved or for his own image mediated through her response to him" (1987, 98). Regardless of gender, Montefiore argues, the beloved, "assigned the role of passive reflecting Other, is thereby feminized":

in any poem where the lover's self is being defined in and through a relationship with a beloved, that process of definition implies the masculinity of the lover and the femininity of the other; which is why . . . the love-poem presents problems to women. (109)

I concur that a woman sonneteer faces significant challenges if she is to inscribe a speaking subjectivity that does not repeat the objectifying dynamics and the hierarchical power structure of the Petrarchan tradition's romantic couple. But Montefiore's ahistorical model does not allow for the alteration in power dynamics that results from different gender configurations in love relationships nor for the difference of female, particularly lesbian, sexuality that Hacker represents.[6]

What one might see as merely the substitution of two lesbians for Petrarch's heterosexual couple or Shakespeare's homosexual one in fact transforms the power dynamics and social significance of the relationships depicted. This is particularly true since all Hacker's love triangles are exclusively female. Eve Sedgwick's analysis of the homosocial elements in Shakespeare's sonnets calls to our attention the ways in which his sequence, as much as Petrarchan heterosexual sequences, reinforces the power structures of heterosexual patriarchy. For all its homoeroticism, Shakespeare's sequence—in which the male characters are bound to each other in a love triangle via their competition for the dark lady's favors—is dominated by "male heterosexual desire, in the form of a desire to consolidate partnership with authoritative males in and through the bodies of females" (Sedgwick 1985, 38). In contrast, the world Hacker creates in *Love, Death, and the Changing of the Seasons* is almost exclusively a (lesbian) woman's world and, for the most part, seems removed from the forces of compulsory heterosexuality. Men appear seldom and in only the most peripheral roles; unlike Rich in "Twenty-One Love Poems" (1978) Hacker downplays the impact of heterosexual patriarchy on the lovers, giving it virtually no role in the disintegration of their relationship. The significance of Hacker's removing her characters from relation to men is illuminated by Wittig's argument that the lesbian escapes from the gender divisions and social systems of patriarchy. Wittig declares in "One Is Not Born a Woman":

> Lesbian is the only concept I know of which is beyond the categories of sex (woman and man), because the designated subject (lesbian) is *not* a woman, either economically, or politically, or ideologically. For what makes a woman is a specific social relation to a man, a relation that we have previously called servitude, a relation which implies personal and physical obligation as well as economic obligation . . . a relation which lesbians escape by refusing to become or to stay heterosexual. (1992, 20)

Establishing a lesbian world is fundamental among the many strategies, often evident as revisions of Shakespearean sonnet conventions, by which Hacker challenges received gender categories. It helps her make a place both for an exuberant lesbian eroticism quite distinct from the phallocentric erotic economy and for relationships that are not merely mirrorings by which the lyric speaker establishes her own identity.

In broad outline, Hacker's plot follows the Petrarchan model. Her speaker is initially the more desiring partner for whom sonnets are partly rhetorical devices for seduction; tracing a wide range of intense emotions, the sequence often records the discomforts of being in love and of experiencing unsatisfied desire. As in Shakespeare's first 126 sonnets, the beloved is significantly younger, marking a potential difference in power between them: the speaker (who refers to herself in the poems as Hacker, Hack, and Marilyn, and whom I will call Hack) is forty-two, her beloved Ray (also Rachel) is twenty-five.[7] Hacker's sequence, like Shakespeare's, is preoccupied with time's passage and with mortality. Several romantic triangles threaten Hacker's relationship, as they seem to have threatened Shakespeare's, and like his fair young man, her fair young woman ultimately becomes involved with another. Before that event, Hacker's speaker, like her forebears', must frequently deal with absence from the beloved, not only because the lovers' New York apartments are separated by four miles, but also because in the year covered by the sequence Hack travels several times to France without Ray (twice in the company of her prepubescent daughter, Iva). Yet unlike the male Petrarchans, Hacker's primary interest is in overcoming metaphorical distances that exist between lovers in a consummated partnership that is fully integrated into their daily lives, what she terms "our doubled dailiness" (1986, 71).

What Hack desires, from the very beginning, is not merely the satisfaction of her erotic desire, or even reciprocal emotional attachment, but a lasting relationship involving shared domestic existence. At the beginning of the sequence, she asks, "What are you doing for the next five years?" (10), and before long she is saying she'd like their relationship to end "when I die / at ninety-seven" (126). While the Petrarchan lover's desire for sexual conquest is often thwarted either by the lady's reluctance or by the moral duty of sexual renunciation, in Hacker's sequence sex is perhaps the most easily attained dimension of what the speaker seeks. As she announces early on, with characteristic colloquialism and sexual explicitness: "Although I'd cream my jeans touching your breast / sweetheart, it isn't lust; it's all the rest / of what I want with you that scares me shitless" (12). When Ray, in the early pages, is still living with another woman, Hack feels free to fantasize about the sexual exploits she and Ray might enjoy but censors her imagination when she wonders about their "dailiness," feeling she doesn't have a right to that (55). Allotting such value to a nonidealizing context for love significantly revises the tradition of the love sonnet and, as we shall see, the distance between speaking subject and silent object on which poems in the male tradition depend.

Hacker's images of romantic fulfillment are domestic, and their apparent triviality provides a parodic reworking of the lofty, moralized Petrarchan norm. Hack longs to have her beloved's "PJs" hung on her bathroom door (13), their laundry thrown in together (178), a common home address (155). Even her erotic fantasies may include a mundane domestic context: "After the supper dishes, let us start / where we left off" begins one vision of the consummation she is still anticipating (50). Figures of homes and houses recur as spaces within which Hack imagines the two as individually fulfilled partners:

> I think the world's our house. I think I built
> and furnished mine with space for you to move
> through it, with me, alone in rooms, in love
> with our work. I moved into one mansion
> the morning when I touched, I saw, I felt
> your face blazing above me like a sun.
>
> (69)

In another poem she imagines them sharing a home in Lacoste:

> It's almost as if we're already there,
> in the narrow stone house, me upstairs
> writing at the splintery pine table,
> you in the downstairs study. . . .
> . . . I'm cooking
> a sonnet sequence and a cassoulet
>
> (25)

Given Hack's desire for a long-term domestic connection, her use of figures associated with heterosexual marriage is perhaps not surprising. The spirit of her invocations, however—ranging from tongue-in-cheek to broad parody—makes clear that she is not aspiring to imitate that patriarchal institution of heterosexual partnership. The first allusion to marriage, which occurs early on when Ray still lives with Alice, is obviously self-mocking:

> I venture it's a trifle premature
> to sign the china-pattern registry
> before you are, at least, at liberty
> to hang your PJs on my bathroom door.
> A funny pair of homebodies we are,
> as wicked as we like to paint ourselves:
> I kiss you till my clit's about to burst
> and catch myself reorganizing shelves.
>
> (13)

Hack's not taking the marriage analogy seriously is apparent, too, in her being taken aback by Ray's speaking, "not kidding," of Alice as " 'my wife' " (34). Hack subsequently characterizes herself in a butch haircut ("short-back-and-sides") as not "the most orthodox of brides" (71) and humorously invokes the marriage bed in a poem recording her feelings shortly after the consummation of their love: "I broke a glass, got bloodstains on the sheet: / hereafter, must I only write you chaste / connubial poems?" (65). Both allusions to marriage may be read as making fun of Ray's locution.[8]

A few pages later, having characterized one of her own poems as an "epithalamion," Hack admits that if she wants to be ironic about "wives" and then appropriate for serious use language associated with marriage, she had better "explain [her]self." Here's what she offers:

No law books frame terms of this covenant.
It's choice that's asymptotic to a goal,
which means that we must choose, and choose, and choose
momently, daily. This moment my whole
trajectory's toward you, and it's not los-
ing momentum. Call it anything we want.

(72)

Hack distinguishes the ongoing voluntary renewal of her and Ray's commitment from the false ideal of marriage's fixed state attained by legal decree and by a single occasion's vows. In her closing statement Hack both signals and accommodates herself to the lack of a single term designating the process of ongoing choice in which she and her lover are engaged. Whatever designation they employ is recognized as a shorthand approximation, its value depending on its being jointly chosen—whatever *we* want. At one point Hack, while "suppos[ing] / you [Ray] want what I want," describes the relationship she desires as "Connecting what gets wilder as it grows / with what's safe, known, quotidian, routine / and necessary as pairs of old jeans" (194); the marriage figure, like the sonnet form itself, provides the safe and familiar apparel with which to clothe something wild, unfamiliar, and subversive.[9]

One of the central ways Hacker incorporates this wildness is through the sequence's very explicit eroticism. Borrowing the descriptive categories Jan Zita Grover sets up in her review article "Words to Lust By," we could say that Hacker's portrayal of lesbian sexuality often has more in common with "bad-girl porn" than with the "good-girl erotica" of lesbian-feminist writings. That is to say, she does not restrict herself, as "good-girl" writing does, to earnest, gentle lovers who "enact their passion in rustic cabins, in nature, in beds"; nor does she often describe sex "by allusion to flowers, fruit, waterfalls, pounding waves, illimitable oceans." Although she also does not go in for sex toys, S/M, and the like, her work frequently fits the "bad-girl" model in that she attends to the mechanics of arousal as much as to the subject's psychological state; she explores role playing and fantasy; she does not rely on heavily metaphorical descriptions of sexual activity; she does not suppress everything culturally associated with maleness; and she employs an "emphatic, workaday vocabulary" (cunt, clit, fuck, etc.) (Grover 1990, 21). In portraying sex graphically with four-letter words, themselves adopted from male discourse, Hacker claims the traditionally male prerogative of voicing sexual desire and flaunting sexual experience. But she goes beyond merely claiming for women the position men have enjoyed: as she invokes male terminology, plays with butch/femme dynamics, or presents the two women in stereotypically heterosexual scenes, she is engaged in a conscious masquerade revealing gender roles as performative rather than as natural, inevi-

table structures. Hack's claim that what "our bodies do together is unprece-
dented" suggests not only that the couple's sexual relationship is the richest she
has ever enjoyed, but that they (and other lesbians) are in fact moving into new
realms of sexual freedom and pleasure. Hacker renders their *jouissance* convinc-
ing largely by revealing the range of roles they feel free to explore—"we do it
once like ladies, once like tramps" (93)—in fantasy or in actual lovemaking.

As a sample of the range of sexual roles represented, here are two poems that
appear on facing pages (the first concludes a crown of six sonnets linked by
repeating the final line of one as the opening line of the next):

> Toward what was after, all our rendezvous
> turned, fine-tuned as a classic Howard Hawkes:
> the silken lady in the black suit walks
> through the hotel bar, smoking. Point of view
> hers: battered tweed with something on the rocks
> near empty, quipping with the bartender,
> glimpsed between bulky shoulders. Pan, then: send her
> around the tables, till the eye-hook shocks:
> "Hi, babe, have you been waiting for me long?"
> Walking west on Twenty-Second Street,
> in wind, near midnight (earlier Godard)
> You held my coat closed, blocked gusts like a strong
> and silent type; the dénouement inferred
> upstairs: denim and silk pooled at our feet.
>
> (82)

> "If I weren't working, I'd sleep next to you
> an hour or two more. Then we'd get the car
> and drive a while, out of Manhattan, to
> a quiet Bloomingdale's in Westchester.
> If we saw anything we liked, we'd buy it!
> We'd try things on, first, in one cubicle.
> You'd need to make an effort to be quiet
> when I knelt down and got my fingers full
> of you, my mouth on you, against the wall.
> You'd pull my hair. You'd have to bite your tongue.
> I'd hold your ass so that you wouldn't fall.
> Later, we'd take a peaceful walk along
> the aisles, letting our hands touch every chance
> they got, among the bras and underpants."
>
> (83)

In the first poem (titled "and Tuesday III"), Hacker places her lovers in thoroughly stereotyped heterosexual roles and allows them to enjoy this play, yet by presenting the scene through camera techniques, she calls attention to the manipulation of the gaze upon which such images depend. Consequently, the couple's impersonation of a heterosexual cliché appears a politically conscious and ultimately subversive act. The academic sobriety of Judith Butler's explanations, however incongruous (as is my own discourse) next to Hacker's outrageous play, provides valuable insight: "The notion of an original or primary gender identity is often parodied within the cultural practices of drag, cross-dressing, and the sexual stylization of butch/femme identities" (1990b, 337).[10] Butler goes on to argue that in fact "part of the pleasure, the giddiness of the performance [of drag, cross-dressing, etc.] is in the recognition of a radical contingency in the relation between sex and gender in the face of cultural configurations of causal unities that are regularly assumed to be natural and necessary" (338). "The proliferation of gender style and identity . . . implicitly contests the always already political binary distinction between genders that is often taken for granted" and promises instead "the possibility of complex and generative subject-positions" (339).

The second poem also opens possibilities for more complex subject positions, though in a quite different way, for here the speaker is the beloved object traditionally silenced in the sonnet sequence. (This is the only poem in the book presented entirely as Ray's voice.) In this poem ("Bloomingdale's I") Ray is the active subject of her own erotic fantasies in which she refuses on several levels the constraints of what is hegemonically proper. She and her lover will not conform to standards of PC lesbian feminism by eschewing the stereotypically feminine love of clothes shopping; they will not restrict their lovemaking to the respectable privacy of their bedrooms, nor reject fetishistic behaviors.

The figure of trying things on in Bloomingdales may provide a metaphor for Hacker's poetic situation. However much the epitome of patriarchal capital consumerism, Bloomingdales is a given in her world, just as the sonnet tradition is a received reality. Yet rather than boycotting either one, she uses them as she wants and for her own kinds of self-definition. Within the establishment, so to speak, she seizes the freedom to "try on" a variety of roles, styles, and behaviors, revealing in the process the performative nature of all subject positions and poetic conventions—even the apparently stable ones whose seeming naturalness bulwarks the status quo.

As if to instruct the reader in the performative nature of sexual and gender identities, the villanelle "Conversation in the Park" (like Petrarch and Sidney, Hacker occasionally interpolates other regular poetic forms among her sonnets) shows Ray moving toward such an understanding in the context of the larger homophobic society (an atypical context, as noted above). Ray opens the poem's dialogue with an attitude not of liberating parody or cocky rebellion, as in the poems just quoted, but of painfully alienated self-consciousness. She asks, " 'Do people look at me and know I'm gay?' " and confesses how it gets her

> "down! The stares—that way
>
> my back aches when I wonder what they say
> behind it . . . But you wouldn't know. You *chose!*"
>
> [ellipses Hacker's]

It seems that Ray regards Hack's appearance—presumably her haircut, her style of dress—as a deliberate announcement of her lesbianism.[11] But apparently Hack would not have thought so, since she replies, " 'Do people look at *me* and know I'm gay?' " Here is the rest of the poem (Ray speaks first):

> "Honey, you look like a twelve-year-old boy.
> But you go down on me the way, God knows,
> only a girl goes down!" "The stairs! That way
>
> out of the park, or else I'm going to lay
> you right here, right now, on the grass!" "Yes, boss!
> Do people look at us and know we're gay?"
> "Why *would* two girls go down the stairs this way?"
>
> (101–2)

Sexual and gender roles—merged in the slang designation of lesbian as "girl"— may be socially coded according to details of physical appearance, but such codes are fluid and depend for their interpretation on context and the interpreter's social position and experience. The only reliable index to the characters' sexual preferences or even their gender is finally performative: it's not clear that a broadly inclusive "they" would recognize either Ray or Hack as a lesbian or as a woman merely by how either one looks; only the couple's lustful dash down the stairs is a clear sign of their immediate sexual orientation.

Significant parallels exist between Hacker's handling of her lovers' sexuality and her approach to the sonnet form itself, for both enact a kind of liberation via excess. In patriarchy's approved representations of female sexuality, as in approved treatments of the sonnet, the potential for wildness has been largely squelched, rendering both, in the terms of Rich's "Love Poem," merely "pretty." Hacker's aggressive irreverence, her ostentatious indulgence in practices many would regard as improper or tasteless, opens up new possibilities in both areas.

The rhyme pattern of the sonnet, whether Italian or English, lends itself to expression of a binary order. Some critics even claim that its two-part structure has served primarily to present first a problem and then its solution or resolution. In Hacker's hands, however, the form does not support a dichotomous intellectual/emotional structure. Her heavy use of enjambment thwarts the rhyme scheme's tendency to divide the octave from the sestet or to divide quatrains from one another; her tendency to employ in the sestet rhyme sounds very close to those in the octave gives a fluid unity to her sonnets (when, according to Paul Fussell, a poet who "understands the sonnet form" is one who exploits its principle of imbalanced halves and who therefore "tries to make the rhyme-words of the final six lines as different as possible from those of the preceding eight" [1979, 115]). Hacker's fondness for the linked series adds flexibility to the length of the units constituting her sequence.

Indeed, Hacker sometimes so pushes the limits of the sonnet that her poems parody the form and the rules determining it. The heterogeneity of her diction is outrageous, mixing archaisms with contemporary urban vernacular, demotic French with highly educated English, Shakespearean allusion with topical references. The significance of the polyphony of languages from which Hacker constructs her poems is suggested when Hack calls attention to herself and her friends being "polyglot queer / women" while Iva who is "pre- / pubescent" is also "pre-polyglot": Hacker links fluency in multiple languages with the flexible self-construction and gender construction her sexually mature lesbian characters are engaged in (52). Hacker's delight in the play of language—in puns, homophones, and the like—echoes that of Shakespeare and other Renaissance sonneteers, but her playfulness goes far beyond her predecessors' as she flagrantly twists and extends syntax, calling attention to the way received forms shape both what is said and how it is said.[12] Midword line breaks and unlikely rhyme pairs—for example, "VIS- / A" to rhyme with "colloquies," "Troj- / an" with "Maleboge," "inadept- / ly" with "re-schlepped"—further highlight the demands of the form and the often arbitrary relation of formal characteristics to semantics.

In both her representation of gender and in the form containing that representation, then, Hacker undermines an ideology of transparent "naturalness." The rules for being a "woman" and generating a proper "sonnet" are ideologically weighted constructions; while not entirely outside either of these, the formalist lesbian poet who is ready to play with both categories and thereby denaturalize them opens the way for different constructions of both gender and generic literary conventions.[13]

That Hacker's lovers, both individually and together, feel free to adopt a variety of conventionally male and female roles signals their consciousness that gender is not given, but enacted. The sequence demands that the reader, too, grant gender's constructedness, allowing the characters to step in and out of roles even as stereotyped as those exploited by Howard Hawkes. Nor is Hacker suggesting an ideal of androgyny or bisexuality. When an interviewer asked Hacker what she thought about Virginia Woolf's notion of the great artist as mentally bisexual, she replied first by criticizing the idea that certain qualities of mind are essentially female and others essentially male, and then added:

> There is, I believe, an enormous spectrum of human possibilities; and none [is] except culturally, more female or more male. The artist must be a whole human being, and that isn't a question of being "mentally bisexual." In my case, it isn't a question of being or wanting to be anything "more" than a woman. I am a woman. I would like to enlarge my own and everyone's definition of what a woman is. (1980, 27)

This is the context for lines like, "You're an exemplar / piss-elegance is not reserved for boys. / Tonight we'll go out in our gangster suits" (1986, 66).

When, following the tradition of the Petrarchan sonneteers, Hacker depicts her lovers in terms of traditional mythology, she does not restrict her metaphorical positionings to female ones. She thereby attempts to expand our acculturated sense of what a woman is, while also acknowledging commonalities between lesbian lovers and other heterosexual or male homosexual lovers who have been portrayed in Western literature. Where Rich's speaker in "Twenty-one Love Poems" insists "no one has imagined us [lesbian lovers]" (1978, 25), Hacker, as is consistent with her attitude toward the sonnet itself, sees the tradition in less exclusive terms. Thus Hack, thinking of her daughter's understanding of the term "lovers" as applying only to couples who have had genital sex (when she and Ray have not yet made love), says, "Two thousand years of Western literature: / potions and swords, the quests, the songs, the trysts, / call us what Iva, if she knew [that we'd not had sex] would not" (33). Without insisting on lesbians' separation from the perspective of those thousand years, her flexible assignment of multiple gender positions undermines the old myths' portrayal of narrow, fixed gender identities. This is the case in "Mythology," where Ray is identified as "Penelope as a *garçon manqué*" who "weaves sonnets on a barstool among sailors"; Iva as both daughter and son, "Persephone / a.k.a. Télémaque-who-tagged-along"; and Hack as "Ulysse-Mamam" (48).

Hacker's portrayal elsewhere of Ray as a "hero" likened to Achilles demonstrates how she can simultaneously claim for women a conventionally male role, mock it, and revise it to generate an expanded sense of womanhood. Hack acknowledges that "hero" is a "big word" but insists ordinary women like Ray and herself "have a claim to" that enlarging label. Taking a revisionary stance, Hack emphasizes the mundane character of heroism, applying the term to coping with "the harder times" in daily living (123). At the same time, she makes fun of the puffery in male heroic images, so that her portrayal of Ray in the hero's role is both sympathetic and teasing: When Ray is a "hero grown morose," Hack observes that "Achilles hung out in his tent and pouted / until they made the *Iliad* about it" (123). And when Ray is troubled about indecision, Hack ironically notes that indecision is "epic":

> Until they made the *Iliad* about it
> nobody would have seen a fit of pique
> as quintessentially *geste héroïque*.
> . . . .
> She whose mind's made up fast as she'd eat cake
> has not got that right stuff of which bards make
> heroes.
>
> (128)

Despite the joking, Hacker seems seriously to suggest that the poet has power to alter our perception of received myths and to shape gendered cultural concepts like heroism.

Expanding our understanding of what a woman is, and in particular what a woman-lover-poet may be, entails embracing a variety of traditionally female roles as well. In *Love, Death, and the Changing of the Seasons,* the speaker's being a mother is integrated into her identity as a lover. The contrast with the role assigned to parenting in Shakespeare's sonnets is illuminating. When Shakespeare's speaker in the "procreation sonnets" encourages his fair youth to become a father, he is concerned only with a narcissistic reproduction of the young man's beauty in his son. Parenting in Hacker's sequence has nothing to do with leaving oneself "living in posterity" (sonnet 6) or with insuring that "beauty's rose might never die" (sonnet 1). Hacker underlines the contrast by alluding to Shakespeare's sonnet 2 ("When forty winters shall besiege thy brow / And dig deep trenches in thy beauty's field") in a poem that opens "Forty-two winters had besieged my brow / when you laid siege to my imagination"; the poem expresses Hack's desire to extend the lovers' relationship—with no mention of anyone's beauty or offspring—another forty-two summers.

Instead of serving as a repetition of her mother, Iva forms the third point in the sequence's most important love triangle. But rather than representing an unstable arrangement of rivalry in which someone will inevitably receive diminished love, this triangle is a potentially stable unit that the speaker attempts to sustain. Hack's hope is that she and Ray can "fill out each other's family"; her love for Ray does not supplant her love for her daughter. "Missing you can't obliterate how I've missed her," Hack frankly tells Ray (188). Thus, as she becomes involved with Ray, Hack remains always concerned about how Iva is feeling. The importance of her maternal love is perhaps most clearly registered in the fact that the poem recording the lovers' long-awaited consummation focuses on Iva and how *she* spent that night in her own room. "Not sure / of what she made of what she thought she heard," Hack goes to her early in the morning so that the poem ends recording a declaration of love not to Ray but to Iva, " 'I love you, you know, down to my last, best word' " (61). Ray and Iva are "my two girls," and Hack, despite the freedom gained during the intervals of Iva's absence, seems happiest when the three are together, for then she has "a family." Iva's presence in the sequence, then, strengthens the emphasis on a domestic ideal while expanding the kinds of love between women the work celebrates.

Hack's loving friendships are also a major focus in the volume, and this too broadens the Petrarchan lover's roles. Not only does Hack emphasize the importance of being her beloved's friend; in addition, numerous poems are composed as letters to friends, most often to Julie in France. Through these epistles Hacker builds a sense of a richly supportive web of lasting relationships, many of them quite intimate without dependence on an erotic bond. When Julie experiences tough times, separation from her is painful just as separation from the beloved might be. Deaths of Hack's friends on both sides of the Atlantic are central events in the sequence; and these crises help the couple counter the imbalances fostered by the inequities of their age and experience. The younger woman takes the guide's role: "my own love," Hack reports, "walks me through / hangovers, death, and taxes like a scout / leader" (114).

In Hacker's representation of Ray and the roles she plays—that is, in her presentation of "the beloved," a tellingly passive critical term—her alterations of the Petrarchan norms are particularly clear. Hacker gives herself what we might call a feminist sonneteer's handicap by presenting a beloved who is not only significantly younger—and often addressed with diminutives such as "little one"—but who is literally the speaker's student; Ray and Hack met in a writing class Hack teaches. These inequities in power and experience would tend to set up a dynamic similar to that between traditional Petrarchan lovers. In examining Hacker's response to the challenge this poses, I will focus on three sometimes overlapping areas: giving the beloved voice and agency; depicting the beloved's physical being; negotiating phallocentric narratives of desire. We shall see that Hacker makes a place in the sonnet tradition for a speaking subjectivity that is not locked into a masculinized position, and that she does much to lend voice, agency, and dimensionality to her speaker's beloved.

That Hacker's sequence is about an affair between two poets, even if one is teacher and the other student, signals the revisionary character of her representation of the beloved, for (as noted in discussing "Bloomingdale's I") this beloved is not the traditional silent other. In the androcentric Petrarchan tradition, as Marilyn Farwell notes, the poet/lover

> is active and creative; he is the one who speaks. The female, the beloved, is acted upon, her usual response to the ardent declarations of her lover being

"no." This answer is not an expression of her own sexual choice, but, rather, it is an expression of woman's symbolic function vis-à-vis men: to help the poet transcend the lower world of change and physicality by reminding him that the real object of his sexual passion is his own creativity. (1988, 106)

In *Love, Death, and the Changing of the Seasons,* both partners throughout their relationship are recording their experience in sonnets and exchanging them, through the mail or in person, as a mode of reciprocal communication. None of Ray's poems appears in the book (though Hack quotes a line from one); however, Hack reports presenting a poem by Ray at a reading of her own work in France, and she shows Julie Ray's poems together with her own. One could perhaps argue that in choosing to publish only her half of this coauthored love story, Hacker has in fact left Ray as silent as Petrarch's Laura; Ray's voice where quoted is either invented or appropriated. Yet the device of keeping constantly before the reader Ray's writerly vocation invites the reader to imagine Ray as possessing a voice and subjectivity that Laura, Stella, and the like did not attain. At one point Hack, who frequently uses popular song titles to sketch her situation, characterizes the members of the writing class as "our back-up group" (119); she thereby situates both herself and Ray as the lead singers. Such narrative details destabilize the tradition of one-sided creativity in which "the active male engenders his poetry upon the body of a passive female muse" (DeShazar 1986, quoted in Farwell 1988, 106).

As for "transcending the lower world of change and physicality," neither Hack nor Ray makes claims about immortalizing her lover through art. Sonnet writing is part of the fabric of their lives, essential to their ongoing conversation and valued primarily as an immediate link between them. Thus, Hack on the transatlantic flight "find[s] a clean page to find you again" (29), and when she misses Ray across the ocean relies on "these few lines connecting me to you" (141). Hack is self-conscious, but unapologetic, about the textualizing drive of "left-brain righteousness that makes me / make of our doubled dailiness an art" (71). Presumably, the mutuality of this activity renders it an enhancement of their relationship.

Ray's being a poet provides another revision of a Shakespearean love triangle: Ray herself in this sequence is in some senses "the rival poet." The poem "Sunday Night" stages a "competition" over who can complete her sonnet first. The complex dynamics of this contest emerge from its being compared to a battle fought by a young Spartan lover, which he wins and in which he dies, in order to save his (male) darling. At the close of this mock-heroic poem Ray swaggers through "victorious," yet the analogy suggests that her triumph is as much a tribute to her lover/teacher as a victory over her. In contrast to the situation sketched by Shakespeare's sequence, if the rival wins here, the speaker is not the loser. The two partners do not in fact occupy such polarized positions as the military metaphors (again a Petrarchan convention) might seem to suggest.

One of the best-known conventions of the Petrarchan sonnet tradition—and for women most problematic—involves objectifying the usually female beloved through celebration, part-by-part, of her various beautiful features. As Nancy Vickers notes in "Diana Described: Scattered Woman and Scattered Rhyme":

> Petrarch's figuration of Laura informs a decisive stage in the development of a code of beauty, a code that causes us to view the fetishized body as a norm and encourages us to seek, or to seek to be, "ideal types, beautiful monsters composed of every individual perfection." (1981, 277)[14]

Distancing her speaker from this dismemberment in the guise of idealization, Hacker takes pains never to have Hack speak of her beloved as beautiful and keeps to a minimum descriptions of her physical attributes. The only characteristic of Ray's appearance referred to with any frequency is her blonde hair; its first mention, in the third sonnet, demonstrates how thoroughly Hacker has appropriated the Petrarchan sonnet tradition. Hacker's lines,

> She hides her blushes in her leonine
> hair, that was more like tinsel than like butter
> when I ruffled it—the feminine
> of *avuncular*[,]
>
> (5)

repeat Shakespeare's gesture in sonnet 130—"My mistress' eyes are nothing like the sun. . . . If hairs be wires, black wires grow on her head." In mocking the exaggerations of a literary tradition of "false compare," Hacker commits an anti-Petrarchism that is firmly within the tradition. At the same time, she reveals how undaunted she is by what others—such as Rich—would see as the masculine bias of the language she has inherited: as used here, "leonine" invokes the characteristics of *male* (maned) lions. Similarly, there is no familiar word denoting "like an aunt," only one meaning "like an uncle." Hacker's appropriation of these terms, like her appropriation of other "male" activities, calls into question our established gender categories, denying that the "male" is in fact male (or the "female" female).

Thereafter, descriptions of Ray's appearance are rare. On the only occasion when loveliness is explicitly attributed to the beloved, what is described is genitals in orgasm as Hack imagines making love to Ray: "with my whole hand, I / hold your drenched loveliness contracting" (21). Here the contrast is most directly with the misogynist portrayal of female sexuality in Shakespeare's poems addressed to the dark lady whose vagina figures as a "hell" in which his (male) angel lover is turned devil, a site of venereal infection (sonnet 144), and a "large and spacious" harbor promiscuously available to all (sonnet 135).

When Hack does provide brief notations of her beloved's physical appearance, she usually accompanies them with comparable descriptions of herself—"my olive skin, your creamy skin" (112), "She's / red-gold, I'm brown" (165)— rendering both partners embodied beings whom readers might envision, neither one the exclusive object of our gaze. On one occasion, writing from France to her beloved in New York, Hack describes herself in order explicitly to remind Ray— and the reader—of the physical attractions she herself offers:

> Not averse to being seen
> as an amelioration of the view,
> I wore that black nubbed-raw-silk *salopette,*
> —but with a lurex cowlneck under it;
> the neckline-to-the-waist take was for you.
>
> (51)

Isolated by a line break, the phrase "Not averse to being seen" suggests that what needs revising in the tradition is the one-sidedness of observation that renders only the beloved an object of visual pleasure.

At the same time, Hacker has her beloved speak out against being used as a "masturbation fantasy." In "What You Might Answer" Hack imagines Ray— still unavailable and reluctant—expressing the kind of resistance the sonneteers' beloveds must have been feeling for centuries:

> "Nobody needs her Frye boots cast in bronze.
> I don't like crowds, and now I'm feeling crowded.
> I can speak tongues, but not the ones your friends
> gossip with you about me in. The end's
> still moot, jackboots. I have to think about it.
> . . . .
> You want a masturbation fantasy?
> Some girls you know put out a magazine
> full of them—but I'm not the centerfold."
>
> (35)

The poem signals Hack's self-consciousness about the dangers of repeating male appropriations when, "horny as a timber wolf in heat" (10), she voices her sexual frustration as traditionally only men might. She is aware that she risks repeating the errors of her male predecessors: rendering her beloved yet another statue on a pedestal, albeit in modernized footwear. Consequently, a later poem finds her choosing not to use Ray as a "masturbation fantasy" when that opportunity arises as Ray, now her bedmate, is rendered passive by sleep. Masturbating while watching her would be easy—the technique is even described, "two fingers along my clit," etc.—"but I don't—take you against your will, / it seems like, and I wouldn't" (100).

In the many times Hack depicts sexual fantasies involving Ray, she attends to Ray's pleasure as much as her own; indeed the two are inseparable. One precon-summation fantasy begins, "First I want to make you come," and describes how she would bring her lover to orgasm by using first manual and then oral stimula-tion and closes with instructions for her lover so that the poem ends, "I want you to make me come" (21). Similarly, she frequently emphasizes her wish to give Ray time and space "to get to me / your way" (80). The poem "Future Conditional" reveals how such regard for reciprocity and mutual pleasure may alter the inher-ited subject/object positions of the sonnet sequence's lover and beloved. Its lan-guage recalls Montefiore's claims about the beloved functioning as a mirroring means of self-definition. Hack, writing from France, begins by urging Ray "let us start / where we left off" but soon moves from the hortatory stance to the future conditional, describing her fantasy of their first genital sex. "Sweetheart," she pleads, "your body is a text I need the art / to be constructed by." Yet having apparently announced explicitly the self-construction that Montefiore finds im-plicit in the traditional love sonnet, Hack proceeds to make this same self-construction available for her lover. As she imagines herself undressing Ray, her own body becomes a text (book) for Ray's use:

> I'll find the hook,
> release promised abundance to this want,
> while your hands, please, here and here, exigent
> and certain, open this; it is, this book,
> made for your hands to read, your mouth to use.
>
> (50)

Opening her legs or the lips of her vagina to expose the clitoris merges with the act of opening the book of sonnets. In the latter act, the reader merges with Ray, suggesting not only an erotic invitation to us but also a textualization that ex-tends even to the reader. No one escapes being textualized, rendered an object by which others may construct their own identities—but by the same token, self-construction becomes an activity common to all. This more abstract version of the "I want to make you come" poem reveals a significant change in dynamics between speaker and beloved made possible simply by an insistence on the equal-ity of their sexual needs and capacities (an equality missing from the heterosexual Petrarchan tradition).

This mutuality is underscored by Hacker's frequent use of a metonymic rhetoric of contiguity and touch in portraying her lovers' connections, rather than a metaphoric rhetoric which, Margaret Homans has noted, hierarchically depends on specular distance between speaker and beloved.[15] Not wanting either of her lovers to be rendered merely objects, Hacker explores the pleasures of a sexuality that is not primarily specular. Once again, however, she sees no need to excise what Homans identifies as the "male" plot of desire or the referentiality to which it is bound, any more than she entirely rejects "male" roles or language for her characters. As we have seen in other contexts, her project is an expansive one: she appropriates a quest plot yet also places new emphasis on the pleasure of touch in women's sexuality.

Distance, according to Homans, is the motive for the (male) sonneteer's writing. This remains true in Hacker's work to the extent that otherness—that is, the lovers' inhabiting individual bodies—itself is a form of distance: Hacker rarely exploits the figure of sameness, a potential disguise of separateness often present in lesbian representation (especially, Grover reminds us, in "good-girl" writing, where it tends to downplay tensions generated by differences, for instance, in class, race, and ethnicity [1990, 22]). But as noted above, the distances that concern her are emotional, not physical or hierarchical, and the story she tells is not primarily the phallocentric story of looking. The spatial figure she returns to several times as depicting her lovers' closeness/separateness is that of asymptotes—lines forever approaching more and more closely, though never in fact touching. For example, in a poem whose opening line ("From you will I be absent as the spring") echoes Shakespeare's sonnet 98, Hack on the eve of departure for France voices her hope that

> the clearer focus of a distancing
> lens will show both of us separately
> comet trails marking your trajectory
> and mine, convergent, or continuing
> asymptotes, toward a human finity
> of works and days.
>
> (137)

While the sixty pages of *Love, Death, and the Changing of the Seasons* that precede the couple's first lovemaking portray a quest similar to that of the Petrarchan male lover—initially, Ray is "just the kind of boy / I would have eyeballed at the bar" (17)—the remaining pages depict a struggle both lovers undertake (at least according to Hack) to reduce psychological and emotional distances: "We've both got work to do / to work our different ways across the distance / between us" (140). Since the goal is a touching on all fronts—

> I want our lives to touch
> the way our minds do. What our bodies do
> together is unprecedented. (Minds
> dreamed it up; can the dichotomy.)
>
> (111)

—even words and gazes may be presented in terms of contact: "wished I could touch / you now with words . . . that there'd be eye // contact and talk across a dinner table" (187). When the breakup does occur, at Ray's instigation, Hack describes the bond she still feels in terms of physical contact and presence that virtually eliminate distance. Yet "I" and "you" remain distinct:

> As my eyes
> open [upon waking], I know *I* am; that instant, feel
> you with me, on me, in me, and you're not.
>
> (209)

Hacker's ways of revising the Renaissance Petrarchans' tropes depicting the beloved in astronomical figures also demonstrate her interest in representing nonphallocentric narratives of sexual pleasure. The traditional metaphors, Homans points out, "depend for their effect on the analogy between the distance between poet and lady—the distance of desire—and the distance between the lady and the stars to which she is compared" (1985, 571–72). Hacker works against this distance. In lines quoted earlier, for instance—"I moved into one mansion / the morning when I touched, I saw, I felt / your face blazing above me like a sun" (69)—the specular economy on which the comparison of beloved to sun traditionally depends merges into a tactile one in which the mutuality of touching and being touched (feeling the blaze) is emphasized. Similarly, shortly after the relationship is sexually consummated, Hack announces, "This is the second morning I woke curved / around your dreaming. In one night, I've seen / moonset and sunrise in your lion's mane" (65). Rather than staring across space at the star/beloved, she sees the motion of astronomical bodies through and "in" the hair of the lover whose body is curved against her own. What Homans terms the "story of looking" here is not one of looking at the beloved, but looking with and alongside her. Nor is Hack the only partner who gazes; Ray has eyes, too, and "What they see sometimes are scabs and scars / on my thin hide. Not always a forgiving / gaze" (166).

It should be apparent by now that Hacker does not aspire to sever her work—or her romantic couple—from the traditions of heterosexual patriarchy; yet her feminist parody and play challenge traditional ideology by undermining patriarchal gender categories. The three poems on "Having Kittens about Having

Babies" (104–6) permit a closing recap of this formalist feminist poet's position both inside and outside hegemonic norms. Ray, wanting her own child, has proposed spending "a few months fucking a high-school friend / or, failing that, cruis[ing] bars and pick[ing] up men / until one takes," believing this arrangement need not impinge on her lesbian relationship. In order to make Ray understand why she finds this proposal outrageous, Hack asks her to imagine a comparable situation involving a hypothetical heterosexual couple in which the man is infertile because the child of his first marriage gave him mumps. Hack apparently assumes that the emotional dynamics and interpersonal responsibilities of her and Ray's situation will be clearer if presented in terms of heterosexual relationships, for which there's a more general agreement about what is acceptable. Through her speaker Hacker suggests that because lesbians have to devote so much energy to forging new patterns, they risk losing sight of some basic obligations that she holds apart from issues of gender and sexual preference: "There are two readings to the text: because / no law defines this love, we are outlaws. / We're not, each to the other, marginal." That Hack and Ray are literally and figuratively outside patriarchal law would not justify behavior violating some more fundamentally human laws of respect for the feelings of those one loves. In the first two of the three poems, then, Hacker seems to caution against exaggerating the difference of lesbian relationships.

Yet after Hack has explicitly presented her situation as "the same" as that of the infertile man in her fictive couple, in the third poem she distances herself from the heterosexual narrative by foregrounding privileges accorded the heterosexual male that no lesbian lover can enjoy. Analogies between heterosexual and lesbian couples are accurate only within certain areas, while the dramatic social differences are materially and psychologically oppressive to lesbians:

> They get to make their loves the focal point
> of Real Life: last names, trust funds, architecture,
> reify them; while we are, they conjecture,
> erotic *frissons,* birds of passage, quaint
> embellishments in margins.

Presenting "we" through "their" eyes enacts the marginalization—the expulsion from the subject position—that Hack is talking about here, and her tone is as angry as it ever gets in the sequence. But she rejects anger for the consolations of her lover, and, after several long kisses restore her composure, she looks to the ways in which lesbians can turn their marginalization to advantage. Refocusing attention away from reproduction and babies, Hack urges:

> Look what we're mak-
> ing, besides love (that has a name to speak).
> Its very openness keeps it from harm, or
> perhaps it wears our live-nerved skin as armor,
> out in the world arranging mountains, nak-
> ed as some dream of Cousin William Blake.

The relationship these lesbian feminists are creating is expansive (open), and the work it is doing is substantial. No doubt Hacker holds similar aspirations for the sonnet sequences they are making. Yet she does not hesitate to identify the visionary character of this work with a man, rather than a woman; in her view neither women nor lesbians have exclusive claims on marginality or productive social change. Nor do free-verse writers—or notably avant-garde ones—have exclusive claims to political engagement; as Hacker once asserted, "If there is such a thing as a New Formalist, s/he may be a black activist as well" (1989b, 4).

Notes

1. This revival is evident in the publication not only of individual volumes of formalist verse but also of formalist anthologies like Philip Dacey and David Jauss's *Strong Measures: Contemporary American Poetry in Traditional Forms* (1985) and Robert Richman's *The Direction of Poetry: An Anthology of Rhymed and Metered Verse Written in the English Language Since 1975* (1988) as well as proformalist critical studies such as Timothy Steele's *Missing Measures: Modern Poetry and the Revolt Against Meter* (1990) and Wyatt Prunty's *"Fallen from the Symboled World": Precedents for the New Formalism* (1990).

2. Ariel Dawson, for instance, claims that "the reemergence of formalism is perfectly harmonious with the yuppie knack for resurrecting elitist traditions" (1985, 5).

3. Statements in a more recent interview with David Montenegro suggest Rich may be moderating her position so as to place more emphasis on the resources of formal tradition. In responding to a question about whether traditional metric implies a frame of mind or limits content, Rich asserts that she never wanted to "get rid of" the iambic pentameter line and adds,

> I guess what I'm searching for always is a way of staying linked to the past, pulling out of it whatever you can use, and continuing to move on. And I'm not sure that a new textual form creates—it certainly *doesn't* create—a new consciousness. It can equally well be said that a new consciousness, a radically divergent one, doesn't necessarily create a new form either. I hate that form/content bifurcation, but sometimes it has to be used, for an attitude, a stance, a positioning of the poet.

She goes on to describe the effectiveness of Derek Walcott's use of iambic pentameter in an explosive "fusion of old form and old consciousness with new form and new consciousness" (1991b, 18–19).

4. In "'Openness,' 'Closure,' and Recent American Poetry," Alan Golding calls attention to the New Formalists' invocation of organicist rhetoric more typically employed by free-verse practitioners, the formalists' putative opponents. The quoted material derives from Golding's paraphrase of Timothy Steele's organicist justification of metered verse (1991, 85).

5. This point is humorously demonstrated by Language poet Charles Bernstein's *The Nude Formalism* (1989).

6. Montefiore acknowledges that the Lacanian model on which her analysis of sonnets as mirror poems rests is "vulnerable to the criticism that it is universalist and ahistorical and that its ready acceptance of such potentially antifeminist notions as the castration complex colludes with the patriarchal bias of their originators" (1987, 104); nonetheless, she finds the model too useful to relinquish in her analysis of women poets' flawed attempts to generate a woman's sonnet tradition.

7. The proliferation of names for the characters in itself points toward the multiple identities/genders that I will argue Hacker opens for her characters.

8. In the context of this essay's larger argument, it is worth noting that in the latter poem, Hack also considers issues of poetic form. While playing upon marriage rituals, she makes fun of organicist, mimetic understandings of poetic form:

> will measured feet
> advance processionally, where before
> they scuff-heeled flights of stairs, kicked at a door,
> or danced in wing-tips to a dirty beat?
>
> (1986, 65)

At the same time, her proclaimed uncertainty about poetic meter and pace points to the sonnet tradition's lack of precedent for treating satisfied, settled love, while nonetheless emphasizing the form's flexibility.

9. In these terms, we can distinguish this project from the more radical one exemplified, for instance, in Wittig's *The Lesbian Body*. As Elaine Marks notes in "Lesbian Intertextuality" (1979), Wittig is creating a new mythology in which the female body and woman's relation to language are thoroughly undomesticated; Wittig wants only the wild, unfettered by the safe and familiar.

10. Sue-Ellen Case makes a similar argument in "Toward a Butch-Femme Aesthetic" (1989), claiming that the butch-femme couple plays on rather than to the phallic economy. Case sees the discourse of camp, associated with the butch-femme masquerade, as a potential key to the liberation of the "feminist subject" who has the agency to change ideology.

11. Perhaps she refers also to Marilyn Hacker's having been a married heterosexual earlier in her life.

12. This is precisely what free-verse advocates like Rich deplore about the use of fixed forms, while claiming that free verse can render poetic form a more genuine extension of content. Hacker, presumably, would see "organic" or "open" forms as no closer to truth or naturalness, only to its pretense.

13. One could invoke here the notion of postmodernism's "complicitous critique" developed by Linda Hutcheon in *The Politics of Postmodernism* (1989). However, Hacker's work seems to me less concerned with commenting upon and critiquing dominant conventions than in opening them up, and Hutcheon's terminology might obscure the playfulness of Hacker's stance.

14. Vickers also makes a similar claim to Farwell's above when she notes, "[B]odies fetishized by a poetic voice logically do not have a voice of their own; the world of making words, of making texts, is not theirs" (1981, 277).

15. In this section I am drawing on Margaret Homans's insights in "'Syllables of Velvet': Dickinson, Rossetti, and the Rhetorics of Sexuality," although Homans, like Montefiore, sees the sonnet tradition as masculine in ways Hacker does not. Homans argues not only that the "I" of the romantic lyric that developed from the Petrarchan love poem is "constitutively masculine . . . because in Western poetic and philosophical traditions, self-expressive subjectivity is represented as a male prerogative" but also that lyrics in the Petrarchan tradition "[depend] on the plot of masculine, heterosexual desire" (1985, 570), which negates women's pleasure. This plot, embodied in a rhetoric reliant on specular metaphor, depends on a distance between speaking subject and silent object. Homans sees Emily Dickinson in some of her poems as having escaped this plot, having imagined "a place from which female sexuality can speak for itself, a rhetoric of female pleasure to replace the silencing rhetoric of male desire" (576). Depending not on distance but on contiguity, and privileging touch rather than sight, this rhetoric relies on metonymy rather than metaphor, since metaphor "assumes a subject-object relation and an order of priority" (585).

DIS PLACE   THE SPACE BETWEEN

M. Nourbese Philip

22 April 1986

Dear C.

I write as an African-Caribbean woman. This consciousness permeates my work—I am referring here to my poetry; True, "Earth and Sound" has no overt reference to my being female, or to feminist issues—which is what I think you're saying, but feminist issues did not impinge on my thinking these issues through, and it would be false to put them in to satisfy current fashion.

Yours truly

M.

Ps. This is not to say that those issues aren't there—for instance, I recollect that my relationship to my environment was very much affected by the severe curtailment of being a female child in Trinidad, I'm sure you know what I mean—home-school-home and on and on. Boys, men had a lot more freedom—this is bound to affect how we respond to place.

CASE STUDY

Facts

In 1985 a black female poet completed an essay, "Earth and Sound: The Place of Poetry," in which she examined the concept and idea of "place" and how the poet attached herself to a place so that she began to write *from* rather than *about* a place. These issues were significant since the poet was in "exile" from her place.

The essay ranged over issues of colonialism, racism, and language, and considered in some detail the work of two writers, Les Murray and Aimé Cesaire, as examples of writers who had found their place and wrote from it. The poet did not deal with the issues of gender or feminism as they relate to place, or the public space.

Issues

Why did the poet write herself—the female body—out of place, the public space of the text? Why did she impose on herself the sentence?
ratio decidendi[1] or how and why the sentence of silence was imposed.

THE BODY

which is to talk about the space that lies between the legs of the female and the effect of this space on the outer space—"place."

In patriarchal societies (the only societies we have known), the female body always presents a subversive threat. By far *the* most efficient management tool of women is the possibility of the uninvited and forceful invasion of the space between the legs—rape.[2] Which is a constant. A threat to *the* space—the inner space between the legs. Even if never carried out, this threat continually and persistently inflects how the female reads the external language of place, or public space—the outer space. One woman raped is sufficient to vocalize and reify the threat of outer space, and the need to protect this inner space means that the female always reads the outer space from the dichotomous position—safe/unsafe, prohibited/unprohibited. How the female poet interacts with the land, the countryside, or the urbanscape—with the outer space in all its variety, or place, in this most physical of senses—is, therefore, entirely affected by gender. She must read place—the outer space—in a gendered language. Is the choice, therefore, either to accept the restriction in physical behavior and available space that the threat of rape brings—limit one's activities to the daytime and to specific places? Or what? The female poet's understanding of place in its most physical sense will be different from, and necessarily a more restricted one, than that of the male poet.

SPACE INNER AND OUTER

All women have imprinted in them the basic politics of male territoriality
—A. Fell 1991, 18[3]

Whether we conceive of the space between the legs as one space, the cunt; two spaces, the cunt *and* the womb; or one continuous space extending from cunt to womb, control of and over this space or these spaces is a significant marker of the outer space. The problematic is whether the threat of the outer space originates there, or whether it is the generative potential of the inner space—its baby-making potential—that threatens the outer space, which in turn seeks to control the inner space.

Space and place—the public space—must be read and interpreted from the point of view of the space between the legs, and in particular from the perspective of how safe the space between the legs is or will be.[4]

The Body. And that most precious of resources—the space. Between. The legs. The black woman comes to the New World with only the body. And the space between. The European buys her not only for her strength, but also to service the black man sexually—to keep him calm. And to produce new chattels—units of production—for the plantation machine. The black woman. And the space between her legs. Is intended to help repopulate the outer space:

> *Female slaves will be provided who, through marriage with the male slaves, will make the latter less eager for revolt, and the number of runaways will be reduced to a minimum.* (Ferdinand, king of Spain, to Miguel Pasamonte, treasurer for Hispaniola, April 1514; quoted in Williams 1963, 155)

The space between the black woman's legs becomes. *The place.* Site of oppression—vital to the cultivation and continuation of the outer space in a designated form—the plantation machine. Harness the use value of the inner space to the use value of the outer space so that the inner space becomes open to all and sundry. Becomes, in fact, a public space. A thoroughfare. The "black magic" of the white man's pleasure, the "bag o' sugar down dey" of the black man's release. *And* the space through which new slaves would issue forth.

"She nuttin but a thoroughfare!" Thoroughfare: Bajan (Barbadian) expression for a woman who is sexually active with many men.

For the black woman, place and space come together in the New World as never before. Or since. To create. S/Place. The immutable and irrevocable linking of the inner place or space. Between the legs. With the outer space—"place" of the New World plantation machine. The Caribbean s/place living its postmodernist realities long before the advent of the theory. If theory it be.

S/Place. Where the inner space is defined into passivity by, and harnessed to, the needs and functions of the outer space—the place of oppression. Run it down:[5] s/place mutating into dis/place, and even further into the *dis place* of Caribbean demotic English. *Dis place:* the outer space—the plantation, the New World. *Dis place*—the space between. The legs. *Dis place:* the result of the linking of the inner space between the legs with the outer place resulting in "dis placement." For the black woman "dis placed" to and in the New World, the inner space between the legs would also mutate into *dis place*—fulcrum of the New World plantation.

A GENEALOGY OF JAMETTES

Jamette[6] from diametre, the diameter, dividing the world between the space and place of respectability and that of the underworld, the lower classes. Jamette—a female belonging to that latter world and class. Jamette! A "loose" woman, a woman of "loose" morals, whose habitat is the street. Jamette! A woman possessing both the space between her legs and the space around her, knowing her place. On the streets of Port of Spain.

We could be starting our genealogy with Nanny of the Maroons.[7] Or we could be going even further back. To Nzinga of Ngola (Angola).[8] Women warriors taking their inner space into the outer space of battle and war where men violate the inner space of women.

Rum shop, cock fight, steel-pan yard, street corner—only jamettes hanging about these places. Men *and* women who above the diameter/diametre would be calling these women out of their names, describing them over the years as wajanks, jackabats, spoats, and hos (whores). We calling them jamettes. For the present. We calling them jamettes but having care not to mistake every jamette for a prostitute. Is what they doing in these places? Only servicing men? Signifying another reality? About the balance between the inner and outer space?

BUT JAMETTES GET RAPED TOO!

THE STREETS

> *The street is the only valid form of experience.*
>
> —André Breton

Biography

Cast of Characters

Boadicea (Jamette, stick fighter, leader of the Don't Give a Damns)
Alice Sugar (Jamette, stick fighter, leader of the Mousselines)
Man Tamer (a *poui*⁹ stick)
Piti Belle Lily (Jamette)
Mossie Millie (Jamette)
Ocean Lizzie (Jamette)
Sybil Steel (Jamette)
Big Body Ada (Jamette)
Darling Dan (Jamette)
Ling Mama (Jamette)
Queen Bee (Jamette)
Myrtle the Turtle (Jamette)
Zinga (Jamette)

Preliminary Notes

Boadicea, the Jamette queen, has just set up her reign of the city streets by fighting and beating Cutway Rimbeau, king of the stick fighters, for showing too much interest in another woman, Piti Belle Lily. Cutway Rimbeau knowing that he's beaten gives Boadicea his stick, Man Tamer. In an earlier fight, Boadicea also beat up Alice Sugar in a fight over Cutway Rimbeau.

Act 1, scene 1

Time: 1865
Everything happening at a crossroads in Port of Spain in a lower-class area. One narrow street running from upstage center to downstage center, where it meeting up with another narrow street running from downstage right to downstage left. All kind of garbage littering the streets. The houses small small and run-down and is fade the paint fade, although you could see somebody building them good. The little windows with their jalousies looking onto the street which not having pavements, and doors opening right on to the road. As the curtain rising everything quiet quiet, but little by little cries and shouts coming from offstage. Suddenly from downstage left a group of stalwart, handsome women bursting onto the stage; two women leading them carrying a red banner with black words— WE DON'T GIVE A DAMN! The women carrying long, heavy-looking sticks, and the way the wood gleaming in the light you could tell the women polish them

up. Some women also carrying stones and rocks, and all of them wearing red head-wraps tie up in some real fancy shapes. The women swaggering around the stage now, their long prettyful skirts trailing in the street and sending up little clouds of dust. They laughing big big and loud and some of them walking with their arms around each other. At a given cue the women start chanting and beating on empty tin cans some carrying with them:

> We don't
> we don't
> we don't give a damn
> we don't give a blast
> we don't give a shit
> we won't give an inch
> not for you or you or you;
> we don't give
> we won't give
> not an inch
> not a foot
> we have we poui stick
> we have we iron
> we have we machete
> and when we done
> is only mousse leave from mousseline.

As soon as they finish singing another group of women bursting onto the stage from downstage right, taking the spotlight and pushing the Don't Give a Damns upstage to the left. These women dressing all in white—fresh wash-an-starch white muslin dresses and white head-wraps giving them their name, the Mousselines. They big just like the Don't Give a Damns and they striding around the stage like they owning it. With the white cloth against their black skin they pretty too bad. Like the Don't Give a Damns, the Mousselines carrying sticks and stones; some even carrying broken bottles too. The spotlight moving from group to group: here, two or three Mousselines standing talking and laughing; there, a bigger group making rude gestures at the Don't Give a Damns, who now on the margins of the stage, muttering under their breath and cutting their eyes at the women in white. The white muslin head-wraps of the Mousselines gather up at the center of the stage, and surrounding them is the red of the Don't Give a Damns and it all set off against the black background. It startling for so. Suddenly, two more women in white entering from downstage right with a banner still wrap up and as they moving center stage they pushing the others back. They unfurling the banner in the spotlight and spelling the word MOUSSELINES. The women in white start singing:

Watch we hard watch we good
keep your eyes pon we—
each one a we have we wood
that good to beat and crack head.
Bottle and stone we know
we sleep pon rock
bottle is we bed
so watch we hard
watch we good
we have we piece a wood
we is the Mousselines
dis town is we own
de Don't Give a Damns
had better begin to give.

They singing loud loud and aggressive and making obscene gestures to the Don't Give a Damns, who muttering louder and louder now. Soon a fierce and brutal fight breaking out between the two groups of women. Sound of stick against flesh, stick against stick, or stone against bone or flesh, is all that filling the theater. Quiet quiet flesh getting cut, and the red staining the stage. Suddenly a shrill whistle piercing the air and someone shouting:

"Police!"

The stage black black now. When it coming up light again, the two groups of women standing together watching the town's law enforcers—all men—coming down the narrow street that running from upstage center to downstage center. The women looking untidy and disheveled, some missing their head-wraps, others having their skirts tear up; some bleeding and a few sitting or lying at the side of the road too hurt to move. Is clear they forgetting their differences facing this new threat. The men, mainly white and brown, all suit up in blue serge uniforms, and careful careful they moving down the narrow street hem in by the houses where these very women living. All the men knowing these women: they meeting them before in similar situations and they frighten of them, especially if they not having other officers backing them up. This is why the men coming down the street slow slow, holding their batons which they know not matching the women's sticks. As the men approaching, the women pulling closer together and making as if to charge. The men back back down the narrow roadway. The women now carrying their furled banners like weapons. This toing and froing happening three times. In silence. Suddenly the jamette, Boadicea, turning her back to the men, lifting up her skirt and baring her behind. All the women doing the same and laughing loud loud and raucous. The men backing off now even further and looking real shocked and angry.

"You're a disgrace to womanhood! All you jamettes—a disgrace, you should be locked up." *One of the officers shouting out.*

"Lock we up nuh, lock we up!" *Is Boadicea who first challenging them like this, then Alice Sugar and the other women picking up the cry:*

"Lock we up, lock we up! We waiting, come and lock we up!"

As the women chanting these words, they moving up the street again toward the men. Boadicea tearing off her dress and now she standing naked like the day she born in front of her troops and the police officers. The women shouting out their approval and everybody tearing off their dresses. Some of the men turning away, their faces disgusted and angry at all that nakedness in front of them. The men pulling back even further. Boadicea waving her dress over her head like a flag, then she turning her back on the police and talking to the women:

"Is fraid we fraid dese men?"

"No!" *the women roaring back at her.*

"Who dese men protecting?"

"Not we, not one o we!"

"Who de street belong to, dem or we?"

"The streets is we own!"

Boadicea turning now to face the men: "You see we here in all we nakedness— you see any of we shame of it? Not one, not one a we shame of we nakedness or frighten of you."

Boadicea advancing slowly on the men as she talking, and the women following her.

"De space between we legs is we own to do with as we please, and we not frighten of dese streets. Dese streets is we own—we have a right to be here and we beating any man who telling we different—just ask Cutway Rimbeau!" *Is clear the men recognizing the name. The women moving faster now and suddenly they charging the men who turning tail and running. The women laughing loud loud like real jamettes. Suddenly the stage black black.*

Act 2, scene 2

The same crossroads as in Act 1, scene 1.
The light spotting a man sitting on a corner, playing a guitar singing:

> Boadicea the jamette who we all know
> Is a real disgrace to we Cariso
> I really can't understand
> Why she didn't take the training of the Englishman
> Roaming all about the vicinity
> Cat and dog passing they mouth on she

Is better she die or lock up in jail
She disgrace every woman in Port-of-Spain.

(Pearse 261, 1956)

THE MISSING TEXT

When a text goes missing in the computer, it is not completely lost—another language is needed to translate the language of the 'missing' text so that it becomes readable once again.

Is it silence that shapes the words of the "missing" text, or do the words shape the silence? How to read the silence? Much like those children's books where pictures of animals and people hide within the larger picture, I hunt the pieces of my silence within the larger text of silence—words. When the missing text is silence, what is the language with which you read the silence? What is the grammar of silence? Start with the word. The poem. The text. To deal in silence one must learn a new language.

On behalf of past generations
the body mediates
fleshing out the shadows of ghosts
soft songs lurk
sometimes so soft—a silence
wails
and the trumpet of words
brings down the Jerichoed walls

of silence

Composition is everything.

—Miles Davis, trumpeter.

It is.
Each poem has its own silence. Technique but the discerning of that silence. And composition—*how* you shape the words around the silence. To understand one's own silence is, therefore, to understand one's words. To understand one's silence one must go to the place of silence. In the words. In the body. *Dis place*—the s/place between the legs!

Jean, Dinah, Rosita, and Clementina[10] were four prostitutes. They all lived in a calypso by Sparrow, the world's greatest calypso man. Jean, Dinah, Rosita, and

Clementina—their space a corner, a street corner, where they posing and selling what all men wanting—a piece of their space, the space between their legs. Jean, Dinah, Rosita, and Clementina—

> bet your life is something they selling
> and if you catch them broken
> you can get it all for nothing
> the Yankees gone and Sparrow, take over now.

Because of the Yankees, Jean, Dinah, Rosita, and Clementina charging a higher price for their space, the place that was theirs and theirs alone. Sparrow man, calypso man, putting them round the corner posing, and believing he could get it all for nothing. Because he controlling the outer space, which controlling their inner space. Jean, Dinah, Rosita, and Clementina—their space, their place, dis place between the legs—public women, women in public on the street corner, round the corner selling . . .
your life   mine and theirs.

EARTH AND SOUND: PLACE OF POETRY

The space and place of silence—the silence around "Earth and Sound"; my own silence locked in my own words—silencing me. The sentence of silence! Césaire, Murray, Walcott, Pound—how they stride around my silence filled with their words—wonderful words. And like past generations, I lurk with Piti Belle Lili and Boadicea—abbreviated traditions—the jamette, the only choice for those with no choice. Earth and sound—the place of poetry in the culture of silence: the silence of black, the silence of woman, the silence of silence.

> silence is
> silence is
> silence is
>
> the sound, the very sound; between the words
> in the interstices of time divided by the word
>
> between
> outer and inner
> space /silence
> is
> the boundary

Why didn't "I"—the female body—surface in the text, or was it there all along? In the silence? "Missing" becomes a metaphor for the silence around the text that omits the woman's s/place. Words crowd her out into silence. Women have, in fact, left their mark on the many silences that surround language—we must, therefore, learn to read those silences.

If we talk of silence and assign to it a validity equal to the word, is it then right to talk of a "missing text," since the text of silence is already embedded in the word? Silence, as in the silence around "Earth and Sound," sometimes says more than the word does. Earth. Sound. And Silence. To read the silence around the text one must become a jamette poet—possessing the space between the legs—the inner space—uncompromisingly—as the outer space.

AS IF

For was there not also the wisdom which had shaped my body up through the years from a single cell?
—Marion Milner, *A Life of One's Own*

The question of possession: true ownership/belonging: is one that will always exercise creole societies: nonnative: and especially the slave Caliban, most dispossessed of all.
—E. K. Brathwaite, "Caliban, Ariel and Unprospero in the Conflict of Creolization"

1.
He walks   gets into his boat
as if
he has always done that
his boat   his space   his place

2.
high heels
push
pushing the body up
away from
earth
thin bodies taking
up
less & less
space

3.
           fetus in place
pushing

pushes body to occupy
                              more

space
dis
tended belly taking
up
more & more
              space

4.
oh, for a race of women
mashing the ground
as if!
they owned it
not like he does

5.
to move
        leaping from occupying space to
occupying the idea
        the thought
to make it your own
taking up
        more & more . . .

6.
the force of baby
    forces
you to
take   more
& more &
more . . .
            space

7.
breasts   thighs   belly   buttocks
flesh swells
ripens into the full
of time filled with
carefully choreographed expansions
of plenitude and ful/
fillment

8.
crazy wild distension of belly   belly
and more belly
that will
not
can
not stop
yet nothing wild here—
everything following
deep codes
yet we take
(up)
space
differently

9.
oh, for a race of women!

10.
he walks
as if
he owns the earth
steps into his boat   his car
his plane
his fighter jet
his idea
his war
as extensions of his
very self
he occupies
possesses them

        car
        house
        children
        women
        ideas
no memory of murder
in his walk
no memory of death
and we who
carrying
and carrying

life
who taking up
space
honestly
carry fear

of our move
                    ments
        expanded   dis
                        tensions choreo
    graphed
            through the centuries and
one hundred years
because we did
                not
                choreo
graph the pain
        the poem

this dance
this song
this lament
we did not
            this idea
he possesses

BUT THE BODY

A history of bodies

—Michel Foucault, *The History of Sexuality*

silence is
silence is
silence is
body and
text
text and
body filaments of silence holding them together
Text Body Silence
Earth Sound Silence
EarthSilenceSoundBodyText

Unlike all other arrivals before or since, when the African comes to the New
World, she comes with nothing. But the body. Her body. **The** body—repository

and source of everything needed to survive in any but the barest sense. Body memory   bodymemory. The African body. Its resources: strength, resistance to disease. The African body. Including the space between the legs, the raison d'être of her importation to the New World.
The African body. At cross purposes with the African body—

> the African body: spirit
> the African body: intelligence
> the African body: memory
> the African body: creativity

: its resources

Time and again these resources impelling her to flee, run from, subvert. The institution of slavery.
Is we bodies saving we—forcing we to live in them. We coming to understand that surviving needing the body. African. Pulling we down: Source of enslavement / road to transcendence: holding we up. The Body African. Is Mind.

> *What I learned from the slave is that I can control my body. Music, movement—this was outside the reach of the oppressor . . . this we could control.* (Rex Nettleford)[11]

So the maroons taking their bodies completely outside the reach and ambit of the white European—but only in those places and spaces where the land allowing it. Mountains!—you having to have them: "I will lift mine eyes to the hills from whence cometh my salvation." Maroonage—the coming together of the exploited physical s/place—"place" and "space"—and the exploited s/place— "place" and "space"—of the body. Maroonage—the coming together. Creating something new—an inner space and place—s/place—of African self-sufficiency that the European, emissary of the outer space, and what Brathwaite calling "missile cultures" continually trying to penetrate.

Foucault (the white, male European) speaks. On sexuality

> *Deployments of power are directly connected to the body—to bodies, functions, physiological processes, sensations, and pleasures; far from the body having to be effaced, what is needed is to make it visible through an analysis in which the biological and the historical are not consecutive to one another, as in the evolutionism of the first sociologists, but are bound together in an increasingly complex fashion in accordance with the development of the modern technologies of power that take life as their objective.* (1978, 151–52)

THE BODY FEMALE and black

= a history of sexuality = a history of bodies
—to harness female reproductive power to the machine of the plantation. The
inestimable value of the space between the legs—the black (w)hole that could
replenish plantations and keep men calm and nonrebellious. *The Handmaid's
Tale* but a vision of the future past in white face.
—to distort the body's impulses and learnt wisdoms
careful choreography of diastole and systole
choreography of birth and death
he walks, gets into his boat his planehas no memory of
murderno memory of death
the   Body   African   the silence at the heart of the word is

                    body—the irreducible—body african
                                    black ivory
                                    piecesofblackgold
                                    piezas
                                    meubles
                                    chattels
                                    things
oh for a race of women
                    African
mashing the ground
dis
tended bellies
careful choreographed expansions of plenty
tude
full
fill   men(t)
and fear

the body female and black = a history of sexuality where biology and history
forever tie up in the black space and place of s/place, birthing "modern tech-
nologies of power that take life as their objective." And take life.
In the New World the African woman creating life and seeing the men—the
white men—taking away her children and selling them. The man who walking,
getting into his boat his plane his ship—taking the product of her body and the
body's wisdoms—her children—like he taking the crops she (dis)tending. Body
and place. Fertilized. Cultivated. Harvested. In the same way. Between parent.
And child. Mother. And child. Father. And child. Rupture. Umbilical cords to

centuries of learning and culture severed. The Body African   Place   The inner space between the legs linked irrevocably to the outer space of the plantation. AfricanBodyPlace

of warfare

resistance:

Some African women nursing for long periods of time postponing sexual relations which postponing pregnancy which postponing children which postponing . . . Silence (Mair 1990).[12]
Some African women nursing—Infanticide!

Re-producing
A-borting

life

—a warping and twisting of the filaments of silence between African and body—
body & text
body becoming text which she learning to read in a
newlanguageandshecomingtounderstandhowtosurvivetextbecomingbodybodi
esdeadbodiesmurderedbodiesimportedbredmutilatedbodiessoldbodiesboughtt
heEuropeantrafficinbodiesthattellingsomuchaboutthemandwhichhelpingfuelt
heindustrializationofthemetropolisesbodiescreatingwealththecapitalfeedingthe
industrialrevolutionsmanytimesoverandoverandoverandoverthebodies. . .

Betweenthelegs   thespace
/withinthewomb   thespace
colonizedlikeplaceandspace

aroundher

thesilenceof
thespacebetween

thelegs

thesilenceof
thespacewithin

thewomb

brokenintowordsofmaster

lord

massa

andsilence

The Body African henceforth inscribed with the text of events of the New World. Body becoming text. In turn the Body African—dis place—place and s/place of exploitation inscribes itself permanently on the European text. *Not* on the margins. But within the very body of the text where the silence exists.

OUR ROYAL WILL AND PLEASURE

Columbus, emissary of the outer space and the Old World, penetrates and enters the inner space of the Caribbean. Violently. From this time on the Caribbean will be described "in terms of," shaped to fit. C(o)untoured to the needs and demands of the outer space.

Jean, Dinah, Rosita, and Clementina, Piti Belle Lily, Boadicea, and all the other jamettes decide—if the space of silence—the silence of the space   between the legs   has to be fractured by massa and his word they would at least decide who would fracture it and they would charge for it.

This is some progress. Perhaps.

Royal Prohibitions

It Is Our Royal Will and Pleasure:

To protect the space that lies between the legs of the female otherwise known as *dis place* and in effort of these ends, *dis place*

- must not be sold
- must not be given away
- must be sold
- must be given away
- must always be given to men
- must not be given to men
- must be taken
- must be sewn closed
- must be mutilated
- must be hidden
- must be a thoroughfare
- must not be a thoroughfare
- must never be given away by the one who possesses it.

Indulgence by the female in any action described above, *on the initiative of the female,* serves to subvert the power of those who control the outer space.

It Is Our Royal Will and Pleasure:

The black male must at all times be prohibited from entering the space lying between the legs of the white female—the white space.

It Is Our Royal Will and Pleasure:

The space lying between the legs of the black female is hereby declared a thoroughfare. A black hole.

white space/black hole

How you interact with the outer space is determined by protection of the inner space. And by whom.

Who is the you?

It Is Our Loving Will and Pleasure:

> don't let nobody
> the mothers teach
> fear
>   but no
> body touch
> you
> there

"Don't let nobody touch you there." The Mothers are right when they making this blanket prohibition, because if they not controlling entry to that space, *dis place,* by markers like the right man, the right color, the right class, and in the right circumstances, you—the woman behind the space—bound to be permanently affected. The Mothers knowing the outer space controlling the inner space which in turn inflecting and affecting the interpretation of the outer space. The Mothers, therefore, intervening—*Their Loving Will and Pleasure*—and ensuring the best. For their daughters. "Don't let nobody touch you there!" So the Mothers teaching fear. Naming the space. Between. The legs—the young girl's legs. The MUSTN'T DO.

But consider. The Black mother under slavery—*her* loving will and pleasure— wanting to protect—"don't let nobody touch you there!"—herself and her daughters. Knowing. Everybody touching her—There! The Black mother naming what the men have. The MUST DO.

"It was a safe place for a girl," she tells me, my friend, describing her childhood on a Manitoban farm, "and yet on moving to the city, I found that my mother had passed on all the lessons of fear":

> don't let
> no!
> body touch
> don't let

> you there!
> nobody touch you
> there

Further Prohibitions Regarding Dis Place:

- those who take these prohibitions to their logical end and prohibit entry to men—those who decide to explore each other's spaces must be dis/placed;
- so too must those who treat the space between the legs as having no monetary value, including loose women, nymphomaniacs, and jamettes;
- as well, those selling the space between the legs will also be dis/placed.

We Hereby Decree under Our Hand and Seal:

that the outer space must *always* determine how safe the inner space is;
that the way in which women know the space around them must always be determined by how safe or unsafe they perceive their inner space to be.

It Is Our Royal Will and Pleasure:

If any number of persons shall find out the Pallenque of the said Negroes, they shall have and enjoy to their uses all the Women and Children, and all the plunder they can find there for their reward. (Modyford 1665)

"Chile you know what dem say about Nanny of the Maroons—that she used to be catching de bullets dat dem baccra firing pon she people right inside she crotch. Beat dat!"

Consider! dis place—the inner space repelling and resisting the aggressive penetrations from the outer space.

SILENCE AND THE SPACE BETWEEN

> silence shapes
>   that space
> between
>   inner and outer
>
> the space between
>   the legs

c(o)unt/ours
            of silence

the outer space of text
borders on the
            inner space
of body

To balance the equation of inner and outer space we must factor in silence.

the text—the silence at the heart of. My text—I writing my own silence . . . and if you cannot ensure that your words will be taken in the way you want them to be—if you sure those you talking to not listening, or not going to understand your words, or not interested in what you saying, and wanting to silence you, then holding on to your silence is more than a state of nonsubmission. It is resisting.

Silence c(o)unt/ours the inner space!

textbody-
body as text
body inscribed
            on text
            on body
to interrupt
    disrupt
    erupt
the text of the new world
is a text of
a history of
            interruptions
                    of bodies
a body of interruptions
bodies of interred
            eruptions

how to interrupt
                disrupt
erupt
    the body

of the text
to allow
the silence
in erupt

*the space between: dis place—defined within the context of fear or control of
penetration whose c(o)unt/ouring has silenced the inner space causing it to col-
lapse in upon itself—*
a black (w)hole absorbing everything around it.

dis place between
the legs
what does it say—this inner space—how read
its silence beyond
fear
of the outer space

Does the inner space exist whole in any language? Other than "threat" and
"fear"? What is the language of the inner space? Beyond the boundaries of
control and fear. Is its language silence? A silence other than the imposed silence.
To read the text that lies "missing" in the silence of the inner space, we needing a
new langauge—the language of jamettes, possessing their inner and outer space.
The be-coming and coming-to-be of a jamette poet.

How to make the black hole (w)hole?
What its shape?
Where begin and end
the (w)hole
of my black silence
collapsing in
upon
itself

:You sound like—fishwife! virago! jamette! The Mothers warn.

How does the inner space
sound
what the sound of
the space
between
the legs

>once found;
>how does the inner space
>sound
>   loud
>like a jamette!
>turning in
>out—
>that inner sound
>found
>loud
>like a jamette!

Words   wombed in silence   wish to speak   in sentences   paragraphs. With no closures

THE BODY RE TURNS

dis/place   dis place   dis place
affecting how we take up space—outer space: fearfully
"no memory of murder in his walk"
agoraphobia: a dread or horror of open spaces. Protection of dis place—the inner space—means all women manifest a degree of agoraphobia—
the paradox: carrying the potential for life within   the inner space we become afraid of the outer space, lurk with Boadicea in the silencing—the space between—inner and outer

Question

what is it about the outer space of my own text ("Earth and Sound") that silenced my inner space—*dis place*?

Answer

If dis place—the Caribbean—is the threatening outer space—*dis place* of oppression, to which they harnessing *dis place* between the legs of the black woman (which also c(o)unt/ouring that inner space by silencing), it making sense that I outing out[13] *dis place*—inner s/place—from the text, metaphor for the outer space—the space of man. Bordered. Controlled. And patrolled. By men. *And* their words.

If "the street . . . is the only valid field of experience" and the street was and is prohibited to women, what is their valid field of experience? The inner space—

s/place—*dis place*? And can the street be the only valid field of experience if what constitutes its experience prohibits, often obliterates through its threat to *dis place,* the presence of women.

At fourteen my son takes up space in ways I never could, and he lets me know this—that he is safe on the streets in a way I, more than twice his age, can never be.

We peeling back layers of silencing and finding what *dis place* is really about. Silence. A different text lying there, a spirit world, an imaginative universe. Marion Milner writes about "an insideness, a kind of womb space where there's both a protectedness, a cocoon, but also something initiating change, an unfolding from some inherent potentiality, a possibility to be realized" (1987, 37); Jessica Benjamin that "the significance of the spatial metaphor for a woman is likely to be in just this discovery of her *own, inner* desire, without fear of impingement, intrusion or violation" (1988, 128).[14]

Diary entry (1988)

I can point to the exact place on my anatomy, the left abdominal area, which I sacrificed for those poems—the kinopoesis of African languages. Tongue, lips, physiology of speech, dismemberment—the body erupted forcibly in She Tries . . . careful choreography- these images of the body are rooted in that experience—the foundation of language is the body—my body. I am finding this out after the fact—seeking out the silences.

Meditations-

> *and fingertips commune with tongue and mouth*
> *seek to know again what once was friend*
> *now is hostile in its dumbness*
> *seek to enter secret ways   now probed*
> *lips spread*
> *see how virgin I am*
> *and tongue tastes*
> *the murder of your blood*
> *is all that would satisfy*
> *now—to drink the blood of my master*
> *and conqueror*
> *confirm the "I" in savage*
> *and freedom in one small drop*

Body must remember song and drum
and story and tale
how it was
and how it wasn't;
it must remember touch
of mother
father, brother and
sister
it must—
remember or seize its ineffable right
and die.
Body must remember the reign of life
and death
that body is not thing
and thing not body
must remember how we knew
and what
was knowing that knew and
knew not
finite end;
and as body remembers to bleed
swell with seed and
child
so body must remember to re-member
the forgotten
the not-known yet known
that each begins and
ends in cell
and between them but a microcosm

a universe drawn tight by memory

THE BODY RETURNS . . . BEYOND THE BOUNDARY

"All she have is two fine leg and a gully,"[15] is how some men describing women.

Caribbean men beating their former masters at their own game, and putting their mark on the outer space. "Two fine leg and a gully"—cricket—shaping the image of the Caribbean in the outer space of the world, where women not even playing the game, let alone going beyond the boundary. "Two fine leg and a gully." To move beyond the boundary of fear—of penetration—unwanted and unwanting—c(o)unt/ouring the inner space—to find the source and sound of our silencing, we must become cartographers of silence, mapping not only the known edges—the boundaries of our inner space—we must be moving beyond the boundary. To take soundings of the deep, where the voice is not one but "the many-voiced one of one voice / ours," polyvocal and many-tongued (Philip 1988, 36).

"You better know your place"—the question at the center of "Earth and Sound." What *is* this place? The body linking the place between—*dis place*—to the beyond of boundary—*Dis Place*.

AIN'T I A WOMAN

If the Black woman's inner space doing the same work as the white woman's inner space—making babies—ain't she a woman? But OUR ROYAL WILL AND PLEASURE saying the inner space of the Black woman nothing but a baby-making factory. Or, they saying she shouldn't be having no more children. Either way they trying to make her less of what they saying a woman is. And even if the Black woman working like a man in the outer space, they still not giving her the rights and freedoms he having.

But still an' all, ain't I a woman?

When Sojourner Truth asking "ain't I a woman?" what is the question? If she working like any man, but is still a woman—or is she?—what making her a woman? The inner space? *Dis place*? Filled with "inherent potentiality." And the loudness. Of the jamette. Possessing the street. The polyvocality—the many-voiced one of one voice that is the sound of *dis place* . . .

"*Oh for a race of Women . . .*"

but women are raced and so too their space. Inner and outer.[16]

CARNIVAL/BACCHANAL/WINING

a race!—of women mashing the ground—dancing and wining[17] their all any and everything, and is carnival time again and the jamettes coming back and pulling all those middle-class and upper-class women onto the streets; the only war now is between the carnival bands and is so the women coming, flowing down the streets with the skimp and scant of their costumes, carrying their staffs—their *lingas* and they wining and wining round and round *dis place*—African and Indian alike—*tout bagai*—wining and wining the *yoni* round and around the *linga*[18] of their carnival staffs and they dancing through the streets—*oh, for a race of women!*—shaking their booty, doin their thing, their very own thing, jazzin it up, wining up and down the streets, parading their sexuality for two (w)hole days—taking back the streets, making them their own as they spreading their joying up and down the streets of Port of Spain . . .

Is the only time of the year that women—old women, young women, thin women, fat women, women women—showing off their sexuality without undue censure or fear, under the benign gaze of OUR ROYAL WILL AND PLEASURE. *Oh, for a race of women . . .*

Act 3, scene 4

The same crossroads as in Act 1, scene 1.
A figure crawls on her hands and knees from upstage center down the street, advancing toward the audience and showing herself to be Boadicea, the jamette queen. Two women with market baskets stand at the intersection of the streets at stage left. As Boadicea approaches the women, they turn their backs, moving away from her toward the audience. They appear to be middle-class women on their way from the market—their baskets filled with mango, paw paw, breadfruit, yams, and other fruits and vegetables.
    First woman: "But just look at her! She's nothing but a nastiness—a thoroughfare—she's got sores all over her body, and she smells too—"
    Second woman: "You never said a truer word, m'dear. All she does is crawl around these streets begging." *The women ignore Boadicea, and linking arms they stroll along the street downstage left all the while talking.*
    First woman: "Yes m'dear, I hear the children really do tease her—they say she's the Devil's disciple herself!" *The woman drops her voice on these last few words, and both of them turn their heads surreptitiously to look at Boadicea, who now follows them.*
    Second woman: "I think she's blind, too, you know—is God's own punishment for her looseness—you remember how she tore off her dress one day on the street?" Both women shake their heads and walk off the stage with Boadicea still following them. The stage goes dark.*

Act 3, scene 6

The curtain rises on a courtroom; upstage center is the judge's bench, behind which sits an old, bewigged and bespectacled white man. His glasses sit low on his nose. He looks a caricature of a judge. At stage right and left are two counsel tables at which sit two lawyers. The lawyer on the right is a white male in a barrister's robe and white wig; the lawyer on the left is a black woman also dressed in a barrister's robe and wig. The white wig against her black skin is startling. At the center in the prisoner's box sits Boadicea, the jamette queen. There are sounds of shouts and cries of women's voices.

"Your lordship," *the lady barrister rises,* "I beg of you to let these women in— they are my client's friends. I assure you they will be quiet." *The gentleman barrister rises:*

"Your lordship, this is entirely unacceptable—we are merely dealing with a motion to confine this, this . . .

"Woman, sir?" *The lady barrister finishes his sentence for him.*

"I can find my own words—I would ask my friend not to put words in my mouth. There is no need for this spectacle, this display of wantonness—these are street women who will no doubt steal whatever they can lay their hands on."

"Is my learned friend afraid that when they're done clearing the courts of its benches these women might also take him away? I can assure my learned friend that he is entirely safe from them—their tastes tend to run to the more muscular—"

"Gentlemen!" *The judge strikes his gavel on his bench.* "Enough of this unseemly bickering. We will proceed." *The gentleman barrister remains standing; the lady barrister sits.*

"Your Lordship, we must make an example of this . . ." *He pauses, then clearly fearing more help from his opponent, he rushes on,* "this abomination of womanhood. She is a stain on this fair city of hers—I mean ours. If we lock her up, then women like her will know that they cannot wander around the streets at will making trouble. It is rumored, Your Lordship, that she even deals in the black arts, what they call *obeah!*[19] I urge you to exercise your responsibility, nay your *duty* and lock her away."

The lady barrister rises: "My plea is a simple one, Your Lordship. This woman—and she does have a name—" *She turns to the man who has just seated himself,* "Boadicea—has done nothing!" *At the sound of her name, Boadicea looks up for the first time.* "She has harmed no one and she's long past the stage where she can do any harm to anyone. Isn't she a woman, my Lord, and aren't there special laws to protect women? All this talk of the devil and the black arts is but hearsay and intended to prejudice your lordship against her. The streets have been her home, and those women out there want to look after her." *As the lady barrister talks, the noise offstage becomes louder and louder; suddenly the door upstage left bursts open and several jamettes rush into the courtroom. They are all armed with sticks and rocks. The judge cowers below his bench, and the gentleman barrister shouts:*

"Enough! Get out! Get out!"

"Is you to get out!" *A buxom woman lifts him and carries him to the door and throws him out. The lady barrister sits at her table, a small smile playing at the corners of her mouth.*

"Come Bo, is Piti Belle Lili, come girl, we going look after you—we not letting none of these damn faysty men—white or otherwise colored—push we or you around. Dis place is not for you or for we. We have we own place—come let we go."

Another jamette: "Woh! dese men lucky oui—dey damn lucky we don't break dey head open and mash up de place." *The women lifting Boadicea, chanting the anthems of the Don't Give a Damns and the Mousselines and carrying Boadicea offstage through the same door they just throwing the gentleman barrister.*[20] *The stage goes black.*

NOTES

1. *Ratio decidendi*—literally the "reason for the decisions"—is the expression commonly used in the reporting of legal cases to identify the kernel of the legal reasoning, as opposed to *obiter dicta*—things said by the way.

2. Anthony Giddens writes that in "pre-modern development of Europe rape flourished mainly on the margins, at the frontiers, in colonies, in states of war, and in states of nature amongst marauding invading armies" (1992, 123). Allegations of mass rape of Bosnian Muslim women in 1992 by Serbian forces as a way of spreading terror and asserting control suggest that these practices defy a simple linkage to premodern times. In a *Ms* editorial on the issue of the rape of Bosnian women, Robin Morgan asks: "If rape in war is a weapon, then what is it in peace time?" (1993, 1).

3. Alison Fell describes women in cities as "under siege, controlled by their fear of men" (1991, 18). In her novel *Virgin Territory,* Sara Maitland echoes this in her description of a nun: "But Sister Kitty had been raped, the weapon held over women's heads always and everywhere" (1984, 66).

4. In *In Other Worlds,* Gayatri Spivak sets up a theoretically useful opposition between the clitoris—a marker of excess—and what she describes as "uterine social organization (the arrangement of the world in terms of the production of future generations where the uterus is the chief agent and means of production)" (1987, 152–53). Society, therefore, perceives the clitoris as a marker of excess and a threat to this order. The clitoris can be seen as not only a marker of excess—of both pleasure and life as in reproduction—but also the external marker of the space between the legs. Clitoridectomy—whether the literal mutilation or more metaphorical psychic attempts to contain and manage women's sexual pleasure—then becomes the inevitable, logical, and rational response by a patriarchal society to this space of excess. It is arguable that even society's overweening interest in the womb is but a sublimation of its fear of this generative female power—a fear manifest most clearly in the abortion struggles.

5. *Run down* or *come down* or *oil down* all refer to Carribean dishes cooked in coconut milk.

6. According to Bridget Brereton in *Race Relations in Colonial Trinidad, 1879–1900,* the men and women who comprised the jamet class in Trinidad were "singers, drummers, dancers, stickmen, prostitutes, pimps, and badjohns in general" (1979, 166–69). Jamette women often worked as domestics in middle-class homes, but middle-class society regarded them as transgressive. Jamet gangs or bands often met and fought for supremacy.

While some prostitues were jamettes, not all jamette women were prostitutes. It would therefore be incorrect to understand "jamette" as being synonymous with "prostitute."

7. Maroons were Africans in the New World who escaped slavery and fled to inaccessible areas where they set up self-contained and self-sustaining communities, most notably in the islands of Jamaica and Dominica, as well as Surinam in South America. During the years of active colonization, maroons fought the Europeans to keep their independence. Nanny, a well-known leader of the maroons in Jamaica, led several battles against the British.

8. Queen Nzinga or Zhinga, leader of the Ndongo people in what is now Angola, was a formidable opponent of Portugese colonization in the early seventeenth century.

9. *Poui—Tebebuia serratifolia*—a tropical hardwood.

10. "Jean an Dinah," a calypso by Francisco Slinger singing under the sobriquet, "the Mighty Sparrow," first performed in 1965.

11. Rex Nettleford is a former Rhodes scholar and a professor at the University of the West Indies; he is also director of the National Dance Company of Jamaica.

12. Many African traditional practices prohibited sexual intercourse during nursing, thereby postponing further pregnancies.

13. To *out out*—Caribbean demotic for erasing.

14. Benjamin critiques Erik Erikson's concept of "inner space" as the receptive and passive half of a phallic dual unity. She recognizes the inner space not only as a passivity, but "as a metaphor of equal importance to 'phallic activity and its representations'" (1988, 128).

15. *Fine leg* and *gully* are cricketing terms for fielding positions. The late C. L. R. James, in his seminal and definitive work on cricket, *Beyond the Boundary*, explored the West Indian psyche and character, and the relationship between the imperial power, England, and its colonies through the game of cricket.

16. Those who police and patrol the outer space treat Black and white people very differently. The most obvious example of this is the police harassment of Black men in the Western world, as they go about their daily lives. Black men's enjoyment of the benefits that come with the male prerogative of territoriality is therefore mediated by policing practices. Space becomes, therefore, not only gendered but raced.

17. Wining is a circular movement of the pelvic region and is a standard aspect of both folk and popular dancing throughout the Caribbean. This overtly sexual motion has been linked to earlier fertility dances of Africa.

18. *Linga* or *siva-linga*, commonly meaning the phallus, although *linga* also refers to the "all-pervading space in which the whole universe is in the process of formation and dissolution" (Mookerjee and Khanna 1977, 35, 36, 55). *Tout Bagai* is a French patois word meaning "everybody." *Yoni* symbolizes the Hindu female principle. It is represented visually by a circle or, in an active state, by a triangle.

19. Obeah is an African spiritual practice which has continued in the Caribbean. Under colonial rule the practice was outlawed and so is still viewed with suspicion, if not contempt, by the middle classes.

20. The real Boadicea, after a life of notoriety, did fall on hard times, becoming a beggar and losing her sight. Andrew Pearse writes that she "died in the 'Hangman's Cemetery' while sitting on the spot where her executed lover was buried some years before" (1956, 261).

"The Erogenous Cusp," or Intersections of Science and Gender in Alice Fulton's Poetry

Cristanne Miller

Debate about the relationship of object to subject, or body to soul, has raged for centuries. Recently, feminist philosophers, critics, and theorists have recast this debate as one on the relation of the sexed and gendered body to perception, language, and power. From theoretical discussions about essentializing (Spivak 1987) or about the woman as object of the male gaze (de Lauretis 1984) to recent studies on topics as diverse as women's relations to food in medieval Europe (Bynum 1987) and the status of women's bodies in the performance of postmodern dance (Wolff 1990), feminists question to what extent women's bodies may constitute the site of a feminist politics. Alice Fulton contributes a new perspective to such debate in her most recent volumes of poetry, *Palladium* (1986a) and *Powers of Congress* (1990). In several poems in these volumes, Fulton uses the epistemological framework of quantum mechanics to address poststructuralist and feminist concerns. Punning on the intersection of physics and physicality, Fulton insists that a body is composed of electrons and neutrons as profoundly as it is of a vagina or penis, skin, feet, eyes, and so on. This insistence allows her to imagine an explicitly embodied and even sexual subject that remains ungendered, thereby calling into question both the adequacy and the necessity of conventional categories of gender construction.[1] Moreover, by describing the physical through a vocabulary for the most part outside categories of social construction, Fulton rejects all systems of dualized or oppositional distinction as the basis for definitions of selfhood. As she writes in "Cusp," identity lies in interstices, in the fluctuating interplay among "the solid abundance" of subatomic particles, individual perception, and the systems of power inherent in all social construction—or in "the erogenous cusp / of mind and world" (1990a, 97, 98).

Quantum mechanics offers a reinvigorated approach to the physical in this poetry, but it also gives Fulton a new kind of poetic authority. Fulton writes within and against the tradition of lyric poetry in which woman's authority has come largely through what was regarded for centuries as her natural or essential position. This was first defined as muse or desired object and then as speaking subject, but only from her again "natural" experience as mother/woman. As Margaret Homans argues in *Women Writers and Poetic Identity*, "Mother Nature" was the only viable model transcending human motherhood available for the nineteenth-century woman poet—a model woefully inadequate because Nature "is prolific biologically, not linguistically" and because she (Nature/the body) is always objectified as other and "may then be possessed or become the property of the [male] subject" or poet (1980, 13, 37). Within this framework, woman is denied full subjectivity as observer; at the same time, because the object is assumed to be essentially different from the observer, there is an assumption that true or "universal" observation demands distinction: the world consists of opposites, the Emersonian "Me" and "Not-me," subject and object, male and female. Quantum mechanics allows Fulton to sidestep these traps of identity and language by giving her a radically different framework for understanding nature, subjectivity, and the subject or self. Her authority comes from rejecting the distinction of subject/object rather than from fully assuming the former's role.

Although the language of science is associated with the masculine sphere (E. Keller 1985), quantum mechanics does not typically gender or trope its objects of experimentation as objects of desire and thus provides a particularly useful model. According to quantum theory, an object manifests itself differently according to the context of the experiment: for example, light behaves as particles under one set of experimental circumstances but as waves under another. Accordingly, it is impossible to know the object of observation except through the mediation of an experimental situation; there is no dualistic separation of object from observer or tools of observation, of nature from knowledge. The object has its own reality, but it can only be known through its behavior during particular acts of observation. Equally important, as the changing behavior of light demonstrates, the object must always be seen in multiple and paradoxical, or what physicist Niels Bohr named "complementary," ways.[2]

Similarly, several of Fulton's speakers are known only through their assertion of conflicting or shifting experiences, identities, and beliefs. Without entering the realms of science fiction or incorporeality, they fall outside of or obviate the need for ordinary fixed categories for personal identity—gender, race, age, and so on. In "The Expense of Spirit," for example, the speaker complains that in "the credits and debits of cold sex" neither "she" nor "he"

Exchange the compliment I mean: to praise the otherness

> Rising or widening next to one's own
> Nude dilations
>
> (1990, 18)

leaving unclear both the gender of the speaker and whether the lovers who should be engaged in praise are of the same or different sexes. Or in "Romance in the Dark," the speaker interchanges first- and second-person "I"s and "you"s with the even more pointedly ungendered "One" and "The Other" or "another." Questions of gender inevitably obtrude because of the reader's socially and critically programmed assumptions, yet they are undercut by their own indeterminacy and multiplicity. For example, one might assume that an ungendered speaker is "universal" hence implicitly masculine—as the literary tradition has insisted for centuries; or one might assume that an ungendered speaker carries the gender of its author, hence that Fulton's are feminine. Given either assumption, one might find evidence within a poem supporting stereotyped associations of particular behavioral patterns with that gender. Yet as Henry Folse insists in explaining Bohr's concept of complementarity, "[D]ifferent phenomenal descriptions must *complement* each other to provide a complete description of the behavior of [an] object" (1985, 242): a "complete description" of Fulton's ungendered speakers "must" consist of a variety of "different phenomenal descriptions."

Trinh Minh-ha's playful formulation of poststructuralist writing in *Woman Native Other* aptly describes Fulton's treatment of these speakers: "Writing, like a game that defies its own rules, is an ongoing practice that may be said to be concerned . . . with creating an opening where the 'me' disappears while 'I' endlessly come and go" (1989, 35); in Fulton's poetry multiple "I"s come and go. Within this openness, Fulton asserts the necessity of attending both to personal experience and to all that lies outside the individual. This insistence on the intersections among social construction, individual experience, and empirical knowledge allies her position with that of feminist critics like Nancy K. Miller (1988), bell hooks (1990), Nancy Hartsock (1990), and Susan Stanford Friedman (1991)—as well as Trinh—who criticize poststructuralism's inattention to authorial presence in a text and to the pragmatic historical and cultural factors of daily life that affect both textual production and all aspects of perception. These issues are raised directly in relation to science by Sandra Harding in *The Science Question in Feminism*. Harding speculates that a "feminist postmodernist epistemology" would

> begin from diametrically opposite assumptions from those routinely invoked to justify modern science's legitimacy. The greatest resource for would-be "knowers" is our nonessential, nonnaturalizable, fragmented identities and the refusal of the delusion of a return to an "original unity." (1986b, 193)

In a 1986 essay, Harding writes more positively that "feminist analytical catego-ries *should* be unstable" (1986a, 647). Through her use of quantum mechanics, Fulton suggests just such an unstable "feminist postmodernist epistemology."

Fulton's poems may also call into question some of the conventions of reading lyric poetry. For example, as I mention above and will discuss below, by giving a first-person speaker embodiment and desire but leaving it ungendered, Fulton challenges traditional and feminist practices of ascribing gender to a lyric "I" and of interpreting a speaker's role in relation to the poet's biography. The reductive implications of the second practice take remarkable form in a tendency of Fulton's own critics to discuss her poems as though they exhibit the poet herself, conflating both speaker with poet and text with body. These critics, moreover, describe the imagined poetic body in excessively gendered terms; "I"/the poem/ Fulton is not just female but exaggeratedly and dismissively so. Holly Prado, for example, writes that "much of [Fulton's] poetry comes across the way a woman does who wears too much makeup: strained" (1984, 9). Calvin Bedient describes the verse in *Palladium* as "high-spirited, but a bit egoistic and noisy" and "look[s] forward to her years of middle-age sag, when her energy will be easier to bear" (1988, 143). Most recently, Mutlu Blaising writes that the "coat" of Fulton's poetry "is woven of 'consumer products,' but [unlike Ashbery's] hers is a skin-tight fit" (1992, 431). Taken together, these reviews evoke an image of Fulton's poems that suggest a clichéd portrait of lower-class sexual display: wear-ing too much makeup and skintight clothes, and being noisy. To the extent that a work defines its audience, I would say that these critics read directly—even perversely—against the grain of Fulton's work, revealing perhaps the determined critical resistance to a separation of speaker, gender, and poet such as that Fulton attempts.

Fulton's verse also contains an unusually wide range and sharp juxtaposition of registers of language—namely, the dictions of slang, science, and religion. By combining a language of defiantly inelegant irreverence and pizzazz with those of highest seriousness, greatest precision, and greatest cultural authority, Fulton may attempt to resist and thereby broaden narrow notions of consistent or natu-ral "voice" associated with the lyric poem.[3] In particular, her combination of highly colloquial slang with technical, scientific language undermines the percep-tion of her "I" as "natural" or common speaker—the criterion of value most consistently maintained for lyric poetry from the Romantic era into the present (Altieri 1984; Perloff 1991). Both vocabularies are idiosyncratic and deflating rather than representative or elevating. The diction of these speakers does not fit any traditional lyric mode or any recognizable pattern of speech.

Through her structures and diction as well as her themes, Fulton raises basic questions about poetics, knowledge, and power. She strikes at what she herself in "To Organize a Waterfall" calls the "dead center" of things that claim "perfection" or to which perfection has been attributed—from theories, to the poem, to divinity itself (1991, 304). And while her primary vocabulary for this kinetic instability comes from science, the conclusion that perfection (a right answer, universal standards) is rarely possible and usually undesirable strikes at the core of the myths of scientific, religious, and aesthetic authority. In a society where women have been expected to attain an apparent moral and physical perfection—as the guardians of family values and the consumers of everything from hair dyes to surgery so as to appear unblemished and youthful—such an argument also liberates women from the false power of "perfect" physicality.

The opening poem in Fulton's *Powers of Congress* reveals the intersections of science, faith, identity, and aesthetics—here, as often in her poems, dramatized within the framework of personal relationship—that are central to her conception of a feminist positioning or subject. "Cascade Experiment" (1990, 1–2) begins:

> Because faith creates its verification
> and reaching you will be no harder than believing
> in a planet's caul of plasma,
> or interacting with a comet
> in its perihelion passage, no harder
> than considering what sparking of the vacuum, cosmological
> impromptu flung me here, a periphrasis, perhaps,
> for some denser, more difficult being,
> a subsidiary instance, easier to grasp
> than the span I foreshadow, of which I am a variable,
> my stance is passional toward the universe and you.

Like the big bang theory in which the universe and life as we know them are sparked from "the vacuum" by a "cosmological impromptu," knowledge here seems at best a mixture of what can be measured (the comet's perihelion), the measurer's positioning or assumptions (faith, meditation), and chance.

"[F]aith creates its verification," the poet writes; "faith in facts can help create those facts"—or, as she puts it more cynically in an earlier poem, "the God of triangles would be / three-sided: we see what we want / to see" ("Peripheral Vision" 1986a, 67). "Cascade Experiment" concludes, "Nothing will unfold for us / unless we move toward what / looks to us like nothing: faith is a cascade . . ."

> Because believing a thing's true
> can bring about that truth,
> and you might be the shy one, lizard or electron,
> known only through advances

> presuming your existence, let my glance be passional
> toward the universe and you.

In this poem, the observations of science—while precise enough to describe "a planet's . . . plasma"—are also potentially as faulty as any belief based on the presuppositions of faith or ideology:

> as when thirteen species
> of whiptail lizards composed entirely of females
> stay undiscovered due to bias
> against such things existing.

There is no way to know the unknown or observe objectively; one can only "believe" in what one has thus far discovered or reasoned to be. As the rhyming of "stance," "advance[s]," and "glance" suggests, this process has to do with action as well as with positionality and perspective: through one's stance or glance, one "advances" (or not) toward the unknown "you." The observer and the object are both in motion, part of the "experiment."

The "passional" quality of this activity further insists that observation is intersubjective. Knowledge stems from powerful feeling—love, hatred, desire—or, as in the Christian Passion, some combination of these feelings with faith. At the same time, Fulton's avoidance of the more normal *passionate* to describe this stance indicates that she does not mean the Romantic spontaneous overflow of feeling; the milder adjective "passional" perhaps reminds the reader that in Fulton's "experiment" of living, interaction with those scientifically defined entities we are either unconscious of or that seem outside the spheres of our lives—electrons and comets—is as essential as feeling to relationship with any "you."

By describing the speaker solely as "I" and couching the primary objective of the poem in the form of an unspecified personal pronoun ("you"), Fulton leaves ambiguous both the speaker's identity and the precise nature of the speaker's quest. Discussing this poem in "To Organize a Waterfall," Fulton writes that "the 'you' addressed throughout is the ultimate power or First Cause: that which ignites the cascade of being, evolutionary on the grandest scale. 'God' is the common abbreviation" (1991, 308). One might with equal reason, however, interpret the relationship of her "I" to "you" as a scientist's search for an object or answer, the speaker's address to a lover, or a poet's appeal to readers—all microcosmic manifestations of the unknowable but passionately desired otherness that we define in seeking it, represented most fully by "God." The poem is an invocation to the imaginative feeling implied by a cascade experiment, which involves extremely unstable particles that decay into smaller particles that also immediately decay: questions lead to finer questions; one reading of a poem triggers another, and so on. The poem contains repeated images of instability, and ends with a plea or prayer to overcome the speaker's own stolid resistance: "*let my glance be passional*" (emphasis added), let me "presum[e] your existence" so that I may know "you"—the electron, comet, lizards, lover, reader, God beyond my knowing.

The ambiguous inclusiveness of Fulton's "you" gives metaphorical form to her conviction that ultimately the world of science or quantum mechanics is not separable from the worlds of religion, daily living, or verse. As she writes in "Of Formal, Free, and Fractal Verse," "a truly engaged and contemporary poetry must reflect" Heisenberg's uncertainty principle and quantum mechanics (1986b, 207). Later, she associates "Cascade Experiment" directly with the uncertainty principle. She summarizes Heisenberg as postulating that "the act of observing changes what's observed" and then describes her poem as implying

> that our preconceptions—the questions asked, the assumptions held before the search—affect what will be found. The behavior and properties of electrons sound like theology as written by the Brothers Grimm: Electrons exist only when they're measured (and why would we have tried to measure them without a prior belief in their existence?) (1991, 309)

The implications of such radical uncertainty for nonscientific thought are clarified by turning to feminist analysis of quantum theory.

Feminist physicist Karen Barad persuasively argues that quantum mechanics, and especially Bohr's notion of complementarity, carries profound implications for our understanding of all frameworks for knowledge. In contradiction to previous descriptions of light,

> twentieth-century experiments [have] seemed to indicate that light behaves as a wave under certain experimental conditions, and as a particle under a mutually exclusive set of experimental conditions. . . . Bohr argued that "wave" and "particle" are classical idealizations that refer to different mutually exclusive phenomena, and not to actual physical objects. (1994, 16)

In other words, quantum mechanics disproves the assumptions of classical science that stable truths may in fact be discovered if we just find the right instrument or method, instead highlighting the interaction of observer or agent with the object under study: "Descriptive concepts cannot properly be attributed to things, but rather characterize the 'intra-action,' the dynamical blurring of constructed boundaries" (17); scientific theories are "partial and located knowledges" (23). As Barad further notes, "[T]he failure of an object/subject distinction leads to a deconstruction of the nature/culture dualism as well. . . . This shifting of boundaries deconstructs the whole notion of identity" (22, 23). Hence, the quantum perspective suggests a way to interrogate not just classical notions of realism in science, but similarly dualistic and fixed notions of race, class, and gender in the realm of social dynamics; quantum theory may provide another route toward the goal of much current feminist social analysis in questioning the boundaries of the personal and the political, the conventions of a bounded, interiorized self, and the classical notions of identity and essence.

Fulton's poem "Cusp" (1990, 96–99) perhaps most clearly unites physical embodiment in an ungendered self and a revisionary aesthetics in what Barad calls "agential realism"—a consciously interactive kind of knowledge that problematizes any notion of "natural, pure, and innocent separations" without seeking the dissolution of all boundaries (27).[4] The speaker of this poem notes that "We recognize what's closest by its power / to obscure what's far" yet, when feeling "transparent," the speaker is quite simply "glad for density"

> which lets one substance hold its place
> to the exclusion of another:
> the pen stay separate from the hand,
> the body independent of the earth,
> the skin allow no ingress,
> and jail and lighthouse
> fail to occupy the same terrain.

Recognizing that she or he will see what is nearest rather than most important or real, the speaker nonetheless rejoices in the ability to distinguish things. Yet the things the speaker chooses to distinguish immediately raise questions about lack of distinction. The pen is not the hand—but isn't the pen-wielding poet also the woman Alice Fulton? Bodies are separate from the earth temporarily, but return at death to the "dust" from whence they (mythically) come. Like the particle and wave, a jail and lighthouse—and whatever concepts they represent—may be complementary as well as mutually exclusive: for example, punishment and guidance may overlap in child rearing or in so-called correctional institutions. Fulton may also play here on the paradox in physics that while two particles may never "occupy the same terrain" waves may and typically do occupy the same space at the same time: competing explanations are mutually exclusive but both necessary. Thus while a statement might be true of an object observed from one perspective, it would be false viewed from another.

Fulton makes this point most strongly by turning to touch—seemingly the truest or most faithful sense but in fact the most deceptive. Contrary to what we gather from common sense, touch stems from the failed attempt of subatomic particles to prevent touching; this is called electromagnetic repulsion. Rather than desiring the intimacy humans seek, in "Cusp," "Electrons make way for a caress":

> The more we press the more our substance
> tries to dodge duress and finds it can't,
> which comes across as touch.
> How odd that the body's deep resistance
> lets us feel another's presence,
> and our presence is bestowed
> by means of protest too.

Far from the Whitmanian notion of singular identity established through a sameness of body and soul represented by touch, Fulton sees "protest" and "resistance" everywhere. The earth that is Whitman's "apple-blossom'd" lover is indifferent or hostile to Fulton's speaker, solidifying her sense of separation from "pen" or earth only through the "failed escapement!" of millions of protesting particles. We cannot trust our senses—physical or "common"—to provide an objective sense of world or self.[5]

Similarly, language provides no solid basis for knowing either oneself as subject or the world. "Cusp," then, does not end like "Cascade Experiment" with a prayer to be open to the unexpected, but instead by giving oneself permission to behave as though the apparent were real. There is "no harm supposing," the speaker hopefully asserts, that things appear and occur because of some ordering principle, that indeed "each knapsack of quanta / in the atom knows its role." And it is in such pragmatic (albeit consciously false) supposing alone, her juxtaposition of lines implies, that one finds an "opaque" perception of self and a basis for the necessarily metaphorical language that underlies religion, poetry, and even science. Immediately following this stanza of "supposing" come the isolated lines:

> "I," the erogenous cusp
> of mind and world, sees the rose
> lining of a bird's beak
> and calls the dawn a churchly blue.

Seeking the separating certainty of touch while the particles of her or his body attempt to avoid it, the speaker finds power only in the consciously fictional creation of metaphor: dawn may not be blue and is certainly not religious, but the " 'I' " "calls" it a "churchly blue" to give some meaning to the phenomenon—which may be called something different on any other morning.

In Fulton's unusual reworking of the poststructuralist commonplace that all meaning in language is constructed, all knowledge and perception, including that of our most basic senses and of our most sophisticated sciences, is analogous to or depends upon the constructions of metaphor. The world is known through subjective observation manifested in language that hypothesizes or constructs relationships and connections we know do not literally exist. As chemist and literary critic N. Katherine Hayles writes, "[T]o speak is to create, or presuppose, the separation between subject and object that the reality would deny"; but as Niels Bohr wrote, "We are suspended in language" (Hayles 1984, 21, 14). The concept of "electromagnetic repulsion," for example, is as metaphorical (and unreal) in its implied granting of desire and agency to apparently stable electrons as the "churchly blue" of the speaker's dawn. The poet, accordingly, may be as important as the scientist in providing conceptions for understanding the world. As Fulton's poetry reiterates, desire, love, but also all understanding of the physical world—including of our own gender, race, age, and so on—exist in an interstitial cusp, a metaphorical but also necessary space between thing and perception, sense and sensation, or concrete knowledge and faith.[6]

While "Cusp" marks an interstice where differing phenomena or constructions of language come together and assume temporary identity or meaning, "Scumbling" and "Palladium Process" dramatize contrasting or complementary aspects of the subject separately (1986a, 61, 62–63). "Scumbling" begins with a first-person speaker "absolved, face to the wall, alive only / in fact"—Fulton's "only" immediately calling attention to the weakness of judging only from "fact":

> All night
> I pretended night was an unruly
> day. I pretended
> my voice. I pretended my hair. I pretended
> my friend. But there it was—"I"—
> I couldn't get rid of that.
> What could I do but let it learn
> to tremble? So I watched feelings hover
> over like the undersides
> of waterlilies: long serpentines
> topped by nervous almost-
> sunny undulations. I had to learn
> largo. I had to trust
> that two bodies scumbling
> could soften
> one another.

Borrowing a term from art, Fulton imagines human development as lovemaking, and lovemaking (or any intimacy) as the process of rendering a color or line softer by either rubbing its edges or lightly covering them with a thin coat of opaque color. "I" becomes less precise and more fully "alive" as it is "scumbl[ed]" in its interaction with others.

Fulton may pun here on two-body and multiple-bodies problems in classical physics: only problems involving two objects exerting mutual force can be solved exactly (with more than two bodies, solutions can only be numerically or approximately solved because of the complexity of the interactions). Unlike the bodies of a textbook physics problem, the two bodies of this poem exert mutual force and thereby become more tentative or "soft[er]" rather than assuming fixed quantities. Similarly, unlike the self as conceived in psychoanalytic theory, which is defined precisely through its contact with otherness, this self—like the line of an oil-pastel crayon—loses its sharpness with rubbing. To gain life beyond mere "fact" (perhaps entry into the psychoanalytic realm of the symbolic or of culture and language), this speaker must acquire less—not more—clearly defined boundaries of selfhood.

To carry quantum theory further into the human arena, one might also argue that Fulton here leaves the notion of two separate bodies altogether behind. Two-body problems in physics assume that elements behave like particles; one might say, however, that this speaker behaves more like a wave interacting with another wave: through "scumbling," these bodies or waves interpenetrate, coming together in one space simultaneously, giving a new twist to the common metaphorical association of waves and sexual orgasm. As Fulton writes at the poem's end:

> I had to
> let myself be gone
> through, do it in the arbitrary light
> tipping and flirting
> with seldom-seen surfaces.

By mentioning "light" together with what seem to be nakedness ("seldom-seen surfaces") and sex, Fulton gives further impetus to a wave/particle reading of this poem. Earlier she compares "feelings" with

> the undersides
> of waterlilies: long serpentines
> topped by nervous almost-
> sunny undulations.

This speaker, who began the poem as a particlelike "pearl"—"imperial" in an isolation resembling the Victorian "pearl" of virginity—now behaves like a wave, fully interpenetrating with another (wavelike) body.

"Palladium Process" (1986a, 62–63) immediately follows "Scumbling" in
Palladium and seems to be a companion poem. It, too, begins with an isolated,
ungendered speaker who is transformed in part through intimacy. At first, this
speaker is "a cloud / chamber," "islanded," "My face, a flag- / stone over
feeling":

> Skirted, stalled,
> in the realm between feeling and expression,
> sensations fell to me as stones fall
> down a well: the wait, the distant clink.

Then, "the mystery simmered":

> love and rage dried and piled up
> like hay in stables that combusts
> in tongues. It took angers, lovers,
> to enfranchise me. There was this difficult rip-
> cord! Then control scattered
> as I edged toward expansion.

Like the speaker of "Scumbling," this speaker "came to life" only after releasing
tightly held, isolating control. Fulton mirrors this release through her own verse
structure, hyphenating words at line ends ("flag- / stone;" "rip- / cord"), as
though she had a strict metrical pattern to match but her language had expanded
beyond that pattern's (or ordinary) boundaries. Unlike the speaker of "Scum-
bling," however, this speaker maintains particle-like behavior throughout her or
his development. Initially a "cloud chamber" tracking the movement of particles,
the speaker undergoes "expansion" and reaches full consciousness, as it were, as
a kind of photographic plate. "A student / of surplus," the speaker is "moved" to
"Shivers" by "dictionaries,"

> tricks
> of the light, dextrous
> evanescent cathedrals, improvident
> constructions, inventories
> like the palladium inventories of
> sun!

These final lines of the poem refer to an aspect of photographic printing using
sunlight rather than artificial light. As Fulton notes in her epigraphs to this
section of *Palladium,* although "the image [is] permanent" when one prints using

both palladium and sun, "because of many variables in paper, chemistry, procedure, and even weather, it is all but impossible [under these conditions] to achieve two prints from the same negative that look exactly alike" (1986a, 53). Instead of (wavelike) losing distinct boundaries or autonomous space, this speaker produces endlessly variable individual forms in interaction with the conditions of her or his existence.

Identity, this poem implies, results from a percolation of chemicals, paper (the proverbial "blank slate"), and sun or conditions of nature beyond human control. As in "Scumbling," here is no oedipal conflict, no psychological development of anxieties or symptoms of "universal" or essential character—no categories of social construction. The clustering of these concepts makes the ungendered speaker into what the title calls a "Process" or experiment, rather than either the subject or object of it: the speaker seems to be photographic plate, particles of light, and observer all in one. Moreover, the speaker is fascinated at the end with similar objects—wondrous things involving multiplicity within sameness: the dictionary, cathedrals, palladium inventories. As a photograph of palladium process, this speaker has boundaries that are "permanent," set. Yet as negative or photographic image, "palladium inventories of / sun" can go through her or him in endlessly new creative ways. Like a reader of dictionaries or gazer at the stars, or like the true scientist that such extensive curiosity suggests the speaker may be, this speaker looks toward the most profound and all-encompassing structures of knowledge and the unknown and rejoices in their "serious / hilarity." This extrovert of "expansion" is the obverse or mirror image of the introvert in "Scumbling." Both poems point to the looseness of individual boundaries at the same time that they focus on a narrative "I." Whether because of intimacy with other human beings or delight in the procession of things in the world, these speakers occupy insistently fluid or multiple positions of identity; neither they themselves nor what they see and feel is defined by fixed categories.

As suggested earlier, reading these two poems through the lens of normative gender categories reveals the limitations of such conventions of reading. For example, assuming a lyric speaker has the gender of its author, one might note that each (female) speaker comes to life through connection or relationship, suggesting in simplified form the line of thought developed through Carol Gilligan's work on moral development and Nancy Chodorow's on infant bonding (Gilligan 1982; Gilligan et al. 1988; Chodorow 1978). In this reading, the speaker is confirmed to be female because "she" develops through connection with others. Such an assumption might be further supported in "Scumbling" by a heterosexist reading of the poem's last lines, in which the speaker's being "gone through" places her in feminine relation to a phallic other. While such a reading is plausible, it ignores the complexity of Fulton's deliberate lack of gender specificity and the implications of the backdrop of quantum theory, which insists that all elements of matter—including this speaker—have the properties of a wave as well as those of a particle—perhaps here of separateness as well as connection, or of the male as well as the female. A gendered reading would have to insist on the essential separateness and difference (hence heterosexuality) of the "scumbling" bodies at the poem's end rather than on their physical and aesthetic mingling. Similarly, in "Palladium Process" the speaker's extreme sensitivity as the primarily reactive cloud chamber and photographic plate might be read as evidence of "her" femininity—a reading supported by Fulton's pun on the speaker's position as "skirted." Yet these assumptions are disrupted by an analogy near the poem's end, where the speaker

> start[s]
> at ordinary things
> the way a 19th-century gentleman might
> start at a glimpse of undraped
> limb.

In either reading, determining the gender of the speaker necessitates contradiction, whereas accepting the speaker's unmarked—whether multiple or unfixed—gender allows the kind of "surplus" and "expansion" celebrated by the "serious/hilarity" of the poem's "Process."

The politics of Fulton's choice to create ungendered speakers become clearer when these poems are examined in relation to other poems that use explicitly female first-person speakers and that take the politics of gendering as part of their topic.[7] Even in these poems, Fulton eschews any uncomplicated association of the biological or physical with gender. Both in her construction of female and of ungendered speakers, then, Fulton strongly marks her difference from feminist poets and theorists who use female subjects to speculate about perception, language, and identity—either referentially, as representing the experience of a real or imagined individual, or metaphorically, as representing extreme possibilities of constructing human experience within the Euro-American psychoanalytic and gender systems.[8]

To cite briefly from one of the best-known writers on female embodiment, Adrienne Rich states in *Of Woman Born* that "[i]n order to live a fully human life . . . we must touch the unity and resonance of our physicality, the corporeal ground of our intelligence" (1976, 62). In some ways elaborating this claim, Alicia Ostriker's *Stealing the Language: The Emergence of Women's Poetry in America* validates physical experience of the individual and collective entity "woman" as the basis for twentieth-century women's poetry. Ostriker reverses Homans's claim for nineteenth-century women poets, that they must at least in part reject their archetypal identification with nature and hence their own femaleness as body—the woman's body serving as the prototypical object within, and characterizing, nature. Instead, she claims that, "when defining a personal identity," contemporary women poets have turned primarily to their bodies to interpret "external reality" and, further, see "the world's body" as "continuous or equivalent with their own": "The idea that other authorities are untrustworthy but 'the body cannot lie' is central here" (1986, 11). As a corollary to her faith in a "body [that] cannot lie," Ostriker finds a fully bounded identity or self in such poetry. For Ostriker, the divided and marginalized self reveals culturally imposed conditions, "the authorized dualities of the culture," to be overcome in a quest for wholeness and autonomy (11). Questioning these dualities both leads toward and takes place in the context of clearly articulated selfhood, leading to the assumption that a reader may indeed know not just what gender but who the unmarked speaker of a lyric poem might be: "when a woman poet today says 'I,' she is likely to mean herself" (12). Ostriker sees women poets writing about themselves, drawing directly from experiences "central to their sex and find[ing] forms and styles appropriate to their exploration" (7).

One may see Fulton's rejection of this notion of experience and selfhood in a sequence of poems with conventionally gendered subjects. Starting with a poem about adolescence ("Cherry Bombs" 1990, 37–40), then moving to a poem about pregnancy and motherhood ("Home Fires, 1943" 1990, 41–43), Fulton indicates her deep "suspicion" of any "lures // to an unfixable forever" such as that culturally defined in the feminine body/self ("Cherry Bombs"). The first of these poems begins:

> At five I knew at twelve
> the body's logic
> would lead to blood, rah-rah
>
> girly pom-poms, breasts, the secondary sex
> signs shaved to lady-
> likeness, arrayed in labial
>
> pleats for the world's ease, a skirt
> on an escalating gender

Complicating the distinction between biological necessity ("the body's logic") and social pressures (to be a cheerleader, skirted, shaved), Fulton describes childhood as a period of learning that gender roles ("lady- / likeness"), more than physical development, restrict one's options; the five-year-old later realizes that it is society's, not the body's, "logic" that "escalat[es]" gender difference. Later in the poem she notes, "It wasn't that I wanted to be not / female. I wanted to be female / as I was"—a condition apparently defined only by its resistance to being "an unfixable forever." Being female "as I was" suggests the ability to develop in as yet undetermined ways—ways that do not equate the feminine with being "arrayed . . . for the world's ease."

"Home Fires, 1943" begins in the past tense with the speaker's address to her earlier self or to some broader "you" of women who have given birth, marking the connections of women's labor rather than the privacy of the speaker's own: "You forfeited the girl / you were, grunting forth the larva of a child." The poem then continues with a dialogue between this laboring "you" and the multiply faced (and gendered) authority figure Dr. Gutzeit/airline hostess/God. Using stanzas shaped like a pregnant woman's bulging stomach or like a graph of the increasing and then decreasing intensity of contractions, this dialogue demolishes popular preconceptions of the glory of birth. In one exchange, for example, "He" speaks in the voice of Romantic essentialism, and the speaker remembers or imagines the appropriate, bitterly pragmatic response:

> "You think
> too much. An infant brings you back to nature. At least give it a try,"
> he'd said. As if a child could be *un*tried. You knew there could be no
> retreat without a death.

The poem ends ambivalently with the speaker-mother holding her own "darling fingered babe" and commenting:

> How private
> his navy iris, a shutter on the interstellar stuff
> he was! Grind the skin of a meteor with
> a dove's and bathe him in it.
> My breathtaker.

The shape and focus of this poem might make one think that Fulton fits Ostriker's description of women writing from their—or at least female—experience. Such a reading would typically give rise to the assumption that, or question whether, Fulton has in fact given birth.[9] Yet, the movement of the concluding lines away from human flesh and into "interstellar" embodiment reminds the reader that the human body is never simply what it seems. Moreover, the poem's running comparison between the unsung heroics of birth and "heroic" war making, together with the conglomerate authority figure that makes labor seem like a cross between recovering from a disease, an innocuously pleasant vacation, and a deeply spiritual experience, suggests that the poet focuses on birthing more as a moment of cultural myth than of personal event. The speaker thinks abstractly during precisely that event mythologized as belonging purely to the body:

The womb's the body's largest muscle, stronger than a fighter's
biceps. It made me able to turn tables breathing theories through
the rotted flower gas.

For her, this is more a cultural than a physiological or private moment.

The following poem, "Our Calling," has no personified speaker and can be
read as commentary on the previous two poems' gender distinctions (1990, 44–
45). This poem uses distinct but interlaced columns to present the dilemma of
understanding oneself through a language that denies many people basic human-
ity and euphemistically disguises its culture's worst horrors. It begins:

> To birth shape from the spill
> > *To* silence *is to kill*
> To raise Cain from the matrix
> > Dislodge disperse dispatch—
> lifting thoughts from nil
> > *the clean words for murder*
> It's our conspiracy to see
> > Overlord's *a lord supreme*
> the world one way

Here the "birth[ing]" of "shape" and "thoughts" becomes shared, as does the
"rais[ing]" of the child "Cain," and a collective "we" arrives at the disastrous
result of "see[ing] / the world one way." While this poem deplores the misogyny
and racism that both silence and kill their "enemies," it insists that final responsi-
bility for the "conspiracy" is "ours." The right side of the poem defines the words
"gossip," "epic," "to man," and "to woman" through reference to hierarchical
gender distinctions, revealing how fully embedded misogyny is in our language
and cultural understandings:

> At worst lies pit the mother tongue
> > Gossip *stands for tales*
> like salt on roads
> > *of birth* epics
> dry-rot the goddess
> > *songs of war in short*
> The world waits for our orders
> > To man *is to make*
> It haunts
> > *active* To woman? *Fill in*

> our heads the atomized
>
> > *the blank*
>
> fuzz of gnats

At the same time, the left side of the dialogue undercuts these sharp distinctions, and the fact that the poem may be read horizontally rather than in vertical columns undercuts them even farther. "We" are different by race and gender (named "*Gook Kraut Cunt Zip Slit*"), yet the poem refers to "our orders" and "*we* call each shot" (emphasis added). Like light, which is both and neither particle and wave, this poem speaks in a universalizing "we" that both reveals itself to be utterly false and shows the depth of complicity "we" in fact share in the racist, misogynistic grounding of "our" language.[10]

The sequence of these poems indicates that, for Fulton, despite the force of gender stereotypes (especially in adolescence), despite the different biological experiences available to the female and male sexes and the forms of empowerment systematically offered or denied them, there is no stable position of identity except as one accedes to it, thereby ignoring other aspects of one's being or responsibility in a complex world. In "Our Calling," Fulton notes that things are "visible only from uncertain . . . personal slants." Positionality informs our knowing, but always as a platform that is itself culturally defined; "Nothing wakes in our head . . . unworded." Even in these poems of more conventional embodiment, there is no "body [that] cannot lie."

This sequence of poems can also be viewed from the perspective of the symbolic relation of female embodiment to language. Rather than link language to the body through a notion of accessible, and hence to some degree transparent, individual experience, theorists like Hélène Cixous and Luce Irigaray see all unempowered speakers as feminine in relation to the phallogocentric structures of hegemonic language, and use the female body to theorize what this symbolic gendering means. Because their references are insistently female, however, the symbolic threatens to become literal.[11] Cixous, for example, refers both to her own experience of a female body and to classical myths of the female—especially Eve—to (en)gender the writing process for those otherwise without a voice.[12] "I was raised on the milk of words," she writes in "Coming to Writing"; "I nourished myself with texts" (1991, 20). Then she describes her own writing through the corporeal images of maternal labor and nursing a child:

> It was the woman at the peak of her flesh, her pleasure, her force at last delivered, manifest. Her secret . . . She gives birth . . . She has her source. She draws deeply. She releases. Laughing. And in the wake of the child, a squall of Breath! A longing for text! Confusion! What's come over her? A child! Paper! Intoxications! I'm brimming over! My breasts are overflowing! Milk. Ink.

Nursing time. And me? I'm hungry, too. The milky taste of ink! (31, ellipses mine)

As Susan Suleiman summarizes in *The Female Body,* Cixous at times imagines an ideal "bisexuality of a 'dual' or even multiple subject," and she attributes women's greater potential than men's for realizing this ideal to historical and cultural causes (1986, 16). Nonetheless, she repeatedly grounds her notion of even this ideal in experiences of the female body.

Similarly, Luce Irigaray both celebrates a dual sexuality in which gender is determined by relationships of power and yet insistently describes nonphallocentric language as initiating in woman's sexuality. In "This Sex Which Is Not One," she reasons that just as woman has "double" if not "plural" sites of sexual pleasure, consisting of parts that are always touching or in touch with each other,

> in what she says, too, at least when she dares, woman is constantly touching herself. She steps ever so slightly aside from herself with a murmur, an exclamation, a whisper, a sentence left unfinished . . . When she returns, it is to set off again from elsewhere. From another point of pleasure, or of pain. . . . For if "she" says something, it is not, it is already no longer, identical with what she means. What she says is never identical with anything, moreover; rather, it is contiguous. *It touches (upon).* And when it strays too far from that proximity, she breaks off and starts over at "zero": her body-sex. ([1977] 1985b, 29)

According to Irigaray, although "she" resides in quotation marks as though there is no such thing as distinct gender, the "zero" position for "her" language is nonetheless "her body-sex."

Some aspects of Fulton's language do evoke a sense of spontaneity and playfulness reminiscent of the fluid emission of Cixous's metaphors or the "contradictory words, somewhat mad from the standpoint of reason" that Irigaray describes ([1977] 1985b, 29). There is wonderful pizzazz in her offbeat metaphors (remember the gendered "skirt" of "labial pleats" in "Cherry Bombs") and a frequent irreverent collapsing of cultural categories (the speaker of "Point of Purchase" hopes that billiards will remain "wily as religion, which is based / on pool-shark smarts" [1990a, 73]). Yet other elements of Fulton's language work strenuously against the application of such metaphors. As described above, by using a scientific vocabulary even occasionally, Fulton evokes the most highly elaborated and determinedly rational code of our culture. Moreover, Fulton's syntax is typically hypotactic, complex in its balancing and modifying clauses, and her sentences are packed full of information—about comets, electrons, nebulas—unimaginable in Cixous's or Irigaray's writing. Through striking enjambment, manipulation of formal elements like rhyme, and imitative and experimental constructions, these poems indicate that they have not been spurted forth from the poet's psyche or self. Fulton's poetry is undeniably playful, and the humor of her wordplay links her formal constructions with the looser aspects of her style. For example, "The Fractal Lanes," a poem that is highly philosophical in content and formal in diction, also contains an anagram spelling out "BOWL-ING DEVELOPS THE RIGHT ARM" (1990, 23), and once one has discovered this comic secret message, as it were, one discovers a number of puns playing against that formality. Yet often even such broad humor and extravagant wordplay underline the craft of the poet.

To give a more extended example, in "Romance in the Dark," Fulton comments on the absurdity of gender distinctions applied simplistically (and traditionally) to language through her use of repeated slant rhymes. In this poem, almost every line ends with a Romance-Latinate polysyllabic word:

> When love becomes a bounty-
> hunt, a panty-
> raiding prop of boys' virility
> or gilt-edged opportunity
> for girls to bed down a commodity,
> one becomes a party
>
> to obliteration: then women are currency
> exchanged between men; men, women's agencies
> of power
>
> . . . *Nebula* can mean opacity:
> so star-struck visions spot affinity
> where none exists. Wanting electricity,
> we settle for fidelity,
> at last admit civility
> will do.
>
> (1990a, 100–101)

Such polysyllables referring to the public or technical world certainly constitute the language of patriarchy if there is one. Yet, ironically, polysyllabic unstressed rhymes like those of this poem are called "feminine," in contrast to the "strong," "perfect," or "masculine" rhymes of monosyllables—as, for example, in *spill / kill* of "Our Calling." By writing a feminist poem with an ungendered speaker in "masculine" language that necessarily creates "weak" or "feminine" rhymes, Fulton must intend to point to the arbitrariness if not outright "hilarity" of such distinctions in language generally and in the terminology of literary analysis. Sex, desire, even an exuberant *jouissance* permeate the world of Fulton's poems, but they cannot be mistaken as having the forms of essentialized embodiment or as marking the identification of such embodiment with particular uses of language.

The contrast between Fulton's and Irigaray's or Cixous's work may be most obvious in "Home Fires, 1943"—Fulton's poem about what Cixous calls "woman at the peak of her flesh." As quoted above, this poem ends with at least a suggestion that giving birth puts an end to a woman's life and is primarily an experience of painful loss of control rather than a metaphor for female creativity: the child is "My breathtaker" and "a shutter on the interstellar stuff," or one who shuts his mother off from all but a mundane life of motherhood. Or, in an alternative reading of this line, the offspring (baby or poem) is itself made of "interstellar," not maternal, "stuff" and hence not essentially bound to the mother but already independent at birth.[13] Giving birth is an act available only to women but not, in either reading of this poem, the defining act of all women or the central event of this individual woman's life. Moreover, putting the birthing mother under the control of an airline "hostess" as well as male authorities makes the conflicting understandings of birth—as either "a little matter / to which men gave form and life" or a mother's heroism in facing bayonetlike pain—more matters of cultural than of biological or gendered conflict. Similarly, there is no "zero" position of gender, physicality, or anything else in "Cascade Experiment," "Cusp," "Scumbling," or "Palladium Process." In these poems, Fulton insists that we simultaneously acknowledge the body, in all its physicality and desire, and break up the categories of its social construction in order to question the most basic ways in which our bodies instruct us about, and connect us to, the world.

In her poems presenting ungendered speakers and employing the vocabulary of quantum mechanics, Fulton imagines the unstable but exhilarating freedom of experiencing one's existence as quantum process. In the poem "Peripheral Vision," Fulton instead imagines a scientist who uses quantum theory to speculate about identity and boundaries while herself remaining firmly within an ordinary narrative frame. This speaker feels isolated from her "colleagues" because "her mind works / toward the marginal, / what's tentative but ready." Although the sentence continues "ready / to take on sound and color," the line break suggests the flexibility of the world as well as of the speaker's viewing: it is "ready," alert— as it were—to several possibilities of "vision." This enjambment has resonance for a typical structural pattern of Fulton's verse as well as for her hermeneutics. Using multiple ambiguous enjambments and frequent syntactic doublings, Fulton signals that her readers, too, must be ready or alert; one must read backward, forward, horizontally, and even vertically (as in her anagrams) to pick up Fulton's complementary meanings and phrases. This may be another way in which Fulton breaks readers' expectations of logical progression while writing in the vocabulary of the discourse that epitomizes logic, or in which she insists on a multiplicity of perspectives—even at the levels of syntax and form.

In the world of "Peripheral Vision," however, "the scientist" is alone in her readiness to meet the world with anything beyond the "black and white" knowledge of the classical scientific method. She alone views nature flexibly, outside a dichotomy insisting that the object observed is separate and opposed to the observing self. The poem (1986a, 66–68) begins:

> The window's a slow-moving liquid.
> In it, the scientist sees another window
> drifting: smaller,
> larger, smaller. It is the opposite
> structure rocking, or her own
> structure or herself.

By referring to this woman as "the" scientist, Fulton suggests that such a poststructuralist perspective in fact constitutes the most accurate (hence scientific) mode of observation, as well as playing against expectations that "the" scientist be male.

The poem continues with the speaker's inability to watch the "film of their last field trip" with her colleagues, because she's distracted by imagining the source of their differences from her—a source she imagines in predictably phallic but unpredictably funny terms.

> She's distracted
> by their black and white extremities,
> the ancillary hands and feet. What blooms
> beneath their suits, snug
> as guilt? Snug as God
> in a hideaway heaven, chanting
> standard tasks: observe, examine,
> isolate.

This speaker suggests that a penis "blooms" beneath each male suit and that this hidden erection (apparently stimulated by watching a film of their own previous pursuit) stands metonymically for the men themselves: it is "snug as guilt" and then—in a suggestive syntactic doubling, again marked by a line break—it and they both are "[s]nug as God / in a hideaway heaven." These scientists "study flirtatious affidavits" in "tracking" the female tiger, isolating and then "spook[ing]" it so they may attach their "collar / with its battery- / driven signal"—a process that sounds like a parody of courtship rituals: isolate and pursue. The lone scientist instead

                    focuses
on the fiery valentine
that is the tiger's nose.
Is there a cover equal to the giveaway
signal? Does the thought admit regret,
resistance?

While both perspectives suggest activities based on a constructed gender system
(capturing and controlling the "other," or sentimentalizing it as valentine), only
the female observer questions her role in its capture—albeit still at the distance of
speculation. She is caught between the (masculine) perspective of her colleagues
and what the poem suggests is her "peripheral"—and "the" scientist's—vision.

As a scientist, the poem's subject calls the "heart a partisan" and the "intellect,
a stickler," wanting "to know / in what sense precisely / the tiger's burning
bright"—or to translate the language of poem into science, the language of
Blakeian "songs of innocence and experience" into data. Yet even her "intellect"
will not hold this "partisan" line of thought "isolat[ing]" heart from head. Claim-
ing that "nature is unchanging, / though it does change," while driving home she
observes all phenomena as being in flux, or through a quantum perspective; she is
unsure what is moving and what is still, what has agency beyond herself: the

                sun slices, horizontally, a line
of trees, or trees skate
past the rooted sun, or cars drift
by the steadfast sun and trees.
What will it be? When God is a round
centered everywhere,
a circumference found nowhere, expanding
the universe, building

new alloys from happenstance and junk.
So constancy won't hold
her.

Not omnipresently "around," but "a round / centered everywhere" and "found
nowhere," the subject of a conditional clause in an unfinished sentence, God
gives no more guidance than the intellect or heart in this mutable world. Does the
sun move and stand still? Where is the "circumference" called "God" that builds
not from sciencelike precise knowledge and instruments but from "happenstance
and junk"? In a lovely weird metaphor for the "ready" and inconstant self, the
speaker's mind at the end is compared to a "radio tower," "underwired with
subtle / stripes and flames, invisible leapaway / music bulleting to distant hit
parades."

The metaphor of electromagnetic waves at the end of this poem may provide a central clue to Fulton's use of science and her exploration of gendered humanity in all these poems. Like light waves, like social constructions, radio waves are everywhere present in an urban, industrialized world and yet are invisible. They are responsible for what we hear and see (or in the case of social constructions, how we interpret our perceptions), yet only highly specialized instruments allow us to perceive them—and then only indirectly through the medium of varying experimental frameworks that stimulate varying behavior in the subject under study, or through the clarifying blur of theory. "Seeing's // such a commemorative gesture," the scientist muses earlier, thinking of scientific instruments more sensitive than the human eye. The radio is such an instrument. As radio, the mind picks up society's signals mechanically. As radio tower, however, the mind also broadcasts multiple "subtle" and "invisible" signals simultaneously; it may "underwir[e]" conventional sounds or perceptions with a "leapaway / music" perceptible to and stimulating minds similar to its own. This mind's creative energies enter the atmosphere like radio waves, like a new music "ready" for its receiver(s), or like the lines of an as yet unread poem.

In physics, the study of light led to the crucial breakthrough in quantum theory proving that light is both and neither wave and particle, and that a subject may not be clearly differentiated from the object being observed. Barad notes the wonderful irony that light has also been a central metaphor for knowledge (1994, 29). In Christianity, light has stood for godhead, revelation, and spiritual guidance; in philosophy, for worldly enlightenment or knowledge; and in gender systems, for male strength—"woman" appears as the reflective moon or light-absorbing earth in relation to "man's" elemental, life-giving sun. By concluding so many of her poems with metaphors of light, Fulton may not only remind us that quantum theory has revolutionized scientific understanding of light but suggest that cultural conceptions of light and truth must be similarly reevaluated. The binaries of Western understanding are also "commemorative"—meaningful historically and useful in practical aspects of living, but not adequate as guides to a contemporary understanding of light, life, poetry, or the universe.

Fulton stresses the paradoxes of human knowledge: the multivalent richness of what we "know," and yet our terrible blindness; the final poem of *Powers of Congress* ends with the earth as "a plinth— / from which we rise, towers / of blood and ignorance" (1990, 108). At the same time, however, there is an extraordinary energy and optimism in the willingness to "advance" "passional[ly] / toward the universe and you" in poems like "Cascade Experiment," "Peripheral Vision," and "Cusp." Fulton implies that our culture's forced recognition of a certain level of ignorance, the lack of a classificatory clarity, the breakdown of duality (wave/particle, subject/object, the inside/outside of touch) may give way to the breakdown of equally powerful social dualities (self/other, black/white, male/female)—and that such change is ultimately life affirming. Similarly, this breakdown of dualities calls into question the relations between poet and speaker, between speaker (or poet) and reader, and between text and interpretation. "The scientist" "knows that // glass is a skittery solid" but still "sees" in it "the opposite / structure rocking, or her own / structure or herself." If quantum theory is also a model for reading, what might I learn to see in what I "know" to be a lyric poem, what elements of myself, or "the opposite," or some fluid thing inbetween? How do its structures, or my reception, change if my mind "works toward the marginal" and "passional[ly]"? Fulton's poems do not propose analytical answers to such questions. By making such questions central to her poetic, however, Fulton suggests that if we cease to perceive and to read through the practices of isolation and binary classification, we may find ourselves at an "erogenous cusp" of understanding that indeed borders frightening vacancy but also makes accessible the extravagant "sound and color" of multiple presently "invisible" worlds.

NOTES

1. Fulton has confirmed her intention to create ungendered speakers in private correspondence. There she states that when "writing 'Between the Apple and the Stars' [1983], I came to these lines in the penultimate stanza: '. . . The scientist passes / a hand like a wand / over the wondrous button. . . . ' And I remember . . . thinking will it be 'her hand' or 'his hand' and deciding on the article instead. This was in 1979 or 1980. It was a decision made consciously, to keep the gender blurred" (letter dated 30 August–9 September 1992; quoted with permission of author).

2. I am indebted to Karen Barad for several conversations about quantum mechanics, and for letting me read an essay of hers on feminist theory and quantum mechanics in manuscript (1994). For a cogent discussion of "complementarity," see Folse 1985. Also useful is Hayles 1984.

3. While slang fits more or less within the Romantic association of lyric poetry with a common speaker, scientific and technical diction does not. As Michael Bernstein argues in *The Tale of the Tribe*, the early nineteenth century dissolved what had previously been considered a " 'reciprocal kinship between knowledge and language,' " redefining poetic discourse as being "absolutely divorced" from the world of fact and daily living, or from the empiricism of science (1980, 6, 5). Similarly, Marie Borroff points out that scientific language tends to have a "solemnity retardant," pragmatic tonal effect, in contrast to the Romantic lyric's tone of transcendence or inspiration (1979, 88). There is certainly precedent for the use of technical scientific language in poetry, especially during the modernist period, but few poets use such language as extensively as Fulton does. For discussions of other poets who do make use of scientific language and theories, see Lisa Steinman 1987, focusing on Williams, Moore, and Stevens; Bernstein 1980, throughout his volume, on Pound and briefly on Olson (241–42); and Conte on Leslie Scalapino (1991, 275–78).

4. Barad (1994) herself notes the overlap between her theoretical argument and Fulton's poetry both by quoting from Fulton in her essay and by borrowing a line from "Cascade Experiment" for her title: "Meeting the Universe Half-Way: Ambiguities, Discontinuities, Quantum Subjects, and Multiple Positionings in Feminism and Physics."

5. It is noteworthy that while Whitman is also betrayed by his nerves—using words like "treacherous," "deluding," "traitor," and so on—they are ultimately in cahoots with the man in leading to his orgasm (1891 "Song of Myself," section 28; the phrase "apple-blossom'd earth" comes from section 21 [Whitman 1982]). Fulton's poem leads to no orgasmic reunification of body and mind or soul.

6. I am not sure this argument works as well for racial as for gender categorization. One might argue, for example, that there is inherent privilege in Fulton's not mentioning this dimension of people's lives, hence that even her ungendered characters are implicitly white. Imagining the kind of free-floating existence depicted in this poem, when it comes with no reminders of the conditions of life left behind, may imply a kind of privilege. At the same time, Fulton's conception of knowledge and presence as "deep resistance" and "protest" recalls—albeit in general terms—the problematic conditions involved in living within the too-fixed categories of "pen . . . hand," "jail . . . lighthouse"—or in more socially powerful terms, black/white, male/female, and so on. To create an unraced character that as clearly opposes or subverts the stereotypes of racial identification as Fulton's ungendered speakers do the conventions of gender, a writer would also have to manifest specific interest in the problematic politics of racial categorization.

7. Fulton also creates male speakers in some poems, and these are equally likely to deal with issues of gender construction—for example, in "Overlord" (1990) or in the third section of "Fictions of the Feminine: Quasi-Carnal Creatures from the Cloud Decks of Venus" (1986a).

8. Another instructive comparison might be drawn with the work of those feminist critics who examine the gendered body in a cultural and historical as well as theoretical light—for example, Hortense Spillers's "Interstices: A Small Drama of Words" (1984) and "Mama's Baby, Papa's Maybe: An American Grammar Book" (1987), and Hazel Carby's *Reconstructing Womanhood: The Emergence of the Afro-American Woman Novelist* (1987) and "It Jus Be's Dat Way Sometime: The Sexual Politics of Women's Blues" (1988). Fulton's frequent central use of contemporary pop culture and the icons of ordinary living may bring her as close to this theoretical stance toward subjectivity and embodiment as to those I discuss here.

9. To my knowledge, she has not.

10. One might argue that "our" functions ironically here and hence marks the distance of many speakers from the implied assumptions of English rather than their complicity. Such a reading saves, as it were, some speakers of English from guilt by association with its worst elements. To the extent, however, that one reads the poem as being less about blame than about the difficulty of countering the racism, misogyny, and violence in a language used even by those who consciously fight such forces, the "our" is necessarily inclusive of all speakers of English. Fulton also ends the poem with repeated emphasis on responsibility: the world is "visible only from uncertain . . . personal slants . . . *except* that from the swarm . . . we forge our terms . . . *except* . . . we call each shot" (emphasis added).

11. There is great debate over the extent to which both Irigaray's and Cixous's work is essentialist in its grounding. Maggie Berg's recent essay "Luce Irigaray's 'Contradictions': Poststructuralism and Feminism" argues persuasively that Irigaray's is not; rather, she claims, Irigaray's "lips" have a "dual and contradictory signification: They do and do not refer to the labia" and hence do not "forg[e] an existential relation between language and the body" (1991, 69). Similarly, Julia Kristeva's quite different theoretical position—which also uses female sexuality and the body to represent the nonhegemonic—has been both attacked as essentialist and defended against this charge. For other excellent, more broad-based discussions of these debates, see Montefiore 1987 on Irigaray; Felski 1989 on Cixous and Kristeva; Benstock 1991 on Kristeva; and Suleiman 1986 on all of these writers.

12. Cixous writes of Eve, for example in "The Author in Truth," translated from the revised version in "Coming to Writing" and Other Essays (1991, 136–82).

13. Of course, one can still read this poem as being about creativity: the poet creates out of painful and confrontational loss of control in an antagonistic social context, and her poem consists of elements beyond those the mother/poet can consciously give—hence "interstellar" as well as genetic offspring. This is not, however, a typical use of the metaphorical intersection of reproduction/production. See Susan R. Suleiman's "Writing and Motherhood" (1985) for an analytical review of several kinds of texts exploring the relation of motherhood to writing, from the psychoanalytic and theoretical to the experiential and pragmatic. Joyce Treblicot's anthology Mothering: Essays in Feminist Theory (1983) also provides multiple perspectives on this subject.

:RE:THINKING:LITERARY:FEMINISM:
(three essays onto shaky grounds)

Joan Retallack

I. PICTURE THEORIES

She moves slowly. Her movements are made gradual, dull, made to extend from inside her, the woman, her, the wife, her walk weighted full to the ground. Stillness that follows when she closes the door. She cannot disturb the atmosphere. . . .

Upon seeing her you know how it was for her. You know how it might have been. You recline, you lapse, you fall, you see before you what you have seen before. Repeated, without your even knowing it. It is you standing there. It is you waiting outside in the summer day. It is you waiting and knowing to wait. How to. Wait. It is you walking a few steps before the man who walks behind you. It is you in the silence through the pines, the hills, who walks exactly three steps behind her. It is you in the silence. His silence all around the unspoken the unheard, the apprenticeship to silence. Observed for so long and not ending. Not immediately. Not soon. Continuing. Contained. Muteness. Speech less ness.

Theresa Hak Kyung Cha, *DICTEE*

In our silence, out of docile bodies and silent minds—out of multiple silences more and more audible—we've constructed theories and accounts of a historical endurance and power we call "women's silence." This is only one of many silences to which an increasingly heterogeneous and problematic *we* is attending after modernism's persistent figure/ground shaking "now." Isn't it, come to think

---

This title is a play on Jerome McGann's "Rethinking Romanticism," in turn, an evocation of Marjorie Levinson's *Rethinking Historicism*. I read McGann's essay in manuscript. I want to thank Marjorie Perloff, Jane Flax, and Francine Rainone, all of whom carefully read and commented on this text-in-process. Our conversations were a source of many improvements to this essay, and none of its shortcomings. Note: my use of the word "feminine" is intended to reflect the cluster of attributes which constitute its current cultural construction in the literature. See pp. 347, 365, and 366 of this essay, and Genre Tallique, quoted on page 359.

344

of it, curious that the twentieth-century project of conceptual reorientation has come so often to silence? There are Wittgenstein's aphoristic and Beckett's elliptical silences; Gertrude Stein's silences of depunctuation and repetition; Kristeva's semiotic silences; John Cage's re-sounding silences; Rosmarie Waldrop's, Hannah Weiner's, Susan Howe's, Lyn Hejinian's, Nicole Brossard's, Tina Darragh's, Diane Ward's, Leslie Scalapino's, Carla Harryman's, Melanie Neilson's, Jessica Grim's, Theresa Hak Kyung Cha's. . . . .poethical silences of countersyntactic and divested forms; as well as testimonies and sacrifices of silence we associate with names like Virginia Woolf, Tillie Olsen, Sylvia Plath, Audre Lorde, Adrienne Rich. . . . . (The cultural silence that befalls radical difference prolongs the obscurity of many of the names I just listed.)

What we've learned from this "coincidence of silences" (as venerable and portentious as a "siege of herons" or a "murder of crows") is that silence itself is nothing more or less than what lies outside the radius of interest and comprehension at any given time. We hear, that is, with culturally attuned ears. This century's *formal* investigations into experiences of silence have meant opening up previously inaccessible or unacknowledged or forbidden territory, where the very act of attending entails a radical figure/ground shift. We have been startled by Cage's discovery that silence is not empty at all, but densely, richly, disturbingly full. Full of just those things which we had not, until "now," been ready to notice; or reluctantly noticing, had dismissed as nonsense or noise. The long postponement of acknowledgment is no accident. It is an indication of just how threatening the articulation of silence is to surface composure, to cultural self-image.

Not an accident, but certainly an intriguing coincidence—to discover the force of silence at precisely this cacophonous moment on the Western Civ time line. A moment of accelerated technological momentum, hell-bent on drowning out silence in every form once and for all. This is no paradox. All those probes and antennas, satellite dishes and cellular phones are designed to make the experience of limit and respite we have called silence as conceptually irrecoverable as the Romantic idea of wilderness. And yet cognitive/intuitive frontiers remain. If silence was formerly what we weren't ready to hear, silence is currently what is audible but unintelligible. The realm of the unintelligible is the permanent frontier—that which lies outside the scope of the culturally preconceived—just where we need to operate in our invention of new forms of life drawing on the power of the feminine.

What is currently most prominently audible/intelligible is, as Judith Butler has pointed out in *Gender Trouble* (1990a), a trap. It is a world authored in the image of Rational/Universal Man—Homo Protoregulator studding a clear and distinct (Cartesian) prose with *man*'s randy, generic pronouns. (Slipping back—do you notice?—after a brief, PC interlude.) We have been presented with a subtle and treacherous "text" declaring itself generic and normative starting point—homo-genius, monolithic, active, authoritative—just as Moses brought it down from the mountain; that is, masculine. Butler sees the generic feminine as "sub-text," either *sub*jugated or *sub*versive (*reactive*) to *the* master-narrative. But we must be cautious about the consequences of such a view. Defining feminine power only as the power of *sub*version valorizes the predominance of the masculine "version." We might note with unsettling, extra-literary logic that if the subversion of rape is seduction, then seduction is an implicit legitimation of rape.

In the unnaturally constructed choreography of cultural survival, text as rational, imperial, constitutive fabric has been understood as logically prior, defining the terms of the intelligible. For Butler, who implicitly accepts the normative status of the "intelligible," and therefore the constraints of this binary textual code, to make gender trouble is to act up as *sub*text: that is, to perform *sub*versions: parody, pastiche, ironic mirrorings, deconstructive replications. Doing this, she feels, exposes the arbitrariness of the phallogocentric text. But this prescription for a performative feminine subtext does not spring the binary trap. On the contrary, it reinforces it by positing its referential stability and by ignoring strong traditions of multivariant feminine texts. To make real gender trouble is to make genre trouble. Not to parody but to open up explorations into forms of "unintelligibility" (unintellig*a*bility?) as feminine frontier.

Textual traditions that have enacted and explored modes culturally labeled feminine have oddly—or, as we shall note, not so oddly—been practiced until recently more by men than by women. *Gender Trouble,* in its strong argument for the social contingency of traits (and bodies) labeled feminine/masculine, can help prepare us for a radical rethinking of the occurrence of "the feminine" in culture. These feminine textual traditions have had tumultuous histories of appropriation and rejection by women and men alike in the long, topiary he(d)gemony of masculinist values disguised as natural forms. It's been suggested by Luce Irigaray and others that "the" feminine is perhaps nothing other than a plural—all that conspires against monolithic, monotonal, monolinear, *uni*verses. Complexities and messes that overflow constrictions of *the* have been labeled variously over the centuries, but most strongly identified with the feminine. As alternative principle, it is importantly the transgressive term in an ongoing Western cultural dialectic between established order and new possibility. We may smart from raw awareness of the invidiously destructive M/F binary, but its internal collisions and combustions have yielded constructively complex and paradoxical forms—mastery, *matery*, and strange powers yet to be named. Our best possibilities lie in texts/alter-texts where the so-called feminine and masculine take migratory, paradoxical, and surprising swerves to the enrichment of both, (n)either, and all that lies between. This is not a vision of androgyny, but of range.

To the extent that such swerves have been abhored they've been identified as feminine; when valued they have been almost entirely incorporated into the myth of dis/e/ruptive male genius (in the Romantic tradition the strong male poet is inspired by a female muse—i.e., *external* feminine element). But as far back as one looks it's there—even prior to Plato's invention of the feminine rationalist, Socrates—in Homer, for instance, as well as in the mythic sources of Attic drama—one finds the paradoxical and ambivalent linking of the feminine with both the yielding and the threatening. From the end of the nineteenth century to the present, the exploding genre (if not gender) project has been located in what is called experimental or avant-garde traditions. Due to the masculinist bias of establishment literary traditions, these labels have often been applied pejoratively to connote the threat of unintelligibility. Perhaps one of the most remarkable things about our present time is that women are finally socially and politically powerful enough to undertake the risks of this "feminine" challenge in their own texts.

A realistic optimism, not just for the feminine but for the complex human, lies in forms that engage the dynamics of multiplicity (three and more). In acknowledgment of difference, yes, but more importantly in generating a proliferation of possibility beyond invidious dualisms. The same global and space information technologies that are disembarrassing us of the illusion of other as "absence" are schooling us in multidirectional coincidence (a pattern, coincidentally, related to Carol Gilligan's "web" image of women's thinking) as a connective principle at least as forceful as monodirectional (hierarchical) cause and effect. In a scientific era recognizing both complexity and the constituting presence of chance in nature, we may be rediscovering that coincidence, that is, everything at any given moment happening at once, is the most remarkable characteristic and most urgent challenge of our teeming global village.

It happens that this has been the condition of women's experience for as long as our histories recount and imply. An interesting coincidence, yes/no? that what Western culture has tended to label feminine (forms characterized by silence, empty and full; multiple, associative, nonhierarchical logics; open and materially contingent processes, etc.) may well be more relevant to the complex reality we are coming to see as our world than the narrowly hierarchical logics that produced the rationalist dreamwork of civilization and its misogynist discontents. I wonder if we may find in the collision of radically destabilizing institutions and emerging feminine forms the energy to make something unprecedentedly, poethically generous of our complex future?

Let's essay into this seismic zone and explore some odd logics in the literary dis/position of women's silence.

She is education history. She. Is water written lament. And cool education written blue. A literate blue. A literate yellow. And arrogance she. Speaks. Forgetting. The first Brazil. Is yellow and so speaking yellow as blue as writing. Lament.

Yellow and blue. Slip. The negative. Bury the negative. Growing written water.
And arrogance. But first. The oversight.
  Carla Harryman, "Dimblue, *After Theresa Hak Kyung Cha's DICTEE*"

FROM IMMANENT TO EMINENT DOMAIN?

First an oversight: The domain of women's silence (of what can/not be spoken/heard) has been until relatively recently almost entirely appropriated—within the domain of Anglo-American feminist thinking—by a literature dominated by visual metaphor: linguistic "as/like" snapshots organized into narrative family-of-woman albums meant to reveal, through startling disclosure (word-image "picturing" lived experience) *her*story. For this project, the task of the feminist novelist, poet, critic has been that of literary photographer and darkroom technician—to record our present experience and expose poorly or un(der)developed images from our long period of cultural latency. A period characterized by the pathos of what has become, in our female captivity narratives, an emblematic, institutional-ized/izable, capital *S* Silence. This silence, metaphorically transmuted into invisibility, but still hissing in the mind's ear, inhabits all our tedious *pression*s, locus of a sinister and insidious absence of power—of having been (passive voice) op*pressed*, sup*pressed*, re*pressed*, de*pressed*, com*pressed*, im*pressed* to the point of participating in our own belittling scorn.

This Enlightenment-based picture theory of female liberation proceeds on the belief that bringing things "to light" is ipso facto deeply therapeutic. Visibility is construed as a sociopolitical force that progressively reconfigures our consciousness so that we can act on the immanent power in our enduring silence. These (at last) *self*-projected images of disenfranchisement should, given the promise of Enlightenment-based psychotherapies, allow us to find voices with which to claim our rightful domain. With a heightened awareness of what we are trying to rise out of, we think we (post-Socratics) know by now that the way up and the way down are radically different: the only way up/out of the condition of chronic, mute oppression is to shatter the silence with raucous, self-affirming self-*ex*pression. "Let there be light" and we will erupt into robust, territorial song! But is there an oversight here? Does it really happen that way, or is this an odd misprism of metaphor?

The major problem with this picture may be that it is just that—a picture theory of understanding and transformation which draws its verisimilitude from the conventions of *de*picting—a distinctly static modeling *from* life with only a limited life principle of its own. To picture may be to transform an image in the mind's eye/"I," but does it transform the processes that make the enactment of change possible?

[Working Note: It has been assumed, in a culture that ties knowledge and free-dom to self-empowerment, that the power of women, like that of everyone else, lies conceptually in the right to self-definition; politically, in the right to self-determination. Add the two together, divide by "I," and you get self-expression, yes/no? It has been part of the chronic dis-ease of women in our society that self-definition was for so long understood as a private matter. Thus, women who daily played the role of domestic or office servant or otherwise diminutive person (often with little-girl body language and undescended voice) seized on auto-biographical forms—diaries, journals, confessional poetry, and novels—all "I"-person genres where the scope did not have to exceed firsthand and self-knowledge—as the field for self-definition cum self-expression.

But suppose we think of self-determination in art as invention, where the power lies in creating not just a self but language games and forms of life that draw on public knowledge and exploration of otherness, thereby re-forming, by their very *active* presence, the public sphere? This might be seen as the realm of imagination, which plays in the arena of the world, as opposed to fantasy, which recedes into the envelope of the mind-I-solate and "I"-solace.[1] This would also mean that the power of women lies not in expressing what has heretofore been stoppered within our cramped domain (scene of our silence) but—in a radical reorientation that may explode the notion of domain as proprietor's home/body/ it/self, substituting the energetic principle of poethical form—social/aesthetic values to live *by*—rather than under, within, or through.]

NOW PICTURING ONLY TWO SIDES OF A PICTURE THEORY OF THE PICTURE THEORY OF LITERARY FEMINISM (THERE ARE MANY MORE)

"When meaning (i.e., what we take to be significant) was pictured as a picture we could talk about its undeveloped negative" (Michelle deCertaigne). We have had a sense that whatever was pictured was real. That proof of existence lay in a discreetly finite set of attributes, rather than the mess of limitless process. We thought that what was undeveloped, that is, all that failed to be stop-timed into managable freeze-frame units, remained or became a negative. Our idea of "development" as calculated leap from one snap-shot to the next must undergo close scrutiny. Genre Tallique, *Glances*[2]

It has been a general practice to evaluate feminist writing in terms of its developed and un(der)developed images of women—to praise poets like Adrienne Rich, Marge Piercy, Audre Lorde, Sharon Olds . . . for the courage of their content—how their writing exposes previously unexposed negatives, female experiences persistently devalued, suppressed, repressed in a world dominated by male logics and values. The image is of a strong female poet creating strong metaphoric pictures to illustrate our generic slave (captivity and escape) narratives; narratives formerly silenced/devalued by a male establishment. But another, and to my mind, equally destructive instance of devaluing must be discussed.

The dark side of this "enlightenment" practice in what has been established as the feminist literary domain has been to criticize or ignore or deny recognition to women writers whose projects have been dedicated to something other than bringing about "therapeutic" exposures. The picture theory of meaning, which has roots in Plato and Aristotle but comes to us most recently from Enlightenment and turn-of-the-century positivist sources, dictates that the picture that is to mean anything at all shall have a fairly simple (this = that) correspondence to what is preconceived as a fully available, intelligible reality. It is further stipulated that this picture shall be an implicative *instance* (no montage allowed) within the deductive genealogy of the reigning metaphysic; internally consistent and coherent (no disruptions in logic or tone) and clearly classifiable (no blurred genres). Craig Owens, in his essay "The Discourse of Others: Feminists and Postmodernism," put it this way:

> Recent analyses of the "enunciative apparatus" of visual representation—its poles of emission and reception—confirm, the representational systems of the West admit only one vision—that of the constitutive male subject—or, rather, they posit the subject of representation as absolutely centered, unitary, masculine. (Foster 1983, 58)

This is surely a model we must question for a feminist enterprise.

. . . Only the women were placing bets.
From instinct and from memory I try to reconstruct nothing. From memory, I broach the subject. And that cannot be from childhood. Only from ecstacy, from a fall, from words. Or from the body differently. Emergency cell like body at its ultimate, without its knowledge, the tongue will tell it.

When Florence Dérive *entered the Hôtel de l'Institut, Montréal, 1980 on rue St. Denis. Snatches of sentences inside. At the registration desk. It was night. Since* Finnegans Wake. *It was night. Itinerant, Florence Dérive such a woman. Brain————memory. The night, numbers and letters.*

Florence Dérive sometimes repeats a certain number of gestures that continue to exist as writing and each time she dis/places ardour and meaning.
Brossard 1990

Interestingly, Brossard's theory as practice moves us away from picturing. The above is not a still form of mirroring. It does not attempt to transport images, more or less intact, from life, to reader as viewer. The disjunctive syntax, the depunctuated grammar, like that of Cha and Harryman, sends ripples through any image that might be forming, keeps it moving in the mind. In place of enlightenment (visual appreciation), the reader is invited to take part in an engagement with the *uses* of language in the generative dark of a Finnegans waking night.[3]

In a picture-book universe nothing much can be found out about the dark side of anything—neither conceptual frameworks nor the moon. Picturing presupposes the recognizable foregrounded figure, i.e. the preconfigured into genus, gender, genre and—with only limited play—all other socially constructed and frontally visible units. It reinforces the authority of current conceptual frameworks, of what can be seen through the established grammatical technology and sequencing of culturally ground/ed lenses. There can be no dark, noisy silence of a *Finnegans Wake* in a picture-book universe—nor can there be the work of Cha, Harryman, Brossard, et al. Theirs is a literature dedicated to what cannot be illustrated. Neither can there be much that is directly, materially linguistic in the use of language as depicter. In that role language must first and foremost be mediator, filter, translucence. We know only what we can glean by representation, that is by removal—from both language as element and in situ scene to be transliterated. The light we see by is as pellucid and secondhand as the light of the moon or the "silver screen."

The ideal product of the literature of depiction is a series of images strung together in a rhythmically unbroken narration, images that appear to reveal (rather than construct) a world. They are designed to create a plenum, to saturate the mind with their convincing presence, to leave an *impression* that not only is there no other logically possible world, but there is nothing left to say about the one depicted. (The admiring reviewer uses words like "skillfully crafted," "deftly polished," "absorbing," "convincing," "lacks nothing". . . .] The reader is not any more spurred to imaginative action than one who has just read to the conclusion of an airtight logical proof. Why act when all the work has quite clearly been done? If existence is nothing more than a set of attributes then "worlds" can be created than which nothing other can be conceived. This is the theological principle of the omnipotent author free of cognitive entropy, or play.

All this is about as far from real life in medias mess as we can get. Could it be, then, that contrary to received opinion, a literature of attributes may not directly empower us to make a joyful, troublesome, gender/genre exploding noise? It certainly may confirm, console, support, justify, "reveal," inform, and—what sounds most active—inspire . . . but what does being "inspired" mean? . . . literally, to be filled with someone else's breath; breath that without an accompanying principle of action expires into fantasy identifications with idealized models. All this can nurture a self-image that feels potent and positive and full of *ideas* for action, but it does not, by its own formal devices, instigate independent imaginative acts.

Women have for centuries been subject/ed to the literature of images—from literary and romance novels to Romantic poetry to movie and fashion magazines. Mostly we have been left with a damaged self-image—a static projection of incompetence and inadequacy, and paralysis—having no sense of how to get from "here" (flawed self) to "there" (idealized image). This is the working of a romantic mechanism—con/fusion with an idealized other—which is, in its updated technological form, central to the electronic media of glamour. As any TV producer knows, the image locks in the viewer's gaze and desire. It is a tool with built-in seduction and persuasion—and, I think, ultimate betrayal. The remainder in the reading/viewing experience fixed to images is the reader/viewer herself—left in a quiescent, fantasy state, entertaining *after*images and *after*thoughts, rather than engaging in active, alternate constructions (e.g., by virtue of playfully indeterminate forms) that can reconfigure a form of life. Could it be that any medium whose chief function is to impress images upon us may be prolonging our cultural latency (our passivication) rather than deconstructing it?

I think we must question "images of women" literary theories in this light (see Moi 1985, 42–49). The extent to which they are founded on positivist or naive realist epistemologies is revealed by their insistence on full disclosure or accessibility. This is an aesthetic that imagines itself into the idea of but one logically possible world, which, coincidentally, is identified by the very internally consistent, narrative or lyrical principles that construct it in the first place. Of course, this connect-the-dots constellation we call our world is no more ontologically present in the cosmos than any other. But the metaphor of mirroring, as brought to us in Aristotle's *Poetics,* still carries enormous weight (see Rorty 1980). It is seen in mainstream literatures as providing unassailable grounds for cultural understanding and political analysis even when the very notion of grounds has become so philosophically shaky, no one would knowingly choose to secure anything to it. It's my feeling that women should be particularly suspicious of mirrors. The retrograde looking-glass world we've been encouraged to inhabit harbors a cultural black hole disguised as "benign" vanishing point.

Interestingly, ironically, the same theories that have destabilized the principles of realist epistemologies and literatures—and are thereby taken by many feminist theoreticians to be inimical to feminist causes—are responsible for the politically vital, postmodern notions of difference and decentered multiculturalism (the fall of "the" metanarrative), which release the power of the feminine from the status of a subtext. Yet the valorization of realist "grounding" and of accessibility, motivated by democratic and inclusive principles, may produce the unintended effect of maintaining women as credulous readers in the passive state (Flax 1992).

I know that the amorous scene has already been viewed and consumed in several of its strategies, I know that, I know that, repeated, it determines the opening and the vanishing point of all affirmation.

Brossard 1990, 41

In traditions of picturing, light is secondhand and written word is destined always to come *after*—after the fact, after the fall of the fact (from Platonic forms or biblical grace of not needing to know), after thought, after image (Jean Baudrillard's vanishing point), and of course, in Harold Bloom's Freuding frenzy, after every other writer's *after*. One would think Bloom's (1973) Romantic image of the male writer in an agon of "belatedness" might be exotic or irrelevant for those of us to whom language has appeared devoid of precedents created in the image of woman—low on *mater*pieces. Instead many of us have found it enviable—a condition to emulate. Hence the effort to establish a rival, mirror-image women's canon.

This ambition attempts to remedy the frightening absence of the feminine in *history*. The cultural memory embedded in all those language games where women have had little if any power has indeed felt like a negative—a sense of the absent (m)other, where the prototypical "other" is woman, where in fact the assumption into culture of the male child is coterminus with an emotional dropping of the *m* from mother. So the poignant title of an emblematic book on "The Emergence of Women's Poetry in America," Alicia Ostriker's *Stealing the Language* (1986), strikes a familiar, ominous note. Since she takes it as conceded that language has not been women's domain, Ostriker concludes that we must pilfer and loot among its male-inscribed artifacts. As in Judith Butler's account of the eminent domain of phallogocentrism, our most active/aggressive role is limited to subversion. We can defiantly expose ourselves as strong women in the pictures we make with "their" language, embed these pictures in forceful stories, and create a new mythology that "portrays" women as heroic models, but this is always done in full cognizance of the degree to which we remain exiles in a foreign tongue.

In her final chapter, "Thieves of Language: Women Poets and Revisionist Mythology," Ostriker writes,

> Women writers have always tried to steal the language. Among poets more than novelists, the thefts have been filching from the servants' quarters. When Elaine Marks surveys the Écriture féminine movement in Paris, she observes that in its manifestos of desire "to destroy the male hegemony" over language, "the rage is all the more intense because the writers see themselves as prisoners of the discourse they despise. But is it possible," she asks, "to break out?" Does there exist, as a *sub*terranean current *below* the surface structure of male-oriented language, a specifically female language, a "mother tongue"?

. . . [A] number of empirical studies in America seem to confirm that insofar as speech is "feminine," its strength is limited to evoking *subjective* sensation and interpersonal responsiveness; it is not in other respects perceived as authoritative; it does not command men's respect. The question of whether a female language, separate but equal to male language, either actually exists or can (or should) be created, awaits further research into the past and further gynocentric writing in the present. (1986, 211; emphasis added)

The contemporary women writers Ostriker valorizes have followed Anne Sexton and Sylvia Plath from a uniquely anguished "I" to an instructively, communally victimized "We"—re/presenting a solidarity of defiant images, which unfortunately remain unresolvable—and therefore inactive—in the alien chemistry of patriarchal language. (Is it because what has in the past been characterized as feminine language has not been authoritative, i.e., respected by men, that Ostriker so summarily passes over its possibilities?) This leaves the structural trap of the "phallogocentric" language intact. Since images created by women do not impress what are still seen as male linguistic arbiters, these images cannot really enter, much less transform the language. Yet they are all we are "allowed," or, to use Ostriker's image, all that is detachable enough to be filched. In Ostriker's Steinbergian languagescape of deeded real estate and men's club, "pride of lions" architectural improvements, we might snatch a *flower, branch,* or *bone* from the masculine metanarrative. Or, better yet, an assertively female vocabulary—*womb, breast, vagina, menses*—but not a dynamic principle—not a grammar or syntax to live by. Sure, says the (male) architect or contractor, you can do what you like as long as you don't fool with anything structural (see Foucault 1979).

If this picture of male, linguistic hegemony were actually the case, then we might be inclined to agree that all we can do is make the best of what we can get away with by theft or subversion. (The degradation implicit in this image is startling!) But this is not only a dismal picture of the politics of gender, it is a questionable picture of language and culture itself—one that shares Butler's mirror image, after Freud-Lacan/Foucault/Rich, of culture as inescapably masculinist and "compulsorily heterosexual":

> That the power regimes of heterosexism and phallogocentrism seek to augment themselves through a constant repetition of their logic, their metaphysic, and their naturalized ontologies does not imply that repetition itself ought to be stopped—as if it could be. . . . [T]he crucial question emerges: What kind of subversive repetition might call into question the regulatory practice of identity itself? (Butler 1990a, 32)

What Ostriker calls for in the face of seemingly insurmountable obstacles to "owning" "the" language is the manufacture of bigger and better (i.e., heroic) female images, turning the "project of defining a female self" into a construction site for a full-fledged, woman-centered mythology—a male hegemonic form which Ostriker thinks we can renovate to represent women authoritatively in the public domain. The project is yet another "subversion" of image into mirror image and swallows Bloom's "strong poet" ethos whole: "Where women write strongly as women, it is clear that their intention is to subvert and transform the life and literature they inherit. . . . [R]evisionist mythmaking in women's poetry is a means of redefining both woman and culture" (211).

But transforming a life is not the same as redecorating a poem or house with stolen or even legitimately acquired accessories. I fear this is a desperate and futile solution in a world-text which constructs the feminine itself as domesticated ornament/image rather than publicly effective, active principle. To the extent that Ostriker fails to link the feminine with dynamic processes already in the language, she condemns the female writer to lurk in the subjective (private), subterranean, subaltern world of subversive self-definition. What is most useful to us now—images of the female or enactments of the feminine?[4]

[Working Note: Is the following a useful distinction?

A use theory of meaning, one that locates the making of meaning in a collaborative engagement with interdynamically developing forms (rather than in the interpretation of a fossil signified), allows exploration of the medium of language itself, and thus the invention of new grammars, where subject-object, master-mater relations can never be presupposed, where nothing ever shrinks and stabilizes into an irreversible "it." The picture is the prototypical "it." "It" lies in obeisance to processes outside "it"self that, left to their own devices, are not compressible into single units. (To counteract just this John Cage pledges to imitate, not nature, but her processes.) What once flowed in all directions at "once" is reduced to the servitude of the inanimate. In the picture all has been isolated in space and stopped in time, reflecting not glorious, multifarious (chaotic)[5] reality, but the vanishing point of the photographer's, painter's, or writer's single-point imagination.]

FIG. 1

I feel you climbing toward me
your cleated bootsoles leaving   their geometric bite
colossally embossed   on microscopic crystals
as when I trailed you in the Caucasus
Now I am further
ahead   than either of us dreamed   anyone would be
I have become
the white snow packed like asphalt by the wind

> the women I love   lightly flung   against the mountain
> that blue sky
> our frozen eyes unribboned   through the storm
> we could have stitched that blueness   together   like a quilt

This is the third stanza of Rich's "Phantasia for Elvira Shatayev" (1978, 4–5). In an epigraph Rich explains that Shatayev was the "leader of a women's climbing team, all of whom died in a storm on Lenin Peak, August 1974. Later Shatayev's husband found and buried the bodies." The "I" of the poem is the voice of Shatayev addressing her husband. The poem ends,

> In the diary torn from my fingers I had written:
> *What does love mean*
> *what does it mean "to survive"*
> *A cable of blue fire ropes our bodies*
> *burning together in the snow We will not live*
> *to settle for less We have dreamed of this*
> *all of our lives*

(6)

It is easy to equate this ill-fated, "heroic" (inspiring?) expedition with a search for the cognitive, emotional, social domain of woman. Shatayev, who in the past trailed behind her husband's assault on Mounts "Blank" (we can imagine him planting flags on countless geological bulges, naming them *his*), has now achieved what might be seen as the ultimate claim to eminent domain—she has, along with her companions, literally become part of the mountain. More importantly, she has become a symbol of the literally monumental: image frozen onto the side of a mountain like the faces at Mount Rushmore. I do mean this seeming contradiction in terms—"symbolically literal." The logical torque here is related to the conjunction of this Romantic/heroic scene with the language of women's self-help manuals ("we will not . . . settle for less") and the language of unrealized fantasy ("we have dreamed of this all of our lives"). The poem contains the entire range from immanent to eminent (as modeled by worldwide machismo) domain. But the symbolically literal is not the literal itself. Like all symbolism it stands "in place of."

What does it mean to be inspired by a poem like this, with its finished surface and Romantic fatalism, to be literarily filled with its breath? Secondhand breath is no more appealing to me than secondhand light. I would rather conspire (active voice) than be inspired (passive voice). To conspire (to breathe together) is to participate in the construction of a living aesthetic event. But this requires a different kind of form—one not so authoritatively intelligible, one that in other wise enacts a continuing articulation of silence.

I chose to look at "Phantasia for Elvira Shatayev" because, like so much of Rich's poetry, it has touched a wide audience. Its passionate, collective self-expression (voices rending the silence of forbidden dreams) may indeed move the reader. But what does it mean to "be moved" (passive voice) by the kind of language game that forms this poem? This is a significantly different dynamic from that of a poetic language game whose unfinished surface requires the reader to behave as fully empowered participant. Think—as Wittgenstein did—of a chess game in which "to move" (active voice), to calculate and imagine, is to collaboratively develop the future configuration in/with which one lives. Here, to understand is to invent, not merely to "get the point."

The didactic implication embedded in the sort of literature that the current pantheon (the new old-girls canon) of received feminist writers represents directs the reader toward the subjectivity of empathetic identification and away from autonomous, critical production. The prompt for female reader as writer (from Ostriker and Butler, as well as Rich et al.) is, after all, toward repetition with a difference (replication of a value structure that valorizes heroics, as well as lyrical forms that mimic logical proofs—where epiphany = conclusion) rather than radical experiments that generate a proliferation of formal possibilities; possibilities that have, incidentally, much less to do with territory, ownership, and rights (all important issues in extraliterary arenas such as courts of law) than with the invention of new, poethical forms of life. Repetition with a difference may just not be different enough.

What's most interesting about the section from Theresa Hak Kyung Cha's *DICTEE* ("Erato   Love Poetry," quoted at the beginning of this essay) is not the picture she presents but the active dis-closure of her language. It seems at first glance to be solidly within the tradition of images-of-women lit, but it presents obvious constructive problems for this kind of reading. The first is how this text is printed in the book; it is part of an interaction of facing pages that only when folded together fill all the space. They are negative mirror images of one another: where one is blank the other is emprinted and vice versa. The act of closing the book, of folding these empty and full spaces into one another, takes on a strangely sexual quality (alerting readers to the odd cohabitations of words and words, ink and paper). But this is no easy sexual union, since one knows, though one will never see it, that this will never be one, continuous text—when the book is closed, the interfacing type will always face in opposite directions.

This text is in Roland Barthes's words, a kind of "lover's discourse": "Language is a skin: I rub my language against the other. It is as if I had words instead of fingers, or fingers at the tip of my words" (Barthes 1978, 73) . . . and yet this language touches only the emptiness of the other (opposite) page. That this text is designed to interpolate itself into emptiness/silence—to let emptiness/silence in—gives it breathing space: possibilities of in- and ex-halation, for writer and reader alike. I'd like to suggest that it is a woman's feminine text (denying any redundancy), which implicitly acknowledges and creates the possibility of other/additional/simultaneous texts. This is a model significantly different from Bloom's competitive anxiety of influence. It opens up a distinction between the need to imprint/impress one's mark (image) on the other, and an invitation to the other's discourse . . .

If we try to look at the relationship between *she* and *he* in "Erato," using the model of depiction, we discover that the silence that is enacted by the syntactical stops and starts of this blurred genre (prose-poetry?) blurs gender as well. It is her/his silence. This is not a PC world, nor is it reactionary. It is really not *a* world at all, but discourse in process—neither simple nor finished. The texts in *DICTEE* in fact operate much more like forms of life than pre-encoded, formally congealed, literary artifacts. Their energies don't come from the projection of images but, to the extent that they enlist images at all, from their grammatical/syntactical, particle-wave interruption. Cha's poetry is not the reflection of a mind that is "made up." It is a permeable membrane—the kind characteristic of living organisms.

A CONFLUENCE OF SILENCES:

We forget that we must always return to zero in order to pass from one word to the next.

John Cage, *For the Birds*

Don't for heaven's sake, *be afraid of talking nonsense! But you must pay attention to your nonsense.*

Ludwig Wittgenstein, *Culture and Value*

Probable probably is the most that they can say.

Gertrude Stein, *How to Write*

Nicole Brossard's, Theresa Hak Kyung Cha's, Carla Harryman's words, the spaces between them, lead us to a prospect—an overview, not oversight—of the medium of language itself, the medium with which we must become so intimate and at home that we stop worrying about ownership and legitimacy (asserting rights of domain) and start using it for the sort of experiment and invention that brings us into transformative interaction with the worlds that languages betroth[6] and create. What I want to suggest, "after Judith Butler," is that to make really productive and useful gender/genre trouble is not to repeat old forms with a difference (parodic or not) but to open up radical explorations into silence—the currently unintelligible—in which our future may make sense.

The question then is not how to exit our silence. Not how we move from immanent to eminent domain. Not how to raise our voices loud enough to be heard in what is currently advertised as "the" legitimate and intelligible forum of patriarchal culture. We already know how to do this: by reflecting the values of established, male-dominated, power structures. Instead, let's think of how we can amplify the knowledge of/in our silence, our not so much *non*sense as additional or other sense, our *im*probabilities, our unintellig*a*bilities . . . creating new forms of intelligibility. This is where our feminist project overlaps with Wittgenstein's, Beckett's, Stein's, Cage's. And with contemporary women writers working within largely unrecognized traditions in active (formal) transgression of genre/gender markers.

They are at this very moment making sense of the unintelligible in their art.[7] And that sense is a breath of fresh air. It strives to avoid the eternal return to hermetic traps in old forms of life tainted by the system(at)ic devaluation of feminine forms. New intelligibilities have been much ignored because what is validated as intelligible, what makes easily accessible sense—what is prized and rewarded[8]—is indeed repetition/replication of structure (a kind of bioconservatism) supporting the aesthetic edifice of an establishment currently enjoying privileges of legitimacy. I want to suggest that there may be more loss than gain when the codes of intelligibility and legitimacy that we know, and that "know" us, all too well are—in an atmosphere of resigned reiteration—appropriated *subver*sively by women's writing. These codes are structural elements in rationalized value systems that derive their force from the extent to which they are constructed and defended in terror of the experimental and the feminine.

NOWFORSOMETHINGNOTCOMPLETELYDIFFERENTNOWFORSO

II. FRENCH FREUD FEMINISM?

What can "feminist" writing possibly mean? Images of the female as persons, strong and weak, admirable and despicable occur in the writing of both men and women. These images, pictures, vignettes, no matter how "progressive" the narrative in which they are embedded, cannot be said to constitute either feminine or feminist writing. Only form—stylistic enactment (aesthetic behavior)—can be feminine. What society has called feminine forms have always been available to both men and women in art as well as life. Feminist writing occurs only when female writers use feminine forms. . . . At precisely that moment of enactment, feminism as polemic disappears: the female writer has entered the world of the living.

Genre Tallique, *Glances*

The use of this quotation and what will follow are hardly intended as an argument from authority. (Who is Genre Tallique anyway!?) On the contrary, it may be that too much authority has vested feminist theory (its rhetorics) to date. And with just that verily patriarchal charge, we seek to escape.[9] Consider vestments of the Freud-Lacan-plex, for instance, playing out its trans-Oedipal love or death masquerade with some of the best and brightest of the intellectual daughters. Positioning feminist theory in an outpost of gendered *post*ness at the very moment when it should be inventing itself anew. Not that I claim freedom from what Tallique has called "this Electracution" (*cette Électrecution),* a sinister cauterizing of the presumed gender wound that invites the feminine to remain transfixed at the mirror stage. (Or in the pre-Oedipal *eros interruptus* of an *écriture féminine* dedicated to "writing one's own body"?)

To be a part of twentieth-century Western Civ is unavoidably to find psychoanalytic narratives winding their *strasse*s and *rue*s through one's mind. In the impacted setting of the psychoanalytic "family romance,"[10] where one's cultural space is delimited by the narrative outline of a nineteenth-century authorial parentage and "name of the father" imprimatur, our understanding of a very curious vanishing point (beyond which lies—who knows what?—everything else!) may be obstructed. Punctuating the grammar of this perspectival artifice, it lies in wait for bounders and transgressors by locating nothing more or less than the farthest reach of the authorial point of view.

In the Freudian master-narrative (and that of his disciple, Lacan), the vanishing point is tagged "resistance" or "denial." Try to pass beyond, and it returns you home, chastened, to the land of single-point perspective. That point for women is simply this: to the extent that we venture onto the post-Oedipal playing field of culture, our every role, every move is defined by the "law of the father" in search of good wife and mother. This is another installment in the fictive creation of the "eternal feminine" within what Butler calls the "heterosexual matrix." She says in a note,

> I use the term *heterosexual matrix* . . . to designate that grid of cultural intelligibility through which bodies, genders, and desires are naturalized. I am drawing from Monique Wittig's notion of the "heterosexual contract" and, to a lesser extent, on Adrienne Rich's notion of "compulsory heterosexuality" to characterize a hegemonic discursive/epistemic model of gender intelligibility that assumes that for bodies to cohere and make sense there must be a stable sex expressed through a stable gender (masculine expresses male, feminine expresses female) that is oppositionally and hierarchically defined through the compulsory practice of heterosexuality. (Butler 1990a, 151)

Beyond the vanishing point lie shocking scenes: in which exposed negatives reveal a dominatrix with polymorphously perverse appetites and ambitions wreaking havoc in the popular maxiseries, "Civilization and Miss Content." For Freud, poly *without invidious comparison* is always safely and emblematically pre-Oedipal:[11] an immature psychological grammar in which subject has not yet bored in on object via singularly motivated, culturally targeted verb. What has occurred for women in this grim fairy tale is something akin to emotional clitorectomy. A situation in which the little girl's assumed complicity in the patriarchal construction of the "eternal feminine" means that she must simultaneously valorize and relinquish her femaleness as both agent and object of desire. The rich polymorphous text of early female experience is thereby reduced to threatened/ing subtext—for women a source of guilt, confusion, self-loathing, enervation . . . When little girls are asked to stop desiring the feminine, and instead to affect it (boys are put in an equivalent position with respect to the masculine), they are no longer exploring vibrant performative gender/genre possibility, but fleeing in fear toward its underexposed image. This regression is astonishingly what is called "development" (maturation) in the psychoanalytic fairy tale. Can we imagine instead a scenario in which maturing, gaining power in one's culture (medium of growth), means actively (disruptively) participating in one's own gender/genre construction by choosing among the multiple logics of a complex, pragmatic realism, rather than passively receiving the imprint of a distilled, idealized, fully commoditized (and phallicized) "symbolic"—that is, *image* of the feminine?

Freud was, perhaps above all else, a great prose stylist. The literary paradigm of psychoanalytic persuasion and plausibility is, as Freud ruefully/pridefully admitted, the novella (see Gay 1978, 51–55). Bruno Bettelheim, in *The Uses of Enchantment* (1977), finds Freud's case studies close to the narrative/symbolic structures of German fairy tales. What this form entails is a persuasive grammar that gathers force from a particular kind of analogical, metaphorical (symbolic) thinking—with the presumption that as/like, and stands-for relations yield "deeply" significant meaning. This is a structure in which symbolic codes stabilize an economy of equivalences and equilibria; one in which, via circularly reinforcing logics, it is easy to maintain an *über*phallus as the equivalent of the entire system. But the symbolic is not the only logical or associative order of meaning. There is metonymy as well as metaphor; there are complex, fluid-dynamically interactive models, as well as equivalences. The phallus that stands alone and apart from the fray, like the Romantic genius or "strong poet" it props up, may spawn a symbolic logic (subject to dire internal phallacy) that is far less useful to the human enterprise than the *mater*ial of a poethical process, neither *pre* nor *post*, but in full medias mess.

Meanwhile there are other compelling forces in Freud's narrative style. It operates very skillfully in the mode of an Aristotelian rhetoric of persuasion. In the psychoanalytic narrative, the rhetorical *ethos* (appeal to respect for the author's character) has been that of courageous patriarchal genius; *pathos* (appeal to our emotions) that of deeply, aesthetically sensitive patriarchal genius; *logos* (appeal to our respect for informative logic) that of rationally masterful, historically knowledgeable, patriarchal genius.[12] It is the confluence of these characteristics in Freud's and, with a different flavor, Lacan's prose that vested the protopsychoanalytic narrative with authority (Ostriker's major concern) and "intelligibility" (Butler's).

The current foregrounding of this narrative form in which author is omniscient translator-interpreter of the symbolic code will perhaps ultimately be most useful in revealing its limitations: its bequest of only one of all possible worlds, its suffocatingly airtight hermeneutics, its aggressive strategy of "surgical" depth charges—spuming, always, into foreordained symbolic (phallic erective, orgasmic, projective) epiphany. Is there room for an "experimental feminine" here, or even for the spirit of a postmodern eclecticism—much less for the invention of new rules? We know that Luce Irigaray was actually expelled from Lacan's seminar when she deviated (rather minimally, as it turns out) from his "law-of-the-father" symbolic order.

In this "progressive" cultural tragedy (drama of the inevitable), we are forever children shaped by the authorial tyranny of the father—sons carrying on the name, the law, the primary text; daughters in dress-up costumes tagged Elektra, Jocasta, Iphigenia, Clytemnestra, Medea. Like all "other" disenfranchised peoples, the daughters can submit or self-destruct. We can rebel, displace, deconstruct, subvert but only in the ongoing *sub*text that is our purported destiny. We cannot author our own play.

Such a model is only plausible if we subject our field of vision to the rules of a metarhetorical perspective, an authority that fastens and maintains a nonrational *sub*text on a nineteenth-century logomotive track where everything either obeys or resists (negative acknowledgment of power) the syntactic impulsion toward recognition of the father as author as father as author. . . . . . .and participates in the ritual culling toward a well-rounded narrative vanishing point—*the* point where/when all that does not hug the textual track is expelled in self-fulfilling linguistic fatalism. With Lucifer, and Luce Irigaray, goes a different light/voice/text only to return as the re-/op-/de-pressed. Isn't this all too familiar? Don't we have to consider that to replicate this (psychoanalytic) model in feminist theory may be to perpetuate an exclusionary and suffocating grammar in which to "make sense," to be "authoritative"/"intelligible," is to underwrite one's subjugation to a system whose very "grounding" is a scorn for the feminine (as negative image of the masculine)—mistrust of the open, multiple, juxtapositional, unexpectedly, teemingly noisy silent? In grounding *the* symbolic order (assumed as *the* only order, even to the point of defining *dis*order) in the long shadow of the name of the father, we surely remain, not "necessarily" trapped in our cultural context—as Butler and other postpsychoanalytic feminists "concede"—but audience to the shadow theater in Plato's misogynist cave. Why then the voluntary subjection of feminist theoreticians to the tawdry outcome of this narrative line?

Oddly, interestingly, the defensive desire for *our* own "grounding" has had the paradoxical effect of making us, as literary feminists, resistant to the use of "feminine forms," which are neither authoritative nor intelligible by current establishment standards. This, I think, is the terminus of a theoretical line whose narrative is entirely constructed on narrow *pre* and *post* axes: pre- and postcultural, pre- and post-Oedipal, pre and post-genital—ignoring the complex, polymorphous, exploded-cartoon contemporaneity of all active thinking experience. In this Western Out-Post (who can outpost whom?) movie, the proverbial (pre- and post-verbal) heroine is still tied to the tracks in the silent film; she *will* be run over by a Freudian-Lacanian logomotive because there are no parallel/other tracks, no sidelines or margins in which the possibility of liberation lurks, no topological warps or additional dimensions in the flatland narrativescape, no choice of vanishing points. Most importantly, there are no alternatives to finding herself in this position to begin with. The possibility of plural possibilities is excluded by the marked telo-singularity of the probable.

[**Working quote: "The critical task for feminism is not to establish a point of view outside of constructed identities; that conceit is the construction of an epistemological model that would disavow its own cultural location. . . . The critical task is, rather, to locate strategies of subversive repetition."** (Butler 1990a, 147)]

In the latest remake of this Classic Western, the woman tied to the tracks may be a feminist who can theorize, parodize, ironize her position but not escape it.[13] This movie is being shot, not in some flimsily constructed studio you see, but on location—*the* "cultural location." This is the outcome of the scenario of *Gender Trouble,* where the proposed response to entrapment in narrowly binary, essentialist gender identities is literally to make gender trouble by means of parody and pastiche—an enactment that, since it is bound to repeat the cultural inscriptions that locate it, may problematize the received metanarrative of gender, but not really complicate it with extra or alternative, that is, radically different, models. The radical swerve of real gender/genre trouble is perhaps possible only when we recognize what has been the continual (constituting) presence of feminine forms in language. That is, that the Freudian-Lacanian logomotive is among many trains of thought entering into the messy *poly*lectics and logues that constitute the live culture of our language.

What I am looking for, then, is a polymorphous startling point (yes, I meant that) from which can spring the possibility of a feminist poethics—an aesthetic practice that reveals, in the course of its enactment, the powers of feminine poetics in female hands. Hands that, freed from holding mirror/speculum to exemplary instances (images) of an immaculately or disgracefully conceived feminine-incarnate, can be caught "red handed," with many, extra-Edenic fruits, at large, in the world. This is not to disavow the necessary investigation and analysis of the boundaries that have defined women's lives (nor of selected, testimonial images within those boundaries), but to suggest that we (a literary "we") are at a juncture where/when the radii of possibili*ties* must stretch beyond the mirror stage.

The room inside me has disappeared. At night, when all is quiet, I no longer hear the pictures shifting on the walls when I walk fast. Only the pump in the basement. I wonder whether the space has folded in on itself like a tautology, or been colonized. You think the wine has washed it out, and it's true that the mirror tilted at a reckless angle. I still have the floor plan with measurements, but now that nothing corresponds to it I can only take it as part of the emptiness I try to cover up with writing. To know my blind spot. I have always wanted to dilate my landscape for the piano and the long labor of losing the self. Though I am too nearsighted for clouds. If I had lived a different image.

Waldrop 1987, 71

We know, with the help of Foucault, Butler, and others that the power to make useful meaning (OE *mænan*—to mean/to moan) of one's historical experience does not lie in discerning outlines of one's "nature" (in fact the only hope for the categorically oppressed lies in constructionist readings of history that expose the political contingency of categories), or in regressive justification of one's role in it, or in retroactively raising collective self-esteem (these are all strategies of victimization), but rather to fuel the project of inventing a polymorphous future. To move from the simple harmonics of moans (whether of pain or jouissance) to a polyphony of exploratory means; from narrative therapy to linguistic experiment; from a picture theory of meaning, where what constitutes object, frame, and focus is always determined in advance by established arbiters, to a use theory of meaning that opens meaning to radical revision "in the act" of moving forward, the invention of multiple language games and new forms of life.

Is it plausible to think of the possibilities of a literary feminism in this way? If it is, then perhaps the sense of entrapment in *the* language-culture with *a* predetermined power structure/symbolic coherence dooming us to *an* "eternal feminine"—defined always in opposition (passive or active) to an equally "eternal" (not to say "universal") masculine—can be superseded, so that we can cancel our ad nauseam encores as an ambiguously grinning, (sub-textual) female repressed. So that we can assume the unambiguously active (textual) project of entertaining the multiple, complex possibilities of our languages and lives. There are of course obstacles. Chief among them has been the picture theory of gender—the essentialist lodging of the feminine in female bodies—as well as symbolic orders from the Freud-Lacan-plex. This has meant, among other things, that in attempting to identify and construct a strong feminine tradition in literature the search for ancestors has been limited to writers who enacted a preordained symbolic code and who could retroactively pass the Olympic committee's hormonal assay as "F."

The most interesting thing about our "different *voices*" may be that feminine modes of thinking as they are currently located and described are, with respect to masculine modes, radically and robustly asymmetrical. Not *post* but *extra,* nurtured in the playing field of complexity, they are culturally constructed as commodious, accommodating, generous, multiple. To invoke the *non* that calls up presence rather than absence, they are at their best nonabsolutist, nonpurist, and nonhierarchical. In not precluding otherness, the feminine as dia- or poly-lectical force that is always an "other" among nothing but "others," leaves us with the humorous prospect that the only thing excluded in principle from the feminine is not even the masculine, but only the devices of exclusion themselves.

NOTES FROM A CONSTRUCTION SITE

(with scenes from a somewhat different film:
figures shift and grounds grow slippery)

> *Gender/genre is pure experiment (as every boundary construction is a gamble, a dare, a hypothetical with consequences). That most have chosen to repeat old experiments does not logically negate the possibility of new forms; it is simply an indication of the degree to which cultures tend to discourage the disruptions of radical curiosity. . . . But there are energetic experimental traditions in our culture as well—in the arts and the sciences. It is in their directions our lucky glance will fall. "Glance," yes. I refuse the word "gaze." The "gaze" as we know all too well turns self and other to stone. The glance has lightness; it can lift off at will, in the gossamer breeze of chance, of un coup de dés, of the unexpected.*
> —Genre Tallique, *Glances*

Gerard Depardieu: [Catherine Deneuve], certain people think you're cold. You're simply direct, frank and unambiguous. People think you're serene and organized: I've never seen anyone so disordered or so capricious with money and belongings. . . . You are stronger, more responsible, more armored than male actors. You are less vulnerable, and doubtless this is the paradox of real femininity. Catherine Deneuve is the man I'd like to be.
Catherine Deneuve: For a woman, I'm quite masculine, you know, in the relations I have toward people, men. All of them, I don't make much difference. And I think it's the way I'm quite straightforward, you know, and he can love me as a man. I understood what [Depardieu] meant, you know, because he has a very feminine quality and I have a masculine quality. I don't try to charm, I have quite strong and straight relations with people. In film it's different. In films you are a character and woman, much more woman than me.
Henry Allen: She doesn't charm. She doesn't have to, with that face: It seems like an aesthetic principle she totes on her shoulders like a jar of water. You find yourself watching her rather than listening to her. The jawline is so long, the face is so big. You find yourself trying to make her smile, to arouse her interest. Not like Tom Sawyer walking a fence for Becky Thatcher, but more like a geisha girl entertaining a Japanese businessman. You try to intrigue this woman who does

> not try to intrigue you. You begin to see what Depardieu meant. You are the
> woman and she is the man.
>
> —Henry Allen, "Deneuve's Masculine Mystique"

In its binary dialectic, feminine/masculine is the Western yin/yang—as ubiquitous and unstable, contradictory and paradoxical as any dualistic principle appealed to for explanations of everything. Depardieu, Deneuve, Allen are caught in a language game that must tag every move M or F. They are, here, on this stage, daring players. But there's still no sign of a form of life that can support polymorphous "persons" whose moves are not self-classifications but experiments in a world of uncompressible possibility. Does such possibility exist? If we abandon the notion of the cultural dynamic as pre-dominantly (phallic) symbolic, can we move toward a new paradigm of culture as *poethical* process, where a primary engagement takes place in transformative interactions with the material presence of heterogeneous bodies and forms? In fleeing a narrowly constructed Ken and Barbie essentialism, can responsively playful social construction broaden the field of genre/gender and spring us from the mind of that bourgeois gentilhomme for whom all that is not *x* is *y*, and vice subversa?

III. GENRE TROUBLE:

THE EXPERIMENTAL FEMININE

I know that it is simplistic. And it is wrong. When one does not recede to the oversight of the western philosophical tradition. But when visa versa? Overseeing the recession of it? I speak my mind or not without receding. In this case memory is a negative. Repetition and jargon.

Carla Harryman, "Dimblue"

We need to recognize the strangeness of what we thought we recognized. The only reliable mirrors are in the fun house.

Dita Fröller, *"New Old World Marvels"*

The "feminine" has for some time located the open and receptive, the materially and contextually inventive. Men, like Joyce, Pound, and Duchamp, could be feminine in their art, but not their life. Women could be feminine in their life, but not their art (note the conspicuous absence of names here). Gertrude Stein, playing the role of scientifically trained investigator and cultivating the demeanor of a Roman emperor, was uniquely positioned to explore the experimental feminine.

Genre Tallique, *Glances*

WHAT!?

First. An oversight.

The experimental feminine draws us on . . . .
. . . .
(long) after *Goethe, Freud, Lacan*

Here's a curious thing. If, as good social constructionists (neither essentialists nor biologists), we note current identifications of "the feminine"—that it is open, diffuse, multiple, complex, decentered, filled with silence, fragmented, incorporating difference and the other (Hélène Cixous, Luce Irigaray, et al.); undefinable, subversive, transgressive, questioning, dissolving identity while promoting ethical integrity (Julia Kristeva, Judith Butler, et al.); *mater*ially and contextually pragmatic, employing nonhierarchical and nonrationalist associative logics— "weblike" connective patterns (Carol Gilligan); self- and other interrupted, tentative, open/interrogative (Sally McConnell-Ginet, Mary Field Belenky, et al.); marginal, metonymic, juxtapositional, destabilizing, heterogeneous, discontinuous. . . . (Genre Tallique, Craig Owens, Page duBois, Janet Wolff)[14] and now if we look for enactments of these modes in the formal strategies of literature, we find first that from the late nineteenth century on they are most often found in work that falls within experimental or avant-garde traditions— that is, anti- or extraestablishment (both modern and postmodern)—and, secondly, that though these modes relate more closely to the life experiences of women, they have been, until relatively recently, chiefly utilized by male artists.

you will have a little voice it will be barely audible you will whisper in his ear you will have a little life you will whisper it in his ear it will be different quite different quite a different music you'll see a little like Pim a little life music but in your mouth it will be new to you

This writing, clear precursor to Harryman, Cha, and others in an experimental feminine tradition, is from Samuel Beckett's depunctuated prose poem, *How It Is* (Beckett 1964). We writers who wish to explore/enact the feminine beyond the punctum of a masculinist vanishing point are always looking for ancestors. Well, oddly enough, here is one—in/on/out of silence:

twenty years a hundred years not a sound and I listen not a gleam and I strain my eyes four hundred times my only season I clasp the sack closer to me a tin clinks first respite very first from the silence of this black sap

Beckett 1964, 24–25

And here's another:

riverrun, past Eve and Adam's, from swerve of shore to bend of bay, brings us by a commodius vicus of recirculation. . . .

You know the rest. Beckett and Joyce, both fleeing their patrimony—the law (the grammar) of the Irish father—for the exile of the (m)other tongue . . . .

But how is it that men come to enact the feminine?

Following the logic of the social construction of gender, can it not quite easily turn out that many of our ancestors in a strong tradition of foregrounding "feminine" processes in writing (which can be traced at least as far back as *Tristram Shandy* in the English novel and to Rimbaud's *Illuminations* in poetry) are men? This is merely ironic, not paradoxical; that is, if we skirt the essentialist M/F trap. The power of feminine forms—not the least of which is the power to deconstruct an institutionalized masculine—has been almost exclusively claimed by men, until the latter half of this century. Because this power is simultaneously admired and despised, and—by definition—trespasses on forbidden or uncharted territory, only those who have had the social backing and poethical courage (or naïveté) to risk both confusion and ostracism by the academy have taken on the challenge. Until very recently women have not had the social (public) power and cultural standing to take such risks without almost certainly disappearing beyond emotional and socially constructed vanishing points. We could extend Virginia Woolf's thought experiment, imagining what would have become of Shakespeare's sister and all her hypothetical progeny, to think of lost female literary revolutionaries—the ones who were told early on that they had missed the point, the ones never heard from (in feminine forms) again.

So, alongside Gertrude Stein, Dorothy Richardson, Djuna Barnes, Mina Loy, and (midcareer) Virginia Woolf, there is the much longer list of men: Andrey Beley (of the four prose symphonies, 1902–1908), and the Russian futurists, Velimir Khlebnikov and Alexei Kruchenykh; Apollinaire, Artaud, Rimbaud, Mallarmé, Marinetti, Cocteau, Tzara, Jarry, Schwitters, Breton, Raymond Queneau, Georges Perec, Sterne, Whitman, Joyce, Beckett, Pound, the Eliot-Pound collaboration in *The Waste Land*, W. C. Williams, Zukofsky (not forgetting the Louis-Celia Zukofsky collaborations in the "Catullus," "A-24," etc.). Jackson Mac Low, Ian Hamilton Finlay, Augusto de Campos, Bob Cobbing. . . . William Burroughs, Gilbert Sorrentino, David Antin, Walter Abish. . . . . The list of course could go on and on.

There are only three women among seventy-seven writers represented in Emmett Williams's *Anthology of Concrete Poetry* (1967); three women of twenty-three writers in Eugene Wildman's *Experiments in Prose* (1969). In Marjorie Perloff's *The Poetics of Indeterminacy* (1981), Gertrude Stein is the only female poet in a lineage spanning the period from Rimbaud's *Illuminations* (1871) to David Antin and John Cage. (Perloff has since written on many of the contemporary women poets who bring this tradition into the present.) Hugh Kenner includes no women in *The Pound Era* (1971), except for a slighting reference to H.D. On the whole, these books are not complicit with mainstream anthologies and criticism in *overlooking* women (at least not before the late 1960s, early 1970s). Women were not in fact very much present (except as handmaidens, models, muses, mid/wives, and mistresses) in the radically experimental literary world until the advent of Language-associated poetries in the 1970s (where, incidently, for the first time, not only the "single" woman, but the wife and/or mother *is* the experimental poet).[15] Two recent Language anthologies have quite different M/F ratios, with women comprising roughly a third of the poets in each: in Ron Silliman's *In the American Tree* (1986), twelve out of forty poets are women; seven of twenty poets are women in Douglas Messerli's *"Language" Poetries* (1987).[16]

If anything, it has become evident since these two anthologies came out that even their M/F ratios do not adequately represent the unprecedented number of women in the new poetry movements in this country. However, most women writers are still writing in styles with mainstream or established genealogies (e.g., the confessional and multigenerational New York schools, the new-old lyric idyll) acceptable to the masculinized academy—writing within the standard/ized stock of poetic genres. Even while espousing a new politics, not forging a new poetics. Woolf herself returned to a conservative (masculine?) style in her last novels after exploring revolutionary feminine forms (indebted to both Dorothy Richardson and James Joyce) in *Jacob's Room* and *The Waves,* and performing that humorous postmodern experiment, *Orlando.* Richardson was of course effectively forgotten in the wake of *Ulysses;* Mina Loy is just beginning to be rescued from oblivion; Stein, both the only high-profile female and the most radically experimental poet of this generation, was ridiculed.

It may seem like a betrayal of the few courageous women who are our clear "feminist" ancestors (Tallique's "female writers who use feminine forms"— Richardson, Woolf, Barnes, Loy, Stein) to acknowledge a "feminine" tradition dominated by males. But it is far worse to deny the presence of the feminine in language (as Ostriker and others do) by missing the fact that the feminine has never been exclusively "embodied" in female writers. It is, of course, entirely a question of power. All forms of power are seized by those best situated to take advantage of them. For sociopolitical reasons made painfully clear by the women's movement, women have not until very recently been in a situation to exercise the power of the feminine, only its *sub*versions.

Even in cultures with greater respect for feminine forms—e.g., in the litera- tures of Romance languages—the power of these forms has been explored mainly by men. Look at France, for example, where Montaigne's untidy, digres- sive *essais* could become a model for the (male) stars of the academy. Recent French intellectual writing (Cioran, Blanchot, Barthes, Baudrillard), and even the deconstructionist movement, despite its strikingly macho surface projections, is strangely feminine. Think of Derrida's self-interruptions, his flirtatious insinua- tions, his coy ironies, his outrageous feints, his calculatedly playful exclamations and interrogatives. He teases out metaphysical pre- and con-texts with as potent a mix of charm and venom as any Bette Davis character. (In this "masquerade" he performs something like Butler's parodical, subversive function.)

Perhaps most characteristic of *Ce sexe qui n'en est pas un* (title of Irigaray's book [(1977) 1985b] is the tendency of the feminine gender/genre to exceed masculine cultural paradigms by its messiness, its multiplicity and complexity. For the fifth (and, as it turned out, last) of his Harvard lectures (*Six Memos for the Next Millennium*, 1988) on the formal qualities he most valued in literature, Italo Calvino begins with a quote from the novel *That Awful Mess on the Via Merulana*, by Carlo Emilio Gadda, and then goes on to talk about Gadda's writing and, more generally, about "multiplicity" as a literary manifestation of imaginative possibility in terms which are not only at times almost identical to Gilligan's "web" metaphor for women's thinking, but comprise a virtual catalogue of so-called feminine modes of thinking. The emphasis below is mine:

> I wished to begin with this passage from Gadda because it seems to me an excellent introduction to the subject of my lecture—which is the contemporary novel . . . as a *network of connections* between the events, the people, and the things of the world. . . . Carlo Emilio Gadda tried all his life to represent the world as a knot, a *tangled skein* of yarn; to represent it without in the least diminishing the *inextricable complexity* or, to put it better, the *simultaneous presence of the most disparate elements* that converge to determine every event. . . . As a writer—thought of as the Italian equivalent to James Joyce—Gadda developed a style to match his complicated epistemology, in that it superimposes *various levels of language, high and low,* and uses the most *varied vocabulary.* . . . What is supposed to be a detective novel is left *without a solution.* In a sense, all his novels are *unfinished* or left as *fragments.* . . . [T]he least thing is seen as the center of a *network of relationships* that the writer cannot restrain himself from following, *multiplying the details* so that his descriptions and *digressions* become infinite. . . . The best example of this *web radiating out from every object* is the episode of finding the stolen jewels in chapter nine of That Awful Mess. . . . He does this by exploiting the semantic potential of words, of all the *varieties of verbal and syntactical forms* with their connotations and tones, together with the often comic effects created by their *juxtaposition* . . . Gadda knew that . . . to "know" is to insert something into what is real, and hence to distort reality. (1988, 105–8)

This is not the language of the "law of the father." What is real here is not abstract principle or a hardcore empirical, "innocent" of theory, but the simultaneity of the whole range in "that awful mess." (Beckett also valorizes the "mess.") The complex realist mess that intermixes vocabularies, syntactic trajectories, linguistic origins, descriptive worlds ("high and low") plays out the formal consequences of foregrounding the material presence of language. Strange and humorous swerves occur when close attention to words reveals peculiar energies; synergistic interactions produce an exploding, multidimensional figure expanding toward chaos—or the "feminine novel." This is a poethical practice that depends on humor in the medieval sense of shifting fluids—in this case the highly fluid con/per/ceptual shifts that are necessary to a lively, informing sense of complexity.

Kristeva locates these fluid humors in what she calls the "semiotic" (not to be confused with "semiotics"), prelinguistic, instinctual, libido-sensual experience of all children. The semiotic, as defined by Kristeva, is the fluid, vitalizing source of the (private) pleasures of jouissance,[17] and thus of all that exceeds and circumvents the (public) grammars of "the law of the father." Interestingly, in *Revolution in Poetic Language* ([1974] 1984) Kristeva argues that the pursuit of the good and the ethical are inextricably tied up with a semiotic-based, avant-garde poetic practice. Having identified poetry with jouissance and "revolutionary laughter," having identified laughter *as* practice, and having quoted Lautréamont's "truth-in-practice" *as* poetry (217), Kristeva writes, "[T]he text fulfills its ethical function only when it pluralizes, pulverizes, 'musicates' [truths], which is to say, on the condition that it develop them to the point of laughter" (233). Kristeva feels that the need for poetry of the sort that "pluralizes, pulverizes, 'musicates'" (233) is urgent for all who would act outside the logics of "the machine, colonial expansion, banks, science, Parliament—those positions of mastery that conceal their violence and pretend to be mere neutral legality" (83). The exemplary writers in *Revolution in Poetic Language* are all men: Mallarmé, Bataille, Lautréamont, Joyce. Kristeva's concession to the identification of the semiotic with "woman" is made via Mallarmé, as prototype of avant-garde practice. For him, she says, the "semiotic rhythm" is "indifferent to language, enigmatic, and feminine" (29).

Despite this call for recognition of an avant-garde poetic practice in dialectical agon with "positions of mastery," Kristeva supports the view that the semiotic (or the feminine) cannot directly enter the (phallic/symbolic) linguistic order. For her the semiotic is logically and developmentally "previous" to language. It can only nuance ("musicate") or interrupt language with "semiotic silence." This insidious view (particularly as it appears in Kristeva's work accompanied by the heavy breathing of psychoanalytic drive theory) is not only counterproductive as an ethical base—which must be part of the public/linguistic realm—but experientially counterintuitive and logically flawed. The process of acculturation and learning a language is not one that takes place at the abrupt terminus of a neatly sealed off "pre-" period. Language is, for most infants, part of their highly charged sonic environment from *their* very first *public* moments after birth. (And not long thereafter, part of their visual world as well.) It is just because the learning of language is in rich intercourse with all the multivaried, sensual experiences—the mess of early infancy and childhood—that natural languages are such rich instruments, such complex forms of life, full of connotative, multiply associative, extrarational dimensions that make them the fluid, vital, permeable, and growing organisms that they are. Language has always overflowed the structures/strictures of its own grammars.[18] But even those grammars exceed rationalist caricatures. They are intimately connected with the complex, messy experience of real lives. The so-called feminine is in language from the start. It is not a *sub*-version, but a vital dimension of the nature of the linguistic—of words that always strike us like chords from the neocortical to the instinctive limbic. The most pressing question at hand is not only why these rich aspects of language have been persistently (invidiously!) identified with the feminine, but much more startlingly, why they have recently been theoretically expunged from the realm of the linguistic altogether.

> *The moment of "I know," this turgid moment in the mind. It has assumed all the consequences of male identity. It must therefore ejaculate: it must impregnate or destroy the other with its teleo-terminal logics. But wait, let's interrupt this trajectory. Attention to the complex discontinuities of the feminine in language will explode the shortest distance between points and turn it into a field of sinuous, labyrinthine lanes.*
>
> —Genre Tallique, *Glances*

MORE GENRE TROUBLE

MULTIPLICITY AND UNINTELLIGIBILITY: THE EXPERIMENTAL FEMININE

> What allows our free will to be a meaningful notion is the complexity of the universe or, more precisely, our own complexity.
> —David Ruelle, *Chance and Chaos*

> The very complexity of the discursive map that constructs gender appears to hold out the promise of an inadvertent and generative convergence of these discursive and regulatory structures. If the regulatory fictions of sex and gender are themselves multiply contested sites of meaning, then the very multiplicity of their construction holds out the possibility of a disruption of their univocal posturing.
> —Judith Butler, *Gender Trouble*

[JR: Pluralize "map" in the first sentence; read "divergence" for "convergence" . . .]
It is she. It is she again. It is preference. Words in the mind on the ground speaking not writing but history in the air. Yellow. For blue. And yellow. For blue

as blue speaking. The first association was arrogance. History and arrogance.
Contemporaneity and oversight. Paring of blue and yellow. Slivers of preference
and literate. As written history might keep. The cool oversight whose soft leaves
water. And later breaking. Slips.

Carla Harryman, "Dimblue"

Yes, and (long) after (even) Wittgenstein, is it not the blue yellow green time to
say "the limits of your language are *not* the limits of my world"? Or better yet, "it
is no more your language than it is my world, and vice versa, with plurals." Ah
the redeeming vice (Ah, the visa!) of verse: to complicate our grammars, to
pluralize our languages and worlds. Verse (OED) "so named from turning to
begin another line."

Here, for instance, is a new line:

> *"A" was for "ox"*
> *The first oxygen conversion occurred as an incline, a*
> *sharp bend as in "wrench". The elements surrounding*
> *it were strong, physically violent ones—wreck, wrestle,*
> *wretch—with the exception of "wren". The next major*
> *activity was "wrinkle", again related to "wrench" with*
> *the addition of "wind". Wrist action proceeded from*
> *there—wrist-lock, wrist-pin, wrist-shot, wrist wrestle,*
> *wristy—preparing us "motor-wise" to write: write our*
> *own ticket, write-down and write-in.*

(Darragh 1981, 5)

And here's another:

> *"elaborative" to "Eleatic" for "D"*
> *"Egg" and "oxygen" both contain "edge", with egg's edge*
> *located at "share" and oxygen's at "shear". The distance*
> *doubles from one to the other along this line: shar et*
> *vb farme atim domin numer iz cti porta acio torti*
> *him sho SHAG low ME L dou sha tio HE min ears cou*
> *ock metim semb dj*

(Darragh 1981, 8)

As Lyn Hejinian (1978) has wriiten,

> *We are parting with description*
> *termed blue may be perfectly blue*

goats do have damp noses
            that test and now I dine drinking with
      others
adult blue butterfly for a swim with cheerful birds
            I suppose we hear a muddle of rhythms in water . . .
                  the streets of traffic are a great success

Coming across Carla Harryman's "Dimblue," being sent by it back to *DICTEE*, reminded of Brossard, Waldrop, Darragh, Hejinian . . . the mind is not put at rest. The traffic of this language is noisy and disruptive . . . full of the formal/ verbal articulation of silence. Neither the streets nor these linguistic bodies go docilely to their preconceived vanishing points. This language does not replicate the science of perspective as we have known it. Nor does it assume the implied movement toward epiphany/conclusion that lyric syntactical momentum has seemed to dictate. It mat(t)ers, not so much as expression of gender but as enactment of genre. That is, the complicated moves it makes take it from expression of female experience to Tallique's "feminine" as aesthetic behavior. It does not deny the consequences of its own material presence by substantiating (and thereby disappearing into) received, masculinized metanarratives. The "it" that mat(t)ers, that behaves like living matter, is language—the material of the writer connected to poethical forms of life. The material in "mattering" is of course linguistic. Nothing can "matter" without words coming alive—spinning contextual, connective, associative webs that not only apprehend the multidimensional realities of what we care about, but enable our variant-radiant intelligences to stretch and transform the complexities of desire and realization.

There's not room for a CATALOGUE RAISONÉ of all the writers who are doing just this. But among the *Cygnes. Paroles souvenus. Deja dit./Vient de dire. Va dire.* (Cha) there are other languages, other worlds:

Ami minden quand un yes or no je le said viens am liebsten hätte ich dich du süfses de ez nem baj das weisst du me a favor hogy innen se faire croire tous less birds from the forest who fly here by mistake als die Wälder langsam verschwinden. Minden verschinden, mind your step and woolf. (Anne Tardos 1992, [n.p.])[19]

OUI. JA. YES.
YES. THIS TIME MOLLY BLOOM'S THE AUTHOR
"IT IS SHE. IT IS SHE AGAIN."
After WOOLF'S roominations

After CARLA HARRYMAN'S *DIMBLUE*
After THERESA HAK KYUNG CHA'S *DICTEE*
After TINA DARRAGH'S *off the corner*
After *et al.*
After the fall of *After the Fall of Adam's Eve*

The most active locus of the exploration and construction of feminine forms in English poetry today is among "Language" and "other" experimental poets. These poets are both male and female of course, but, if Tallique is onto something, it is the women among them who—for the first time in large numbers using "feminine" formal processes—are presenting us with our strongest, most challenging models of literary feminisms. These poetries, these poethical practices—ironically marginalized in established feminist circles—are the experimental feminine that, in active exploration of multiplicity and unintelligibility—in the articulation of silence—draw us on.

Notes

1. D. W. Winnicott makes this important distinction between imagination as playful "work," negotiating a reality principle, and fantasy—daydreaming without consequences—in, for example, *Playing and Reality* (1984).

2. All quotes attributed to Genre Tallique are from *Glances: A Pre-Post-Eros Supposition (Les coups d'oeil: une supposition pré-post-éros)*—prepublication manuscript. All translations are mine.

3. This movement from a picture theory of language to a use theory draws on and parallels Wittgenstein's move from the positivist ambitions of the *Tractatus Logico-Philosophicus* to the *Philosophical Investigations'* use theory, where language is seen as an activity inextricably intertwined with forms of life.

4. I wholly agree with Judith Butler's emphasis on the performative as enactment rather than expression, but not its conflation with performance—a backslide into an old female trap.

5. As understood by the new "complex," non-linear sciences—a balance of order and disorder characterized by pattern bounded unpredictability.

6. I owe this idea to Jerome McGann, who, in correspondence, wrote of truth as "troth."

7. In fact I want to argue that the most original and vital writing being done by women in this country today has come from a very different sort of literary tradition, one that has to do, not with mirroring, but with inventive poethical enactments. By the term, "poethics," I refer to a practice of theory and literature that, following Wittgenstein, takes the primary force of language to be the way in which its uses are enactments, rather than portrayals, of forms of life. For discussions of this kind of tradition, read Marjorie Perloff's *Poetics of Indeterminacy* (1981), *Poetic License* (1990), and *Radical Artifice* (1991); Linda

Reinfeld's *Language Poetry* (1992); Charles Bernstein's *Content's Dream* (1986) and *A Poetics* (1992); Peter Quartermain's *Disjunctive Poetics* (1992).

8. All of the leading lights in the received feminist canon have received prizes, awards, tenured professorships, and endowed chairs from the literary and academic establishments. They are clearly not seen as fundamentally threatening to business as usual in the masculinized academy.

9. I want to distinguish between *patriarchal*—which denotes masculinist authority in the hands of male persons, and which I take to be the closest male equivalent to *feminist*—and *masculine*, which denotes traits found in women as well as men.

10. See Freud's "Family Romances" (1909), which, though one of his briefest essays, securely seals the fate of his progeny to reenact their thralldom to his authority. My reason for conflating Freud and Lacan in a per*plex*ity for women is that the authority of the "law of the father" is already fully established by Freud; Lacan has merely to append the phallic-symbolic with its linguistic permutations.

11. This has been noticed as the only space left, in Freudian-Lacanian psychoanalytic theory, for a feminine not yet under the law of the father. Hence the *pre*mie nature of those modes generically identified with the feminine by the psychoanalytic French feminists— pre-Oedipal, precultural, prelinguistic, presymbolic, that is, generally *pre*(mature?)—in the semiotic of *jouissance,* unable to intermingle with cultural logics or articulate itself linguistically. It is at this point that one must question the whole psychoanalytic structure, breathe in the air outside it, no? Perhaps we must move *forward* into the "unintelligible" that is pushing at the developmental edge of what can be articulated, rather than moving regressively into the prelinguistic, which can—by definition—never be articulated.

12. That Freud was indeed both intellectually and morally courageous, as well as aesthetically and intellectually vital and brilliant, is reason for admiration but not necessarily persuasion.

13. Kierkegaard, iconic ironist himself, (ironically?) makes the point that irony is necessary to productive critique but is not itself a move to a new form or stage of development.

14. For an analysis of ancient Greek constructions of the feminine, and their movement from metaphor to metonymy, see duBois 1988. Janet Wolff writes interestingly of modernist and postmodern constructions of the feminine (1990).

15. This is a radical shift in the gendered demographics of experimental poetry, and directly reflects societywide shifts in gendered demographics following World War II, and the medical and civil rights developments that made it possible for women to take control of their reproductive processes.

16. In a more recent anthology of experimental poetry, *The Art of Practice* (Barone and Ganick 1994), twenty-three of the forty-five poets included are women.

17. In post-Lacanian psychoanalytic theory, jouissance is the literal *je ne sais quois* experience of pre-Oedipal sensual pleasures. It is thought to be lost to direct articulation since its source is pre-symbolic/linguistic. It is also widely identified with the feminine, though Kristeva stresses that it is/has been experienced by, and is therefore available to, both men and women.

18. A fact lost to most linguistic scientists, which may be the reason why French

psychoanalytic theories of language, with their reliance on Saussure, consign language to a rationalist symbolic realm.

19. Tardos's text engages with a representative four (English, French, German, Hungarian) of the multiplicity of languages that articulate our globe, creating a web structure of crosslinguistic, intercultural "unintelligibility" that acts as a field of generous and suggestive semantic play.

Works Cited

Abel, Elizabeth. 1989. *Virginia Woolf and the Fictions of Psychoanalysis*. Chicago: University of Chicago Press.

Addison, Joseph, and Richard Steele. 1965. *The Spectator*. Ed. Donald F. Bond. Oxford: Clarendon Press.

Adorno, Theodor. 1974. "Lyric Poetry and Society." *Telos* 20 (spring): 56–71.

———. 1978. *Minima Moralia: Reflections from a Damaged Life*. Trans. E. F. N. Jephcott. London: NLB.

Allen, Henry. 1993. "Deneuve's Masculine Mystiques." Washington Post, 2 January, D2.

Allen, Paula Gunn. 1991. "Deer Woman." In *Talking Leaves: Contemporary Native American Short Stories*, ed. Craig Lesley and Katheryn Stavrakis, 1–11. New York: Laural.

Altieri, Charles. 1984. *Self and Sensibility in Contemporary American Poetry*. Cambridge: Cambridge University Press.

Altman, Meryl. 1992. "A Prisoner of Biography." *The Women's Review of Books* 9, nos. 10–11 (July): 39–40.

Alurista. 1980. 1971. *Floricanto en Aztlán*. Los Angeles: Chicano Studies Center.

———. "From Tragedy to Caricature . . . and Beyond." *Aztlan* 11:89–98.

Alurista et al., eds. 1976. *Festival de Flor y Canto: An Anthology of Chicano Literature*. Los Angeles: University of Southern California Press.

Anzaldúa, Gloria. 1987. *Borderlands/La Frontera: The New Mestiza*. San Francisco: Spinsters/Aunt Lute.

Arac, Jonathan. 1985. "Afterword: Lyric Poetry and the Bounds of New Criticism." In Hošek and Parker 1985, 345–55.

Ardis, Ann L. 1990. *New Women, New Novels: Feminism and Early Modernism*. New Brunswick: Rutgers University Press.

Atwood, Margaret. [1976] 1987. "Circe/Mud Poems." In *Selected Poems, 1965–1975*. Boston: Houghton Mifflin.

Auerbach, Nina. 1984. "Robert Browning's Last Word." *Victorian Poetry* 22:161–73.

Baker, Peter. 1991. *Obdurate Brilliance: Exteriority and the Modern Long Poem*. Gainesville: University of Florida Press.

Bakhtin, Mikhail. 1981. *The Dialogic Imagination*. Ed. Michael Holquist, trans. Caryl Emerson and Michael Holquist. Austin: University of Texas Press.

Barad, Karen. 1994. "Meeting the Universe Half-Way: Ambiguities, Discontinuities, Quantum Subjects, and Multiple Positionings in Feminism and Physics." In *Making a Difference in the Natural Sciences: Eliminating Gender and Related Biases in the Content and Practice of Science*, ed. Bonnie Spanier. Bloomington: Indiana University Press. Forthcoming. Typescript.

Barone, Dennis, and Peter Ganick, eds. 1993. *The Art of Practice: Forty-Five Contemporary Poets*. Elmwood, Conn.: Potes and Poets Press.

Barthes, Roland. [1953] 1967. *Writing Degree Zero*. Trans. Annette Lavers and Colin Smith. New York: Hill and Wang.

———. [1957] 1972. *Mythologies*. Trans. Annette Lavers. New York: Hill and Wang.

———. 1975. *The Pleasure of the Text*. Trans. Richard Miller. New York: Farrar, Straus and Giroux, Noonday Press.

———. 1978. *A Lover's Discourse: Fragments*. Trans. Richard Howard. New York: Hill and Wang.

———. [1967] 1986. "The Discourse of History." In *The Rustle of Language*. Trans. Richard Howard. New York: Hill and Wang.

Baudelaire, Charles. 1961. *Oeuvres Complètes*. Paris: Editions Gallimard.

Beckett, Samuel. 1964. *How It Is*. New York: Grove Press.

Bedient, Calvin. 1988. "The Wild Braid of Creation." *Sewanee Review* 46, no. 1:137–49.

———. 1990. "Kristeva and Poetry as Shattered Signification." *Critical Inquiry* 16 (summer): 807–29.

Beilin, Elaine V. 1987. *Redeeming Eve: Women Writers of the English Renaissance*. Princeton: Princeton University Press.

Benjamin, Jessica. 1988. *The Bonds of Love: Psychoanalysis, Feminism, and the Problem of Domination*. New York: Pantheon Books.

Benjamin, Walter. 1968. *Illuminations*. Ed. Hannah Arendt, trans. Harry Zohn. New York: Harcourt, Brace and World.

———. 1983–84. "Theoretics of Knowledge, Theory of Progress." *Philosophical Forum* 15, nos. 1–2:1–40.

Benstock, Shari. 1986. *Women of the Left Bank: Paris, 1900–1940*. Austin: University of Texas Press.

———. 1991. *Textualizing the Feminine: On the Limits of Genre*. Norman: University of Oklahoma Press.

Berg, Maggie. 1991. "Luce Irigaray's 'Contradictions': Poststructuralism and Feminism." *Signs* 17: 50–70.

Bernstein, Charles. 1986. *Content's Dream: Essays 1975–1984*. Los Angeles: Sun and Moon Press.

———. 1989. *The Nude Formalism*. Illus. Susan Bee. Los Angeles: Sun and Moon Press.

———. 1992. *A Poetics*. Cambridge: Harvard University Press.

Bernstein, Michael André. 1980. *The Tale of the Tribe: Ezra Pound and the Modern Verse Epic*. Princeton: Princeton University Press.

Berryman, John. 1956. *Homage to Mistress Bradstreet*. New York: Farrar, Straus and Cudahy.

Bersani, Leo. 1984. *A Future for Astyanax: Characters and Desire in Literature*. New York: Columbia University Press.

Bettelheim, Bruno. 1977. *The Uses of Enchantment: The Meaning and Importance of Fairy Tales*. New York: Vintage Books.

Bhabha, Homi K., ed. 1990. *Nation and Narration*. London: Routledge.

Black, Max. 1962. *Models and Metaphors*. Ithaca, N.Y.: Cornell University Press.

Blasing, Mutlu Konuk. 1992. "The American Sublime, c. 1992: What Clothes Does One Wear?" *Michigan Quarterly Review* 31:425–41.

Bloom, Harold. 1973. *The Anxiety of Influence*. New York: Oxford University Press.

Bordo, Susan. 1992. "'Maleness' Revisited." *Hypatia* 7, no. 3:197–207.

Borroff, Marie. 1979. *Language and the Poet: Verbal Artistry in Frost, Stevens, and Moore*. Chicago: University of Chicago Press.

Boym, Svetlana. 1991. *Death in Quotation Marks: Cultural Myths of the Modern Poet*. Cambridge: Harvard University Press.

Braidotti, Rosi. 1987. "Envy: Or with My Brains and Your Looks." In *Men in Feminism*, ed. Alice Jardine and Paul Smith, 233–41. New York: Methuen.

Brathwaite, E. K. 1977. "Caliban, Arielm and Unprospero in the Conflict of Creolization." In *Comparative Perspectives on Slavery in the New World Plantation Societies*, ed. Vera Rubin and Arthur Tuden, 41–63. N.Y.: New York Academy of Sciences.

Breckenridge, Jill. 1986. *Civil Blood: Poems and Prose*. Minneapolis: Milkweed Editions.

Brereton, Bridget. 1979. *Race Relations in Colonial Trinidad, 1879–1900*. New York: Cambridge University Press.

Brisman, Leslie. 1979. "Back to the First of All: 'By the Fire-side' and Browning's Romantic Origins." In *Robert Browning: A Collection of Critical Essays*, ed. Harold Bloom and Adrienne Munich, 39–58. Englewood Cliffs, N.J.: Prentice-Hall.

Brodine, Karen. [1981] 1990. "Woman Sitting at the Machine, Thinking, A series of work poems." In *Woman Sitting at the Machine, Thinking, Poems, 1978–1987*. Seattle: Red Letter Press.

Brooks, Gwendolyn. [1968] 1987. *Blacks*. Chicago: Third World Press.

Brooks, Peter. 1985. *Reading for the Plot: Design and Intention in Narrative*. New York: Vintage.

Brossard, Nicole. 1990. *Picture Theory*. Trans. Barbara Godard. New York: Roof Books.

Brown, Rosellen. 1977. *Cora Fry*. New York: Norton.

Browning, Elizabeth Barrett. [1900] 1974. *The Poetical Works of Elizabeth Barrett Browning*. Ed. Harriet Waters Preston. Boston: Houghton Mifflin.

Browning, Robert. 1970. *Poetical Works 1833–1864*. Ed. Ian Jack. London: Oxford University Press.

Browning, Robert, and Elizabeth Barrett Browning. 1969. *The Letters of Robert Browning and Elizabeth Barrett Browning 1845–1846*. Ed. Elvan Kintner. 2 vols. Cambridge: Harvard University Press.

Buck-Morss, Susan. 1977. *The Origins of Negative Dialectics: Theodor Adorno, Walter Benjamin, and the Frankfurt Institute*. Hassocks, Sussex: Harvester.

Burke, Carolyn. 1985. "The New Poetry and the New Women: Mina Loy." In Middlebrook and Yalom 1985, 37–57.

———. 1987. "Getting Spliced: Modernism and Sexual Difference." *American Quarterly* 39:98–121.

———. 1990. "Mina Loy (1882–1966)." In Scott 1990, 230–38.

Butler, Judith. 1990a. *Gender Trouble: Feminism and the Subversion of Identity.* New York: Routledge.

———. 1990b. "Gender Trouble, Feminist Theory, and Psychoanalytic Discourse." In *Feminism/Postmodernism,* ed. Linda J. Nicholson, 324–40. New York: Routledge.

———. 1992. "Response to Bordo's 'Feminist Skepticism and the "Maleness" of Philosophy.'" *Hypatia* 7, no. 3:162–65.

Bynum, Caroline Walker. 1982. *Jesus as Mother: Studies in the Spirituality of the High Middle Ages.* Berkeley and Los Angeles: University of California Press.

———. 1987. *Holy Feast and Holy Fast: The Religious Significance of Food to Medieval Women.* Berkeley and Los Angeles: University of California Press.

Calvino, Italo. 1988. *Six Memos for the Next Millennium: The Charles Eliot Norton Lectures 1985–86.* Cambridge: Harvard University Press.

Cameron, Anne. 1987. "The Sickness That Has No Name." In *The Annie Poems.* Madeira Park, British Columbia: Harbour Publishing.

Campbell, David A., ed. 1982. *Greek Lyric.* Vol. 1. Cambridge: Harvard University Press.

Carby, Hazel V. 1987. *Reconstructing Womanhood: The Emergence of the Afro-American Woman Novelist.* New York: Oxford University Press.

———. 1988. "It Jus Be's Dat Way Sometime: The Sexual Politics of Women's Blues." *Advances in Discourse Processes.* 30:227–42.

Case, Sue-Ellen. 1989. "Toward a Butch-Femme Aesthetic." In *Making a Spectacle: Feminist Essays on Contemporary Women's Theatre,* ed. Lynda Hart, 282–99. Ann Arbor: University of Michigan Press.

Caserio, Robert. 1979. *Plot, Story, and the Novel: From Dickens and Poe to the Modern Period.* Princeton: Princeton University Press.

Cervantes, Lorna Dee. 1981. *Emplumada.* Pittsburgh: University of Pittsburgh Press.

Cha, Theresa Hak Kyung. 1982. *DICTEE.* New York: Tanam.

Chernin, Kim. 1983. *In My Mother's House: A Daughter's Story.* New York: Harper and Row.

Chin, Frank, Jeffery Paul Chan, Lawson Fusao Inada, and Shawn Wong. 1975. *Aiiieeeee: An Anthology of Asian-American Writers.* Garden City: Anchor.

Chin, Marilyn. 1987. *Dwarf Bamboo.* Greenfield Center, N.Y.: Greenfield Review Press.

Chodorow, Nancy. 1978. *The Reproduction of Mothering: Psychoanalysis and the Sociology of Gender.* Berkeley and Los Angeles: University of California Press.

Christian, Barbara. 1989. "The Race for Theory." In *Gender and Theory: Dialogues on Feminist Criticism,* ed. Linda Kauffman, 225–37. Oxford: Basil Blackwell.

Cixous, Hélène. 1972. *The Exile of James Joyce.* Trans. Sally A. J. Purcell. New York: David Lewis.

———. [1975] 1980. "The Laugh of the Medusa." In Marks and Courtivron 1980, 254–64.

———. 1991. *"Coming to Writing" and Other Essays.* Ed. Deborah Jenson. Trans. Sarah Cornell et al. Cambridge: Harvard University Press.

Clayton, Jay. 1989. "Narrative and Theories of Desire." *Critical Inquiry* 16:33–53.

———. 1990. "The Narrative Turn in Recent Minority Fiction." *American Literary History* 2, no.3 (fall): 375–93.

Clayton, Jay, and Eric Rothstein. 1991. "Figures in the Corpus: Theories of Influence and Intertextuality." In *Influence and Intertextuality in Literary History,* ed. Jay Clayton and Eric Rothstein, 3–36. Madison: University of Wisconsin Press.

Clifton, Lucille. 1983. "A Simple Language." In *Black Women Writers (1950–1980): A Critical Evaluation,* ed. Mari Evans, 137–38. Garden City, N.Y.: Anchor Books.

———. 1987a. *good woman: poems and a memoir, 1969–1980.* Brockport, N.Y.: BOA Editions.

———. 1987b. *next: new poems.* Brockport, N.Y.: BOA Editions.

———. 1991. *quilting: new poems 1987–1990.* Brockport, N.Y.: BOA Editions.

———. 1993. *The Book of Light.* Port Townsend, Wa.: Copper Canyon Press.

Coltelli, Laura. 1990. *Winged Words: American Indian Writers Speak.* Lincoln: University of Nebraska Press.

Conte, Joseph M. 1991. *Unending Design: The Forms of Contemporary Poetry.* Ithaca, N.Y.: Cornell University Press.

Cooper, Helen. 1988. *Elizabeth Barrett Browning, Woman and Artist.* Chapel Hill: University of North Carolina Press.

Dacey, Philip, and David Jauss, eds. 1985. *Strong Measures: Contemporary American Poetry in Traditional Forms.* New York: Harper and Row.

Dahlen, Beverley. 1985. *A Reading (1–7).* San Francisco: Momo's Press.

———. 1989. *A Reading (11–17).* Elmwood, Conn.: Potes and Poets Press.

———. 1992. *A Reading (8–10).* Tucson: Chax Press.

Daniel, Samuel. 1950. *Poems and a Defence of Ryme.* Ed. Arthur Colby Sprague. New York: Routledge and Kegan Paul.

Darragh, Tina. 1981. *on the corner to off the corner.* College Park, Md.: Sun and Moon Press.

Darwin, Charles. [1871] 1983. Excerpt from *The Descent of Man and Selection in Relation to Sex.* In *Women, the Family, and Freedom: The Debate in Documents,* ed. Susan Groag Bell and Karen Offen, 1: 409–11. Stanford: Stanford University Press.

Davidoff, Leonore, and Catherine Hall. 1987. *Family Fortunes: Men and Women of the English Middle Class, 1780–1850.* Chicago: University of Chicago Press.

Davis, Natalie Zemon. 1980. "Gender and Genre: Women as Historical Writers, 1400–1820." In *Beyond Their Sex: Learned Women of the European Past,* ed. Patricia H. LaBalme, 153–82. New York: New York University Press.

Dawson, Ariel. 1985. "The Yuppie Poet." *Associated Writing Programs Newsletter,* May, 5–6.

DeFrees, Madeline. 1990. *Imaginary Ancestors.* Seattle: Broken Moon Press.

DeKoven, Marianne. 1989. "Male Signature, Female Aesthetic: The Gender Politics of Experimental Writing." In *Breaking the Sequence: Women's Experimental Fiction,* ed. Ellen Friedman and Miriam Fuchs, 72–81. Princeton: Princeton University Press.

de Lauretis, Teresa. 1984. *Alice Doesn't: Feminism, Semiotics, Cinema.* Bloomington: Indiana University Press.

———. 1987. *Technologies of Gender: Essays on Theory, Film, and Fiction.* Bloomington: Indiana University Press.

Del Castillo, Adelaida R. 1977. "Malintzin Tenepal: A Preliminary Look into a New Perspective." In *Essays on La Mujer,* ed. Rosaura Sanchez, 124–49. Los Angeles: Chicano Studies Center Publications.

Deloria, Ella. 1932. *Dakota Texts.* New York: AMS Press.

Dembo, L. S. 1966. *Conceptions of Reality in Modern American Poetry.* Berkeley and Los Angeles: University of California Press.

Derricotte, Toi. 1983. *Natural Birth.* Trumansburg, N.Y.: Crossing Press.

DeShazar, Mary K. 1986. *Inspiring Women: Reimagining the Muse.* New York: Pergamon.

Dickie, Margaret. 1986. *On the Modernist Long Poem.* Iowa City: University of Iowa Press.

Dickinson, Emily. 1955. *The Poems of Emily Dickinson.* Ed. Thomas H. Johnson. 3 vols. Cambridge: Harvard University Press, Belknap Press.

———. 1958. *The Letters of Emily Dickinson.* Ed. Thomas H. Johnson. 3 vols. Cambridge: Harvard University Press, Belknap Press.

Diehl, Joanne Feit. 1978. "'Come Slowly—Eden': An Exploration of Women Poets and Their Muse." *Signs* 3:572–87.

———. 1990. *Women Poets and the American Sublime.* Bloomington: Indiana University Press.

Di Prima, Diane. 1971. *Revolutionary Letters.* San Francisco: City Lights Books.

———. Loba: Parts I–VIII. Berkley: Wingbow Press.

Dore, John. 1983. "Feeling, Form, and Intention in the Baby's Transition to Language." In *The Transition from Linguistic to Prelinguistic Communication,* ed. Roberta Michnick Golinkoff, 167–90. Hillsdale, N.J.: Lawrence Erlbaum Associates.

Doubiago, Sharon. 1982. *Hard Country.* Minneapolis: West End.

Dove, Rita. 1986. *Thomas and Beulah.* Pittsburgh: Carnegie-Mellon University Press.

duBois, Page. 1988. *Sowing the Body: Psychoanalysis and Ancient Representations of Women.* Chicago: University of Chicago Press.

DuPlessis, Rachel Blau. 1985. *Writing beyond the Ending: Narrative Strategies of Twentieth-Century Women Writers.* Bloomington: Indiana University Press.

———. 1989. "No Moore of the Same: The Feminist Poetics of Marianne Moore." *William Carlos Williams Review* 14, no. 1:6–32.

———. 1990. *The Pink Guitar: Writing as Feminist Practice.* New York: Routledge, Chapman and Hall.

———. 1991. *Drafts.* Elmwood, Conn.: Potes and Poets.

———. 1992. "'Seismic Orgasm': Sexual Intercourse, Gender Narratives, and Lyric Ideology in Mina Loy." In *Studies in Historical Change,* ed. Ralph Cohen, 264–91. Charlottesville: University Press of Virginia.

Eagleton, Terry. 1990. "Nationalism: Irony and Commitment." In Terry Eagleton, Fredric Jameson, and Edward W. Said, *Nationalism, Colonialism, and Literature,* 23–39. Minneapolis: University of Minnesota Press.

Easthope, Anthony, and John O. Thompson, eds. 1991. *Contemporary Poetry Meets Modern Theory.* Toronto: University of Toronto Press.

Eliot, T. S. 1952. *The Complete Poems and Plays.* New York: Harcourt, Brace.

Ellis, Sarah. [1838] 1839. *The Women of England: Their Social Duties, and Domestic Habits.* 2 vols. Philadelphia: E. L. Carey and A. Hart.

———. 1843. *The Wives of England: Their Relative Duties, Domestic Influence, and Social Obligations.* New York: D. Appleton, and Philadelphia: George S. Appleton.

Erdrich, Louise. 1984a. *Jacklight.* New York: Holt, Rinehart and Winston.

———. 1984b. *Love Medicine.* New York: Holt, Rinehart and Winston.

———. 1988. *Tracks: A Novel.* New York: Holt, Rinehart and Winston.

———. 1989. *Baptism of Desire, Poems.* New York: Harper.

Erkkila, Betsy. 1992. *The Wicked Sisters: Women Poets, Literary History, and Discord.* New York: Oxford University Press.

Farwell, Marilyn R. 1988. "Toward a Definition of the Lesbian Literary Imagination." *Signs* 14:100–18.

Fell, Alison. 1991. "One Night a Stranger . . ." *New Statesman and Society,* 25 October, 18–20.

Felski, Rita. 1989. *Beyond Feminist Aesthetics: Feminist Literature and Social Change.* Cambridge: Harvard University Press.

Fetterley, Judith. 1978. *The Resisting Reader: A Feminist Approach to American Fiction.* Bloomington: Indiana University Press.

Finkelstein, Norman. 1991. "The Problem of the Self in Recent American Poetry." *Poetics Journal* 9 (June): 3–10.

Flax, Jane. 1992. "The End of Innocence." In *Feminists Theorize the Political,* ed. Judith Butler and Joan W. Scott, 445–63. New York: Routledge.

Folse, Henry J. 1985. *The Philosophy of Niels Bohr: The Framework of Complementarity.* Amsterdam: Elsevier Science Publishers.

Foster, Hal, ed. 1983. *The Anti-Aesthetic: Essays on Postmodern Culture.* Seattle: Bay Press.

Foucault, Michel. 1978. *The History of Sexuality.* Trans. Robert Hurley. Vol. 1. New York: Random House.

———. 1979. *Discipline and Punish: The Birth of the Prison.* Trans. Alan Sheridan. New York: Vintage Books.

Franco, Jean. 1989. *Plotting Women: Gender and Representation in Mexico.* New York: Columbia University Press.

Freud, Sigmund. 1965. "Revision of the Theory of Dreams." In *New Introductory Lectures on Psychoanalysis,* ed. James Strachey, 7–30. New York: W. W. Norton.

Friedman, Susan Stanford. 1986. "Gender and Genre Anxiety: Elizabeth Barrett Browning and H.D. as Epic Poets." *Tulsa Studies in Women's Literature* 5 (fall): 203–28.

———. 1989. "Lyric Subversion of Narrative in Women's Writing: Virginia Woolf and the Tyranny of Plot." In *Reading Narrative: Form, Ethics, Ideology,* ed. James Phelan, 162–85. Columbus: Ohio State University Press.

———. 1990a. *Penelope's Web: Gender, Modernity, H.D.'s Fiction.* Cambridge: Cambridge University Press.

————. 1990b. "When a 'Long' Poem Is a 'Big' Poem: Self-Authorizing Strategies in Women's Twentieth-Century 'Long Poems.'" *LIT* 2:9–25.

————. 1991. "Post/Poststructuralist Feminist Criticism: The Politics of Recuperation and Negation." *New Literary History* 22, no. 2 (spring): 465–90.

Frye, Joanne S. 1986. *Living Stories, Telling Lives: Women and the Novel in Contemporary Experience*. Ann Arbor: University of Michigan Press.

Fulton, Alice. 1983. *Dance Script with Electric Ballerina*. Philadelphia: University of Pennsylvania Press.

————. 1986a. *Palladium*. Urbana: University of Illinois Press.

————. 1986b. "Of Formal, Free, and Fractal Verse: Singing the Body Eclectic." *Poetry East* 20–21 (fall): 200–213.

————. 1990. *Powers of Congress*. Boston: David R. Godine.

————. 1991. "To Organize a Waterfall." *Parnassus* 16, no. 2:301–26.

Fussell, Paul. 1979. *Poetic Meter and Poetic Form*. Rev. ed. New York: Random House.

Gardner, Thomas. 1989. *Discovering Ourselves in Whitman: The Contemporary American Long Poem*. Urbana: University of Illinois Press.

Gay, Peter. 1978. *Freud, Jews, and Other Germans: Masters and Victims in Modernist Culture*. New York: Oxford University Press.

————. 1984. *The Bourgeois Experience: From Victoria to Freud: Education of the Senses*. New York: Oxford University Press.

Gerhart, Mary. 1992. *Genre Choices, Gender Questions*. Norman: University of Oklahoma Press.

Giddens, Anthony. 1992. *The Transformation of Intimacy*. Stanford: Stanford University Press.

Gilbert, Sandra, and Susan Gubar. 1979a. *The Madwoman in the Attic: The Woman Writer and the Nineteenth-Century Literary Imagination*. New Haven: Yale University Press.

————. eds., 1979b. *Shakespeare's Sisters: Feminist Essays on Women Poets*. Bloomington: Indiana University Press.

————. 1988. *The War of the Words*. Vol. 1 of *No Man's Land*. 2 vols. New Haven: Yale University Press.

Gilligan, Carol. 1982. *In a Different Voice: Psychological Theory and Women's Development*. Cambridge: Harvard University Press.

Gilligan, Carol, Janie Victoria Ward, and Jill McLean Taylor, with Betty Bardige, eds. 1988. *Mapping the Moral Domain: A Contribution of Women's Thinking to Psychological Theory and Education*. Cambridge: Harvard University Press.

Ginsberg, Allen. 1956. *Howl*. San Francisco: City Lights.

Glancy, Diane. 1991. *Lone Dog's Winter Count*. Albuquerque: West End Press.

Golding, Alan. 1991. "'Openness,' 'Closure,' and Recent American Poetry." *Arizona Quarterly* 47:76–91.

Gómez-Quiñones, Juan. 1974. *5th and Grande Vista (Poems 1960–1973)*. New York: Editorial Mensaje.

Grahn, Judy. 1978. *The Work of a Common Woman*. New York: St. Martin's Press.

————. 1982. *The Queen of Wands*. Trumansburg, N.Y.: Crossing Press.

———. 1987. *The Queen of Swords*. Boston: Beacon Press.

Grassi, Carolyn. 1989. *Journey to Chartres*. Redding Ridge, Conn.: Black Swan Books.

Greene, Gayle, and Coppélia Kahn. 1985. "Feminist Scholarship and the Social Construction of Women." In *Making a Difference: Feminist Literary Criticism*, ed. Gayle Green and Coppélia Kahn, 1–36. London: Methuen.

Greer, Germaine, Susan Hastings, Jeslyn Medoff, and Melinda Sansone, eds. 1988. *Kissing the Rod: An Anthology of Seventeenth-Century Women's Verse*. New York: Noonday Press.

Grossman, Allen. 1992. "Summa Lyrica: A Primer of the Commonplaces in Speculative Poetics." In *The Sighted Singer: Two Works on Poetry for Readers and Writers*. Baltimore: Johns Hopkins University Press.

Grosz, Elizabeth. 1989. *Sexual Subversions: Three French Feminists*. Sydney, Australia: Allen and Unwin.

Grover, Jan Zita. 1990. "Words to Lust By." *Women's Review of Books* 8 (November): 21–23.

Gubar, Susan. 1981. "'The Blank Page' and the Issues of Female Creativity." *Critical Inquiry* 8:243–64.

H.D. 1961. "Marianne Moore." *Egoist* 3, no. 8 (August): 118–19.

———. [1944–46] 1973. *Trilogy*. New York: New Directions.

———. [1961] 1974. *Helen in Egypt*. New York: New Directions.

———. 1979. *End to Torment: A Memoir of Ezra Pound*. Ed. Norman Holmes Pearson and Michael King. New York: New Directions.

———. 1983. *Collected Poems 1912–1944*. Ed. Louis L. Martz. New York: New Directions.

Hacker, Marilyn. 1974. *Presentation Piece*. New York: Viking Press.

———. 1980. "An Interview with Marilyn Hacker." Interviewed by Karla Hammond. *Frontiers* 5:22–27.

———. 1986. *Love, Death, and the Changing of the Seasons*. New York: Arbor House.

———. 1989a. "'Begin to Teach.'" Review of *Time's Power*, by Adrienne Rich. *Nation* 249:464–67.

———. 1989b. "An Invitation to My Demented Uncle." *Ploughshares* 15:1–5.

Hadas, Pamela White. 1983. *Beside Herself: Pocahontas to Patty Hearst*. New York: Knopf.

Haigwood, Laura E. 1986. "Gender-to-Gender Anxiety and Influence in Robert Browning's *Men and Women*." *Browning Institute Studies* 14:97–118.

Hannay, Margaret Patterson, ed. 1985. *Silent but for the Word: Tudor Women as Patrons, Translators, and Writers of Religious Works*. Kent, Ohio: Kent State University Press.

Harding, Sandra. 1986a. "The Instability of the Analytical Categories of Feminist Theory." *Signs* 13:645–64.

———. 1986b. *The Science Question in Feminism*. Ithaca, N.Y.: Cornell University Press.

Harjo, Joy. 1983. *She Had Some Horses*. New York: Thunder's Mouth Press.

———. 1989. *Secrets from the Center of the World*. Sun Tracks Series. Tucson: University of Arizona Press.

———. 1990. *In Mad Love and War*. Middletown, Conn.: Wesleyan University Press.

Harris, Marie, and Kathleen Aguero, eds. 1987. *A Gift of Tongues: Critical Challenges in Contemporary American Poetry*. Athens: University of Georgia Press.

Harryman, Carla. 1991. *In the Mode Of*. La Laguna, Canary Islands: Zasterle Press.

Hartsock, Nancy. 1990. "Postmodernism and Political Change: Issues for Feminist Theory." *Cultural Critique* 14:15–33.

Hayles, N. Katherine. 1984. *The Cosmic Web: Scientific Field Models and Literary Strategies in the Twentieth Century*. Ithaca, N.Y.: Cornell University Press.

Hejinian, Lyn. 1978. *Writing Is an Aid to Memory*. Berkeley: Figures.

———. 1987. *My Life*. Los Angeles: Sun and Moon Press.

———. 1992. *The Cell*. Los Angeles: Sun and Moon Press.

Henderson, Katherine Usher, and Barbara F. McManus, eds. 1985. *Half Humankind: Contexts and Texts of the Controversy about Women in England, 1540–1640*. Chicago: University of Illinois Press.

Herbert, George. 1974. *The English Poems of George Herbert*. Ed. C. A. Patrides. London: J. M. Dent and Sons.

Herrera-Sobek, Maria. 1990. *The Mexican Corrido: A Feminist Analysis*. Bloomington: Indiana University Press.

Hesiod. 1953. *Theogony*. Trans. Norman O. Brown. Indianapolis: Bobbs-Merrill.

Hirsch, Marianne. 1979. "The Novel of Formation as Genre: Between Great Expectations and Lost Illusions." *Genre* 12:293–311.

———. 1989. *The Mother/Daughter Plot: Narrative, Psychoanalysis, Feminism*. Bloomington: Indiana University Press.

Hirsh, Elizabeth A. 1989. "Imaginary Images: 'H.D.,' Modernism, and the Psychoanalysis of Seeing." In *Signets: Reading H.D.*, ed. Rachel Blau DuPlessis and Susan Stanford Friedman, 430–51. Madison: University of Wisconsin Press.

———. 1994. "Back in Analysis: How to Do Things With Irigaray." In *Engaging With Irigaray*, ed. Carolyn Burke, Naomi Schor, and Margaret Whitford. New York: Columbia University Press, forthcoming.

Hobby, Elaine. 1989. *Virtue of Necessity: English Women's Writing, 1649–88*. Ann Arbor: University of Michigan Press.

Hogan, Linda. 1978. *Calling Myself Home*. Greenfield Center, N.Y.: Greenfield Review Press.

———. 1981. *Daughters I Love You*. Denver: Research Center on Women.

———. 1983. *Eclipse*. Los Angeles: UCLA American Indian Studies Center Press.

———. 1985. *Seeing through the Sun*. Amherst: University of Massachusetts Press.

———. 1988. *Savings*. Minneapolis: Coffee House Press.

———. 1990. *Mean Spirit*. New York: Random House.

Holland, Norman N. 1978. "Dr. Johnson's Remarks on the Death of Cordelia." In *Psychoanalysis and the Question of the Text*, ed. Geoffrey H. Hartman, 18–44. Baltimore: Johns Hopkins University Press.

Homans, Margaret. 1980. *Women Writers and Poetic Identity: Dorothy Wordsworth, Emily Brontë, and Emily Dickinson*. Princeton: Princeton University Press.

———. 1983. "'Oh, Vision of Language!': Dickinson's Poems of Love and Death." In *Feminist Critics Read Emily Dickinson,* ed. Suzanne Juhasz, 114–33. Bloomington: Indiana University Press.

———. 1985. "'Syllables of Velvet': Dickinson, Rossetti, and the Rhetorics of Sexuality." *Feminist Studies* 11:569–93.

———. 1986. *Bearing the Word: Language and Female Experience in Nineteenth-Century Women's Writing.* Chicago: University of Chicago Press.

Hongo, Garrett. 1982. *Yellow Light.* Middletown, Conn.: Wesleyan University Press.

———. 1988. *The River of Heaven.* New York: Alfred A. Knopf.

hooks, bell. 1990. *yearning: race, gender, and cultural politics.* Boston: South End Press.

Hôsek, Chaviva, and Patricia Parker, eds. 1985. *Lyric Poetry: Beyond New Criticism.* Ithaca, N.Y.: Cornell University Press.

Houlbrooke, Ralph. 1984. *The English Family, 1450–1700.* London: Longmans.

Howe, Susan. 1982. *Pythagorean Silence.* New York: Montemora.

———. 1983. *The Liberties.* In *Defenestration of Prague.* New York: Kultur Foundation.

Huff, Cynthia. 1988. "Private Domains: Queen Victoria and Women's Diaries." *Auto/Biography Studies* 4:46–52.

Hull, Gloria T. 1987. *Color, Sex, and Poetry: Three Women Writers of the Harlem Renaissance.* Bloomington: Indiana University Press.

Hull, Suzanne W. 1982. *Chaste, Silent and Obedient: English Books for Women, 1475–1640.* San Marino, Calif.: Huntington Library.

Hutcheon, Linda. 1989. *The Politics of Postmodernism.* London: Routledge.

Irigaray, Luce. 1985a. *Speculum of the Other Woman.* Trans. Gillian Gill. Ithaca, N.Y.: Cornell University Press.

———. [1977] 1985b. *This Sex Which Is Not One.* Trans. Catherine Porter with Carolyn Burke. Ithaca, N.Y.: Cornell University Press.

———. 1991. *The Irigaray Reader.* Ed. Margaret Whitford. Cambridge: Basil Blackwell.

———. 1993a. *je, tu, nous: Toward a Culture of Difference.* Trans. Alison Martin. New York: Routledge.

———. 1993b. *Sexes and Genealogies.* Trans. Gillian C. Gill. New York: Columbia University Press.

James, C. L. R. 1993. *Beyond a Boundary.* Durham, N.C.: Duke University Press.

James, Louis, ed. 1976. *English Popular Literature 1819–1851.* New York: Columbia University Press.

Jameson, Anna. 1834. *Memoirs of Celebrated Female Sovereigns.* 2d ed. 2 vols. London.

Jameson, Fredric. 1981. *The Political Unconscious: Narrative as a Socially Symbolic Act.* Ithaca, N.Y.: Cornell University Press.

Jardine, Alice. 1985. *Gynesis: Configurations of Woman and Modernity.* Ithaca, N.Y.: Cornell University Press.

Johnson, Guy. [1930] 1968. *Folk Culture on St. Helena Island.* Hatboro, Pa.: Folklore Associates.

Jones, Ann Rosalind. 1990. *The Currency of Eros: Women's Love Lyric in Europe, 1540–1620.* Bloomington: Indiana University Press.

Jordan, Constance. 1990. *Renaissance Feminism: Literary Texts and Political Models.* Ithaca, N.Y.: Cornell University Press.

Juhasz, Suzanne. 1976. *Naked and Fiery Forms: Modern American Poetry by Women, a New Tradition.* New York: Harper and Row.

———. 1986. "Writing Doubly: Emily Dickinson and Female Experience." *Legacy: A Journal of Nineteenth-Century American Women Writers* 3, no. 1 (spring): 5–16.

———. 1989. "Reading Doubly: Dickinson, Gender, and Multiple Meaning." In *Approaches to Teaching Dickinson's Poetry,* ed. Robin Riley Fast and Christine Mack Gordon, 85–94. New York: MLA.

———. 1993. "The Big Tease." In Suzanne Juhasz, Cristanne Miller, and Martha Nell Smith, *Comic Power: Performance and Audience in Emily Dickinson's Poetry.* Austin: University of Texas Press.

Julian of Norwich. 1978. *A Book of Showings to the Anchoress Julian of Norwich.* 2 vols. Ed. Edmund Colledge and James Walsh. Toronto: Pontifical Institute of Mediaeval Studies.

Kamboureli, Smaro. 1991. *On the Edge of Genre: The Contemporary Canadian Long Poem.* Toronto: University of Toronto Press.

Kamuf, Peggy. 1982. "Replacing Feminist Criticism." *Diacritics* 12, no. 2 (summer): 42–47.

———. 1988. *Signature Pieces: On the Institution of Authorship.* Ithaca, N.Y.: Cornell University Press.

Karlin, Daniel. 1985. *The Courtship of Robert Browning and Elizabeth Barrett.* Oxford: Clarendon Press.

Kaufman, Shirley. 1984. *Claims: A Poem.* New York: Sheep Meadow Press.

Keats, John. 1978. *The Poems of John Keats.* Ed. Jack Stillinger. Cambridge: Harvard University Press, Belknap Press.

Keller, Elizabeth Fox. 1985. *Reflections on Gender and Science.* New Haven: Yale University Press.

Keller, Lynn. 1988. "Poems Containing History: Some Problems of Definition of the Long Poem." Paper presented at Modern Language Association Convention, December.

———. 1992. "'to remember / our dis-membered parts': Sharon Doubiago and the Complementary Woman's Epic." *American Literary History* 4 (summer): 305–28.

———. 1993. "The Twentieth-Century Long Poem." In *Columbia History of American Poetry,* ed. Jay Parini, 534–63. New York: Columbia University Press.

Kelly, Joan. 1984. *Women, History, and Theory: The Essays of Joan Kelly.* Chicago: University of Chicago Press.

Kelso, Ruth. 1956. *Doctrine for the Lady of the Renaissance.* Urbana: University of Illinois Press.

Kendrick, Dolores. 1975. *Through the Ceiling.* London: Paul Breman Heritage.

———. 1984. *Now Is the Thing to Praise.* Detroit: Lotus Press.

———. 1989. *The Women of Plums: Poems in the Voices of Slave Women.* New York: William Morrow.

Kenner, Hugh. 1971. *The Pound Era.* Berkeley: University of California Press.

Keyes, Claire. 1986. *The Aesthetics of Power: The Poetry of Adrienne Rich.* Athens: University of Georgia Press.

Kim, Elaine H. 1994. "Poised on the In-Between: A Korean American's Reflections on Theresa Hak Kyung Cha's *DICTEE.*" In *Writing Self Writing Nation: Essays on Theresa Hak Kyung Cha's "Dictée,"* eds. Elaine H. Kim and Norma Alarcón, 3–30. Berkeley: Third Woman Press.

King, Margaret L., and Albert Rabil, Jr., eds. and trans. 1983. *Her Immaculate Hand: Selected Works by and about the Women Humanists of Quattrocento Italy.* Binghamton, N.Y.: Medieval and Renaissance Texts and Studies.

Klepfisz, Irena. 1982. *Keeper of Accounts.* Watertown, Mass.: Persephone Press.

Knoepflmacher, U. C. 1984. "Projection and the Female Other: Romanticism, Browning, and the Victorian Dramatic Monologue." *Victorian Poetry* 22:139–59.

Koethe, John. 1991. "Contrary Impulses: The Tension between Poetry and Theory." *Critical Inquiry* 18:64–75.

Kolodny, Annette. 1985. "A Map for Rereading: Gender and the Interpretation of Literary Texts." In Showalter 1985, 46–62.

Kristeva, Julia. 1980. *Desire in Language: A Semiotic Approach to Literature and Art.* Trans. Thomas Gora, Alice Jardine, and Leon S. Roudiez. New York: Columbia University Press.

———. 1981. "Women's Time." Trans. Alice Jardine and Harry Blake. *Signs* 7:13–35.

———. 1982. *Powers of Horror: An Essay in Abjection.* Trans. Leon Roudiez. New York: Columbia University Press.

———. [1974] 1984. *Revolution in Poetic Language.* Trans. Margaret Waller. New York: Columbia University Press.

———. 1989. *Black Sun.* New York: Columbia University Press.

———. 1991. *Strangers to Ourselves.* New York: Columbia University Press.

LaCapra, Dominick. 1983. *Rethinking Intellectual History: Texts, Contexts, Language.* Ithaca, N.Y.: Cornell University Press.

Lanyer, Aemilia. [1611] 1991. *Salve Deus Rex Judaeorum.* Transcribed by the Brown Women Writers Project, Brown University. Typescript.

[Lanyer, Aemilia]. 1993. *The Poems of Aemilia Lanyer.* Ed. Susanne Woods. New York; Oxford: Oxford University Press.

Laslett, Peter. 1984. *The World We Have Lost: England before the Industrial Age.* 3d ed. New York: Scribner's.

Lawrence, Karen. 1980. *The Inanna Poems.* Edmonton, Canada: Longspoon Press.

Lazer, Hank. 1987. "Critical Theory and Contemporary American Poetry." In *What Is a Poet.* Tuscaloosa: University of Alabama Press.

Lee, Li-Young. 1986. *Rose.* Brockport, N.Y.: BOA Editions.

———. 1990. *The City in Which I Love You.* Brockport, N.Y.: BOA Editions.

LeGuin, Ursula K. 1981. "It Was a Dark and Stormy Night; or, Why Are We Huddling about the Campfire?" In *On Narrative,* ed. W. J. T. Mitchell, 187–95. Chicago: University of Chicago Press.

Leighton, Angela. 1986. *Elizabeth Barrett Browning.* Bloomington: Indiana University Press.

Lerner, Laurence. N.d. "Private Feelings: Public Forms (Are Elizabeth Browning's Letters Literature?)." In *Disciplines and the Canon*, ed. Jay Clayton, Jean Bethke Elshtain, and H. J. Schultz. Typescript.

Levertov, Denise. 1971. "Staying Alive." In *To Stay Alive*. New York: New Directions.

Lewalski, Barbara K. 1985. "Of God and Good Women: The Poems of Aemilia Lanyer." In Hannay 1985, 203–24.

———. 1991. "Re-writing Patriarchy and Patronage: Margaret Clifford, Anne Clifford, and Aemilia Lanyer." *Yearbook of English Studies* 21:87–106.

———. 1993. "Imagining Female Community: Aemilia Lanyer's Poems." In *Writing Women in Jacobean England*. Cambridge: Harvard University Press.

Li, Victor P. H. 1986. "The Vanity of Length: The Long Poem as Problem in Pound's *Cantos* and Williams' *Paterson*." *Genre* 14:3–20.

Limón, José E. 1983. "The Rise, Fall, and 'Revival' of the Mexican-American Corrido: A Review Essay." *Studies in Latin American Popular Culture* 2:202–7.

———. 1986a. "La Llorona, The Third Legend of Greater Mexico: Cultural Symbols, Women and the Political Unconscious." In *Renato Rosaldo Lecture Series Monograph* no. 2, ed. Ignacio M. Garcia, 59–63. Tucson: University of Arizona Mexican American Studies and Research Center.

———. 1986b. "Mexican Ballads, Chicano Epic: History, Social Dramas and Poetic Persuasions." Working paper no. 14, Stanford University Center for Chicano Research.

———. 1986c. "The Return of the Mexican Ballad: Américo Paredes and His Anthropological Text as a Persuasive Political Performance." Working paper no. 16, Stanford University Center for Chicano Research.

———. 1992. *Mexican Ballads, Chicano Poems: History and Influence in Mexican-American Social Poetry*. Berkeley and Los Angeles: University of California Press.

Livesay, Dorothy. 1968. *The Documentaries*. Toronto: Ryerson Press.

———. 1987. "The Documentary Poem: A Canadian Genre." In *A Family Romance: Critical Essays*, ed. Eli Mandel, 267–81. Winnipeg: Turnstone Press.

Lloyd, David. 1986. *Nationalism and Minor Literature: James Clarence Mangan and the Emergence of Irish Cultural Nationalism*. Berkeley and Los Angeles: University of California Press.

Longford, Elizabeth. 1964. *Queen Victoria: Born to Succeed*. New York: Harper and Row.

Lorde, Audre. 1984. *Sister Outsider: Essays and Speeches*. Freedom, Calif.: Crossing Press.

Lowe, Lisa. 1994. "Unfaithful to the Original: The Subject of *Dictée*." In *Writing Self Writing Nation: Essays on Theresa Hak Kyung Cha's "Dictée*," ed. Elaine H. Kim and Norma Alarcón, 35–69. Berkeley: Third Woman Press.

Lowell, Robert. 1973. *History*. New York: Farrar, Straus, and Giroux.

Loy, Mina. 1923. *Lunar Baedecker*. Dijon, France: Contact.

———. 1982. *The Last Lunar Baedeker*. Ed. Roger L. Conover. Highlands, N.C.: Jargon Society.

Mair, Lucille Mathurin. 1990. "Recollections of a Journey into a Rebel Past." In *Caribbean Women Writers: Essays from the First International Conference*, ed. Selwyn R. Cudjoe, 51–60. Wellesley, Mass.: Calaloux.

Maitland, Sara. 1984. *Virgin Territory.* London: Joseph.

Mandel, Charlotte. 1988. *The Life of Mary, a Poem-Novella.* Upper Montclair, N.J.: Saturday Press.

———. 1991. *The Marriages of Jacob, a Poem-Novella.* Marblehead, Mass.: Micah Publications.

Marks, Elaine. 1979. "Lesbian Intertextuality." In *Homosexualities and French Literature: Cultural Contexts/Critical Texts,* eds. George Stambolian and Elaine Marks, 353–77. Ithaca, N.Y.: Cornell University Press.

Marks, Elaine, and Isabelle de Courtivron, eds. 1980. *New French Feminisms: An Anthology.* Amherst: University of Massachusetts Press.

Marlatt, Daphne. 1983. *How Hug a Stone.* Winnipeg: Turnstone Press.

Marlatt, Daphne, and Robert Minden. [1974] 1984. *Steveston.* 2d ed. Edmonton: Longspoon Press.

Marlatt, Daphne, and Betsy Warland. 1988. *Double Negative.* Charlottetown, Canada: Gynergy Books.

Martin, Stephen-Paul. 1988. *Open Form and the Feminine Imagination: The Politics of Reading in Twentieth-Century Innovative Writing.* Washington, D.C.: Maisonneuve.

Mayer, Bernadette. 1982. *Midwinter Day.* Berkeley: Turtle Mountain Foundation.

———. 1984. *Utopia.* New York: United Artists Books.

McCarthy, Desmond. 1982. "New Poets, T. S. Eliot." Review of *Ara Vos Prec,* by T. S. Eliot. In *T. S. Eliot: The Critical Heritage,* ed. Michael Grant, 111–17. London: Routledge and Kegan Paul.

McCorkle, James. 1989. *The Still Performance: Writing, Self, and Interconnection in Five Postmodern American Poets.* Charlottesville: University Press of Virginia.

McDowell, John H. 1972. "The Mexican Corrido: Formula and Theme in a Ballad Tradition." *Journal of American Folklore* 85:205–20.

———. 1981. "The Corrido of Greater Mexico as Discourse, Music, and Event." In *"And Other Neighborly Names": Social Process and Cultural Image in Texas Folklore,* ed. Richard Bauman and Roger D. Abrahams, 44–75. Austin: University of Texas Press.

McGrath, Lynette. 1991. "Metaphoric Subversions: Feasts and Mirrors in Amelia Lanier's *Salve Deus Rex Judaeorum.*" *LIT* 3:101–13.

Mermin, Dorothy. 1989. *Elizabeth Barrett Browning: The Origins of a New Poetry.* Chicago: University of Chicago Press.

Messerli, Douglas, ed. 1987. *"Language" Poetries: An Anthology.* New York: New Directions.

Michie, Helena. 1992. *Sororophobia: Differences among Women in Literature and Culture.* New York: Oxford University Press.

Middlebrook, Diane, and Marilyn Yalom, eds. 1985. *Coming to Light: American Women Poets in the Twentieth Century.* Ann Arbor: University of Michigan Press.

Miles, Josephine. 1967. *Style and Proportion: The Language of Prose and Poetry.* Boston: Little, Brown.

Millay, Edna St. Vincent. [1931] 1988. *Fatal Interview.* In *Collected Sonnets of Edna St. Vincent Millay.* Rev. ed. New York: Harper and Row.

Miller, Betty. 1953. *Robert Browning.* New York: Charles Scribner and Sons.

Miller, James E. 1979. *The American Quest for a Supreme Fiction: Whitman's Legacy in the Personal Epic.* Chicago: University of Chicago Press.

Miller, Nancy K. 1982. "The Text's Heroine: A Feminist Critic and Her Fictions." *Diacritics* 12, no. 2 (summer): 48–53.

———. 1988. *Subject to Change: Reading Feminist Writing.* New York: Columbia University Press.

Milner, Marion. 1987. *A Life of One's Own.* London: Virago.

Modyford, Sir Thomas. 1665. "Resolutions from the Council of War." In *Article of War by Governor Sir Thomas Modyford and Council.* 15 August 1665.

Moi, Toril. 1985. *Sexual/Textual Politics: Feminist Literary Theory.* London: Methuen.

Molesworth, Charles. 1990. *Marianne Moore: A Literary Life.* New York: Atheneum.

Monroe, Jonathan. 1987. *A Poverty of Objects: The Prose Poem and the Politics of Genre.* Ithaca, N.Y.: Cornell University Press.

Montefiore, Jan. 1987. *Feminism and Poetry: Language, Experience, Identity in Women's Writing.* London: Routledge and Kegan Paul, Pandora Press.

Mookerjee, Ajit, and Madhu Khanna. 1977. *The Tantric Way.* London: Thames and Hudson.

Moore, Marianne. 1924. *Observations.* New York: Dial Press.

———. 1967. *The Complete Poems of Marianne Moore.* New York: Macmillan, Viking Press.

———. 1986. *The Complete Prose of Marianne Moore.* Ed. Patricia C. Willis. New York: Viking Press.

Moraga, Cherrie, and Gloria Anzaldúa, eds. 1981. *This Bridge Called My Back: Writings by Radical Women of Color.* New York: Kitchen Table, Women of Color Press.

Moretti, Franco. 1987. *The Way of the World: The Bildungsroman in European Culture.* London: Verso.

Morgan, Robin. 1993. Editorial. *Ms.,* March–April, 1.

Morrison, Toni. 1983. "Rootedness." In *Black Women Writers (1950–1980): A Critical Evaluation,* ed. Marie Evans, 339–45. Garden City, N.J.: Anchor Books.

———. 1984. "Memory, Creation, and Writing." *Thought* 59, no. 235 (December): 385–90.

———. 1989. "Unspeakable Things Unspoken: The Afro-American Presence in American Literature." *Michigan Quarterly Review* 28:1–34.

Mulvey, Laura. 1989. *Visual and Other Pleasures.* Bloomington: Indiana University Press.

Munich, Adrienne Auslander. 1984. "'Capture the Heart of a Queen': Gilbert and Sullivan's Rites of Conquest." *Centennial Review* 28, no. 1 (winter): 23–44.

———. 1987a. "Queen Victoria, Empire, and Excess." *Tulsa Studies in Women's Literature* 6 (fall): 265–81.

———. 1987b. "Robert Browning's Poetics of Appropriation." *Browning Institute Studies* 15:69–77.

Mura, David. 1989. *After We Lost Our Way.* New York: Dutton.

————. 1991. Interview by Lee Rossi. *On the Bus* 6–7:263–73.

Murray, David. 1989. *Literary Theory and Poetry: Extending the Canon.* London: B. T. Batsford.

Nelson, Cary. 1981. *Our Last First Poets: Vision and History in Contemporary American Poetry.* Urbana: University of Illinois Press.

Newton, Judith Lowder. 1989. "History as Usual? Feminism and the 'New Historicism.'" In *The New Historicism,* ed. H. Aram Veeser, 152–67. New York: Routledge.

Nowottny, Winifred. 1965. *The Language Poets Use.* London: Athlone Press.

Olson, Charles. 1983. *The Maximus Poems.* Ed. George F. Butterick. Berkeley: University of California Press.

Ostriker, Alicia Suskin. 1980. *The Mother/Child Papers.* Santa Monica, Calif.: Momentum Press.

————. 1985. "The Thieves of Language: Women Poets and Revisionist Mythmaking." In Middlebrook and Yalom 1985, 10–36.

————. 1986. *Stealing the Language: The Emergence of Women's Poetry in America.* Boston: Beacon Press.

Owens, Craig. 1983. "The Discourse of Others: Feminists and Postmodernism." In *The Anti-Aesthetic: Essays on Postmodern Culture,* ed. Hal Foster, 57–82, Seattle: Bay Press.

Paredes, Américo. 1958. *With His Pistol in His Hand: A Border Ballad and Its Hero.* Austin: University of Texas Press.

————. 1964. "Some Aspects of Folk Poetry." *Texas Studies in Language and Literature* 6:213–25.

————. 1976. *A Texas-Mexican Cancionero.* Urbana: University of Illinois Press.

Parker, Pat. 1978. *Movement in Black.* Trumansburg, N.Y.: Crossing Press.

Patterson, Annabel. 1987. *Pastoral and Ideology: Virgil to Valéry.* Berkeley and Los Angeles: University of California Press.

Paz, Octavio. 1961. *The Labyrinth of Solitude: Life and Thought in Mexico.* New York: Grove Press.

Pearse, Andrew. 1956. "Mitto Sampson on Calypso Legends of the Nineteenth Century." *Caribbean Quarterly* 4, nos. 3–4:250–62.

Perloff, Marjorie. 1981. *The Poetics of Indeterminacy: Rimbaud to Cage.* Princeton: Princeton University Press.

————. 1985. *The Dance of the Intellect: Studies in the Poetry of the Pound Tradition.* New York: Cambridge University Press.

————. 1990. *Poetic License: Essays on Modernist and Postmodernist Lyric.* Evanston, Ill.: Northwestern University Press.

————. 1991. *Radical Artifice: Writing Poetry in the Age of Media.* Chicago: University of Chicago Press.

Peterson, William S. 1977. Introduction to *Sonnets from the Portuguese: A Facsimile Edition of the British Library Manuscript,* by Elizabeth Barrett Browning, ed. William S. Peterson. Barre, Mass.: Barre Publishing.

Philip, Marlene Nourbese. 1988. *She Tries Her Tongue: Her Silence Softly Breaks.* Charlottetown, Canada: Ragweed Press.

Pizan, Christine de. [1405] 1982. *The Book of the City of Ladies.* Trans. Earl Jeffrey Richards. New York: Persea Books.

Poe, Edgar Allan. [1846] 1984. "The Philosophy of Composition." In *Essays and Reviews.* New York: Library of America.

Pollard, A. W., ed. 1911. *The Holy Bible: A Facsimile of the Authorized Version Published in the Year 1611.* Oxford: Oxford University Press.

Poovey, Mary. 1988. *Uneven Developments: The Ideological Work of Gender in Mid-Victorian England.* Chicago: University of Chicago Press.

Porter, Carolyn. 1990. "History and Literature: 'After the New Historicism.'" *New Literary History* 21, no. 2:253–72.

Pound, Ezra. 1918. "Others." *Little Review* 4, no. 11 (March): 56–58.

———. 1926. *Personae.* New York: New Directions.

———. 1950. *The Letters of Ezra Pound 1907–1941.* Ed. D. D. Paige. New York: Harcourt, Brace and World.

———. [1929] 1954. "How to Read." In *Literary Essays of Ezra Pound.* London: Faber and Faber.

———. 1960. *ABC of Reading.* New York: New Directions.

———. 1979. *The Cantos of Ezra Pound.* New York: New Directions.

Prado, Holly. 1984. "In Verse." *Los Angeles Times Book Review,* 8 January.

Prins, Yopie. 1991. "Elizabeth Barrett, Robert Browning, and the *Différance* of Translation." *Victorian Poetry* 29: 435–51.

Prunty, Wyatt. 1990. *"Fallen From the Symboled World": Precedents for the New Formalism.* New York: Oxford University Press.

Psomiades, Kathy. 1991. " 'Subtly of Herself Contemplative': Aestheticism and the Woman Poet." Ph.D. diss., Yale University.

Quartermain, Peter. 1992. *Disjunctive Poetics: From Gertrude Stein and Louis Zukofsky to Susan Howe.* New York: Cambridge University Press.

Quilligan, Maureen. 1991. *The Allegory of Female Authority: Christine de Pizan's Cité des Dames.* Ithaca, N.Y.: Cornell University Press.

Rawick, George. 1979. *The American Slave: A Composite Autobiography.* Westport, Conn.: Greenwood Press.

Rebolledo, Tey Diana. 1987. "The Politics of Poetics: Or, What Am I, a Critic, Doing in This Text Anyhow?" *The Americas Review* 15, nos. 3–4:129–38.

Reinfeld, Linda. 1992. *Language Poetry: Writing as Rescue.* Baton Rouge: Louisiana State University Press.

Rich, Adrienne. 1973. *Diving into the Wreck: Poems 1971–1972.* New York: W. W. Norton.

———. 1976. *Of Woman Born.* New York: W. W. Norton.

———. 1978. *The Dream of a Common Language: Poems 1974–1977.* New York: W. W. Norton.

———. 1979. "When We Dead Awaken: Writing as Re-vision." In *On Lies, Secrets, and Silence: Selected Prose 1966–1978.* New York: W. W. Norton.

———. 1986a. *Blood, Bread, and Poetry: Selected Prose 1979–1985.* New York: W. W. Norton.

———. 1986b. *Your Native Land, Your Life.* New York: W. W. Norton.

———. 1989. *Time's Power: Poems 1985–1988.* New York: W. W. Norton.

———. 1990. "'Sliding Stone from the Cave's Mouth.'" *American Poetry Review* 19 (September–October): 11–17.

———. 1991a. *An Atlas of the Difficult World, Poems 1988–1991.* New York: W. W. Norton.

———. 1991b. "Adrienne Rich." In *Points of Departure: International Writers on Writing and Politics,* Interviews by David Montenegro, 5–25. Ann Arbor: University of Michigan Press.

Richards, Earl Jeffrey. 1982. Introduction to *The Book of the City of Ladies,* by Christine de Pizan. New York: Persea Books.

Richman, Robert. 1988. *The Direction of Poetry: An Anthology of Rhymed and Metered Verse Written in the English Language Since 1975.* Boston: Houghton Mifflin.

Riddel, Joseph N., ed. 1978. Special issue on the long poem in the twentieth century. *Genre* 11 (winter).

Rorty, Richard. 1980. *Philosophy and the Mirror of Nature.* Princeton: Princeton University Press.

Rose, Mary Beth. 1988. *The Expense of Spirit: Love and Sexuality in English Renaissance Drama.* Ithaca, N.Y.: Cornell University Press.

Rosenthal, M. L., and Sally M. Gall. 1983. *The Modern Poetic Sequence: The Genius of Modern Poetry.* New York: Oxford University Press.

Rosenwasser, Rena. 1992. *Isle.* Berkeley, Calif.: Kelsey St. Press.

Rowse, A. R., ed. 1978. *The Poems of Shakespeare's Dark Lady* [Aemilia Lanyer]. London: Jonathan Cape.

Ruelle, David. 1991. *Chance and Chaos.* Princeton: Princeton University Press.

Ruskin, John. [1865] 1907. "Of Queens' Gardens." In *Sesame and Lilies, The Two Paths, and The King of the Golden River.* London: J. M. Dent.

Sadoff, Ira. 1990. "Neo-Formalism: A Dangerous Nostalgia." *American Poetry Review* 19 (January–February 1990): 7–13.

Saldívar, José D. 1991a. "Chicano Border Narratives as Cultural Critique." In *Criticism in the Borderlands,* ed. Hector Calderón and José D. Saldívar, 167–80. Durham, N.C.: Duke University Press.

———. 1991b. *The Dialectics of Our America: Genealogy, Cultural Critique and Literary History.* Durham, N.C.: Duke University Press.

Saldívar, Ramón. 1990. *Chicano Narrative: The Dialectics of Difference.* Madison: University of Wisconsin Press.

Sánchez, Marta Ester. 1985. *Contemporary Chicana Poetry: A Critical Approach to an Emerging Literature.* Berkeley and Los Angeles: University of California Press.

Schwab, Gail M. 1991. "Irigarayan Dialogism: Play and Powerplay." In *Feminism, Bakhtin, and the Dialogic,* ed. Dale M. Bauer and S. Jaret McKinstry, 57–72. Albany: State University of New York Press.

Schweickart, Patrocinio P. 1986. "Reading Ourselves: Toward a Feminist Theory of Reading." In *Gender and Reading: Essays on Readers, Texts, and Contexts,* ed. Elizabeth A. Flynn and Patrocinio P. Schweickart, 31–62. Baltimore: Johns Hopkins University Press.

Schweik, Susan. 1991. *A Gulf So Deeply Cut: American Women Poets and the Second World War.* Madison: University of Wisconsin Press.

Scott, Bonnie Kime, ed. 1990. *The Gender of Modernism: A Critical Anthology.* Bloomington: Indiana University Press.

Scott, Joan. 1986. "Gender: A Useful Category of Historical Analysis." *American Historical Review* 91, no. 5:1053–75.

Sedgwick, Eve Kosofsky. 1985. *Between Men: English Literature and Male Homosocial Desire.* New York: Columbia University Press.

Sexton, Anne. 1971. *Transformations.* Boston: Houghton Mifflin.

Shakespeare, William. 1961. *Sonnets.* Ed. Douglas Bush and Alfred Harbage. Baltimore: Penguin.

Shange, Ntozake. [1977] 1980. *for colored girls who have considered suicide/when the rainbow is enuf.* New York: Bantam.

Shepherd, Simon, ed. 1985. *The Women's Sharp Revenge: Five Women's Pamphlets from the Renaissance.* New York: St. Martin's Press.

Showalter, Elaine, ed. 1985. *The New Feminist Criticism: Essays on Women, Literature and Theory.* New York: Pantheon.

Siebers, Tobin. 1988. *The Ethics of Criticism.* Ithaca, N.Y.: Cornell University Press.

Siegle, Robert. 1989. *Suburban Ambush: Downtown Writing and the Fiction of Insurgency.* Baltimore: Johns Hopkins University Press.

Silko, Leslie Marmon. 1976. "A Conversation with Leslie Marmon Silko." *Sun Tracks: An American Indian Literary Magazine* 3:26–32.

———. 1981. *Storyteller.* New York: Little, Brown.

Silliman, Ron., ed. 1986. *In the American Tree.* Orono, Maine: National Poetry Foundation.

Sitwell, Edith. 1927. *Rustic Elegies.* New York: Alfred A. Knopf.

Smith, Joseph. 1991. *Arguing With Lacan.* New Haven: Yale University Press.

Smith, Paul. 1988. *Discerning the Subject.* Minneapolis: University of Minnesota Press.

Sowernam, Esther [pseud.]. [1617] 1985. *Esther Hath Hang'd Haman.* In Shepherd 1985, 85–123.

Speght, Rachel. [1617] 1985. *A Muzzle for Melastomus.* In Shepherd 1985, 57–83.

Spillers, Hortense J. 1984. "Interstices: A Small Drama of Words." In *Pleasure and Danger: Exploring Female Sexuality,* ed. Carole S. Vance, 73–100. Boston: Routledge and Kegan Paul.

———. 1987. "Mama's Baby, Papa's Maybe: An American Grammar Book." *Diacritics* 17, no. 2:65–81.

Spivak, Gayatri Chakravorty. 1987. *In Other Worlds: Essays in Cultural Politics.* New York: Methuen.

Spivak, Kathleen. 1974. *The Jane Poems.* New York: Doubleday.

Sprengnether, Madelon. 1990. *The Spectral Mother: Freud, Feminism, and Psychoanalysis.* Ithaca, N.Y.: Cornell University Press.

St. Aubyn, Giles. 1992. *Queen Victoria: A Portrait.* New York: Atheneum.

Steele, Timothy. 1990. *Missing Measures: Modern Poetry and the Revolt against Meter.* Fayetteville: University of Arkansas Press.

Stein, Gertrude. [1935] 1985. "Poetry and Grammar." In *Lectures in America.* Boston: Beacon Press.

Stein, Richard. 1987. *Victoria's Year: English Literature and Culture 1837–1838.* New York: Oxford University Press.

Steinman, Lisa M. 1987. *Made in America: Science, Technology, and American Modernist Poets.* New Haven: Yale University Press.

Stephens, Michael. 1986. *The Dramaturgy of Style: Voice in Short Fiction.* Carbondale: Southern Illinois University Press.

Stephenson, Glennis. 1989. "The Vision Speaks: Love in Elizabeth Barrett Browning's 'Lady Geraldine's Courtship.'" *Victorian Poetry* 27:17–31.

Stern, Daniel. 1985. *The Interpersonal World of the Infant: A View From Psychoanalysis and Developmental Psychology.* New York: Basic Books.

Stevenson, Anne. 1974. *Correspondences: A Family History in Letters.* London: Oxford University Press.

Stock, Noel. 1970. *The Life of Ezra Pound.* New York: Pantheon Books.

Suleiman, Susan R. 1985. "Writing and Motherhood." In *The (M)other Tongue: Essays in Feminist Psychoanalytic Interpretation,* ed. Shirley Nelson Garner, Claire Kahane, and Madelon Sprengnether, 352–77. Ithaca, N.Y.: Cornell University Press.

———, ed. 1986. *The Female Body in Western Culture.* Cambridge, Mass.: Harvard University Press.

———. 1990. *Subversive Intent: Gender, Politics, and the Avant-Garde.* Cambridge, Mass.: Harvard University Press.

Swetnam, Joseph. [1615] 1985. *Araignment of Lewde, Idle, Froward, and Unconstant Women.* In Henderson and McManus 1985, 198–216.

Takaki, Ronald. 1989. *Strangers from a Different Shore: A History of Asian Americans.* Boston: Little, Brown.

Tan, Amy. 1989. *The Joy Luck Club.* New York: Ivy Books.

Tardos, Anne. 1992. *Cat Licked the Garlic.* Vancouver: Tsunami Editions.

Taylor, Linda. 1992. "'A Seizure of Voice': Language Innovation and a Feminist Poetics in the Works of Kathleen Fraser." *Contemporary Literature* 33:337–72.

Thomas, Keith. 1958. "Women and the Civil War Sects." *Past and Present* 13:42–62.

Thompson, Dorothy. 1990. *Queen Victoria: The Woman, the Monarchy, and the People.* New York: Pantheon.

Tomlinson, Charles, ed. 1969. *Marianne Moore: A Collection of Critical Essays.* Englewood Cliffs, N.J.: Prentice-Hall.

Tovar, Ines. 1975. "'Roses are Rosas': Juan Gomez-Quinones—A Chicano Poet." *Mester* 5:95–100.

Treblicot, Joyce, ed. 1983. *Mothering: Essays in Feminist Theory.* Totowa, N.J.: Rowman and Allanheld.

Trevarthen, Colwyn. 1979. "Communication and Cooperation in Early Infancy: A Description of Primary Intersubjectivity." In *Before Speech: The Beginning of Inter-*

personal Communication, ed. Margaret Bullowa, 321–47. Cambridge: Cambridge University Press.

Trinh, T. Minh-ha. 1989. *Woman, Native, Other: Writing Postcoloniality and Feminism.* Bloomington: Indiana University Press.

Turner, Victor. 1974. *Dramas, Fields, and Metaphors: Symbolic Action in Human Society.* Ithaca, N.Y.: Cornell University Press.

Vendler, Helen. 1980. *Part of Nature, Part of Us: Modern American Poets.* Cambridge: Harvard University Press.

Vickers, Nancy J. 1981. "Diana Described: Scattered Woman and Scattered Rhyme." *Critical Inquiry* 8:265–79.

Victoria, Queen. 1908. *The Letters of Queen Victoria: A Selection from Her Majesty's Correspondence between the Years 1837 and 1861.* Ed. Arthur C. Benson and Viscount Esher. 3 vols. London: John Murray.

———. 1912. *The Girlhood of Queen Victoria: A Selection from Her Majesty's Diaries between the Years 1832 and 1840.* Ed. Viscount Esher. 2 vols. London: John Murray.

———. 1985. *Queen Victoria in her Letters and Journals.* Ed. Christopher Hibbert. New York: Viking.

Wakoski, Diane. 1984. *The Collected Greed (Parts 1–13).* Santa Barbara, Calif.: Black Sparrow Press.

Wald, Priscilla. 1990. "Displaced Personae in Theresa Cha's *Dictée.*" Paper presented at Modern Language Association Convention.

Waldrop, Rosmarie. 1987. *The Reproduction of Profiles.* New York: New Directions.

Walker, Cheryl. 1991. *Masks Outrageous and Austere: Culture, Psyche, and Persona in Modern Women Poets.* Bloomington: Indiana University Press, 1991.

Wall, Cheryl, ed. 1989. *Changing Our Own Words: Essays on Criticism, Theory, and Writing by Black Women.* New Brunswick, N.J.: Rutgers University Press.

Waller, Gary F. 1985. "Struggling into Discourse: The Emergence of Renaissance Women's Writing." In Hannay 1985, 238–56.

Warland, Betsy. 1987. *serpent (w)rite (a reader's gloss).* Toronto: Coach House Press.

———. 1990. *Proper Deafinitions: Collected Theorograms.* Vancouver: Press Gang Publishers.

Weeks, Jeffrey. 1981. *Sex, Politics and Society: The Regulation of Sexuality since 1800.* London: Longman.

Werner, Craig. *Adrienne Rich: The Poet and Her Critics.* Chicago: American Library Association.

Whitford, Margaret, ed. 1991a. *The Irigaray Reader.* Oxford: Basil-Blackwell.

———. 1991b. *Luce Irigaray: Philosophy in the Feminine.* London: Routledge.

Whitman, Ruth. 1973. "The Passion of Lizzie Borden." In *The Passion of Lizzie Borden: New and Selected Poems.* New York: October House.

———. 1977. *Tamsen Donner: A Woman's Journey.* Cambridge, Mass.: Alice James Books.

———. 1986. *The Testing of Hanna Senesh.* Detroit: Wayne State University Press.

———. 1992. *Hatshepsut, Speak to Me.* Detroit: Wayne State University Press.

Whitman, Walt. 1982. *Complete Poetry and Collected Poems*. Ed. Justin Kaplan. New York: Library Classics of the United States.

Williams, Eric. 1963. *Documents of West Indian History 1492–1655*. Port of Spain, Trinidad and Tobago: PNM.

Williams, Sherley Anne. 1982. "Letters from a New England Negro." In *Some One Sweet Angel Chile*. New York: William Morrow.

Williams, William Carlos. 1963. *Paterson*. New York: New Directions.

———. 1986. *The Collected Poems of William Carlos Williams*. Ed. A. Walton Litz and Christopher MacGowan. Vol. 1. New York: New Directions.

Wilson, Rob. 1991. "Falling into the Korean Uncanny: On Reading Theresa Hak Kyung Cha's *Dictee*." *Korean Culture* 12, no. 3 (summer): 33–37.

Winnicott, D. W. 1965. *The Maturational Processes and the Facilitating Environment*. Madison, Conn.: International University Press.

———. 1984. *Playing and Reality*. New York: Tavistock-Methuen.

Wittig, Monique. 1992. *The Straight Mind and Other Essays*. Boston: Beacon Press.

Wolff, Janet. 1990. *Feminine Sentences: Essays on Women and Culture*. Berkeley and Los Angeles: University of California Press.

Woodham-Smith, Cecil. 1972. *Queen Victoria: Her Life and Times 1819–1861*. London: Hamish Hamilton.

Woods, Susanne. 1993. Introduction to *The Poems of Aemilia Lanyer,* ed. Susanne Woods. New York and Oxford: Oxford University Press.

Woolf, Virginia. 1929. *A Room of One's Own*. New York: Harcourt Brace.

———. 1953. "Modern Fiction." In *The Common Reader*. New York: Harcourt Brace Jovanovich.

———. 1958. "The Narrow Bridge of Art." In *Granite & Rainbow, Essays*. New York: Harcourt Brace Jovanovich.

Wylie, Elinor. 1928. *Nets to Catch the Wind*. New York: Alfred A. Knopf.

Yamada, Mitsuye. 1976. "Camp Notes." In *Camp Notes and Other Poems*. San Lorenzo, Calif.: Shameless Hussy Press.

Yau, John. 1989. *Radiant Silhouette: New and Selected Work, 1974–1988*. Santa Rosa, Calif.: Black Sparrow Press.

Yorke, Liz. 1991. *Impertinent Voices: Subversive Strategies in Contemporary Women's Poetry*. London: Routledge.

Contributors

Rachel Blau DuPlessis, Temple University, is the author of *The Pink Guitar: Writing as Feminist Practice* (1990), *Writing Beyond the Ending: Narrative Strategies of Twentieth-Century Women Writers* (1985), *H.D.: The Career of that Struggle* (1986), and the editor of *The Selected Letters of George Oppen* (1990). She is writing a book on modern poetry.

Susan Stanford Friedman, Virginia Woolf Professor of English and Women's Studies at the University of Wisconsin-Madison, is the author of *Psyche Reborn: The Emergence of H.D.* (1981) and *Penelope's Web: Gender, Modernity, H.D.'s Fiction* (1990), the co-editor of *Signets: Reading H.D.* (1991), and the editor of *Joyce: The Return of the Repressed* (1993). She is writing a critical study of modernism.

Elizabeth Hirsh teaches at the University of South Florida in Tampa. She has published articles on Victorian poetics, feminist theory, and twentieth-century women writers. She is currently completing *Re-Producing Modernism: Irigaray, Formalism, and the Place of the Woman-Writer*.

Margaret Homans is professor of English and chair of Women's Studies at Yale University. Her publications on nineteenth-century women writers include *Women Writers and Poetic Identity* (1980) and *Bearing the Word* (1986). She also publishes on contemporary feminist theory and fiction, and she is at work, with Adrienne Munich, on a book on Queen Victoria.

Akasha (Gloria) Hull is professor of Women's Studies and Literature at the University of California, Santa Cruz. Her numerous publications include *Color, Sex, and Poetry: Three Women Writers of the Harlem Renaissance* (1987) and *Healing Heart: Poems 1973–1988* (1989).

Elaine A. Jahner is professor of English at Dartmouth College. Most of her publications address issues related to Native American cultures, languages, and literatures. She has taught and lectured extensively in the United States and in Europe. Currently she is completing two books on issues of cross-cultural literary criticism.

Suzanne Juhasz is professor at the University of Colorado, Boulder. Her books include *Comic Power in Emily Dickinson* (with Cristanne Miller and Martha Nell Smith, 1993); *The Women and Language Debate: A Sourcebook* (with Cristanne Miller and Camille Roman, 1993); *The Undiscovered Continent: Emily Dickinson and the Space of the Mind* (1983), and *Naked and Fiery Forms: Modern American Poetry by Women* (1976).

Lynn Keller, professor at the University of Wisconsin-Madison, is the author of *Re-making It New: Contemporary American Poetry and the Modernist Tradition* (1987) and of several essays on twentieth-century women poets. She is writing a book on recent women's long poems.

Teresa McKenna, associate professor at the University of Southern California, has published articles on Chicano/a literature and edited "Mexican Folklore and Folk Art in the United States" (Special Issue of *Aztlan*, 1982), *The Broken Web: The Educational Experience of Hispanic American Women* (1988), *CARA: Chicano Art Resistance and Affirmation* (Exhibition Catalog, 1991). University of Texas Press will publish *Migrant Song: Studies in Contemporary Chicano Literature and Politics*.

Cristanne Miller, professor at Pomona College, is the author of *Emily Dickinson: A Poet's Grammar* (1987), *Comic Power in Emily Dickinson* (with Suzanne Juhasz and Martha Nell Smith, 1993), *The Women and Language Debate: A Sourcebook* (with Camille Roman and Suzanne Juhasz, 1993), and is now completing *Questions of Authority: The Example of Marianne Moore*.

Janel Mueller is professor of English and Humanities at the University of Chicago and editor of *Modern Philology*. Until recently she published primarily on male-authored Renaissance prose, especially by Donne and Milton. Now she is editing the works of Queen Katherine Parr, Henry VIII's last consort, and selected letters of Queen Elizabeth I.

M. Nourbese Philip, a writer and lawyer living in Toronto, has published four books of poetry: *Thorns* (1980), *Salmon Courage* (1983), *She Tries Her Tongue: Her Silence Softly Breaks* (1989, winner of the Casa de las Americas Prize), *Looking for Livingstone: An Odyssey of Silence*. Her most recent works are *Frontiers: Essays and Writings in Racism and Culture* (1992) and *Showing Grit: Showboating North of the 44th Parallel* (1993).

Joan Retallack, Butler Chair Professor of English, SUNY Buffalo (1993–94), is the author of many essays and two books of poetry—*Circumstantial Evidence* (1985) and *Errata Suite* (1993). *How To Do Things With Words* is forthcoming from Sun & Moon. Wesleyan University Press will publish her conversations with John Cage and a book of poetry, AFTERRIMAGES.

Shelley Sunn Wong is assistant professor of English and Asian American Studies at Cornell University. She has published articles on twentieth-century American poetry and fiction and is presently working on a book, *Notes From Damaged Life: Asian American Literature and the Discourse of Wholeness.*

Index

407